Library of Congress Cataloging in Publication Data

Millar, George Reid.
Horned pigeon
by George Millar.
p. cm.–(Classics of World War II. The secret war)
Reprint. Originally published: Garden City, N.Y.: Doubleday, 1946.
ISBN 0-8094-7266-X
ISBN 0-8094-7267-8 (lib. bdg.)
1. Millar, George Reid. 2. World War, 193901945–Personal narratives, British.
3. World War, 1939-1945–Prisoners and prisons, German.
4. World War, 1939-1945—France.
I. Title. II. Series
D811.M5157 1988   940.54'86'41–dc 19   88-29518 CIP

Time-Life Books Inc. offers a wide range of fine music series,
including *Your Hit Parade*, original recordings from the '40's and '50's.
For subscription information, call 1-800-621-7026 or write Time-Life Music,
P.O. Box C-32068, Richmond, Virginia 23261-2068.

HORNED PIGEON

A pigeon which had been released from a wicker cage in a foreign country was flying through the evening sky when he overtook a crow.

"Where are you going?" asked the crow.

"Home," replied the pigeon, annoyed that he must slow his speed to answer this dull bird.

"And what do you expect to find there?"

"Home."

"But how do you know that your home will still be where you left it?"

The pigeon had already flown on, and the crow looked down for any old place to land.

HORNED PIGEON

BY

GEORGE MILLAR

Author of
"MAQUIS"

WILLIAM HEINEMANN LTD
MELBOURNE :: LONDON :: TORONTO

FIRST PUBLISHED 1946
REPRINTED 1946, 1953

PRINTED IN GREAT BRITAIN
AT THE WINDMILL PRESS
KINGSWOOD, SURREY

CHAPTER I

SOMETHING made me stop on the thickly carpeted stairs. I stopped and listened. I heard her weeping in desperate, uncontrollable, wailing bursts.

There were fourteen steps up, back to her room. Red-carpeted steps with brightly-polished brass stair-rods. The crying crescendoed as I opened the door, washed all round me as I stood beside the bed.

She lay, face smothered in the pillow. A bedside light shone into her reddy-brown curls. She gasped and stifled and retched with the agony of her crying. I will not forget it. I stood beside the bed as though I were in a torture-chamber. My insides formed themselves into tentacles that tried to grasp at the rings let into the walls of the torture-chamber.

How glad she was to see me again. She caught at me as though I were going to stay with her all night, as though I were going to stay with her for ever, as though we were destined to grow old together. As though I were not sailing the next day. Yet when the crying stopped the tears still pushed their slow way out from her eyes, her curving body with its long, delicate back still shuddered to the terrible rhythm of the sobbing that had possessed her.

I did not know whether the sadness that filled me was her sadness or mine. It was an agonising sadness. She called me by her names. She said that she would pray for me. She begged me to look after myself, not to get killed. We spoke of the years when we had lived together and worked together. I told her that I would soon be back (knowing, as well as she, that this was false), that the war would soon be over, that soon we should be living in Paris again with Félicie and another big poodle (since Vicky had been killed), and the bright copper pans in the kitchen and the trim Palais-Royal gardens beneath our windows. She had cried so much that she was exhausted, like an emotional child. She was easy to handle. I soothed her and undressed her and put her to bed. I sat on the bed and when she slept I slid my hand from hers and left the room.

This time when I listened on the staircase I only heard the noise of a man's razor strop. Such a banal noise in the silence of that quiet "family" hotel. I hated to think that a man who shaved before he went to bed, or any man for that matter, was occupying a room so close to my suffering wife.

At the bottom of the stairs I passed through the place where the hotel regulars sat. They were elderly people. Many of the women wore velvet with diamonds in ugly settings and often ropes of pearls as well. Some of the men wore square-toed shoes. There were two tables of bridge. The old women's eyes looked as hard as pebbles. So different from the undefended, weeping eyes of my wife upstairs. The old women had had their lives, had probably had everything except death. Now their eyes had hard shells to them like the round eyes of dead cod-fish. Anne's eyes were soft and myopic. Anne was still around thirty. She had plenty of suffering ahead of her.

It was 1941, September. Russia had just been attacked by Germany, and her resistance was already considered a miracle. Britain was still in her desperate stage, with Churchill fiercely lashing her on. But the old women's eyes did not light up at the sight of my battle-dress. Perhaps the war made them think too much of their stockbrokers. And I took a whiff of the war, and the suffering and frustration and joy and development which it brings to young people, into the stuffy, expensive place where they sat. And out of it into the street.

But was my sadness partly shame and self-hate as I hurried back to the transit camp on foot and in the tram-car? It was easy for me to hurry. I knew this ugly British port, for I had been born within twenty miles of it. I knew that I must catch a yellow tram in Sauchiehall Street. Was there no exhilaration in the breeze with its salty heaviness, in the untamed bellow of a tug pushing its blunt, handsome nose under the bridge?

Yes. The exhilaration was there. I wanted the freedom and the adventure of the desert battle. And I was ashamed of my shallow wanting, my feeble boy scout longings, when I compared them with the sadness in my wife, who could have none of these things, who must stay in Britain, alone, to face dullness and boredom. The tug's bass voice spoke for me, not for her.

The carbolic, polish, and sweat smell of well-kept soldiers and the smell of often-stirred dust permeated the air of the transit camp. Three other officers shared my room. They were already in bed, but talking. I checked over my clothing before I got into bed. Like a bride looking at her trousseau. In eleven hours I would be on the ship, and I was excited. But as I laid my head on the pillow the sadness crept back into me, or into my consciousness, for it had really been there all the time. It stayed with me until 1944.

*   *   *   *   *

I was snobbishly annoyed at being obliged to approach the docks marching, at the head of fifty well-dressed, well-disciplined men with a sergeant-major. I would have preferred to have approached as I once did in the old days, stealthily in a car. That time I had Jim stop the car on the corner, gave him a pound note, and walked guiltily down towards the freighter. Nobody saw me. I adopted the roll of the sailor. When I got into the forecastle there was a smell of stale drink. And somebody said as I dumped my old kitbag: "What the hell threw you up, Sonny?" That was on S.S. *Gregalia,* though, and I considered her a handsome freighter and myself an interesting ordinary seaman, I suspect. Now I had to go on a passenger ship belonging to a line which, as an ordinary seaman, I had always detested for its priggishness, its bugle-calls to over-large meals, and its scarlet pickles of passengers. It was an ostentatious ship of some twenty thousand tons. Over-funnelled, as was the fashion when she was built. She carried three of the things, two of them dummies.

Officers of my own and another, a cavalry regiment, circulated on her many decks and on the quay. I knew all of them. There were R.A.F. officers too. I knew none of them. My party was the last to arrive. We had been packing away my battalion's vehicles on the smart Clan ship that was to carry them to Egypt.

Soon we were steaming slowly down the Clyde, past Erskine, where my grandfather had helped to make a refuge for the wounded of the first World War. I had seen them there. It was wonderful how they played billiards, pushing themselves around the tables in their wheeled chairs. The fat table-legs were softly padded so that the wounded would not tear themselves open again on the corners. Admirable, the wounded were. So admirable that you forgot to be sorry for them when you were inside the boundary wall with them under the knotted oak-trees beside the Clyde, where the big ships moved so stiffly between the soggy fields.

Now my ship moved like that, carrying some of the wounded-to-be of the second World War. They were extremely cheerful, for, like me, they were excited by the prospect of change. Our own men, being Londoners and quicker-witted than the troopers of the cavalry regiment, and the majority of the airmen, excelled in the verbal sallies which shot from our ship to the people on either bank of the river.

They also excelled in the sallies that greeted their first sight of the quarters they were to occupy for some two months, on the

3

way to Egypt via South Africa. They were a fine lot, our men, and thoroughly reasonable. But at first sight the troop decks seemed almost uninhabitable. And the contrast between these makeshift quarters with the accommodation offered to the officers was too obvious. My men were in the holds. I was in a first-class cabin. It is true that I shared it with Charlie, another second-lieutenant. In peace-time I should have been alone in it (if I could afford the fare). We officers had what seemed to be at least normal first-class meals of the British hotel and steam-ship variety—five-course breakfast, six- or seven-course lunch and dinner, with all the trimmings, including waiters and a heavy classical décor with sham Corinthian columns. We had a bar with stewards who were over-worked fetching cheap peace-time concoctions. The favourite was a strong rum cocktail called a "depth-charge". Our men lived in squalor below the water-line. Their food was worse than their food ashore. Why do men suffer such differences in their living conditions?

I repeatedly asked myself this question as I worked with my own men on the promenade deck on which they were allowed to set foot only when it was a question of training. I saw then that they still appeared to consider me as a reasonable being, although I tolerated my own superior living conditions and raised no active or effective protest against the discomforts of theirs.

They learned a great deal on the ship. After the first four days the convoy was far enough out into the Atlantic for them to be used to the movement on the water and to the menace of sub-marines. And on the ship we were away from our vehicles, the monsters that normally demanded sixty per cent of the men's attention. I had forty-two men, eleven Bren-carriers, two armoured scout cars and six motor-cycles in my "scout" platoon. The riflemen were quick and eager. If they had a fault perhaps they were over-intelligent for soldiers. Now, on the starboard side of the promenade deck they made good progress. My superior officers happened to be good. They left us fairly well alone on the promenade deck.

One day Jimmy, the colonel, came walking past while my men and I were debating the motion "I would rather fight in the R.A.F." I spoke myself for the Army while the leading speaker on the other side was a former itinerant vendor from White-chapel. He won. The men liked the R.A.F. blue (if anything beyond their refusal to have me kept me out of the Air Force that colour did), they liked the R.A.F. food, and they preferred the R.A.F. pay scale. The colonel only smiled at their verdict

4

and walked on, a spry little man in shorts and softly padding, crêpe-soled shoes. He thought me a little odd, did the colonel. But my platoon were good, anyone could see that. No credit to me. The whole company and the battalion were good.

I had never greatly liked Corporal Shelmerdine, and I hated going to see him in prison. So I took one hundred cigarettes to give him (and then only gave him fifty, thinking the larger number might make it look as though I were trying to buy back his favour). He was a big, beautiful, precocious corporal, with waxy fair ringlets.

He had attempted to use a code in his letters home. It was an absurdly simple code and I noticed it whenever he began to try it. (One of my duties was to censor the platoon's mail.) The corporal was sending home military secrets to a girl. They were drab little military secrets, but dangerous all the same. So he spent most of the trip a prisoner.

"I want to thank you, sir," Shelmerdine greeted me when I walked into his cell.

"What on earth do you mean?"

"For finding me out, for getting me punished." He looked at me with dulcet, blue eyes. "All I ask now is a chance to start afresh."

I had a horrible feeling that a cinema organ was about to play on the other side of the bulkhead. A horrible feeling that Shelmerdine might continue in this odious vein.

Why had I run him in? I could have frightened him quite well enough myself. I suppose I had run him in partly to revenge myself on him for assuming that I, the censor, was stupid or careless enough to let his silly code through. And as An Example, I told myself priggishly.

For I was in some ways a model and conscientious junior officer. Nevertheless, I had Corporal Shelmerdine on my conscience all through the hot weather, especially off the submarine-haunted Gold Coast and in the Red Sea.

Yes, I was, or seemed to be, a model officer. Only I was not so nice as the majority, perhaps, of my brother officers thought. A minority thought the reverse because sometimes my tongue had run away with me during training in England. Mike, my company commander, had ordered me to desist from extolling the virtues of the three-inch mortar and the failings of the two-pounder anti-tank gun, the obsolete weapon with which the tanks and anti-tank regiments of our prized armoured division were still armed. Other officers who had caught me in particularly obstreperous mood in the mess-tent at Tidworth one summer evening had reported my "Red Ragings" to the colonel, who had "cautioned" me in his orderly-room the following day.

An entirely model officer was young Charlie, who shared my cabin with me. He was fresh from Eton with a long straight nose and a long straight yellow moustache. Everything he did was methodical and serious. He obeyed every handbook published for the British Army. He was intelligent, I think, but his code was so rigid that he occasionally seemed a little ridiculous. He and I had only one thing in common. We both worked hard with our men. I don't know what Charlie thought of a queer charlatan like me. I know what I thought of him. He was splendid. He was killed, later, in the desert.

Lots of Charlies were among our officers. And I was glad. They make the best officers. All of us were well behaved at nights despite the amenities of the ship's bar. So were the officers of the cavalry regiment that accompanied us. You would expect that. All of these officers were "the right sort". Which meant that their parents had all had sufficient money to send them to the more expensive schools. At nights the R.A.F. officers showed up unfavourably. They were less well-behaved, less polished, less agreeable than the soldier butterflies. But their crudities did not make me cease to regret that the R.A.F. had turned me down at the beginning of the war. I wanted to be a fighter pilot.

It is agreeable to belong to what is known as a good regiment. It is good to be proud of the regiment, and to feel that you must behave up to certain standards because of the regiment and its history and the men who fought in it in other wars. It is an additional responsibility, and the soldier should be given all possible responsibilities. I was extremely proud of my regiment, and of my distant emotional fellowship and close professional fellowship with Charlie and the other officers who would obviously all of them, if put to it, die well.

Their company did not please me on the ship. During my training period in England I had spent most of my leisure time with Anne. Now at sea almost every night I wrote to her. For I could drive from my head neither the memory of her last tears nor the guilt in my heart because I myself had desired the parting.

If destiny, half-way across the Atlantic, had turned the convoy for home I should have written to Anne: "How wonderful, how wonderful." But I would still have sought the new adventure of the desert. I would have been furious to see England. In my letters to her I found some satisfaction. In my letters and in my leisure hours hidden above the boat deck and at the base of one of the false funnels, soaking in the sun and annoyed by the soot from the real funnel, I surveyed my past life day after day after day.

The sun, the prohibited sun (for our doctor and senior officers forbade us to bare even our heads to it), that soaked into me as the convoy zigzagged from the Gold Coast round to Port Said, helped me to remember our life together in which the sun had played an important part.

I was just back from the Pacific when I met Anne for the second time in the spring of 1935. We had met before a year or two earlier and I had made advances to her which she had rejected, judging me accurately to be a young and uninteresting philanderer. This time, though, her judgment wavered, for I was straight back from the sea and wild foreign parts and making the most of my health and vigour that came from the sun and from much hard physical work.

Anne had an affectionate nature, and an impetuous one. We ran away together, to a cottage in Sussex. Sometimes we drove up to London to attempt to sell the film scripts I wrote. I sheered away from the film companies when our money was done, partly because I was disgusted with what we saw of them, but largely because, however inefficient they might be in other respects, they appeared to have as low an opinion of my scripts as I had of them. In my last interview in the film world a gentleman with a slightly unusual name offered me a job as "The Peasant Lad" in a film called *Rembrandt*. He told me that it was a good walk-on part since I would have the privilege of spitting in Rembrandt's beer. The part, said the gentleman, might lead to great things, even to juvenile leads.

Faced with such a future, I stirred myself from the sugary lethargy into which I had settled since the acquisition of Anne. We drove into London, settled ourselves in a bed-sitting-room in a backwater of South Kensington called Manson Place, and, in order to eat and pay the rent, sold my car. The Jew who bought it in Great Portland Street only paid me twelve pounds ten shillings.

The twelve pounds ten was finished on the day before I was due to report at the studios to practise spitting into beer at the rate of payment of three guineas per working day. That day,

7

although I had determined never again to be a newspaper-man (I had worked once for nearly a year on a Glasgow evening paper), I went down to Fleet Street and landed a reporter's job in the first office I walked into, that of the *Daily Telegraph*. The job came to me through the friendship of an Australian, Ronald Monson, whom I had met on a strange attempt to salvage the *Lusitania,* and through the spontaneous good-will of the stout Scots news editor, McGregor. That night when I got back to the bed-sitting-room Anne told me that she too had got a job.

I had bluffed considerably with McGregor to get my job, and I have always been bad at confessing ignorance or asking for help. My work on the *Telegraph* was often a nightmare to me in the first few months. A lot of luck with my news stories consolidated me on the paper, however.

Anne had been ill during much of the first year we were together. I suppose it was a year that neither of us will forget. A year of quarrels between two ungoverned characters, a year of love and of growing affection. It was an invaluable year for me, for through necessity I worked at one thing long enough to learn to enjoy the work.

Our world for two had moved on happily. In Fleet Street and elsewhere they thought we were a nice young couple. We were very devoted. We had enough money to spend good holidays in the sun. The war caught us in Paris, but well prepared. Paris was exactly where I wanted to be. I had long made up my mind that when war came I would be a war correspondent. But when I had sampled this employment on the French fronts I decided vehemently that I wanted to be an airman. I was told coldly at the Air Attaché's office that I was "much too old" (twenty-nine). Next I wanted to join the Navy, but I had tried that some years before the war when they started the new Supplementary Reserve, and they had refused me when they found that I was slightly colour blind. The only thing left was the Army. By the time that I had joined that the German armies had bitten into the heart of France. Anne and I met on a quay at Bordeaux. She had been driving an ambulance on the French front, while I had been following the Government cavalcade from Paris through Tours to the terrestrial stopping-place, Bordeaux.

We came out of France on the *Madura*, one of the many "last ships" (according to writers) that left Bordeaux. It was a very overcrowded ship and I loathe crowds. Perhaps it was the fall

8

of France. Perhaps the tendency of my compatriots to put all the blame on the French and the tendency of the French to put all the blame on us. Perhaps it was my overflowing urge to be a soldier now instead of a newspaper-man. At any rate, on this journey there was a coldness between us. Anne could not fully understand my longing to cease being a war correspondent. We discussed it, and I agreed bitterly that it probably *was* simply the herd instinct. We discussed it endlessly, lying on her inflated rubber mattress beside the submarine look-outs on the crowded boat-deck. Sometimes my friend Geoffrey Cox was beside us. He was, I thought, the best newspaper-man on board. He too had caught the fever to join the Army. Perhaps he had caught it from me. Tom Delmer too, elephantine, holding court from a groaning deck-chair, had a whiff of the fever. Delmer, intelligent, sybarite and wanderer among newspaper-men, was destined, although he did not know it, to work for his country and to eat powdered eggs for four years in England.

Whatever made me want to join the Army, there was no stopping it. And Anne, although she still thought I would be more "useful" as a correspondent, soon got to the stage when she could boast of my "altruism" or "patriotism" in public.

Altruism and patriotism, indeed. Nothing could have been farther from the truth than either of these nouns. I had always been fond and proud of Britain. But since the age of fourteen, revolted by the shillings-and-pence conservatism of the over-comfortable Scottish bourgeoisie from which I am sprung, and by the jingoism taught me at one of the smuggest of public schools, I had learned to hate the word "patriotism". And no unbiased person could seriously call me altruistic, as you will find out if you read this book.

The coldness of our trip from France to brave, strangely inspiring, post-Dunkirk Britain soon passed away. Anne came up to Aberdeen and kept various homes for me while I sailed through four months in the ranks of the Gordon Highlanders and struggled through three months in an officers' training unit. She supported me through the boisterous gaiety of the ranks, a time full of kilts and white, pure-malt whisky, and through the depression of being an officer cadet in winter-time in a Wales that seemed to work hard to snub the humble cadet (and his not so humble wife, tall and red-haired with a temper to match).

While I was a junior officer in Tidworth and in the smoky wastes of Swindon, through the tedious time of training and

9

then the sudden urgent rush to get ready for Africa, our marriage had continued firmly.

It was true, I reflected when I searched back through the summer days at Swindon, and especially when my memory lit on warm Sunday afternoons when we had driven away to rest beside the source of the Thames, that Anne had been jealous of my new affection for the Army. It would have been difficult to find in all Britain a much more enthusiastic second-lieutenant than myself, an otherwise disillusioned thirty-year-old. She noticed the incongruity. I did not.

I was perfectly happy in England, training with our armoured division on Salisbury Plain. Then one day we were summoned to the big tent the battalion used for Church Parades. It was raining and there was a smell of wet battle-dress. The whole battalion was there, silent, correctly dressed. It had no idea why it was there.

"Well," Jimmy, the colonel, as dapper as a ringmaster below the big wet tent, said to us all. "We're off."

We were leaving for Egypt. Then I could not understand how I had been content to sit in England. An impatience to be off seized me, consumed me. Even the delight of getting new weapons (I mean unused weapons, there was nothing new in their design), new vehicles and everything else needed for my platoon, down to new ear-plugs, failed to stifle the urgency of the desire to get out to the desert.

And here I made a mistake. I attempted to hide my desire from Anne. After six years of honest dealing with her, for I had been honest I think, I attempted to lie to her, to pretend that I did not want to go. She saw through it of course. And perhaps it shook her confidence in me. We had begun our life together as jealous lovers. With the passing of time the survival of our love had given us confidence in ourselves and in each other. Now Anne saw that I had a new craving.

"Fighting in the desert is the only thing that can cure you," she said. "This soldiering of yours seems like a drug. When I saw at Aberdeen that you actually enjoyed drilling on that absurd concrete square, I just could not believe it. Since then it has got worse and worse. It will have to be burned out, cauterised."

She came to this despondent conclusion when we were on embarkation leave in Devon. We found mushrooms on the slopes behind the inn and prawns at the mouth of the creek below it. We ate and drank and were alone together. Sometimes I wanted to think of what lay immediately ahead, embarkation. But I pushed such thoughts from my head, and for a week we were happier than we had been when we first ran away together. Was it my guilty conscience lurking slyly in the background with the promise of foreign travel and the desert that prompted me to be more affectionate and more possessive with my wife than I had ever been before? At the time I certainly did not think so. But I thought repeatedly of the injustice of war. Why should it sometimes be so fascinating, so interesting for the young man, and always so stultifying, so drearily dull, for his young wife?

The climax of our parting began at "The Sloop Inn" and ended in the Glasgow Hotel, two odd *mises-en-scène*. But what a multitude of domestic tragedies must have been staged in those war years in just such places.

The hotel bedroom. Such rooms can bring an agony into my heart that was never there before the war. The wash-basin, the fumed or varnished furniture, the black telephone between the twin beds, the tart notices on the walls, the noises from other rooms, from the bar, from the lifts.

The war threw young people into surroundings that dissolved their roots. But the urgency, the burning sadness of a parting with the possibility of death beyond the parting, can fade away the horror of most surroundings. Sometimes they fade the soullessness of the hotel bedroom, drown its monotonous "Next, please".

The ship, the convoy, thrummed on while my reflections hovered behind us in the past.

Steamy Freetown, suburban Capetown, oily Aden, they passed without entangling me in any ideas, loyalties or excitements outside my wife and the Army. How could they? The sound of Anne's tears was still with me, not once but many times each day; and late into the night the sound came back to me, and I wondered about her. At Capetown young second-lieutenants became quickly involved with the convoy hostesses who waited in their large American cars to swoop screechingly on the new bodies that were arriving to pass the time for them. I watched, from an enjoyably aloof position of not caring, some of the younger ones, excited no doubt by the thought of approaching death, entwine their fresh hearts and sentiments with those of the convoy hostesses.

There was one second-lieutenant in my company, slow, fresh-faced, serious for his age. He fell in love, he kissed a girl for the first time, he danced in the moonlight, and he mooned about the girl for the rest of the trip. The girl was not worth five minutes of his mooning. She was an affected, hard, experienced convoy hostess. She probably regretted that she had chosen such a sweet and simple boy from this convoy. She would make up for it with the next arrivals, pick a more naughty specimen.

"Say something, can't you say something, stupid?" I heard her ask him one night in Capetown's night club as he sat gazing at her with wondering, silly eyes. This second-lieutenant survived the North African campaigns, but I do not know whether he returned to Capetown.

There was another who did not survive. A livelier youth, the one I liked best of all the young ones. He had a girl, of course; he had met her at the Capetown races. She was a better girl than the other, fresher, more attractive, more juicy. This officer also imagined that he was in love. He dragged me along with him to the girl's home because he noticed that I had no girl, and thought that I must be sad and lonely.

His girl tried to make me kiss her while we were listening to gramophone records in her house. He never knew about it. I expect he thought about that girl when he was dying, when he had dashed himself and his youth against the steel tide of the German Afrika Korps. I expect he thought about her before his parents and other people who had truly loved him. When I later heard that he was dead his death hurt me. Then I thought of the girl, and I knew that his thoughts had been of her, but that did not hurt me. Perhaps his last thoughts helped him.

What responsibilities they had, the convoy hostesses. And rich and poor (though many of the poor in those South African parts are coloured people, and the whites asked the convoys kindly not to mix with *them*) they nobly played their part. When I got my forty-two men together on the promenade deck after leaving Capetown I found them whole-heartedly grateful to the place.

"Sorbo", a dashing White Russian officer in my battalion who spoke frequently of the Kirghesian sheep that drag their fat-containing tails behind them on little sleighs, gave supplementary physical training to a voluntary class of officers on the boat deck early each morning. His exercises were good and he was a good teacher. The exercises made some difference to my life, for I was to remember them later, when I needed them. I did P.T. also with my platoon every day, and in my spare time I learned Morse, read and sunbathed and worked on the manuscript of a book called *Convoy,* a manuscript that I think I knew was destined to be destroyed, either at my own hands or at somebody else's.

Aden pleased me more than Capetown. There were no fluttering girls in it, only the smell of fuel oil, tinned food and expensive whisky at the club, and a tired and dusty-looking garrison. Aden suited my mood. But the young ones, after Capetown, thought it was hell. Doubtless they longed for more convoy hostesses at Aden. Alas, the convoy hostesses in that oily place expected something more jingling than a delightful way of speaking the King's English, twirling a moustache, or waltzing, in return for *their* company.

Some time before Capetown we had learned that the big attack had begun in the desert, and we knew as we left Aden and steamed up the Red Sea for Port Said that the attack was progressing bloodily but well. I remember Tommy, one of the other scout platoon commanders, exclaiming one day at breakfast beneath the Corinthian columns: "George, the devil of it is that we are going to be too late."

"Too late for what?"

"Why, to get into it. Don't you see? These damned New Zealanders and people are going to clean up the whole show before we get a look in."

"What, right through to Tripoli?"

"Yes, why not? They say we've got plenty of air power this time."

"Perhaps plenty for the moment when we are near our bases, but it won't be plenty when they get up beyond Benghazi."

"But look at the mass of stuff waiting to come from England, and they say that in the States the weight of material is simply fantastic."

"Quality of material counts in war now almost more than weight. The Germans have better tanks than we are likely to have for a long, long time. As for the material, and particularly the material for the air, that was meant for us, but we shan't get a smell of it. It must go against the Japs."

"You mean because of Singapore?"

"Yes."

"I think there will be plenty for both theatres," he maintained stoutly. "Winston said in his last speech that this offensive was going through."

"No offensive, and certainly no speaker, is infallible."

"You're not suggesting the old boy could be wrong? I begin

to believe stories that you're a Red. Well, anyway, we shall put up a good show, shan't we?"

"Yes, we will."

"And this grape-fruit is delicious. I do like grape-fruit for breakfast."

I think Tommy ate just three more grape-fruit in his life because there were three more breakfasts before our arrival in Port Said.

My battalion had been as well schooled as any in desert warfare, as well schooled at it was possible to be away from the desert, since our other "regular" battalion had been in North Africa before the business with Mussolini began, and had played a big part in Wavell's first advance. We had had the benefit of their advice over in England, and two or three of them were waiting to knock any odd corners off us when we arrived at Port Said. You could pick them out a mile away from the quay, strange, wild-looking men in well-cut cord trousers and rubber-soled boots. Their hair was long and matted. They had an artificial look about their faces, for their sand-smoothed skins looked like beauty advertisements. They eyed our gear with the superior airs of old residents. I had known one of them in the training battalion only a few months before. Now his right arm was bent in a sling.

Port Said was a rush and a flurry, with mountains of equipment to stuff into trains. We ate a hot, slushy Army stew in the docks. Then we were shuffling through the Egyptian night in a shaky old train. We officers travelled in squashed discomfort in carriages like third-class carriages on local lines in Britain. The men were in long, unpartitioned carriages with wooden seats and a lot of dark water slopping about on the floors. The cold was sharp. They stood it humorously.

Until next morning, when we fell in beside a station to be taken in trucks to our camp outside Alexandria. Only half of my men were able to leave the station. The others were helpless with a local disease called "gippy tummy". While I got the remainder into trucks and led them away I wondered vaguely why it had not hit me. I had already had dysentery, caught in an outpost in front of the Maginot Line in 1939 while I was writing about the French Army, and the disease had persisted through the ice-bound Paris winter of that first year of war. It had returned to me the following year while I was a cadet in North Wales. Anne, an excellent cook, had fought it off with milk puddings and a special diet. I had expected to be the first man in the battalion to get "gippy tummy", a young brother of dysentery. So when Sergeant Drummond dashed off with half the men and an extremely hasty apology I had a happily smug feeling of security and strength.

We were driven to a dust bowl beside a military road through the desert. No tents had yet been erected, all that lay ahead of us. But there were a few isolated little buildings dotted about the desert, buildings about half the size of a self-respecting shelter on a golf-course. My pains came on while we were falling in again to detail the company off for tent erecting.

They were terrible pains. A prey to them, I wandered into the desert, but to wander out of view of the battalion would have taken me half a day. I made use of the only cover in the landscape. Next day I learned that I had defiled "A" Company's cookhouse, but nobody else ever knew that I was the guilty party. "Gippy tummy" never bothered me again. I had too much to do. The training period was over. Now we were at war.

Now my longings were to be fulfilled.

CHAPTER II

BLOUNT and Skinner and I. We were a happy trio, bumbling across the Egyptian, and then the Libyan, desert in our carrier.

Blount was called "Moody" by the other men. He was an old soldier with all the old soldier's vices, I suspect, although the only one that was apparent in the desert was a disinclination to move swiftly in any direction and an overweening passion for the only available beverage—tea. He was by no means the best man in my platoon. Why had I chosen him from all the others for my own driver? Firstly, I think, because he was a very wonderful driver. Secondly, because something in his battered face, with its "Bugger-all-the-officers, and-that-goes-for-the-sergeants-too . . ." look appealed to me. He never said much, but he had a nice sour sense of humour which was automatically directed against authority in any form. This was natural enough since three times he had risen to sergeant's rank himself, and had been "broken" for one reason or another. Shortly before my arrival in the company he had held the important job of Transport Sergeant. Now he was plain Rifleman Blount again. "Back," as he remarked to me himself, "in the aristocracy of the Army." The sergeants and other N.C.O.s disliked "Moody".

The trouble with him was that he knew all the answers, from every Army point of view.

Jack Skinner was a different type. He came from the grey ranks of the white collar workers. While Blount took the line that it was best to leave anything undone for the maximum possible time in the hope that somebody else would do it, Skinner was a fusser, a man-with-conscience. Skinner was a biggish fellow, sturdily built, with a large, pink, intelligent bun-face, extremely wide at the height of his prominent cheek-bones. He had a drawling voice, which, with his fussy ways, occasionally maddened me. But he was a first-class signaller and a most useful and helpful soldier.

Skinner and I were both good at what the Army calls "making things", which is what the civilian would call "finding" or even "stealing" things. Apart from his tools, which he had to pay for if lost, Blount never "made" anything. Nevertheless, our carrier was certainly one of the best-provisioned vehicles in the desert. Of course a lot of the stuff was legitimately bought by me in Alexandria before we began our long approach march into battle. Things like tinned fruit and vegetables and chocolate I had bought there to improve our rations when we ate all three beside the carrier (or to improve their rations when I was not there—that kept "Moody" in a good humour). Other things like potatoes and onions I had "made" from the food-dumps round Alexandria and on the way up to the fighting. They were kept on my "mother truck", and were available to the whole platoon.

I remember being happy in the desert because I occasionally began the day with a type of breakfast food especially recommended for constipated people. Not that I was constipated, but with a lot of condensed milk and sugar this food was good. I remember being happy because: one morning I remembered to shake my boots before putting them on, and this time a scorpion *did* fall out; because there was half an onion to put in our bully stew beside the carrier one evening; because my pipe-stem broke and Sergeant Henwood "made" another from one of the riflemen and brought it up all fresh and hot because it had been boiled "to remove all pollution, not to mention infection, sir". I remember being happy because one afternoon I shot particularly well and the rest of the platoon disgraced themselves, and unhappy because one afternoon they surpassed themselves and I shot badly. But most of my unhappiness came—as to a worker in the England of the Industrial Revolution—through machines.

They had taken away my motor-cycles when we got to the desert. On the approach march I only had the eleven carriers, two heavily-armoured little Daimler scout cars (said to have been Field-Marshal Rommel's favourite vehicle for desert reconnaissance), and the "mother truck". This was a three-ton Chevrolet supplied under Lease-Lend, and I think it was the only vehicle that never gave any trouble. It was loaded up with all the platoon extra kit, a few of my things (including the nearly completed manuscript for the book *Convoy*, two photographs of Anne in leather frames, and a good many books, including the autobiography of Benvenuto Cellini with some writing by my father on the title-page), and the platoon's reserves of food, water, and petrol. Any spare men rode on the "mother truck" with Cobb, my batman, and Mercer, the spectacled mechanic from the Ordnance Corps.

Most of my carriers were new when we started the thousand-mile trek across the desert. In my opinion the carrier was a poorly designed thing, already out of date when the war began; but every time I said anything like that to my brother-in-law in the War Office he jumped down my throat. In 1941 he even drew a picture showing the whole of the British Army (bar the tanks) in carriers.

All I knew was that they were a constant worry to me. When we were on the march I would search around my different sections to find out where one was missing. For some reason (possibly stepped-up maintenance) they did better in the desert than they had ever done for us in England, until we got into the soft sand, where the ordinary 30-h.p. engine struggled wonderfully against the overload of driving one of these heavy things constantly in bottom gear, and then gave up or blew up.

On our marches I normally had my sections spread round the advancing column, advance-guard, rear-guard, and on the flanks. This made hard work in the halts. For whereas the ordinary motor platoon commander would have his four trucks in a 400-yard square, I might have miles to travel between my sections. At this time the British Army was still operating under the correct assumption that the enemy had control of the air. We moved across the desert in a state of dispersal that was ludicrous. The order was, "At least 400 yards between vehicles", and orders with us had to be rigidly obeyed. The amount of petrol that this order cost the Army must have been fantastic. Also the greatly over-deployed formations were unsuitable and unwieldy for fighting.

On the approach march we still had our company officers' mess with us. (This was before the day of 'Alamein.) The mess was a three-ton Ford which had been roughly fitted up by the Ordnance in Alexandria with a long table running down one side, two petrol cookers, and some cupboard space. When I had the time (which was not often) I would get to the mess for lunch at the midday halt. And I ate there in the evening.

There was an advantage in the system. It brought all the company's officers together, and it facilitated the giving out of orders. We ate no better than the men, except that from the Egyptians the mess secretary had bought extra tinned things and a supply of whisky and gin; and from the wily and grasping inhabitants of Benghazi we had bought at enormous cost a quantity of Italian tinned food and liquor, relinquished by the Italian officers on their second precipitate retreat from that town. The drinks were mostly sweet liqueurs like triplo secco and Italian kümmel with square white crystals floating in it. Our messing was very expensive.

Mike, my company commander, was a regular soldier, and a good one. He was a smallish man with a moustache as stiff as his self-discipline, and a liking for bitter invective. Mike never hesitated to damn anything, and he was always chary of praise—two high qualities in a company commander. He kept us all thoroughly in order, although his second-in-command, Noel, had only joined the company after our arrival in Egypt, and Mark or myself might well have been troublesome, since we were both old and opinionative for second-lieutenants. Mark, violently and sensually attractive in a faintly debauched way, was in the early thirties, and had lived much in Paris and everywhere else. He was quiet, well-read (and well supplied with interesting books). Bill and John, the other two motor platoon commanders, were both very young, and quite charming.

There was no doubt that Mike and all his officers worked harder than any of the N.C.O.s or men in the company. For that reason it was a good company, and a reasonably happy one, although Mike was always ready to make all of us sorry for ourselves whenever we needed driving.

Most people bore some petty physical cross in the desert. Mine was a tender skin, which rapidly developed desert sores. Mike's was his nose, for he had sinus trouble. He was the greatest nose-blower that I have heard. He slept always in a bivouac beside the mess-truck and his own 8-cwt. wireless truck. I would hear him snuffling and blasting as I walked across to the mess in the darkness before we broke out of our close night's formation (called either a "leaguer" or a "laager" when I was there) into the widely dispersed daylight formation.

"Reading," he would hiss—for apart from his own nose he was a strict disciplinarian about noise—"bring me a handkerchief." And Reading, his batman, a sharp, long-nosed little Londoner, would come running with an enormous silk square.

It was cold on those winter mornings before the sun was over the edge of the desert. I feel my ears nipping now when I remember them. We would "shake out" in a hurry as the dawn came near, all of us in vehicles riding swiftly out through the low ground mist. The tanks looked medieval, with the pennants on their antennæ waving as they pushed aside the sensitive mist. We were well-trained, and moved automatically out to our widely-spaced stations like child dancers going through the lancers. Once shaken out, the men would have to wait beside their vehicles until Mike gave the signal that cooking-fires might be lit.

Then I would watch them begin their cooking, tea, tinned bacon, and fried bread. When that was under way I was free to jump into a scout car and drive myself over to the mess. We often ate breakfast standing by the lowered tail-flap of the truck, since it was cold and dank inside. The tea was good then in the chill morning, very thick and syrupy, with a lot of sugar and condensed milk in it. How disagreeable it sounds, but I suppose the cold strong air of the desert, unpolluted by the fetid smells of man and beast, unsoiled by the dust from ash-cans and coal fires, would have made stranger things than this beverage and the "health food" seem better than the purest of coffees, the finest of *croissants*.

Before breakfast, Reading would have set up our "pedestal" some fifty yards down wind from the mess-truck. The pedestal was a lavatory seat fitted on top of a wooden box from which the lid and the bottom had been removed. At first this erection had been surrounded by a three-walled screen made of poles and sacking. But this was soon discarded as a ridiculous appendage, which indeed it was, for the very openness of the desert brought about an easy camaraderie in these things, or would it be more accurate to say that it broke down the stupid inhibitions which are normally pumped into the heads of children, to be normally retained by adults? At any rate, there was something quite enjoyable in sitting on this pedestal, whether the brigadier happened to be calling or not.

One of Mike's most persistent watchwords was the charming one: "A Clean Desert." This caused great amusement among the men, who probably had memories of the litter on the holiday beaches of Brighton and Ramsgate. But nevertheless they were obliged whenever we moved to see that the desert was left "as they found it".

I remember Mike standing in front of a tall corporal and shouting fiercely at him, pointing an accusing finger meantime at the shingle: "What is that, Corporal Digby? What is that, what is that, what is that?"

"That, sir, Major Elgar, sir? That, sir, er, is um, is what-d'you-call-it, is *excrolument*, sir."

"Ex. . . . Well, dig it in, man, whatever it is," Mike snapped. "Now look here, Mark," he continued, for with him the officer always took the final rap. "This is really too much. How many more times will I have to din into you the necessity for a really clean desert?"

After breakfast we would probably soon be on the move. There were three places in the carrier. Blount drove. I sat or stood beside him and navigated with my oil compass and the mileage on the speedometer. Skinner was behind us with his big radio set in the deep rectangular compartment beside the engine. I usually had head-phones on too. Driving a carrier over rough going was hard work. Sometimes I would take over from Blount or get Skinner to do it. It was very hot in the back, a dry, throbbing heat from the panting engine. In the day, when the sun was up, Skinner always sweated there, but when it was a case of a night drive, or an early morning start, we all liked to take a spell in the back. And we all did, unless I was navigating for the column or something like that.

One morning, while I was stretched out in the back and more than half asleep, a staff car cruised silently up behind my carrier, and a general whose name was well known then stood up on the front seat and pushed his long neck out of the roof to look down upon me. Skinner was driving at the time and Blount, temporarily "commanding" the carrier, stood in easy posture beside him. It was very cold and very early. Blount was wearing a Balaclava helmet in lieu of a cap. I saw the general when it was too late, so feigned deep sleep.

"What is that officer doing in the back? Is he dead?" the general screamed at Blount above the roar of the carrier.

"The lootenint is on radio watch, sir," answered Blount.

"But he's asleep."

"That's right, sir. That's why he switched the radio off. Order just came over the radio detailing Lootenint Millar to get all the sleep he could in view of last night's operations and the operations which may be anticipated to-night," Blount lied brilliantly.

"Who gave that order?"

"May have been de-emanated from you, sir, for all I know. Came over in a code name, that's all I know."

"Don't you normally salute people like me?"

"Of course, sir, when I am correctly dressed."

"Who gave you permission not to wear a hat?"

"Orders are that we must wear hats after O-eight-hundred hours, sir: on account of the cold in these here vehicles without windscreens, we are permitted 'elmets, wool, to cover our ears till then," Blount riposted, eyeing the general's comfortable car.

I expected to hear more of this encounter, but never did. Perhaps the general had important things to think about.

So passed our normal day, bumping and bouncing.

A short halt. Jump out to examine the track pins.

"Time to brew up, sir?"

"Better have another go at that Bren."

"Cleaned the Bren last halt we did, sir. While you was away bawling out number three section."

"What's that signal? Did you catch it?"

"Officers immediately to Company H.Q., sir."

"Call up Carter, and keep in station this time if they move before I'm back."

Billy Carter comes fussing up in my scout car. He is one of my best men. A Londoner with a knocked-about face that nobody can help liking.

"How's she going now, Carter?"

"None too good, sir. Too delikit for this place these things are."

He always said that, and his scout car always kept going because he cherished it.

I liked best to be out in front of our column, which was usually made up of our company with a battery of twenty-five-pounders of the Honourable Artillery Company, some anti-tank units with two-pounders mounted on three-ton chassis, and anti-aircraft units with Bofors.

When I was away out in front there was always a chance of getting a shot at a buzzard or a beautiful gazelle. Sometimes I would hurry far ahead of the column and then switch off and listen to the silence until the rumble approached. And if they said anything about it afterwards I replied that I was practising advance-guard work, jumping from feature to feature. Which in a way was true.

Just before dark we would go into laager. Someone would signal with a flag and then all the vehicles and tanks (if there happened to be any attached) would mysteriously swerve and quicken or slow their progress until every vehicle was one of an orderly spaced file, and there would be perhaps a dozen parallel lines of vehicles racing along. Then another signal, and all the vehicles would be stopped and closed up into tight little lines, nose-to-tail, with ten to twenty yards between lines. So well-trained were the vehicles that they seemed to laager like circus animals. And Mike, standing upright in his armoured White Car, was glaring round under his faded and greasy old green side-hat, was noticing if any vehicle was as much as three feet out of place. I never, of course, discussed Mike with the two men in my carrier. Such a thing would have been unforgivable. Nevertheless, I knew perfectly well that soldier-for-the-duration Skinner disliked his company commander, failed to understand the major's passion for detail, whereas old-soldier Blount both understood and appreciated him.

In fact I once overheard Blount discussing the officers with Craker, another carrier-driver.

"Mike," Blount said. "You know where you are with that bugger. He don't waste no time arsing about."

There was no time wasted once we were in laager. The guards were out at once, their Brens positioned to sweep out from each side of the square. Maintenance began on my vehicles, and I would wander down the line of carriers talking to the men and noting any breakages and losses.

The men in the carriers had a harder day than the men in the trucks, and when the day was over they had more work to do on their vehicles and less men to do the work. Yet the extra work gave them a kind of pride in their carriers. They despised the tame trucks that crept silently about the place like over-fed rabbits. I would have liked to have seen them with something better to ride in than the carriers. But I enjoyed at the end of the long day looking into the overworked engines, proud that they were clean, and that the drivers worked so cheerfully on them.

Meanwhile Cobb would be putting up my bivouac beside my own carrier. Cobb, my batman, had been chauffeur to an elderly man before the war. He was a dark, wrinkled man of Kent, a good worker. Some people (I was among them myself before the war) deplored the fact that there were still batmen in a British Army that was pretending to become democratic. But it is completely logical to have servants for your officers. If they are reasonable officers they work harder than their men, and they have no time to look after themselves. Furthermore, there are some people in the world, and some men in the Army, who have a genius for serving, and who ask to be servants. All our batmen were volunteers for the job, and when you wanted one there was no shortage of volunteers. Cobb was one of the best and most useful men out of the forty-two in my platoon. He was a good mechanic and a good shot, he was willing, and he was everywhere.

When all the work was finished, and the men were bedding down, I went to the mess, climbed into that warm, smoky, covered truck, where the others might be drinking whisky or eating stew. Whisky was rationed to one glass a night. Sometimes we had gin or some of the Italian drink. Only three of us drank regularly, Mike, Mark and I. Whisky was good in the cold night air, and on top of the sleepy tiredness that possessed me whenever I saw the men going to bed. When we had eaten, Mike always had some comments on the day's work, and sometimes orders for the next day.

Rations, petrol and water arrived during the night in the colour-sergeant's trucks, and I usually got some mail. Anne wrote me every day, and with every mail I got several air-mail post-cards and some letters too, almost all of them from her. It was fine to get the letters, and I replied almost every day. But her letters told me little, except that she was lonely and unhappy in the country near Winchester. I read them usually inside my sleeping-bag by the light of a hooded torch. The kapok sleeping-bag was all that I carried in my valise, for I had taught myself years before to dispense with a pillow and a soft place to lie on. And the bivouac kept the wind away from me, and indeed kept away everything that existed outside, my men, the enemy, the desert. When I crawled into the bivouac (it was a standard Army issue, about two feet high and six feet long) I felt that I was back in my own world again, with my own thoughts and private responsibilities.

It was not that I disliked the desert world outside. On the contrary, I liked it, I almost loved it. Even now I occasionally get a nostalgia for its lean emptiness, although I suppose I can go just as usefully to many more interesting places than the Libyan Desert, with companions as interesting as Mike and Blount and Skinner. My sleeping-bag was fresh and comfortable since I had had two inner bags made from sheets, and these were regularly changed and washed by Cobb. But I did not undress because we might be turned out in the night, and indeed sometimes were, and because of the piercing cold. Nevertheless, I never remember a bedroom, a hut, or a tent that I preferred to my bivouac. Perhaps it was the result of the day's work. Under Mike it was practically impossible to leave things undone. The men had bivouacs ("bivvies" they called them) too. But usually the carriers arranged themselves in pairs and the men stretched the handsome tarpaulins I had "made" before we left England to make small, airless huts between the vehicles. They preferred to squeeze in there together. I could hear them sleeping when I went to bed.

Anne was much in my thoughts at nights then. Although she wrote so frequently her letters were not filled with news, with facts and happenings and surroundings, the kind of material with which I could build a picture of her life near Winchester. Thus, she lived in a rented cottage, it was a lovely cottage or a perfectly foul cottage—I forget which—but she never told me what kind of front door it had and whether sash or casement windows, what sort of desk she sat at to scribble her air-mail post-cards to me and what, if anything, she could see from the window as she racked her brains to find something to fill a post-card's space. Her correspondence alarmed me. It was undisciplined. She savagely loathed the war, and I knew that the war would persist for a very long time. It was dangerous to batter oneself against anything so strong, so inexplicable. Better to swim flaccidly with the current, like her husband.

Blount, Skinner and I were all married. I remember discussing marriage with them on the side of the Wadi Fareg. The Wadi Fareg was a long, dry cut that ran roughly east and west, and was situated well into the desert and south of 'Agheila. When our column arrived up at the outpost lines near the western end of this wadi a cavalry regiment of armoured cars was patrolling there every day. But the armoured cars were not standing up to the strain of working in the soft sand, so the patrolling had to be done by the carriers of my platoon instead. Two patrols were sent out each morning at dawn, one under me and one with another officer from Jimmy's headquarters. We were fortunate at that time, my company, to be in a column with the usual odds and ends of gunners and things, but commanded by our own colonel. There were a good many Germans about at the western end of the wadi, around a place the lancer regiment called "the grouse moor", and running north from there they were digging, or pretending to dig, a defensive line. Behind the line we had no difficulty in seeing each day large movements of what we called M.E.T.—mechanised enemy transport. You could not mistake them. All our vehicles, armoured and otherwise, were a pale yellowish colour. These were darker, more sinister, less civilian-looking vehicles. We saw a good deal of heavy artillery drawn up by the big half-tracks that the Germans had so successfully developed. There was an enormous contrast between our side of the line with its tiny, scattered columns and their side with all this activity. I knew that our own tanks, owing to a great shortage of petrol, were halted many, many miles back. So apparently were the R.A.F. Enemy aircraft were always active over us, and strafed patrols whenever they noticed them.

The wadi varied in width from one to two miles and had high precipitous sides. There were a few places in the sides negotiable by carriers. The main trouble was that the bottom of the wadi, as well as the whole area on the southern side in which we were operating, was the softest of soft sand. The carriers could not stand up to such going. My own, which had gone well through the desert, was beginning to knock even under Blount's expert, if lethargic, nursing. We were running very short of vehicles. The majority were victims of the soft sand. Two had been knocked out by the vicious little Italian Caproni biplanes, things that flew so slowly that they were accurate for ground-strafing.

On this particular day, I remember, I only had one other carrier on patrol with me. We had taken up a position somewhere on the north side of the wadi and I was observing the enemy through my glasses. Our own carrier was hidden in some scrub immediately below us. Blount lay beside me, half asleep. Skinner came fussing up with our lunch, bully sandwiches made with Army biscuits, and tea from my big thermos flask.

"Can we smoke, sir?" asked Blount.

"Yes, but keep down in the bottom of the bowl."

"Give us a fag then, Jack." Skinner was one of the world's providers. He always had everything. Blount was one of the world's consumers.

"That makes twelve you owe me. When can you pay me back?"

25

"When the Army from Cairo to Benghazi cuts down its smoking and decides to send some forward for the boys in the line. Is it true that them as knows where to give bribes can get hundreds of ration cigarettes back there, sir?"

I wondered how they had got hold of that story. It was true that the supply situation was bad at that time, and that there was bungling somewhere. But I pretended to be busy with my glasses.

"Jerry busy to-day, sir?"

"Yes, very."

"Think he's going to come out from behind that line, sir?"

"Maybe."

"Do the brass-hats know about all those Jerries in there, sir?"

"Yes, they do. It comes out on the Brigade Intelligence report every day—'One thousand M.E.T. observed on the move between Wadi Fareg and 'Agheila'."

"Coo, then they must be laying a trap for him," said Skinner.

"Yes, Softie," said Blount from the bottom of the bowl. "And we're the bait."

"Oh no, we're not," I told them. "They can't get at us over there on the soft sand. If they send a big column out here, it's bound to keep to the hard going. That runs right along this stony ridge where we are now. Over on the other side of the wadi they'll be bogged down if they try to come at us. The only things that could really get in amongst us would be tanks, and they won't waste tanks on our little column, especially when we can shoot at them with twenty-five-pounders. If they come out we'll retreat parallel to them, and shell them across the wadi."

"Hope they don't come out," said Skinner. "I want to go right through to Tripoli, like Churchill said. Tripoli by Easter, then home leave with the wife and kid."

"Well, I hope they *do* come out," Blount said, "so we can be out here in peace, see. And no messing around with wives and kids while there's a war. I've had enough of home for a few years. And what, may I ask, encourages you to believe we may get home leave after Tripoli?"

"It'll be such an event. Papers'll be full of it. We'll all be blinking heroes. Won't we, sir?"

"Yes, for one day. To-day's heroes are to-morrow's wash-outs. The public forgets as quickly as the newspapers. Besides, it won't be finished at Tripoli."

"Trouble with you amatcher soldiers," said Blount—and his words were politely directed at Skinner—"is that you are

26

married men first and in the Army next. You make me sick. Never get away from the babies' nappies, you don't. Always whining about your loving wives. What do you know of women? You never saw the world. You always been sheltered in your clurk's job. There's only one kind of women, and that's bad women. There's only one way to behave with them. Treat them hard while you're with them, and leave them cheerfully when the troopship sails."

"Marriage," Skinner said, rather sententiously for a signaller, "is the finest thing on earth . . ."

"Yus. So you and the rest of the husband and father class spend all your time now moping and moaning for your loved ones in England. You become that sentimental you're less than men. At the same time you're just as willing as any proper men to have a bit of fun on the side. Now I believe in being frank with my old woman. She knew I was glad to leave in the course of duty. She won't await any letters from me unless I want something. Her money will be all right while I'm gone, and even if I don't come back."

"But you give her nothing to hold on to," said Skinner. "What would you do if she was unfaithful to you?"

Blount laughed so immoderately that I had to caution him for making too much noise. "Her, unfaithful," he said. "Why, I'd murder her. And don't think all your icing-sugar moping and letters will help to keep your wives straight. Women are stupid in many ways, but they're sharp on things like that. They see through you, Jack. You can't put icing-sugar ropes round a woman a couple o' thousand miles away. Can you, sir?"

"No, you can't," I agreed in principle.

That evening on our road home the carrier engine gave a wheeze and died on us. So I walked on to the column laager, pulled out Jones with his carrier, and drove back on a compass bearing through the darkness to the other carrier. We spent most of the night transferring the wireless and gear from Blount's vehicle to Jones's. Before dawn I was back at the laager to pick up two other carriers to patrol the wadi again.

I had seen Blount for the last time.

That morning when dawn came we saw that the Germans were on the move. A great column, most of it armour, was silhouetted on the north side of the wadi. The front of the column was already well past the place where Blount had spoken on marriage. Soon shells were whistling over from our twenty-five-pounders, and some German guns were replying. A few

German armoured cars and half-tracks towing anti-tank guns peeled off their column to watch us.

But they would hit us from the air. There were clouds of Stukas in the sky, all of them well to the north of us.

That afternoon they hit us. My "mother truck" went, manuscript and all, but I do not remember feeling sorry about the manuscript. I was thinking more in terms of petrol. Then our mess-truck went, closely followed by the colonel's mess-truck. The mess-trucks blazed with a weird assortment of coloured flames—probably, we thought, caused by burning cherry brandy, kümmel, and triplo secco; but the men bitterly remarked that our company mess-truck far outdid the battalion one in the power of its blazing. They claimed that this was due to the company's rum ration which Mike had been hoarding.

"I'll issue out your rum when you have done, or are about to do, something to deserve it," he had told them. His remark was now freely remembered by the riflemen as, crouching on the shingle, they fired with Brens and rifles at the swarms of Stukas and Messerschmitts, followed by attendant Capronis like cheap carrion birds, which savagely bombed, cannoned and machine-gunned us.

"What have we done to deserve this?" they asked the desert heaven and their officers as they watched the flames.

After that I lived entirely with Skinner and Jones on the carrier. We were alone most of the time. On the second day of the long withdrawal mine was the only carrier left out of eleven. Most of them were knocked out by the heavy going. Doing rear-guard to the column, which was moving fast, we fell a long way behind. Jones was a canny driver, who nursed his engine and refused to be hurried whatever happened.

One night we arrived so late that Mike had apparently given up hope of seeing us again, for he clapped me on the shoulder and said that he had been worried about me.

By this time the British tanks had been ordered into action against the German armoured columns. They had been ordered to "Destroy the enemy", and they had bravely attacked, had bravely faced destruction. I remembered that I had not been allowed to mention the virtues of the three-inch mortar and the failings of the two-pounder gun in the mess back in Tidworth. It was supposed to be a virtue in an Army officer to "make do" gladly with what arms he had, instead of straining to get the best arms. I saw some of the cavalry corpses in the burned-out tanks, and I wished that I had shouted myself black in the face about the failings of the two-pounder gun before I left London. These men had been blasted to bits before they had a chance to fire a shot, blasted by the superior guns of an enemy who was fighting with years of pre-war planning and with army brains and factories combined.

Jimmy, the colonel, was a soldier. It was a pleasure to work for him. When he sent me out on my last patrol I was glad to go. He could have sent me anywhere. Retreating is a difficult business. But Jimmy was calm and flexible. It seemed to us that he could do anything.

I was having a wash at the back of my carrier when I got the order to go out. A dry wash. There was no water to spare for luxuries. But I had an "electric" type razor that worked by hand, and I cleaned some of the dust off myself with a rough towel.

The colonel came up himself because there was trouble with the radio on my carrier. Skinner had nursed his set. But with all the sending that he had done on the rear-guard work, the radio was "a bit tired", he said. Jimmy, although he had all the responsibility for the column and all the rest of the work of an officer to do too, looked fresh and confident. He spoke in a soothing voice, different from his voice on training.

Tommy was there too. Jimmy had wirelessed to get him and his scout platoon sent down to help my carriers in their patrolling on the soft sand. Tommy had met us on our withdrawal. He was a tall, violently keen youngster with heavy black eyebrows. It was he who had been frightened on the ship that the battle would be finished before we got there.

Now he begged Jimmy to let him go instead of me.

"George gets doing all the patrols," he said. "Please let me have a go, Jimmy."

"No," answered the colonel, and he gave me more orders about rejoining the column, and the direction he would take if they moved on. I checked on the compass bearing he had given me for that, and there were great clouds of black smoke on it, just east of Benghazi. The dive-bombers must be breaking up our soft vehicles, I thought. Tommy was sulking. His eyebrows closed over his eyes.

We bumped and rattled away. Two carriers. Sergeant Robeson was in the other. He was Tommy's platoon sergeant, and one of the best men in the battalion. I had coveted him for my own platoon, and I was glad to see his little birdy head in the other carrier. We had been warned that there were Germans

B

about, and I moved carefully. Robeson was some 500 yards out on my right. We moved in bounds. I would go forward half a mile, then stop and observe through my American binoculars. When I stopped, Robeson would leap-frog up and pass on in front of me. All we saw on the trip were some British and South African corpses and a few burned-out trucks. We found a gallon and a half of good drinking water on one of the trucks.

The object of our patrol was to make contact with Charles Column, which was falling back, parallel to my own column. I had a pin-point in the desert for the rendezvous. I waited there and they never appeared. Other columns did, but not Charles. Much more serious than that, our radio broke down. Skinner said it was a valve which could not be replaced. I sat there and waited for two hours after the agreed time for the rendezvous, then we turned back.

On the run back to where we had left the column I chased three gazelles, firing occasional short bursts with the Bren at them. But they were too fast for a carrier, and I had no luck. The dust spurts were all round them. The column needed food by that time, and gazelle is among the best and most tender flesh in the world, or so it always seemed after weeks of bully beef.

The column was not there when we got back. But I noted that its tracks all led off on the bearing Jimmy had left me. There was a lot of thumping up there, but no smoke-cloud. It was five o'clock.

"Time for a cup of char, sir?" asked Sergeant Robeson.

"Yes, but we've no time to cook. I would like to catch the column before nightfall. I'll give you ten minutes."

We did not find our column, and before dark closed in we were crossing a hilly and scrubby part of desert where there had evidently been a tank battle. So among the blackened, sad remains of British "Crusader" and "Honey" tanks we lost the tracks of our column. That was our undoing. The column (although we had no means of knowing it) had been obliged to change direction and force its pace. Already it was far to the east and south of us, and with every rev of our engines we widened the gap, for we were thrusting right up into the centre of German strength, while they, informed and instructed by a higher command with aerial vision, were running before that power centre.

Night showed me that we were in a nasty fix. The enemy was in clumps all round us. It was easy to see them at night, for whereas we British kept a dead silence and showed no light, the Germans, who lacked our excellent compasses and our ability to navigate in small groups, guided their supply vehicles into the laagers by firing streams of coloured Very lights.

My five companions saw the lights of course, and were as quick to grasp their significance. But nothing daunts the Londoner. These men were hungry, and they decided to turn our bad situation into a temporarily good one. There was so little hope of our surviving the following day that we might as well eat all we could hold. No point in saving. Robeson, who excelled as a cook (as well as in every other role), made us some kind of stew; and the "follows", I remember, were tinned "yellow cling" peaches supplied from my carrier. To top the whole thing off, Robeson made us coffee. Delighted by this wonder meal, the riflemen went quickly to sleep. We had a roster, with each man, including myself, taking sentry-go for one hour. We slept stretched closely side by side in the lee of my carrier, so that one touch could wake the lot of us. I slept well, for I was very, very tired.

Before dawn we were on the move again. But we did not get far. By midday my carrier was in flames.

Skinner and I crawled over the brow of the hill, and the German half-track drawing a gun was nearly at our carrier. While we were momentarily halted by this sight we saw Jones's head pop up above the camouflage netting, and then disappear down into the carrier again. One of the Mark IV tanks that we had been watching on the other side of the ridge came cruising up; he stayed in a hull-down position near the top of the ridge. But the men on the turret could just see our carrier, and they might see us. We kept low.

"Where the hell did those devils spring from?" I was cursing myself. Cursing that I lay there so helplessly. That we had gone away from the carrier on foot.

Down in the hollow were hidden the two trucks we had met that morning, with two officers and some men from my own battalion in them. The tank behind us edged a shade farther forward, closer. Skinner and I got lower down in the thin camel scrub. Jones was lifting himself slowly in the carrier now, his hands up. He had been working on the engine. The Germans, six or seven of them in steel helmets, strutted round the carrier for a minute. They asked Jones in pantomime to drive it away. He refused. They threatened to shoot him. He still refused. So they pulled him out and tossed in a hand-grenade. A blaze began immediately the grenade punctured the twin petrol-tanks. The tank rattled and clanked a little closer; Skinner and I were now less than fifty yards from it. You would never have believed that the crew did not see us. I could plainly hear them talking. They were discussing—in German, of course—the merits of Players and Gold Flake cigarettes.

The two trucks in the hollow were also burning now. There was a volley of scattered rifle-fire from around the trucks where Vic and Jeffery and their men were lying. One of the half-tracks came flying past us, so close that it nearly ran over our feet. The rifle-fire was accurate. We heard one or two rounds ricochet off the steel sides of the half-track, and the Germans inside it were keeping well down. Then, away to the left of us, we saw Vic leading his men away in open order and at the double. The tank behind us must have seen them too. But he did nothing. Rommel's Afrika Korps were on the start line of their long advance, and had no particular desire to clutter themselves with prisoners. A man on foot in the desert would soon starve to death. After a time the tank moved away a little distance. Skinner and I lay still. There was no sign of Vic and his men now. But over in the direction where they had been running another big German column was slowly crossing the desert. Most of their trucks were captured Ford 3-tonners. We could hear another convoy on the far side of the hill; and between us and them there was the inquisitive tank and several others, perhaps five or six.

When it was nearly dark we stood up, doing the cabman's exercise to warm our arms and shoulders. We crossed to the still smouldering carrier. Most of what had not been burned had been blown to bits by the hand-grenades and anti-tank mines she had carried. But we found a haversack and enough tins to keep us going for some days. We had a meal then and there beside the wreckage of what had been home a few hours ago. Skinner tried to comfort me. I felt better when we could stand up and walk.

We headed north-east on the stars. I told Skinner we would walk all night and dig ourselves in before daylight came. We would lie up all day, unless there was any sign of transport to be had for the taking.

"Don't worry. We shall make it easily," I told him. And I meant it. We were fairly well equipped. We had two full water-bottles, our boots were sound, and each of us had a .38 revolver with twelve rounds. Then we had the compass in case the weather got bad, and I had great hopes of picking up an abandoned vehicle and making it go, or perhaps stealing a German truck during the night. Our other hope, a fairly feeble one, was to get in touch with Senussi tribesmen, most of whom were friendly to the British.

We walked through the night, resting at ten minutes to every hour, and religiously starting off again at the hour. Both of us were still sleepy after many days and nights of hard work and anxiety. It became extraordinarily difficult to go on again once we had sat down. I had to waken Skinner each time. At the end of six hours' walking, we heard trucks behind us. When we dropped flat we saw them sky-lined. They stopped and waited in silence, as the German supply columns were trained to do. A shower of green flares went up all round us. We seemed to have walked right into the open space, some 600 yards across, between three or four laagers. At 2.30 a.m. all these laagers began to hum with work. Flares were constantly going up. Trucks and little scout cars ran past us, carrying messages from one laager to the other. Skinner was already asleep, lying uncomfortably on his face in the shingle. I woke him, and painstakingly, with our hands, we dug a hole for ourselves in a spot where some camel scrub gave a little cover. A great deal of the noise around us was made by tank engines. Whenever we slacked in our digging I told Skinner we had to get that hole so deep that a tank could pass over us without squashing us. We did it, after an hour's scraping and digging with sharp-edged flat stones. I cut some bushes. We lay in the hole, clinging to each other, and covered ourselves with the bushes. Even at the bottom of the hole we still felt the icy wind that now swept the desert. The sweat we had on us from digging soon became glacial.

I was wakened by the increased noise of tanks and Skinner saying to me: "Thank God we dug deep, sir."

The tanks were rumbling past us in close column. They were so close that the shaking of the ground broke off stones from the sides of our hole, and I was afraid of a serious cave-in. I looked at my watch. Four o'clock. But then Rommel was always in favour of the early morning pounce. There were a lot of them. Both Mark IVs and Mark IIIs, much more formidable than any tanks we had to stop them. Following the tanks went the soft vehicles.

When they had all gone it was six o'clock, and nearly light. I took the compass-bearing of their course and reckoned, rightly I think, that they were making for Derna.

Skinner's face, which had a good deal of loose flesh on it, was shaking laughably from the cold. I myself was hardly in better shape. The cold night had brought on "gippy tummy". We breakfasted on a tin of condensed milk. Then it rained. With the icy wind and rain we could not remain hidden there. We must walk or die.

"In some ways it's a good thing," I said to Skinner. "Visibility is poor, and we don't risk so much, walking. Then the rain will prevent us from getting too thirsty."

Skinner tried to agree, but his teeth were chattering so briskly that he found speech impossible. We walked very fast for the first fifty minutes, and at the end of that spell I felt a little tired and stiff, but I was still perishingly cold. Skinner was even colder. Our battle-dress was soaked through. The wind was in our faces. We walked again.

We walked ourselves into a state of numbness. At first I carefully kept to the fifty minutes' walking, ten minutes' rest. As the hours walked past us I found that the rests stretched to quarter of an hour, sometimes twenty minutes or half an hour. The moment we sat down both of us fell asleep. We awoke automatically, not because we were rested, but because of the cold. Then we walked again.

We walked through small battlefields littered with piles of cases of expended shells, mortar bombs, and cartridges, and with occasional carcases of vehicles. In the first day we examined perhaps twenty such carcases. But the Germans were being thorough. When a vehicle became a casualty they destroyed it or had it towed back immediately by their recovery sections.

After each vehicle inspection we walked on a shade more despondently. Each vehicle showed signs of that super-military thoroughness. I decided that our best hope was to find a German truck at night and overpower the driver.

The weather was what was going to beat us. Cold uses up a man's energy. And there would be no question of sleep that night.

"What are the odds against a fine day to-morrow?" I asked Skinner.

"About fifty to one against, I should say, sir."

"So should I. This rain looks set for a week."

"Irony of fate, isn't it, sir? The folks back home will be thinking of us dying of thirst on the hot sands, and the worst things of all are the damp and cold, not to mention the blisters."

"The funny thing is that I *am* thirsty."

"Same here, sir. What about a short one, next halt?"

"Well. Just one mouthful each."

"That's the ticket, sir."

"We shall have to keep going to-night, that's certain."

"You said it."

"So our best hope, as I see it, will be to find a German laager and steal one of their trucks. We've got our two pistols. We should have an excellent chance in the dark."

"I couldn't agree more, as the major would say, sir."

"Yes, he would, wouldn't he? Wonder how the column is. Hope they're all right."

"They're doing no bleeding walking. If I ever get out of this packet I'll walk no more so long as I draw breath."

We walked fairly steadily through the day, and in the evening we came on a well-worn track made by German vehicles. This track was even sign-posted every quarter-mile or so. The sign had a big J on it. We agreed to follow the track in the hope that it would lead us to concentrations of German vehicles that night. We did not walk on the track, we followed it by keeping the J signs on our left.

We walked and walked and walked. Then, in the cold, and although it was still raining, we lay down to sleep. We lay in a weapon-pit dug either by British or German troops, probably British, I thought. There had been mortar bursts all round the weapon-pit.

Sleep in such cold and damp neither rests nor refreshes. All the muscles stiffen against the discomfort, and the body cannot find relaxation. But we slept for quite a long time. When we awoke I found it difficult to remember where I was. There was a singing in my ears, I was not hungry, and my "gippy tummy" was worse. Skinner was in bad shape too.

All that we felt we could eat was one small tin of condensed milk between the two of us. We drank one mouthful of water each. Then we walked on, and the day wore past in the old fifty-minute drudgeries. I began to hear violins playing in my ears. Sometimes a single violin playing Beethoven's "Concerto", sometimes an orchestra, sometimes millions of violins a long way away, a sea of sound. My "gippy tummy" bothered me whenever we halted now. The track began to draw us towards it. There was no traffic on the thing, anyway. We had been beside it for æons of time and nothing had passed. In

35

fact I was wondering whether it would ever lead us to any vehicles.

There seemed to be a battle going on about fifty miles to the north-east of us. Apart from that, everything was so empty, so desolate, that we might have been walking on the driftweed of the Dead Sea. Finally we just walked along the track itself. By this time our feet were raw, and it was much easier walking on the track than through the camel scrub. The violins played me along.

The German convoy came up behind us and was within sight of us before we realised that it was there. My mind must have wandered because I remember thinking that if we just walked calmly on without paying any attention to the convoy, the Germans would pay no attention to us. Skinner seemed to be just as vague.

Five or six trucks stopped beside us, and we were surrounded by a group of excited German soldiers with levelled rifles. One of them spoke French to me, and his words brought me back to reality.

"Raise your hands," he was saying. "Or you will be shot."

We raised our hands above our heads. They pushed forward eagerly to examine and finger our clothing. One of them told Skinner to take off his gold wedding-ring. I protested hotly to the one who spoke French.

"So you understand German," he said. "And you speak good French. Who are you? Airmen, I suppose?"

"Do you want our names, ranks, and numbers?"

"All right, all right, keep calm, officer."

He was a sergeant, an elderly, decent-looking man. One of his men poked at Skinner with the muzzle of his rifle, and asked if they were not going to kill us.

"Kill them?" answered the sergeant reasonably. "You don't understand war, my son. They are more valuable alive. Besides, look at their fair hair and blue eyes. They look just like Germans . . ."

"God forbid," I interrupted, but in French.

"Now, now, officer. Please be reasonable. Look, men," he went on to the group. "They must have been in the desert for days. Where is that spare coat? This one is an officer."

One of them went to a truck and came back with a British greatcoat. He handed it to me with clumsy friendliness. Something in the friendliness opened some duct inside me. I felt tears, tears of shame, rushing to the back of my eyes. I passed the coat to Skinner, who put it on. When I noticed his face alongside the dirty but hearty faces around us I was quite startled. Skinner looked like a corpse that had been dug up out of wet sand.

The sergeant clucked his tongue sympathetically when he saw that I was still coatless.

"You, Hans," he shouted. "Give the officer that New Zealand coat. Come on now, what are you waiting for?" Hans was the man who had felt like shooting us. He peeled off the New Zealand coat and gave it to me with a dirty look. At this further generosity I again had to fight down an inclination to weep.

We were helped into the back of a truck, with three Germans for guards. They were loutish young men, very friendly to us. They offered cigarettes and oranges. Both of us were too upset to accept. Now that we were out of the wind and sitting down, I realised fully the enormity of what had happened. If I could have killed myself I would have done it. For a free man to be suddenly a prisoner is terrible. It must resemble castration. It seemed to me that everything was lost. A blinding hate for our curious and kindly guards filled me one instant. And next instant I felt like a small boy who arrives at a new and fearsome school, and wants to cry every time anyone addresses a word to him, especially a kind word.

We were driven to an airfield with Messerschmitt 110s clustered on one corner of it. A lot of dirty-looking air crews came to gape at us. "That's an Army officer," I heard them tell our sergeant. "Better send them on to the advanced company of the infantry."

"Can't you send them in one of your trucks, sir?"

"No. You found them, you take them. You can spend the night with that company, then move on in the morning."

"Just as you say of course, sir," answered the sergeant, but when he came back to give orders to the drivers he was in a bad temper. "They've been hanging around here all day while we've driven a hundred and fifty kilometres, but *we* have to take the damned prisoners on and cover an extra sixty kilometres into the bargain," he said angrily. "Besides, these hellish forward troops never have any food to spare. I was hoping to eat some decent British tinned stuff to-night." I wondered if he was regretting his humanity when he had forbidden the other to think of killing us.

It was late when we drove up to the forward company. They

37

had two or three Spandau machine-guns on the ground, pointing at a number of prisoners, perhaps one hundred, who squatted in a big clump. Most of them were South Africans, recognisable by their light-coloured steel helmets. A good few were coloured. They looked most pathetic.

When they saw us they did a surprising thing. They burst out laughing. The Germans around us echoed their laughter. In fact ripples of laughter spread over the encampment.

"What are they laughing at?" I asked Skinner, who had been shouting to a few of the men whom he evidently knew.

"They say we look like snow-men, sir. And one of them said we were Tutankhamen and Nefertiti."

Skinner's friends came across to speak to us, but our guards angrily pushed them clear of me.

"*Offizier, offizier,*" they kept repeating. The sergeant explained to me in French: "Sorry, officer, but we don't allow men prisoners to mix with officers."

"How childish," I answered (though of course we had the same rule in the British Army), and the sergeant agreed with me. He handed me over to another N.C.O., who led me to a truck in which a German major was washing his feet in a bowl that held two pints of dirty water. The N.C.O. told me to climb into the truck. So I did. Then the major screamed to me to get out. So I did.

"But this is an officer, sir," the N.C.O. told him. Whereat the major stuck a wizened head on the end of a long neck out of the back of the truck, and asked me in slow English to step inside.

"Heartiest apologies, lieutenant," he said. "Forgive me, I did not recognise your uniform. You are so very, very dirty I thought you were a soldier." He spoke correct English, but uttered the words with excruciating slowness. Sometimes he would pause for as long as a minute while he silently searched for a noun or selected the tense of a verb. His French was better, more fluent, at any rate. He asked me politely to sit down, apologised, and continued to wash his feet. When he had finished that he fed me on a dixieful of rice stew. He ate himself a complete tin of Italian meat, which he opened and consumed with the aid of his dagger. I had difficulty in eating, and fought against alternating currents of sullen rage and tearfulness. The kinder he was the worse I felt.

He was a regular Wehrmacht man, risen from the ranks. He had fought in Poland, Holland, Belgium, and France before joining the Afrika Korps. This new attack, he told me smoothly, was to go right through to Russia, crossing the Suez Canal as quickly as possible.

"We are the right fork of the pincers," he explained. "The left fork is working through Russia approaching Stalingrad now." He wagged a horny finger under my nose. "You smile, lieutenant. You think we cannot pass the Suez Canal. But you have nothing to stop us. Germany is invincible on the ground and in the air. Really, the efforts of your factories are lamentable. I admit that your trucks are better than ours, but your tanks! Why, your poor tank crews might as well fight with bows and arrows. Then again, let us admit it frankly, you British are charming fellows. But no soldiers, just amateurs. Your navy now. That's something. There you have a discipline equivalent to that of our Wehrmacht, and a spirit.

"With your navy and our army and air force our two countries could lick the rest of the world." This was the first time that I heard a German express this view. But it was one that was commonly expressed, at any rate in the Afrika Korps. I must have heard it from them fifty times in the short time that I was their prisoner.

The major lay down for the night on a mattress covering the floor of the truck. He told me to lie on one of the benches and gave me two of his many blankets. Maddeningly he talked on and on in his slow English while I tried to get to sleep. Whenever I temporarily succeeded he would shake me with his heavy hand.

"Do I say that correctly?" he would ask. "Is the verb correct?" So he hammered on at me. He let me know that he thought the war would be ended that year. When it was over he planned to go to England, to the Isle of Man, where his father had been a prisoner of war from 1916 to 1918.

"He was well treated by your people," he said. "My father always told me: 'The French are rotten, no good. But the British are fine people. The only people in Europe who resemble Germans, who are fit to be friends with the Germans.'"

"Utter nonsense," I told him angrily. "It is the French and the British who spiritually have much in common."

"You only say that because you are upset, and you feel now, wrongly, that we are enemies," he replied, with maddening calm. "Do not feel upset, it will only make your imprisonment an agony. I am a professional soldier. With me soldiering is no game. If I am taken prisoner then it is just part of my job. I may be taken in this advance, who knows? In that case I will expect to be well treated by the British. In war the soldier must keep to the rules when dealing with soldiers—of course with civilians or outcasts like Jews, more stringent steps may be necessary.

"At any rate, you will be well treated by us. The trouble is that we shall be obliged to hand you over to the Italians, who are the most unmitigated swine. They add to their incompetence as soldiers by maltreating their prisoners. They are useless, scented creatures, popinjays, degenerate, merely the jackals of Rommel's desert army."

"You do not propose to settle down in conquered England?" I asked him bitterly. But he noticed no bitterness.

"Oh no," he answered simply. "I shall retire from the army after the war and settle in South Africa, a country where life is reasonable and where there flourishes a traditional love for Germany. I shall have a house with a veranda and a comfortable income."

"From what source will your income be derived?"

"Why, that is simple. Before the war all Englishmen were rich and all Germans poor. After the war it will be the Germans' turn to be rich."

At this interesting stage in our conversation the major was turned out of his bed. There was a lot of swift talk which I did not bother to understand. Then the lorry moved off. An *Aspirant* rode in the back with the major and me. He held a *Luger* pistol ready in his hand.

"Forgive the guard," the major said. "But I can take no chances with you. Indeed, you would despise me if I did. We have only a short journey, then you will perhaps see North Africa's Man of Destiny."

There were a great many officers in the low, dark tent. They stood very stiffly, politely, their uniforms and their rugged faces stone-coloured in the lamplight. They might have been German officers carved out of rock or hardwood. Rommel came through the crowd for a moment to look at me. His face swam before my eyes, but before all these people, watching me, I was intent on being cold and dignified in spite of the dirt that covered me. Rommel asked the major if I spoke German, and the major told him, Yes, a few words.

The general looked at me for a moment or two. There was no compassion in his hard, worn face. I looked straight into his face, not caring what he thought of me. Then he spoke softly.

"He looks tired out," he said to the others. "Some of these Britishers have covered fantastic distances on foot in the desert." Then he raised his voice and spoke to me slowly and distinctly.

"Do you like whisky?"

"Yes, General."

"Bring some whisky," he called to an orderly. The orderly brought me nearly half a glass, neat. It was Johnny Walker, I recognised by the taste. I drank it at once, for I was suddenly afraid that there would be a toast. Rommel did not drink, but most of the others did.

"You will be well treated, Lieutenant," Rommel told me. "War with us is an impersonal thing. All my men have orders to treat prisoners correctly. But under an International Agreement we are obliged to hand over all prisoners, except sometimes airmen, to the Italians, our Allies." The last word was spoken with soft, hissing emphasis, and a rustling titter swept the polite wedge of officers around us.

"War is strange indeed," the general went on. "Sometimes the soldier wonders that he is fighting with so-and-so against so-and-so. Well, adieu, Lieutenant. Good luck and the condolences of all officers in this tent." The crowd in uniform, crowd of worshippers hewn from stone, closed around the great man. The major took me back to the truck, made sure the young *Aspirant* was awake to guard me, and dived back into the tent. I fell asleep while I listened to the murmur of voices and wondered what lives, German and British, depended on that eager talk.

When I awoke the truck had moved. We had apparently left the major at Rommel's headquarters, and now there were half a dozen German N.C.O.s and an interpreter with me in the truck. The N.C.O.s were taking off the cover and mounting two Spandaus, pointing forward, on the roof of the driver's cab.

"Don't worry, Lieutenant," said the interpreter in deep, fruity, American accents. "You won't have to walk, but the men will, poor bums. We got no transport but this old washout. They will walk thirty kilometres to-day. It's the only way we can get them back. There is neither food nor water here for them."

We set off, jolting down the trail cut by the German tanks, but going back. The prisoners struggled in an untidy, complaining column ahead of us. After a time some of the South Africans began to fall by the roadside. The Germans stopped the truck and loaded them in, one by one. They told me that they had not seen food for days.

"Quite true," the German interpreter agreed, when I complained. "How could they see food? We only have the company's reserve rations on this truck, and the company only had its fighting rations. They had to be kept for the advance."

About half of the South Africans who now lay in our truck were feigning injuries or exhaustion in order to get the lift. Several of them told me so. This was all right until other cases fell out. I had to turn some of the first "casualties" off the truck in order to give rides to their more exhausted brothers. This caused bad feeling. When I walked alongside the struggling column (for the guards would not allow me to walk in it) I heard some cries of "Bloody officer," and others still more outspoken. This pained me because it occurred in front of the Germans. I was glad when they ordered me back on the truck again. The interpreter then harangued the whole column.

If any more men fell out they would have to be shot, he said. Also the marching speed must be increased. At a halting-place that was now only twelve kilometres distant all prisoners would get water, soup and bread. But if the column did not increase its speed they would not get there before nightfall.

We got there, but no food arrived, and water came only in the shape of rain. The Germans put up the cover again, and we sat in the back of the truck, eating, and then sleeping, sitting bolt upright on the benches. They were polite with me, offering me first helpings of everything that they ate, dark, sticky brown bread, tinned meat, good cheese packed in tubes like toothpaste, jam and coffee. They ate much less than British soldiers, it seemed to me. Then they were very much dirtier than my own men, both in their persons and in their weapons. Several of these German N.C.O.s were lousy, although they had only just left their own lines to begin the attack. They carried more authority than our N.C.O.s though, and they seemed better fitted for it, more conscientious.

They were slightly contemptuous of me, I felt. And the interpreter, who stayed always at my side, was treated with open disdain.

"The others dislike me because I worked for fifteen years in America," he admitted to me. "They say I am crazy because I know Britain and America are stronger than the Nazi Government believes or says."

"What did you do in America?"

"I was a 'cellist on Broadway."

"Why did you leave America?"

"Blood is strong with us Germans. I had to leave when the war got going and they tore through Poland. Also I have a great hatred for the Jews."

"Then why did you live in America, where Jews are not persecuted?"

"Have an orange, Lieutenant, and quit talking about Jews. That always makes me feel ill."

I accepted his orange, as I accepted all the other food, and put it in my pocket. I was trying to accumulate a little store, to give to Skinner and the other men, who were still unfed twenty-four hours after arriving at the halting-place. While we remained there a few Italian officers from their *Ariete* armoured division, which was scattered over our desert horizon—peacefully resting some fifty miles behind the leading German tanks—came over to have a look at us.

Highly scented, in their waisted uniforms and polished riding-boots (without spurs) they danced about among the prisoners, and finally came to mock at me in jibbering English. When they had made some remarks about Churchill and the British as a whole, a German sentry came along with his rifle held in a horizontal position, and using it as a broom, he swept these perfumed crows away. I was delighted to see that there was every evidence of schism among the Axis soldiery. The Germans were openly contemptuous of their Italian allies, while the Italians could scarcely conceal the loathing and fear in which they held the Germans.

An Italian truck-driver turned out to be a better man than the *Ariete* officers, although he wore sandals instead of polished riding-boots. I travelled back through Agedabia in the cab of his big Lancia diesel truck. About fifty prisoners, with some German guards, occupied the back.

This Italian handed to me, and to the German guard who sat beside me, his thermos which held hot coffee. And when we had emptied that he handed me an enormous flask which was chained to his steering column. The contents made me choke, and then made me cheerful, for it was full to the screw-cap with potent *anis,* and I like that taste well enough. Fortified with this strong spirit, I arrived at the German interrogation centre.

It was a small bowl in the sand-hills on the left of the supply road built by Mussolini from Tripoli to Agedabia and on to Egypt. There were some hundreds of prisoners squatting there, but I was the only officer. They pushed me into a small box-shaped, and hideously camouflaged tent. While I sat on the sand inside, two German officers brought me a whole loaf of their brown bread and a full tin of delicious Italian peach jam. They endeavoured to pump me a little, but in a most amateur fashion. Thus:

"What part of England do you come from, old man?" asked one of them when I had given them my name, rank, and number.

"I am sorry, I cannot answer that question."

"Oh, nonsense, my dear fellow," insisted the other German. "My friend here only asks because he has greatly lived in your beautiful country, and he has many friends in all regions of it."

"Under the international rules governing warfare I am only obliged to give you my name, rank and number."

"We know, we know, old man. You are only behaving correctly. As we should behave in your unfortunate circumstances. Well, for you the war is ended."

"Looks like it."

"And your men, those poor fellows down there. So many of them fair-haired and with frank, blue gazes. To think that we should be fighting against such men, and that our Allies are the Japs, yellow men, while you fight with the Russians against us. . . . It's so unnatural. . . ."

"Not unnatural at all. The Russians are our brothers. Side by side with them the British face German tyranny and cruelty. We are proud to fight beside them. We shall be proud to live in amity with them when the war has been won and the Teutonic bullies lie putrefying with their yellow brothers in the dust."

"Are you taught to say all this?"

"Indeed, no, it is quite spontaneous."

"Then you are a British Communist?"

"I am not."

"Well, we must go now. *Bon appetit.*"

They walked away, a serious, wooden, silly-looking couple. But their senior officer was having better luck with the other prisoners. This German intelligence officer was clearly a more dangerous person. He did not wear German uniform. Instead he strolled about among the prisoners in shorts and a khaki shirt which bore no insignia. He was a medium-sized dark man with a charming, tired smile, and he spoke English like a South African. While he talked to the men he handed out bread and jam and the kind of platitudes they wanted to hear as they

44

guzzled the first food they had seen for days. Soon some of them were showing him photographs of their wives and children. Wherever he went there seemed to be laughter and good fellowship. I watched this, seething, through the entrance to my absurd brown-and-blue tent. When I tried to walk out to scowl at least at the too-voluble prisoners I was rudely thrust back inside.

Then they packed us into trucks. By now the good-fellowship act of the intelligence officer was wearing thin. The prisoners, their spirits coming back in a rush with the food, were beginning to guy him. They did this by profiting from his friendly overtures. Soon they were calling him "Fritzy" and "Sunny Jim". I heard one grizzled and filthy private ask him: "What's your name, chum?" Another replied: "Why, it's Jerry, ain't it, Jerry?" This ponderous witticism was accompanied with a slap on the shoulder that sent the German reeling. His thin, intelligent face went chalk colour with rage; and when we left in the trucks he was standing screaming hoarse insults and orders at us in that peculiar, mechanical voice that German officers and N.C.O.s adopt when they berate their inferiors in rank.

It is extraordinary what bread and jam can do. I sat in front with one guard and the driver. The thirty prisoners behind sang all the way down the strategic road to 'Agheila. It was a difficult trip, for the road had been badly mauled by the R.A.F., and there was a constant stream of war material pouring up in the other direction. To make things worse, the German driver did not know how to drive. He frankly admitted that he had just learned, and the truck's steering was extremely worn. After grazing first an ambulance, then a staff car, and finally a tank, the old Ford arrived, heaving, at an adobe building in a square in 'Agheila.

My German guard, still one of the Afrika Korps men, held out his hand, and after a second's hesitation I shook it. I was immediately glad that I had thus unbent, for he gave me an orange and a stick of excellent German chocolate.

"Eat them at once," he advised me. "Otherwise the Italians will steal them from you. Also take my advice and hide that handsome watch of yours."

A swarm of little Italian soldiers in Dr. Livingstone sun-helmets, with grotesque crimson plumes waving from them, came rushing out of the adobe building, and thrust us inside with little, maddening pats from their ever-moving claws. After standing in a queue with the men, taking my turn to be interviewed, I was dragged in front of a stout major. He was seated behind a small desk in a low room that smelled badly of wet clothes, brilliantine, and dirt.

"Rank?" he asked.

"Second-lieutenant."

"Ah. An officer."

He looked up at me, studying my uniform. Suddenly he leaned forward and shrieked in Italian: "The green rope is mine."

"But you had the last, the pocket-knife," complained the thin captain who stood behind him. Then I understood. They wanted my regimental whistle-cord. The major leaned forward and tugged at it, and the whistle attached to it came out of my breast pocket.

"You cannot take that," I told him in English.

"Cannot? You don't understand the position."

"Yes, the whistle-cord is part of my uniform. You may not take it under the Geneva Convention."

"Ah," he exclaimed. "But the whistle is part of your military equipment, and I am entitled to relieve you of that." He was so pleased with his own intelligence that he took the whistle, left me the cord, and did not have me searched. So my watch, fountain-pen, and money escaped their attentions.

It was raining when they pushed me with a batch of thirty men into a barbed-wire cage. The ground underfoot was squelching mud, and there was scarcely room to sit or lie down, so tightly was the space (perhaps one hundred square feet) packed with men. I went to the entrance to protest.

"*Ufficiale, ufficiale,*" I repeated to the sentries, knowing that this meant "officer", and hoping (how green I was) that they would either let me out or would send for one of their own officers. Instead they only mocked my words, repeating them like parrots. And two of these dignified soldiers put their pale tongues out at me.

There was a small building that looked like an English coal-cellar in one corner of the cage. Skinner found me raging at the sentries, and led me over to the building.

"You ought to go inside, sir," he said. "There are three other officers in there, and some sergeants."

So I tried to go in, but the floor was quite covered with bodies. I could not turn anyone out of that refuge, where the air felt quite warm and dry. Skinner made room for me beside him outside, on a bank; and a little South African (whose unknown

46

name be praised) insisted on sharing his one blanket between the three of us.

Thus, lying on excreta and in the rain, I passed my first night in Italian hands.

CHAPTER III

EARLY next morning I wandered round and round the cage before the other prisoners were afoot. My suspicions of the night before were confirmed. We were shut up on a native refuse-dump and open latrine. It was not surprising therefore that from this moment my "gippy tummy" developed into something more like dysentery. When I think back to my first two months in Italian hands it is the dysentery that looms up, pushing other things into the background, as a sandstorm makes you forget the desert. I will try not to write again of dysentery, for it is a tedious disease. For nearly two months I was ill. Sometimes I was helpless as a child before it can walk, before the armour on its skull has hardened. Sometimes the disease was only a pastime. Because of it I was less than a man. There was no strength in me. Only an interest in survival, and in a time when I would be well again inside.

When they had issued us with our first Italian hard rations, a four-inch-square, yellowish-whitish dog biscuit and a tin of meat, they pushed us into trucks again. The native refuse-dump had to be cleared at once for more British arrivals.

This trip (although we did not realise it) was a luxury one for myself and the other three officers. We occupied the back of a big Lancia truck with only two guards for company. There was plenty of room, and the day began brilliantly when Denis Patchett, of the Queen's Bays, stole a large lump of Parmesan cheese from one of our guards and shared it with the rest of us. I had known Denis by sight in England. He was a regular cavalry officer. Now, like the rest of us, he was shaggy and filthy, but usually ready to laugh, like any Irishman, at his own misfortunes.

Richard Carr, a young, broad and heavily built officer, adjutant of the celebrated Long Range Desert Group, later became one of my best friends, but I did not take an instant liking to him. He seemed to be sad and ponderous. When I first saw him in his dusty British Warm, with his great black head hanging forward, I took him for a padre. My third companion was Tonks, a self-possessed young regular from the 10th Hussars.

I realised, when I had their company, how lonely I had been since my capture, and how much any company can help a man to face a hostile world. Our truck was swiftly, skilfully driven west, hurtling us away from our own people. In half a day it slashed a slice off the map and we found ourselves mounting under orange-trees to the cavalry barracks at Sirte. Cavalry. Patchett and Tonks were convinced that we would be better off here.

We were pushed into a room which had nothing in the way of furniture except two or three rush mats on the stone floor. With these we made ourselves a bed for the four. Patchett had stolen a blanket and Tonks, lucky man, had got away from his burning tank with his officer's valise—blankets, soap, tooth-brush and all.

Among the phallic obscenities scrawled on the walls by filthy-minded Italian *soldati* were little notices written by British officers. I saw the name of Clifford Wheeler, one of the officers in my battalion. He had gone through a few days before.

"Watch the 'Pope's nephew', he'll try to make you tight," someone had written on the wall.

When I entered the room the tall dark officer stood swaying a little, as though he were stretching up from the balls of his feet.

"Do sit down, Millar," he said, with an Italian-American accent. "Bad luck being captured, but you'll be O.K. when you get back to Italy. Have you any complaints about your treatment so far?"

"Yes. The Germans treated me like a soldier. The Italians have gone out of their way to insult me and the men with me."

"Tut. Never mind. In Italy you will be treated like a lord. Here, in the front line, feeling runs a little high. Your Australians pushed their Italian prisoners around terribly, you know. We shall never forget that. Indeed, after the war there will be some competition among Italians to join the Army of Occupation in Australia.

"But this is stupid," he went on, struggling to regain his suavity. "Let us talk like Christian brothers and not like man-made enemies. I am the Pope's nephew."

"Felicitations."

"Thank you. Now through my uncle's influence I can send messages from the Vatican to your family, your home town,

48

your girl friends, anywhere. They go by radio. Just give me details now, and within a day or two your folk will know that you are O.K."

"I can only give you my name, rank and number."

"But I seem to know your regiment. Let me see." He stared at my green side-hat. "I remember. That badge belongs to the, to the . . . Now don't tell me . . ."

"Don't worry. I won't."

"Aha. But it is so easy for me to find out," he said with a smile, and he carefully drew a sketch of the horn on my hat. Then he gave me leave to go.

Next time I heard his voice he was shouting at the men, who were given the same quarters as the lousy horses (and I think he had temporarily forgotten that he was the "Pope's nephew").

"Whadya think this is?" he shouted. "The Goddamn Waldorf-Astoria?"

Next morning we were paraded in the stable-yard ready to climb on trucks. Three Sikhs, tall, noble-looking men, saluted Patchett, the senior British officer, and told him that they could not use the single open latrine which had been used by hundreds of prisoners. Their religion forbade them to enter the defiled place.

Patchett complained to the "Pope's nephew" (who was there to see the last of us), demanding that the Sikhs be given other accommodation. The "Pope's nephew" laughed. The Sikhs looked at this big, laughing white man, and they did not understand. They could not see that he was laughing at their pain. Patchett lost his temper.

"Waiter, *garçon, Herr Ober, cameriere,* boy, *mozo,*" he shouted at the laughing Italian.

The "Pope's nephew" suddenly stopped laughing.

"Put these four so-called officers on the trucks, with the men," he said to the guards. Then to us: "Why should you ride alone like gentlemen? I am keeping these three natives. They will stay because I have a job for them—they will clean out the latrines."

"Please, sir," said one of the Sikhs. "If this officer makes us do that we will die. . . ." But the truck drove away, leaving them standing there, three tall, still figures among the smaller, jerking Italians. Why should men be so cruel, so mean? I asked myself if I could have acted like the "Pope's nephew" in similar circumstances, and I answered myself in the negative. But who knows?

49

I remember our next stopping-place, Misurata, not because of its squalor and beastliness, but because there was an Italian officer, the commandant, who took a liking to me. His liking crystallised into endless conversations in French about the rights of man and the bursting need for expansion of the Italian people, and—more concrete crystallisation—it produced for me almost at will loaves of bread and tins of jam. Sometimes he even gave us coffee from his own officers' mess.

The prison, or transit camp, at Misurata had been an Italian native barracks. The four of us slept in a tiny cell, eight feet by five, which had once been occupied by an Askari soldier, his woman, and his children. But the stay was coloured by the generosity of my quickly-made Italian friend. For months we were to remember Misurata in terms of bread and jam. We remained there for two days. At the end of that time the commandant said good-bye to me like this:

"I am a business man in Milan. I build new houses, new cities. You will remember my name and we shall meet after the war. You are a patriot now, and I am a patriot. But after the war we will be brothers in the sight of God and man. You swear that you will remember my name?"

"I swear it." Then he gave us each another loaf, another tin of jam. I watched his plump, rather ridiculous figure in its striped breeches as, framed in the back opening of the truck, it dwindled to the size of a pea on the long straight road lined with orange-trees. Alas, I had not even memorised his name.

We arrived at Tarhuna two days later, after sleeping the intervening night in a cyclist's rest-house, an ancient tower in an olive grove. In the cyclist's rest-house we had all picked up fleas so strong and so numerous that they made sport and rations of us for weeks. Our journey had been comfortable, for with my few words of Italian I had made a friend among the guards, whose brother was a prisoner of war in South Africa. The guard gave us a little food, all that he had. But he also took us out of the back of the truck and put us in the big cab alongside the driver.

That made six of us in the cab, and we had a good time. The driver handed out a bit of Salami sausage and a small flask of wine. Then he threw back his heavily jawed head and trumpeted the Italian version of "Lily Marlene". He told us that the girls would be wonderful in Italy. That we would occupy villas by the blue sea. That the war would pass with music, feasting, dancing—pass so smoothly that we would regret the brusque interruption of peace. He told us this in French. Before the war he had been in the Milan post office. And once he had gone to Paris for two nights. But I did not care for his talk about Paris.

Now I had nearly "achieved" the journey to Tripoli that we had dreamed about since Jimmy told us in the wet tent at Tidworth: "We're off." They did not deposit us at Tripoli itself, but at this village called Tarhuna, some distance inland. At Tarhuna they had hurriedly made a transit camp for prisoners of war out of some buildings of an ordnance depot used by the Afrika Korps.

When we were herded into the barbed-wire pen Clifford Wheeler and Hugo, one of our company commanders, fussed over me.

"My God!" Clifford said to me when he had looked at me. "What have you done with your hair?"

"Oh, is that all? I had it cut short, nearly shaved, in fact, because I could not keep it clean in the desert."

"And Mike did not mind?"

"Of course he did. But he could not grow it for me."

"Now you must tell me all about everything. . . ."

And I did, for the second time (since Patchett, Carr and Tonks had earlier demanded an account of my experiences and had regaled me with theirs). As I talked to Clifford and the crowds of news-seekers that clustered round, I realised just how boring a man can be when he talks about himself. And the new-prisoner bore is possibly the worst of all bores as he describes (seeks to excuse?) his capture.

CHAPTER IV

I suppose that if I ever return to Tarhuna, and it has not been destroyed by British bombing or gunfire, the building where we were housed may look quite pleasant with its veranda, its pantiles, and its olive-trees. It had originally been an Italian officers' mess, and it may conceivably be spruced up to fulfil that function again.

It certainly seemed pleasant enough, luxurious even, to me then. We slept, fifty British officers, on double-decker iron beds around three sides of a long room. People were kind to me. A clean-looking youngster in the 60th Rifles, Jimmy le Coq, gave me his sleeping-bag. Clifford lent me soap and shaving things.

The tall, serious doctor who gave me medicine, Frank Haines, gave me also a clean shirt. Angus Maude, who had been in the City office of the *Daily Mail*, gave me a pair of socks.

When I arrived I had nothing clean. Now I could lie on my bed, the possessor of a shaven chin, a clean shirt, and clean socks. The other rooms we used were the dining-room, which had a couple of trestle tables in it, the kitchen, a store where the two British cooks slept, and the wash-room. In the wash-room there was running water in two small basins, and two latrines. I had not realised that I was still very thirsty, but now that there was water for the drinking, I found myself almost constantly beside the tap, lapping up the water like an exhausted dog.

We were searched whenever we arrived, aggressively searched by an unpleasant Italian officer aided by two sergeants. Feeling was bad between the prisoners and the Italians. Four of our officers, who had been caught hiding Egyptian money, had been dragged off to the punishment cell just before our arrival. And in the Tarhuna punishment cell there was starvation diet.

A reassuring thing about this place was that the British were organising themselves and offering a solid front against the Italians. The most important man amongst us was Bellamy, an elderly, comfort-loving captain in the Service Corps. He was messing officer and he drew the rations from the Italians each day. The rations were extremely skimpy, we thought, although actually they were more copious than the rations we were to receive in Italy later. We got about two hundred grams of bread a day, and enough meat, macaroni, rice, beans and odds and ends for Bellamy, aided by his cooks, to give us each one-third of a dixie of stew twice daily. Then there was a little coffee for the morning and just enough sugar to sweeten the coffee.

Furse, the senior cook, was nothing short of a genius. He had been employed in the kitchens of the Berkeley Hotel, London, and before joining up at the outbreak of war had been concocting sauces at Gleneagles Hotel in Perthshire. He was a bitter-looking, dark-jawed creature, with the whitest, oiliest skin I ever saw.

Another important figure was the padre, also a bitter-faced man. He seemed to be proficient at his job, although I doubt if he reached such heights of proficiency as Furse did in another sphere. I have no liking for tub-thumping religion. I prefer the reasoned kind, and this padre was apt to ring the easy, patriotic bell when he officiated at his services which were held in our bedroom (so that it was impossible to entirely avoid them if you wanted to be warm in bed after dinner). But he was important even to atheists among us because the Italian authorities were obliged, under the Geneva Convention, to let us have some money. They doled this out parsimoniously, but there was still enough for the padre to go to the native market, accompanied by a guard, and buy filling things like dates and figs. I remember the padre also because he was a heavy smoker, and he used to pick up discarded cigarette-butts from the floor in order to eke out his ration (we got fifty Italian cigarettes a week). And most of all I remember that he had a weak bladder, because at the bottom of his bed there was always hanging a glass receptacle that looked like a goldfish bowl. It was a chilly walk to the latrines at night.

Our two doctors were exceptional. Frank Haines was in the thirties, and serious and ponderous enough in his movements to have been in the sixties. Gordon Hooker was in the twenties, a quicksilver creature who always preferred running to walking.

The most wonderful thing about our two doctors was that they were generous and big in all things. Both of them had come into prison fully equipped with clothing and other semi-necessaries. When I arrived they had already given away almost everything they possessed. I don't suppose there was one among the fifty officers who had not reason to be grateful to the two doctors. Also they constituted themselves "sanitary officers", and they made the latrines work every day—a horrible task; but they calculated that we were seriously under-nourished, and feared an epidemic of dysentery, typhus, or diphtheria. They were good men, and they helped me and other weaklings by the example of their practical goodness.

The nights were almost unbearable at Tarhuna. In the darkness you learned that men who seemed normal during the day were still living a nightmare. Ian Campbell, for instance. In the day-time he was a pleasant, well-built pilot with a long nose, whom we therefore sometimes called "Schnoz". He was an Etonian, and he wore a sailor suit that was much too small for him—clothing that had been provided when a Messerschmitt had shot his Blenheim down into the sea. At night in Tarhuna Ian screamed and fought in his sleep—fought to get out of the cockpit of an aircraft that was submerging deeper, deeper in the green water, then struggled up with bursting chest, up to the surface where he floated, in the blood of his victims.

My trouble was less romantic than Ian's. I snored. I had not done it before. At any rate, I had not been aware of it. And a little later I think I cured myself of it. But at Tarhuna there was nothing to be done. Whenever I got to sleep I was wakened with a prodding stick or a well-aimed boot in the night.

The windows had to be kept shut at nights by order of the Italians, and the foul air soon penetrated from the wash-room. I lay awake hour after hour then, looking at the windy Tripolitanian moon through dirty glass, listening to the shrieks and moans, the snores and softly spoken words of my sleeping companions, and to the incessant clop of rubber soles on the stone floor as officers heaved themselves from their beds, stuck their bare feet into their desert boots, and padded the trail to the wash-room.

Often I thought of Anne as I lay there in the dark. And I thought that she would be pleased if the letters I had written already from this prison ever reached her, if she knew that I was a prisoner, and therefore no longer in danger. I was glad too, after the first few days, that I was still alive. Alive to enjoy the taste of macaroni swill, to enjoy an occasional black Italian cigarette, to enjoy the sunshine on the sand outside our building. Alive to hate the nights—the interminable nights that only ended when Jock, the Guardsman, came round with flat-sided Italian Army aluminium mugs of coffee. I would have saved a scrap of bread from the night before, and perhaps some dates as well, or half a sweet potato. And it was luxury to sit up in bed and breakfast. Luxury to be able to talk again to the companions who surrounded me. Luxury to be able to hate the sharp way that Maude always said to his friend in the next bed: "Morning, *toad.*"

When I use the word "luxury" I cannot but think of Hugo at Tarhuna. Hugo not only possessed two books (one a detective novel and the other a book by his mother about his mother), but he also had a *new* battle-dress, complete with our green regimental facings around the collar. This battle-dress had been in his valise when he was captured, so had the books.

Now Hugo shone forth as a smart officer among a lot of caricatures. The uniform of the British officer in the desert was already diverse enough, with such normal variations as bush shirts and corduroy trousers. The uniform of captured officers, tattered and filthy, with bits missing here and there, was fantastic. Clifford and I were proud of Hugo in his new battle-dress; he was a credit to the regiment.

But I think I envied him his tooth-brush more than the uniform. I used to attempt to clean my teeth with twigs torn from the trees. There was little to do inside but have Italian lessons from Cross, a Reuter correspondent who had been captured near Benghazi, or play "submarines" against Richard Carr. Books were so scarce that you were lucky to be able to borrow one bad one a week.

Outside the building the Italians had left us just enough space for the fifty officers to walk about all at once, provided they observed a few simple traffic rules. There was sand underfoot, and in one place pedestrians had to avoid the remains of a formal garden with low privet hedges. Around our exercise space was the usual barbed-wire fence, and around the outside of the fence were the Italian sentries—more of the species I had seen at 'Agheila, with Dr. Livingstone sun-helmets. Practising my slowly-budding Italian on them, I learned that they were veterans of Mussolini's Abyssinian victory. They were unconvincing—and unconvinced—veterans.

Our own men were prisoners in the big building on the other side of the entrance roadway. They were very miserable, for they were so overcrowded that they were sleeping even in the latrines. They had no beds, and few of them had bedding. Their food was worse than ours, because, although the rations were the same, their food was cooked by the Italians, who, naturally, were less painstaking and imaginative than our Furse.

Up the entrance road between our two compounds drove vehicles of the Afrika Korps, proudly showing their delightful palm-tree insignia—vehicles worn in the desert battle and sent back for overhaul. And down the road drove the same vehicles, crudely patched up. The Germans manning the depot lived in a big building half visible through the trees, a building which was part barracks, part hospital. Several of our own British wounded were there, wondering, fearing that their wounds, encased in white plaster, were going gangrenous.

When the Germans went to eat they marched smartly in column with a long loose step and a jerking bass song. Occasionally a German officer, walking past our compound, would talk to one of my fellow-officers across the wire. Most of us had reacted to the skilfully correct treatment the Afrika Korps had given to prisoners taken in that advance. And certainly none of us could help contrasting the manly kindness of the German fighting man with the petty hatred of the scavenging Italian behind the German fighting screen. I used to argue (for I had lived long enough in France to feel some racial dislike and mistrust for Germans) that if the scavengers had been Germans, not fighting men but second- or third-line troops, they would have treated us just as badly, and in a more exasperatingly thorough and Teutonic fashion than our strictly Latin guards.

Looking north, from our small compound, past the red tennis-court (disused that year), we could see the handsome portico of the new Italian officers' mess. The interesting thing about the portico was that it contained a heavy machine-gun mounted on a tripod and sighted on the door of our building. So that in the event of trouble (or annoyance?) the Italian commandant could leave his newspaper or his table, walk to the front door, and kill Britishers by simply flicking forward the safety-lever and squeezing the trigger. The sighting of this gun bore out two of his favourite expressions which were reported to us by sentries who appeared to find us distasteful, but their commanding officer more distasteful still. The expressions were:

"A comfortable soldier is a good soldier," and: "When the British are dead they are great, when they live they menace all expanding peoples."

The diet and sanitary conditions provided under his régime at Tarhuna must have brought greatness to many Britons. He was killed later, I was told, shot by one of his own men. But now I have forgotten even what he looked like. I am a bad hater. Ogres are dull.

Imprisonment and constant hunger began to spread meanness among the weaker-minded prisoners. You could watch the growing bickerings and petty hatreds. You could see, as the days dragged past, the growing shine of greed and envy in the eye of the man who looked upon his neighbour's dixie, his neighbour's loaf. But the arrival of another big batch of British officer prisoners showed that the meanness, the worst disease of prison life, went deeper than was apparent. Because our community, the community which had been so generous to my own little party of four, turned sour on the newcomers.

They arrived (as we had arrived) coated in the dust of the desert, and without blankets, dixies, knives, spoons, all the little essentials of prison life. Our community had existed for about a fortnight. Long enough, a fortnight, for the seeds of prison selfishness to take root and sprout. In prison you are always afraid that what little comfort exists for you will somehow be taken away. Now the newcomers seemed entirely detestable. We formed a clique that kept itself to one room, while the new officers—and they were more numerous—were allowed to get on as best they could in another room in which the Italians dumped the necessary number of beds. At first we were of the opinion that these newcomers should make their own cooking and meal-time arrangements. But in the end this was a little too much. Bellamy was too good an organiser to allow such wastage of fuel and man-power. So the old lot ate in a "first sitting" while the newcomers sat scratching themselves on the veranda outside, watering at the mouth, sniffing at the odour of Furse's stew, and occasionally shooting ardent looks through the dining-room window.

I distinctly remember the following conversation between two majors. The first major, an old inmate, had just eaten, the cooks and volunteer helpers had whisked away the dixies for washing, and the second major, his appetite at fever-point, was waiting for their reappearance.

Second major: "I say. Is it good to-day? I seem to smell tomato in it."

First major: "Really?"

Second major: "Good bulk, is there? One-third of a dixie?"

First major: "Can't say. Had I known that you wanted a bulletin, I would have undertaken a Gallup Poll."

Second major: "Couldn't possibly put you to such trouble. And there is no need to inquire whether the farinaceous matter was in the form of rice or macaroni."

First major (drawling): "Indeed?"

Second major: "No. I can see the rice in your moustache. It is as visible as the dandruff in your beard. Furthermore, everybody knows that what you eat on first sitting bears no relation to what we 'outsiders' eat on second sitting, especially where quantity is concerned."

First major: "Trust one of your damned lot to make offensive remarks of that nature. I shall report you to the senior British officer."

Second major: "I shall report *you*." (A clatter of dixies from the dining-room.) "After lunch."

It is easy now to sniff at our selfishness. Men and women who sniff easily at such things are men and women who have never feared that they were slowly starving to death. The new arrivals brought an old disease with them—lice. While most of us, sufficiently rested now from our battle fatigue to be longing for a move, walked up and down or round and round talking endlessly about the way we had been made prisoner, the new ones

57

sat limply in the sunshine pulling lice out of their shirts.

The urge to move was strong, even in me, and I was weak, and knew that the journey would be an ordeal. We knew that escape from Tarhuna to the British lines, still apparently moving back to Alexandria, was impossible. The desert distance between was too vast. Any friendly Italians who spoke to us said that we would be well off in Italy. That was it. Italy. We longed for Tripoli then, and the ship that was to take us to the land of promise. Ancient, cultured, civilised, beautiful Italy.

That was why Trig Tarhuna was such a disappointment.

We were carted in ambulances right into the southern suburbs of Tripoli. We thought they were taking us to a ship. Sometimes we could see the Mediterranean, and no sea had ever looked fresher, more desirable. Then, swinging right, the ambulances mounted through olive groves to a strange-looking fortress, half barbaric, half modern. It was a white fort with many slits in the walls that might have been designed for bowmen. Soaring above the adobe agglomeration was a skeleton tower surmounted by a sentry-box.

We were ushered, we officers, into a stone pen which was smaller than a self-respecting Georgian drawing-room. Off the sides of this pen opened seven cells. We were told to divide ourselves into groups of eight. We must sleep eight to a cell.

Behind us, deeper inside that foul prison, we could hear the shouts of rage of our men as they were shown to their quarters, which presumably were worse than ours. Many of them also had dysentery. The stench of that disease hung over the ramparts. Apart from our cells and the inner court-yard we were provided with an exercise space, a small sloping field.

If you eliminated from your consciousness the barbed wire that surrounded the field, and stood with your back to the fort, it was a lovely field sloping as sweetly as the shoulders of one of John Leech's ladies into the olive groves and orchards that themselves swept in a continuous, smooth current to a corner of the blue sea, and to the white buildings of an outlying port of Tripoli. Little children with goats and wizened sheep often came to play on the free side of the barbed wire. The Italian sentries, lounging outside the wire with long rifles slung on their shoulders, told the children that we were mad, dangerous, and dirty. The children eyed us with wondering hatred, and we smiled back. We were certainly dirty. About half of us wore beards, and about six per cent of the beards were successful. There was one squadron-leader who had a beautiful red one, yellowy-red shot with deep chestnut, a strong, pointed, jutting beard. The man was starving. His face was falling away from his cheek-bones, was dragging at the bags beneath his eyes so that too much bilious white showed below his eyeballs. But that beard of his was alive, vivid, full of the self-advertising virility of a Casanova or a Frank Harris. I have forgotten the squadron-leader's name. But not his beard. He shaved it off later, and when I deplored this he explained that he had never liked it, that it had not expressed his real personality. And perhaps after all he was right. You always felt that George V was waiting behind his beard. But this wonderful, sharp, red beard was waiting in front of the squadron-leader. This beard, and the others, annoyed the Italian authorities. And the children, peering through the wire, looked at us as though we were lepers and it was our own fault.

When you turned your head and took in the other two sides of the field, where the boundaries were the walls of the fort, you were pulled, breathless, through the bright winter sunshine to the land of death. One wall was the backcloth to execution. Roughly at chest height the wall was spattered and pitted with bullet-holes, and lower down it was splashed with old, faded blood. Probably Senussi blood. The Italians had a great deal of trouble with the Senussi (but the Senussi had worse trouble with the Italians). It was not a dignified setting for firing-squads. The ground was not even flat. In fact the men facing the rifles must have stood with their right feet some three inches higher than their left feet. And the slope ran up to a mound of sandy earth topped by the steps leading through to our quarters. This mound suppurated and gave forth a ghastly smell, since the one latrine in our quarters was a primitive arrangement between the execution wall and the prison court-yard inside. Its contents seeped into the mound.

And yet, and yet. I look back to Trig Tarhuna as a happy memory. Mankind is great, and there are great memories picked out of stench and squalor.

There were several factors that made Trig Tarhuna good.

Firstly, we all regarded it as the final stepping-stone to Italy, where we expected our lives to be better. We were leaving every day. We stayed there ten days, and learned this lesson. The Italian will say *"domani"* (to-morrow) when an Englishman will talk about the weather.

Secondly, the Italian commandant who said *"domani"* in this case was a kind and good man. He was a thin, sensitive

Northerner who had worked in peace-time for Cook's travel business. He was horrified himself by the prison, and he tried every minute, every second, to think of ways to give us pleasure, to improve our conditions, to see that the guards did not insult us. Sometimes he walked round our field, often he came fussing into our court-yard. His brown eyes were deep pools of compassion, his thin legs, in embarrassment at our living conditions, seemed to endeavour to wriggle out of their high, incongruous boots. He must have had his reward in our reaction to his kindnesses. At that time the most hardened of us would have reacted to anyone who gave us (out of kindness) five cubic centimetres of soup.

And thirdly there was friendship again at Trig Tarhuna. It was forced upon us. The others in my cell were: Richard Carr and Denis Patchett (who had made the trip from 'Agheila with me), Clifford Wheeler, Teddy Key (of the Northumberland Hussars), Nigel Witt (a pre-war stockbroker), and the two doctors. Eight of us in a "bedroom" that would have been cramped for one. Fortunately the bedroom was unfurnished. We made a communal bed, and lay in two lots of four with an interlocking system, so that you slept with the feet of the lot sleeping the other way round on either side of your head. The door of each cell was locked early in the evening. Then time was hard to pass. We played all sorts of games, crouching solemnly round the edges of the tiny floor. Frank Haines had an old torn pack of cards. Very often this priceless possession was out on loan to another cell. When it was not we played round after round of whisky poker and other still more nauseating games. Sometimes we played bridge, and even I (who have disliked the game since I was obliged to play it as a child) played with keen enjoyment. But mostly I remember playing guessing games, or spelling games, or just telling stories. The audience was so receptive that it was as easy as telling fairy-stories to children. Then we used to read aloud, each man reading two pages of a book, then handing it to the man on his left. We did all this to postpone the moment when we must lie down on the floor and sleep. Inexorably that moment would arrive.

It was bitterly cold at nights. We heard the sentries stamping at the top of their queer tower. The pale light of their searchlight stabbed at intervals through the miniature window of the cell. The Italians put a big piss-pot into the cell, but after the first night we forbade the use of this thing. We drew up an agreement to leave the cell all at once. Usually around four in the morning we would all stand up, batter on the door and yell. Eventually a sleepy Italian sentry, freezing in the court-yard and smelling heavily of garlic, sour wine and black tobacco, would let us go one by one to the latrine. One of the trials of prison was your inability to control your bladder. This may have been caused partly by nerves (as many believed), but the main reason was probably the extremely liquid nature of the diet. At any rate, it was like being a baby or a dotard. One night when the guards took longer than usual to open the door, one of us was compelled to seize and fill the dixie from which he would later eat.

Thanks to the good offices of the Italian from Cook's, we ate more copiously at Trig Tarhuna, though the food was prepared in the Italian kitchens, and therefore tasted less clean and less good than at Tarhuna. In the mornings we had sweetened coffee. We would all be awake of course long before the coffee arrived— awake, shivering and miserable. Soon after the coffee the sun would come over the battlements behind us, and it would be warm enough to wash a little at the tap in the court-yard. Then to the field whence, back turned to the fort and the blood-stains, you could look at the corner of the Mediterranean and remember happier times beside, on and in that blue, tideless sea.

My last, yes, my very last, real holiday had been spent on it in the month of June, 1939, when Anne and I had sailed up and down the coast in an old British-built yawl called *La Lame*. I remembered Anne fishing from the deck. She liked hunting things. All her ancestors had been soldiers. She was completely double-jointed. Instead of sitting, as a stiffer woman might have done, with her bare feet hanging over the side, she always crouched, like an Asiatic, sitting on her heels. And while she fished I was usually in the water, twisting, turning, letting it stroke my body, stroke away the unhealthiness of my work in cities. We had trouble with the crew. With the cook, dark and sinister, who charged me not twice, but six times the value of everything he bought. He claimed that he had invented a hand-grenade made of glass which the French Army was going to use. Then he would be a millionaire. Trouble, of a cleaner kind, with the deck-hand, who claimed to have been round the world in sail. While we knew him his movements were completely governed by those of his young wife. When we arrived at a new port this woman was always standing waiting for us on the quay, extremely, fantastically *mignonne* in her tiny shorts, and with her breasts poking aggressively at us below her shirt. The sailor led our party up and down the coast at the tails of her abbreviated shorts.

But there is a big difference between the free man who looks at a sea and the prisoner. Sometimes I dreamed that the navy would rescue us on the trip across the sea—*domani*. . . .

For lunch we always got two-thirds of a dixie of swill-water in which meat had been boiled, and a 250-gram loaf of bread. But the wonderful meal came in the evening, when we had a cup of thin red wine each and some macaroni with a little meat in it. Once each of us actually had a full dixie of macaroni. Some of us were sick when we had eaten such unusually copious meals.

They brought round a travelling establishment to give us hot showers. They even gave us each a small tablet of grey stuff, a substitute for soap. We stood on the slimy duck-boards and rubbed and scrubbed ourselves. I was surprised at the drawn, knobbly look of my body. I would never have recognised it if it had been laid out with a lot of other bodies on a marble slab.

While we bathed, our clothes were put through the portable steam delouser. That finished any pretension they had to being uniforms. The desert was hard on clothing. It sandpapered and faded all materials. Now the delouser shrank and crushed each garment in a million ugly creases. Now we looked like villains. We were fit to show to the Italian mainland in the role of British thugs.

Next day we sailed.

CHAPTER V

WHEN I saw the ship in Tripoli harbour I instantly liked her. She was a fine, rounded freighter of about 7,000 tons, with German anti-aircraft weapons clustering the poop, the forecastle head and monkey island.

They ferried us out to her in pinnaces. We were mixed up with a crowd of happy Italian and German soldiers going home on leave. They were so happy that they forgot to be rude to us. I stood in the pinnace next to a young Italian lieutenant. 'He was fussing round with his kit, and when he had established that all his bags were there, he took care of his appearance. As he dusted his boots, pulled out the creases in the back of his coat, and finally ran a comb through his oiled curls, I remembered that I myself—though in a less spectacular fashion—had once been extremely pleased with my uniform, and extremely proud of it. I contrasted myself then, preening around London and Salisbury Plain, and myself in the pinnace, dirty, unkempt, hungry, weak and smelly. And the thought cheered me. I always had a subdued liking for untidiness, and a hatred for clothes that must be clean and pressed and correct.

The ship had steam up, and as we came on board we were sent below. We officers were lucky. There were only 106 of us. We were put only one deck down in number one hold, next to the forecastle-head, where there was a lavatory which we were allowed to use in the day-time. Our poor men were crowded deep into the other holds. If the ship had been torpedoed or sunk by bombing all of them would undoubtedly have perished. Many of the men had dysentery, and the scenes below in their holds were appalling. The ship, which had been built for fruit-carrying, must have been irreparably soiled by the presence of this wretchedness.

Rations were issued as the ship sailed. Two of the hard, square dog-biscuits and two tins of meat each. Two days' rations for a five-day trip. The Italians gave us no blankets. A few of the hatch-covers were broken. On the first night it was fairly heavy weather, and rain and spray showered down on us as we rolled about on the deck in the dark, dusty hold. I was not worried by sea-sickness, like many of my comrades. In fact, the cold and the salty air seemed to do me good. We clung together in our little group of eight, formed at Trig Tarhuna. So long as you were certain that you were sharing things you felt that anything could be faced.

All the Italians and Germans, crew as well as passengers, wore their life-jackets, and slopped about the decks with their boots unlaced from the moment that we left Tripoli until the ship was firmly tied up in Naples Harbour. It surprised and amused us that the Germans should obey such a craven order, at least in so far as the boots were concerned. But the bo'sun, a wrinkled old Genovese, told us that there had been thirteen ships in the line to which this ship belonged. Now British submarines and air-craft had sunk the other twelve.

One day in the lavatory I heard a tinkle and realised that a gold stopping placed some years before in one of my bigger top teeth was now on its way to the bottom of the sea. This was symptomatic. Without vegetables, milk, or butter, our teeth were beginning to fall to bits. The large open cavity caused me discomfort for nearly two months. It helped to pass the time, as a boil on his neck might help to distract the attention of a man who loses a leg.

Off the queer, rocky island of Pantelleria, alive with German aircraft and airmen, our ship was obliged to pick its way through a large group of floating British mines. Messerschmitts, with long-distance petrol-tanks hanging below their shapely bellies, dived down to cannon the mines, and the Germans on board opened up at the bobbing round shapes with their 20-mms. Two dashing, flashing Italian destroyers escorted us to the lovely harbour of Palermo. We stayed there for twenty-four hours, and one of the Italian ship's officers went ashore and bought some tangerines for us, bless him. Gordon Hooker had some Italian money, and he got enough tangerines and jam for all of our party of eight to taste them.

We passed Capri in the morning. It was raining on the island, though our deck was dry. Then the Italian guards, who had grown lax with us, and had allowed us, and the men too, to spend much of the day on deck, pushed us all below, and closed the hatches.

"Why is this done?" Teddy Key asked the bo'sun.

"Our captain is a Neapolitan," replied that old man. "He says that the Bay of Naples is the most wonderful sight in the world. One hundred times more wonderful than the seven wonders of the earth. One hundred times too wonderful for a lot of damned British prisoners to see for nothing."

"Why, the mean old blighter."

"Not so mean when you work it out. He used to be captain of a pleasure-steamer. Then the British paid good money to see the Bay of Naples. Why should he spoil the market? If you see it now, maybe you won't come back."

There were great crowds of young German soldiers on the quay. They were well equipped, and looked serious, as though they knew that a great ordeal lay ahead of them—although the news from the desert could scarcely have been better from their point of view, and most of them must have been certain that this time Rommel would quickly overrun Egypt and Suez. Perhaps it was just strain between them and the Italians. The Germans were making no effort to disguise their over-weening superiority complex. And even the Neapolitan dock-workers (not the least simian of Europeans) were showing openly that the Germans were unwelcome there.

Before we had time to take in the scene we were marched off the ship and formed up on the quay. Already we were beginning to collect the prisoner-of-war's agglomeration of junk. It may be difficult for the ordinary reader to understand this. I must therefore explain that I was taken prisoner with nothing. If they set food in front of me I had nothing to eat it in, I had nothing to eat it with. If they offered me water (or something better) I had no drinking vessel. Prisoners are not provided with necessities like other soldiers. So I learned to provide for myself by being watchful and cunning, by searching rubbish-heaps, by darting on something, claiming it, cleaning it, pocketing it.

My most treasured possession, for example, on arriving at Naples, was an empty jam-tin which I had picked up on board ship. The beauty about this tin was that it was big, it could hold nearly a pint and a half. It was an easy shape to clean, and I could either eat out of it or drink out of it. I had beaten down the ragged edges with a marline-spike until they could not cut my lips. I had scoured it with sand. A beautiful tin! Just the bulge of it, there in my New Zealand greatcoat pocket, made me feel good.

So we all carried what appeared to be junk in one form or another. And the ones with heavier equipment had to be helped. Clifford Wheeler and the two doctors had valises. An officer's valise is heavy enough for a fit man. I helped Clifford with his. Our Neapolitan martyrdom began.

They marched us in threes through the dockside streets. We were going to the delousing-pen, and we wanted to hide ourselves. But we had to march through the streets with women and children and civilians who looked at us with hard brown eyes. Sometimes they laughed at us, and sometimes they shouted or spat or turned away in quiet disgust. My big Army boots felt so heavy that I could scarcely move them. My insides were on fire. My arm, attached against its will by the hand that obstinately grasped the strap of Clifford's valise, seemed to be stretching until the arm socket was free, the valise held only by the skin on my shoulder.

When we reached the baths where we were to be cleaned up for residence in Italy, I sat on a bench and cold sweat broke out on me so swiftly that I could feel it running down my back. As I sat there in the changing-room, while other people hurriedly tore off their clothes to rush in and find the best showers, I became aware that I had a battle on my hands. I had a battle for my life. There was a germ inside me that could kill me. I must fight the germ, and to do that I must rest my muscles, my heart, and my stomach. I must ride the discomforts, smooth them over, or, better still, let friends smooth them for me.

From that moment I believe that I began slowly to get well and strong again. When the others had finished I gave my clothes to the delouser and wandered into the shower-room, feeling, with gratitude, its steam upon my bare skin. I looked so pathetic that a man with whom up to that moment I had exchanged no words loaned me his razor with some precious English shaving-soap. I was last out of the showers. I did not have to fight for my clothes. They were the only ones there. I put them on slowly. Each movement was a floating, a relaxation. The movements were geared down now, they cost me no effort, for I was fighting the germ with my brain. When I got outside into the muddy street, the others were already fallen in in threes, impatiently waiting. Big Frank Haines held up his leather gloves. He had left them in the pocket of his greatcoat when it went through the delouser. Now the gloves had shrunk to the size of small doll's gloves. I began to laugh. But laughter tore at my inside. I stopped.

I remember no more until I found myself sitting in a railway carriage. The train ran slowly through Naples. Once it stopped alongside a narrow street where a man was playing a guitar. The train jolted on and I relaxed, consciously at first. I forced my limbs and my mind to loosen themselves until there was nothing tautened in me, until I lay in the corner seat, a human hulk that swayed loosely to the jerking of the train.

When it stopped again we knew it would move no more that night. Gordon Hooker slept in the rack to give the rest of us more room. My sleep was deeper, more beneficial, than any sleep I had known since Rommel's attack.

Next morning it was raining when they formed us up again and marched us off to our first prison camp in Italy. It was *Campo* 66, the transit camp, at Capua, but we did not know that as we walked through the slums from the station. It was a long walk, so they took our luggage on a cart. Sometimes I thought I would not be able to keep up with the others. We marched in step. At last the column swung in under the cross-beam of a dirty wooden gateway that reminded me of a film I had seen of a concentration camp in Germany.

They stopped us outside a barbed-wire enclosure surrounding a hut. A British officer came out of the hut to look us over. He was sleek and birdy with his plastered fair hair and the warm tartan scarf (hunting Stuart) round his throat. It was Tony Hay, of the Long Range Desert Group. Richard knew him.

"You're a queer-looking lot of birds," Tony shouted. "Where are you from?"

"Tarhuna. What's this place like?"

"Hungry. It's a dump."

We were interviewed by Hutcheson, a New Zealander whose face was a cross, the vertical being formed by the knife-like face itself, the horizontal by a virile red moustache. He was adjutant of the prisoners of war. He took down our names, dates of capture, etc.

"The Eyeties ought to do this," he told us. "But I expect some of you are very tired and want to get to bed. If we left it to them you'd be standing by all night."

Captain Ucelli, tall, fair-haired Italian Guards officer, who stood beside Hutcheson watching us, sizing us up, looking at the valuables we "declared" as though we were going through customs, did not blink an eyelid at this. He understood every word. (He had been at school in England, in fact he was the school contemporary of one of the officers in our party, I cannot remember which one. I do remember that they disliked each other, and that they never spoke to each other.)

While this was going on a few old inhabitants who were prisoners from my regiment came to talk to Clifford and myself. They were kind and helpful and most eager for news from outside. Precious little we could give them. Our men marched past to the other ranks' compounds beyond our own. I saw both Skinner and Jones. Both of them walked firmly. I had confidence that Skinner would keep them both going, he so excelled at "making" things.

Before we could go to bed we had to collect mattresses and bedding. I was just able to carry these back to the hut. Old prisoners were playing bridge opposite my bed. They scarcely bothered to glance at me. They looked a little glazed. But perhaps that was my fault. Everything looked a little glazed. We were overcrowded. Our beds went right down the side of the hut, and they were practically touching, side to side. But we had sheets and a big Red Cross blanket each. The old prisoners told us that those blankets were manufactured from spun glass. Wonderful.

The Italians gave me a pair of pyjamas sent out by our Red Cross. They were pink-striped pyjamas of wool, with no collar. There was a little red cross over the right breast and a smart label of which I was proud. "Made in Australia," the label said.

Everyone else was fussing round, it seemed. But I knew that I must go to bed. A tall man with a pointed beard stood beside the bed.

"Are you George Millar of the *Daily Express?*" he asked. He was Rex Reynolds, a South African fighter-pilot shot down in Greece. He had been in newspapers before the war. He said he would bring me a pipe and some tobacco from the Italian canteen the following morning.

"And some books," he said. "Do you play bridge?"

"Not when there are books."

Later I woke up. I was sweating, and felt much better. Teddy Key was sitting on the next bed, looking at me. He was a delightful young man—serious and kindly. He had got a Scholarship to Oxford and came from one of the finest counties, Northumberland, and always thought the best of everyone, even me.

"Will you come to my birthday-party, George?" he asked, inclining his kindly head, a head a shade big in proportion to his muscular body.

"When is it?"

"To-morrow. Tea-time."

"I shall be delighted. The only birthday present I can give you is a tin of Eyetie meat."

"Wonderful. That is just what we need. We are a little short of meat. To-morrow at four o'clock, then."

"Thank you so much, Teddy. I've just realised that we're in Italy. It's such a long time since I was in Italy. Far up in the north, and it was summer. . . ."

"The two doctors have gone off to try to get some medicine," he said. "If I were you I'd go sick. They might send you to hospital. They say you get better food in hospital, and money to buy things from the real shops."

"I shall be all right now." And I knew that I was going to be well. There were bugs in that hut. I felt them biting. But nothing could keep me awake.

CHAPTER VI

A MAJOR in the Northumberland Hussars, a coal-owner, but one of the kindest of men, had presented Teddy with a bag of rice which had been smuggled all the way from the head-line town of Benghazi. With this rice, a few tins of the Italian meat, and some vegetables stolen from the Italian plot which fringed our barbed wire, Teddy cooked a meal for eight persons. It was raining outside, I remember, and while we ate a priest came in to ask us to fill in forms for the Vatican radio.

He was a powerful-looking man, with strangely swaying eyes, and we had been warned that he acted as a stool-pigeon for the Italian authorities, but I never saw anything wrong with him beyond a somewhat over-rich approach to fair-haired boys, and a habit of laying a plump and greasy hand on your shoulder or upon your knee, where it made a bulge in the surface of the bed-clothes.

Teddy's was the first of many birthday-parties I enjoyed in prison. It was the worst (in so far as food was concerned) and the best of all I think because we needed the food so badly, and we knew what sacrifices he had made to save enough to feed us.

After that they moved our group, many of whom were sick, to a building called the infirmary, which had been full of older prisoners when we arrived. They were obliged to take our places in the bug-infested hut. In the infirmary we had proper hospital beds with sheets and blankets. It was a long building with a corridor in the middle and beds that stuck out from the walls. At one end was the entrance, then two or three small rooms in which the senior officers settled themselves, then our long room, and at the other end the wash-place and lavatories.

In the last-named place and in my bed I spent most of the first ten days at *Campo* 66. During that time I fasted to cure my dysentery, and hoarded every possible scrap of food for the building-up period that would follow the fast. There was not much to hoard.

Breakfast was a tinful of watery tea—saved from former issues of Red Cross parcels. Lunch was some kind of macaroni or rice mess, and extremely little of it; and the evening meal was the same, only less. At lunch-time we were usually issued also with one hundred grams of bread (rather less in size than a man's clenched fist), an orange, and a small amount of solid Italian jam. The food (apart from the bread) was sold to our messing officers by a thin, black-suited vulture of an Italian contractor who came rattling out from Capua in a mule-cart each morning. We must have made his fortune.

At any rate, I was able to save up my bread and jam. I did not speak about my fast to the others, for I knew from experience that few Englishmen—even Englishmen who read and believe in the Bible—think of fasting as anything but madness, and only a few cranks realise its power.

It was not an unpleasant existence since fasting, after the first four days or so, makes life ethereal, sensitive, interesting. I was able to lie in bed and suck enjoyment from the conversations I overheard, from books, from the comfort of my clean bed and pyjamas. While I lay thus Gordon Johnstone, another officer in my regiment, arrived. He had been wounded in the arm, and had been in hospital in North Africa and Italy.

He arrived, I remember, carrying a cardboard box filled with small Italian luxuries which he had been permitted to buy in hospital, things like fish-paste and meat extract, and even some cocoa.

I am prone, when talking of people I know, to exaggerate them in one way or another. Usually, I fear, I tend to emphasise their baser qualities and emotions, on the principle perhaps that a scoundrel is often a more interesting character than a good man. But in Gordon's case I had built up a picture of a man of character and of diverse talents, musical, linguistic, and so on. I had spoken much of him to my companions (and Clifford, who always eulogised everyone in his own regiment, had vouched for my words): in fact I had given Gordon tremendous advance publicity. And I was delighted to see him live up to it, becoming immediately the dominant figure of our group. He was entirely qualified for such a position. But it amused me to see that my crude spate of words had given him a powerful initial thrust.

He was a charming person, Gordon. A fine musician, cultured, travelled, and yet in private life he had been, of all things, a chartered accountant in the City of London. He was a creature of contrast. A friend of everybody, a friend of nobody. You could not get to know him because he was indefinite. He floated away from you on the river of his convictions—convictions based as far as I could make out on the ideals of a Gentleman in Victorian England. Gordon had a strangely pink-and-white face, at once a baby face and an old man's face. His body, too, was weak in some parts, strong in others, a body which disliked exercise and liked chocolate. Gordon began to give us German lessons.

When my fast ended, and I felt what over-romantic nature-cure faddists in England name the "call of hunger", I went to the doctors and got some medicine. This killed the dysentery in me and I steadily began to pick up strength again.

I had noticed as I lay in bed that the prisoners were dividing themselves into two types, the type that did things—either worked or took exercise, or both—and the type who lay on his bed and played cards. The second type was so unattractive that, despite my own great talent for doing nothing, I was obliged to range myself with the others. I therefore divided my time between giving French lessons, learning Italian and German, and walking about the compound, often alone.

Prison, especially the initial part of it, was harder for me than for most of my friends because I cannot say that I genuinely like my fellow-men. And I detest communities. This probably comes from my hatred for my wasted years at school, the unhappiest period of my life. My life at home, with my mother, my brothers and my sister was, on the contrary, a particularly happy one. Unconsciously I believe that I had come to associate unhappiness with an exclusively male community, a set of rules, and the feeling that one was obliged to work as a part of a machine, or a "team", as they always unpleasantly emphasise at school and in the Army. Why then did I like serving on ships, why did I enjoy the Army, and Cambridge? Neither on the ships, nor in the Army, nor at Cambridge was my life purely masculine. Quite apart from the sexual aspect, I think that women are more necessary to some men than to others. And certainly freedom of movement is essential for the happiness of some men, while for others it only constitutes a worry.

To live inside a perimeter of barbed wire was a constant agony for me. Even as a small child I was a creature of wide movements. I was a sulky child, and if I sinned in the family circle I preferred to run away and hide in the woods. I have the restlessness of the Scots. It is the monotony of a steady existence, of fixed and secure prospects, that wears me down. I was unfitted to be a happy prisoner.

Walking up and down, up and down the muddy compound at Capua, I tended to draw myself away from the close friendship of our group of eight, the friendship forged in the stench of Trig Tarhuna. While Gordon Johnstone, for example, increased his purely superficial, but sincere, contacts, while warm-hearted Teddy Key stretched wide his not unselective gift of true friendship, I gradually withdrew myself until there was no depth of feeling in any of my relationships.

And the mountains outside, with the snow and the pine-trees on their precipitous sides, brought longings for freedom, for my wife, and for the privilege of fighting, of ceasing to be helpless and useless.

Our prison, a shoddy and unbeautiful clump of huts, tents, and cheap cement and wood erections, squatted in a small plain of absolute flat muddiness. The drab plain was accentuated because it was surrounded by the sudden mountains that encased it in a curve. At night the far shoulders of the mountains were red with the light from Vesuvius.

During much of the day I worked at languages, drumming them into my brain with what grammars and vocabularies the camp could offer. Working like that gave me the feeling that hope was not dead, that I was fitting myself for the future, working for Anne, bringing her closer. Already we had begun our Italian ration of letters home, one small letter and one post-card each week. Already I was beginning to long for the replies, to ache for them, to wonder whether my wife still lived, and whether she knew that I lived, and for her.

Although it was now only March, the sun came out on one day in three, and it was a strong sun, warm enough for us to take our shirts off and soak in it. I began to get brown, and to look after my body. Some of the people there did sporadic physical training, but I knew that I would not be fit for that for a long time. My strength was only gradually seeping back, since the diet was both insufficient and unhealthy. I was even subject to relapses of dysentery.

When they issued us with new battle-dress sent out from England, I cut off all the insignia from my old one, including the rhinoceros of the First Armoured Division, borrowed Gordon Hooker's "housewife", and sewed them all on to the new one. I now felt so presentable that I decided to attempt a beard. Despite my thirty-one years I had not much confidence in my power to grow one, but I tried, and it gave me a day-to-day interest (like the cavity in my tooth).

Now I had eaten my stored bread and jam, and I was as hungry as any of the others. It became a question of ekeing out the rations. We did this in various ways. Firstly, you could cut the peel with a razor-blade from your oranges and boil it up with your jam ration to increase the bulk (and the doctors said orange-skin was nourishing). Secondly, you could sometimes steal vegetables from the Italians' "more food for victory" plots around the prison, and quite often you could find some nourishing potato or turnip peelings around the garbage-can at wrong end of the mess-tent. These things could be boiled on the small electric stoves that heated the infirmary. Lastly, there was the canteen.

An officer prisoner was paid in special camp currency (or *buone*) according to his rank. The second-lieutenant got 750 lire per month, the lieutenant 950, the captain 1,100, and so on. Out of this he had to pay his messing bill. Now the mess in all the camps I was in was run (quite fairly) by a messing committee elected by the prisoners. Since prisoners were always hungry, they always asked the messing committee to spend the maximum amount on food. And since there was usually a dishonest Italian contractor in the vicinity who was only too willing to profit from the situation, the messing committee normally spent the maximum amount. This maximum was limited so that the second-lieutenant could just pay it, but only just.

Again in most camps a canteen was run. This meant that the Italian authorities, sometimes an officer, sometimes even a priest, sometimes a sergeant, sold goods (including food like sweets and fruit whenever he could get them) to the British, who in their turn sold them, without profit, to the individuals who wanted them. What happened was that everybody wanted any food that was going, but the second-lieutenant often had no money to buy it.

And the second-lieutenants were naturally (apart from exceptions like me) the youngest officers, the ones who really needed the food. In *Campo* 66, since we were near Naples, and many of the Italian staff were corrupt, a certain amount of food came into the canteen and was distributed among the officers. There were small quantities of chestnuts, onions, boiled sweets, biscuits, jam. But everything was so expensive that the second-lieutenant was always torn between his greed and his pocket. When the junior officers could not buy their quota the food was sold to the seniors who could.

Another canker soon became apparent in the food situation. The other ranks prisoners were living in abject misery in compounds visible from our own. The fortunate ones were in huts where, although they had to contend with dirt, overcrowding and vermin, they were at least dry. But the overflow, which included Skinner and Jones, were living in Italian tents, badly-made, camouflaged tents which invited the entry of every cold breath of air, which soaked up every drop of rain or snow and then sprinkled the moisture in icy drips over the men.

There was only one thing that could alleviate such misery—tobacco. Cigarettes never meant anything to me; and if they had I hope that I should still have given them under such circumstances to my two men. Most of the other officers did likewise, although to many of them it meant a severe sacrifice. But there were others, some of them of field rank, who played a more sinister game.

The men were unpaid. They were waiting at the transit camp to be sent away to work, in factories or on the land. They were often employed on fatigues around the camp. And they were on a different scale of rations, much larger than the officers' scale. For example, they got from four to five times more bread than we did. Bread was the thing that was most lacking in the officers' diet. Our bread ration was not enough to keep a miniature poodle alive. Furthermore, we were getting jam, but not enough bread to spread it on.

Instead of giving their cigarettes to the men, therefore, some of these officers *sold* their cigarettes for bread.

What had we fallen to? When you looked around the compound, and saw some British officers scrabbling in the rubbish-heaps for food while others carried on this atrocious black barter with their own troops, you wondered where the demoralisation of prison would end.

The British Red Cross sent out food parcels on the scale of one parcel per prisoner per week.

Fascist Italy had made many advances and improvements in transport, but Mussolini had been unable to alter the national character. And although the Italian peasant, labourer, tradesman, or artisan, remained a good and conscientious worker, the Italian organiser was remarkably lazy and incapable. Also much of the country's transport network was strained to the limit by German troop movements and German demands for Italian food and manufactured goods for the German people.

After nearly two months of semi-starvation imprisonment, we were given at *Campo* 66 an issue of Red Cross parcels on the scale of one parcel to every three men. They were Canadian parcels—the best of all, since they contained butter, an excellent powdered milk, and more chocolate, cheese, and biscuits than parcels from any other country. In an atmosphere tense with hunger and greed, the chosen officer from each group of three queued up at the store and came back with his cardboard box. Then came the process of dividing everything into exactly equal quantities. The prunes had to be counted, and lots drawn to decide which officer out of the three would have six prunes instead of five. The butter, the cheese, the chocolate had to be meticulously cut into three.

Of all the petty hurdles of prison life, I think that this instinct to make certain that you were not being tricked when food was divided was the hardest to surmount. At Capua the bread was not baked in small enough loaves to give each officer a loaf. Instead there might be one-and-a-half loaves to divide among eight officers. The bread was carried back by each group to the infirmary. The groups then waited to borrow Jimmy le Coq's knife, since that was the sharpest blade in the camp. Then the bread would be cut into eight portions, and we had a roster to determine which officer had first choice. I remember waking in the morning and asking myself: "Why is to-day a good day?" and remembering: "Oh yes, I am first on the bread roster to-day." All that for a few crumbs.

While I slowly rebuilt my strength at Capua some of the older prisoners (none from our lot) had escaped. The initial business of getting out of this camp was surprisingly easy. It was the only easy camp that I visited. Yet the Italian authorities took a serious view of these escapes, and invariably changed the colonel commandant when one occurred.

All the escaper had to do was to put his name down for the dentist. The dental parades were not counted, either on leaving the compound or on returning. And in the dentist's waiting-room someone had discovered a cavity under the floor, where it was possible to lie hidden until nightfall.

While I lay in bed I saw first Bethune-Williams of the 60th and then my bearded acquaintance Rex Reynolds led down to our latrines from their punishment cell just beyond the front door of the infirmary. Bethune-Williams was disguised as an Italian soldier, Reynolds as a man on a walking tour. Neither of them had stayed out very long. There was snow on the ground and conditions were difficult outside. They reported that the Italian peasant was suspicious, the Italian policeman alert.

Some of the older prisoners were hoarding the remains of their former Red Cross parcels. But I decided that it would be stupid to save my own small first issue of Red Cross food. I had to get well before indulging in such luxuries. So I ate it very, very slowly. One ounce of cheese lasted me for ten days. The chocolate went faster. That was irresistible. There were no more parcels at Capua.

One morning in April big Ucelli, the interpreter, shouted on roll-call:

"You are leaving here to-morrow. Going to an old monastery

which has been made into a new concentration camp (a literal translation of the Italian *campo di concentramento*). I can assure you that it is a very lovely place, one of the world's beauty-spots. . . ."

"Never mind the beauty, what about the food?" somebody shouted back.

"I believe the food will be good there," he answered politely. "There, things will be properly organised, and the monastery lies in a richly fertile valley."

When the men heard that we were leaving they began, many of them, to get worried. Their conditions were already so insanitary that they feared they might be left to die if the officers were taken away. Naturally our senior British officers, helped by Hutcheson, the excellent adjutant, had done all they could to attempt to bully the Italians into giving the men better conditions. With little apparent success. The Italians said: "Yes, *domani*," and did nothing.

Now Skinner and Jones asked me if they could come along with the officers, since a number of batmen were to accompany us to the new camp. I told them that if they stopped where they were they would soon perhaps be working on some farm where they would be able to eat copiously and to cuckold the Italian owner, away with the army in Egypt. In their place I should have stayed on. But since both of them wanted the security and immediate improvement in conditions that coming with us would probably give them, I got Clifford, who had more influence than I with the high-ups, to see that my two men were included in the party.

Before leaving Capua I managed to steal some food from an Italian cart passing the doctors' hut where I was being vaccinated, and the mess catering officer gave me a little more, since following my motto, "Never Hurry for a Train", I was still hanging about when the others had fallen in to march to the station. So I had two cardboard boxes of food and junk to carry.

Walking down to the station I realised that I had progressed during my stay in Capua. I had eased myself away from dependence on my friends; I had practically cured the dysentery. The summer could not be far away, and Ucelli said the monastery was beautiful.

I faced the future with some confidence.

CHAPTER VII

Worn out though I was by a long journey and by the tediously strict search we were obliged to undergo on arrival, I still count my entry into the vast court-yard of the monastery at Padula as the second greatest moment in my twenty-month career as a prisoner of war. The greatest moment came at the end.

The Certosa di Padula was monumental. It even claimed to be monumental. The book written about it said that it had the largest cloisters in Europe. Dressed in a ponderous Doric order, they ran right round the court-yard.

Opening off the cloisters were suites of chambers, formerly inhabited by the monks, now to be inhabited by our senior officers. And directly over the cloisters, with an exterior dressing of coarse Ionic pilasters, was the former ambulatory, really nothing more than four wide, high, immensely long corridors corresponding with the four sides of the court-yard. The level of the red-tiled floor of the ambulatory was about forty feet above the paving of the cloisters—paving worn in places by the constant traffic of monks, lay brothers and, latterly, tourists.

It was in the ambulatory, or the wings, as the four corridors were named by us, that the junior officers were to sleep.

Another five or six prisoners had now joined our original party of eight formed at Trig Tarhuna. The place where we were to sleep had been reserved for us by an eager member of the party who had rushed up into the wings and chosen a part of Wing 3, because it would get most of the sun. The drawback was that it would also get most of the smell, since we were at the end of the wing situated beside the lavatories serving Wings 2 and 3.

Having dumped my few belongings between the beds of Clifford and Gordon Johnstone, I departed to look at the wonders of our new prison.

Our vast inner court-yard was the last, and by far the biggest, of a series of court-yards. You entered it from the former working part of the monastery through a great door with an inscription in Latin which said: "He who enters these portals renounces the world." Or words to that effect. This doorway was now shut and guarded. Living on the other side of it, in a maze of court-yards, corridors, and old, high, stone-floored rooms, were the Italian officers and men who were responsible for keeping us alive and keeping us in.

If you turned right at the doorway you walked down a long blank wall. Behind this wall was the former refectory, now our

77

dining-room, a heavily panelled, pompous, vulgarly religious place which made the Church of England padres' mouths water.

Next to it was the kitchen, the monks' kitchen, with huge boilers, and cooking equipment not less than two hundred years old. Furse and Bellamy stood raging in front of this rusted iron apparatus. I moved on, along the same wall, to find Italian workmen partly dressed as soldiers (or soldiers partly dressed as workmen) who were struggling to install hot showers and the necessary devices for such contrivances demanded by the Geneva Convention for treatment of war prisoners.

My tour of inspection was interrupted while the Italians held roll-call. We fell in by wings in a long line stretching nearly the length of the draughty cloister running from the entrance to a vast, ceremonial stone staircase at the far end of our court-yard.

This staircase, a tremendous piece of baroque masonry, mounted in a double sweep to the level of our wings above the cloisters. Its three colossal, empty stone windows looked out on a view that could not have been more beautiful, down a valley heavy with crops and precious trees, and teeming with livestock. On either side of the valley, which had once been a mosquito-infested swamp, and then had been drained and developed by the monks, rose stony hills. The dramatic contrast between the softness of the lovely valley and the brutal hardness of the hills was increased by the villages which clung, like limpets, to the hill-sides, as though they refused to occupy one hectare of the rich soil off which they lived.

Immediately above the monastery itself was perched the village of Padula, one of the richest in the whole valley. As we stood on roll-call we could look up to the balconies, the weathered grey walls and the pinky-red pantiles of the terraced village. Sometimes, while they called our names down in our prison, we saw a woman hanging washing on the lines rigged on her high old balcony. Or a man standing looking down on us with his arm around the waist of a plump *signora*.

Barbed wire and sentry-boxes in profusion circled the great, confused plan of the monastery, like a tight-fitting girdle, except immediately beyond the ceremonial staircase, where the wire perimeter swept out to leave for our day-time use a rough field amply large enough for football. Seven olive-trees stood there; and it was altogether a most agreeable field with a fine view of the village and the hills to the south. We could not see any of the village streets, since the place was constructed like a hat, or a candle-snuffer, with the outer windows looking far over the valley, the inner windows leaning over narrow, hidden streets. It did us good to see the village. Especially at night when the lights were on. Then you felt that there must be a decent home life continuing in many of these houses, despite the war, despite the suffering. You felt that there must be a few honest men and women up there who paused as they ate, or as they swallowed their pre-prandial vermouth, and said: "I wonder how the prisoners fare? Cold and hungry, I'll bet, poor devils."

On the train journey to this new camp we had passed down the coast from Naples to Salerno, and then branched inland. There had been no unfriendly incidents; and the country, the sea, the villages, the dusty roads, the oxen had been so full of beauty that, added to the solid stone beauty of our new prison, I had a deep impression of a friendly Italy outside—an impression that went much deeper than the hasty flickering perspectives of war-time. It was an impression that remained with me throughout my time in Italy, that remains with me now. From behind the barbed wire I used to look at the hills, and think that one day Anne and I might build a small house on such and such a spot. We would have two Italian servants, a man and his wife. And two mules for riding over the hills. Sometimes we would ride one hundred miles, to deserted beaches by the sea—beaches where we could bake big potatoes in seaweed ovens (as I used to do at Pamplonne) and bathe without clothes if we felt so inclined.

If I felt happier in the monastery than in other prisons, my happiness was shared by few of my comrades. Most of them looked at the place from the practical point of view, and decided that it was a hole. It was bitterly cold, both in the wings and in the dining-hall, where, as prisoners poured in from other transit camps, we were obliged to eat in two sittings. Soon there were nearly 500 officers and 60 British batmen in the camp. The kitchens were quite inadequate to deal with such numbers. The latrines were inadequate. The water supply was inadequate. The food was inadequate.

The Italian staff were not able to organise a reasonable system for roll-calls. It was a bleak and stormy month of April, with blustering winds, torrential rain. We spent much of the time standing shivering in greatcoats beneath the damp cloisters, waiting for our names to be called.

We had no resources of body energy, no reserves of food and warm clothing to face this ordeal. My own assets, which I totalled up after I had passed through the searchers on entering this prison, were a wrist-watch (bought in Alexandria for five guineas), a good fountain-pen (bought in Paris in 1940 for 500 francs), and a pigskin belt, bought in Piccadilly. Then I still had my big tin for drinking; I had an almost new battle-dress, an old and skimpy greatcoat, my green side-hat, two pairs of pyjamas and some handkerchiefs (from the British Red Cross), two doubtful pairs of socks, and a pair of leaking Army boots that had once thumped the barrack square at Brig o' Don, Aberdeen.

The evenings were difficult to pass. Sorely conscious of our empty stomachs, we crouched together in the semi-dark wings, wondering when Red Cross food parcels would arrive. One of us had been lucky in a draw at the canteen which had already opened (although there was little in it but highly perfumed brilliantine and large boxes of talcum powder). This officer had drawn the right to buy a bundle of firewood.

At intervals down the wings the Italians had installed box-shaped red tile stoves with asbestos pipe chimneys that rose straight for eight feet, then angled back and through the outer wall of the building. There was not enough wood to make a proper fire. But we could take turns of placing our hands on the stove. And inside the stove itself we could place two Italian troops' dixies, and thus heat something to drink before going to bed.

Twelve of us shared this "brew", as we called it. For some days we had things to put in the hot water. Gordon Johnstone still had two teaspoonfuls of cocoa bought in hospital. I had a little cornflour and a few meat cubes, bought from the canteen at Capua. The day arrived when there was nothing. I had heard of mint tea, and there was plenty of mint down on the mossy grass in the big court-yard. I picked a couple of fistfuls, cut it up very small, and made an infusion. The drink was not liked. After that we went to bed cold as well as empty.

The stairs began to take their toll of us. Living in the wings, you had to go downstairs four times a day, twice for roll-call and twice for meals. The going down was all right. But coming up put a queer, inflating pain in your heart. It felt as though the heart was a bag filled with helium gas. And every step up the baroque staircase worked a pump that created a vacuum around your heart. As the vacuum grew the heart expanded. One day it would reach the limit and you would roll down the stone staircase. It was a beautiful tomb of a staircase. But what would Anne say? Those days, we paused often on the way upstairs to admire the view down the cold valley. Most of the time we worried only about the discomforts of blue noses, cold fingers and toes. For the first time since my schooldays I had chilblains. The doctors said this was due to lack of calcium in the diet.

Towards the end of April I went into the cells for the first time. We were all supposed to be in our quarters by 10 p.m. One night the Italian orderly officer, doing his rounds with the guard, caught me after curfew in Room 6, where I had been invited to pass the evening. Richard Carr, Denis Patchett, and Clifford Wheeler, all fairly senior captains, had been moved down from the slums in the wings to the greater comfort of this quarter.

The Italian captain had me dragged out into the dimly-lit cloisters, and I thought that he was going to murder me. He was a *Bersaglieri* captain, an enormously strong, apoplectic creature. Like many of the Italian soldiers whom I met, he could be quite agreeable one moment and bursting with hysterical rage the next. When in the second condition the creatures were dangerous. This officer, with two sergeants, literally carried me the length of the cloisters and through to the Italian office. There Captain de Stephani, then the senior interpreter, and a more solid type of man, calmed his brother officer and told me to go to bed.

Next day I was sent to the "cooler".

The cooler at Padula was then a double cell, formed of what had been a kind of reception office when the monastery was a money-making concern, with large agricultural responsibilities and property in the towns. One cell, which had a table and two chairs in it, looked through a heavily-barred window to the dark cloisters of a small cobbled court-yard. The inner cell had a window looking on to the entrance passage. It contained two beds.

Since the electric light was good in the cells, and I had books and interesting company, I thoroughly enjoyed my time there, and was sorry to go out into the big prison again.

My companion was Alasdair Cram, who had been given the same sentence as myself for some equally trivial offence.

Cram was an escapologist. He had already escaped once, from a transit camp in Palermo; and he had spent about eight days making his way on foot across Sicily to the south coast in the hope of stealing a boat and reaching Malta.

He had been caught on the coast. He was a good talker; and

81

as he described his experiences to me I got a vivid picture of his fierce will pushing his body on its painful way across the mountains, sleeping with shepherds, eating oranges from the trees and sour milk cheese picked up at cottages. Cram was working up for another escape, I soon saw, though he was much too cunning to tell me anything about it. He had arrived in Italy earlier than our lot, and had had time to make a small store of food. He was in himself admirably equipped for escaping. An intelligent individualist with a thick yet wiry body. He professed to be a mountaineer, and claimed that he knew the Alps well.

In civilian life Cram had followed the legal profession in Edinburgh; and indeed he had an Edinburgh face—a hard face, pinkish and determined, with a high curving forehead surmounted by a rather awkward crop of fair curls. His eyes were stony, uninterested, but suddenly sharp if he saw that you had something vital to say.

He spoke good Italian with a Scot's accent, and he also spoke German. He had done interesting and peculiar things, like living alone on an island off the west coast of Scotland.

His physical training was somewhat typical of his individualism. Cram did the exercises of Professor Müller, and he did them thoroughly. Each morning at 7.30, when he was not in the cooler, he went down into the great court-yard, stripped naked and went through Müller's routine. The last part of the professor's excellent programme consists of "rubbing". At first Cram used to have an excited, sometimes a caustic, audience when he did the rubbing, which consisted of starting low down on each leg and rubbing in strangely voluptuous movements right up to the base of his neck. Because he held the same name as a German tennis-player, Cram was always known in prisons in Italy as "the Baron".

The day that the Baron and I came out of the cooler it happened that the canteen made a big issue of boiled sweets. Then the canteen brought off another coup which illustrated the contrast between Italy's ill-controlled war-rationing system and Britain's. It was able to purchase (from Turin, I think) two huge casks of excellent condensed milk. The first issue to all prisoners was "one jam-jar per officer" (half a pint). Six hours after the issue about one-third of the officers were on their backs, very sick. The sweet stuff was too strong for their starved stomachs. But in a few days everybody felt better for the milk. You could almost feel your teeth hardening as you drank it. By this time I was having treatment from Robby, a Harley Street dentist. The treatment consisted in stuffing cotton-wool in the cavity. The Italians had promised dental equipment. It arrived a month or two later, just before the Swiss, who represented the "Protecting Power", visited the camp.

After the milk and the Baron's inspiring talk, I began to do physical training myself. There were several classes each morning; but I have never liked classes, and I preferred to do my own routine. From the day that I began I scarcely missed a morning during my imprisonment. I worked out a system of exercises from the British Army P.T. and Professor Müller's system, mixed in with Swedish exercises taught me by Sorbo Soboleff, the Russian. The exercises were mostly loosening and stretching ones, with some hard work for the stomach and legs. I thought I might need my legs again some day.

The Baron's imperturbability taught me a useful lesson. All my friends were inclined to scoff at my exercises. They thought I was doing it to gain "the body beautiful". I let them think it, and I forced myself to use their disparaging comment as a goad. I have always been apt to be far too attentive to praise or ridicule.

There was still no news of food parcels, and hunger grew until it was really difficult to think of anything else. One incident, illustrating this, has remained in my mind. The senior British officer, a distinguished soldier, tall and thin, with deep nests of wrinkles round his eyes, made a long speech to the assembled officers. His speech dealt exclusively with food, the possibilities of the canteen, finding a new contractor, the local black market, and so on. He described an interview with a Naples contractor.

"This man claims that he can produce for the camp up to three hundred cakes a week," said the S.B.O. "I fear that the cakes are small. Little bigger than my index finger. But they appear to be made of a mixture of nuts and dried fruit, and they are coated with sugar icing. I call them 'Little White Mice'."

* * * * *

A certain senior officer whom I had befriended and helped on numerous occasions happened to be walking with me around the paddock one sunny evening. And I noticed that, although I am normally a good walker, I could not keep up with him. In fact, I wanted to fall down, to allow myself to collapse. My heart was labouring, and it was only by a strenuous effort that I managed to keep going. He took me back to his rooms. He

83

shared these rooms with other senior officers. While my friend asked me to correct some work that he had been doing, my nose, which is ultra-sensitive, picked up a fascinating smell in the air. Searching in the files of my smell memory, I suddenly came upon this one.

"Hullo," I told myself. "That smell is boiled egg."

Sure enough, when my friend put his exercise-book away in his drawer, I heard a rolling noise, and shooting a quick glance inside before he had time to shut it, I saw three hens' eggs. He said nothing. I said nothing.

Up in the wings twenty-year-old Jimmy le Coq was lying on his bed, looking as grey and cold as a shroud. He could have done with one of the eggs.

The eggs were still on my mind when I stood in a queue outside the canteen the following morning. We were queueing for boiled sweets. Now, as I stood there, two senior officers, one of them my friend, came out of the canteen, each with his rationed quota of sweets, about a handful. The two stopped beside me, and one of them said to a young Welsh second-lieutenant who stood behind me: "What about letting me buy your sweets?"

"No, sir. I want them myself. I'm hungry."

"But you can't afford it. I don't know how you manage to buy sweets on a second-lieutenant's pay." He moved down the queue offering to buy. He found two takers. There were murmurs of rage from the shivering queue.

Incident number three was unconnected with food. There was a certain rubicund major in my own regiment who had never favoured me with a word since my arrival, nearly two months earlier, at Capua. I admired what I knew of this officer; I should have been grateful if he had talked to me. But I felt that he disliked me because my clothes were dirty, because I had dysentery (although he could not know that), and dragged around Capua like a self-commiserating shadow. One morning rude messages about my beard reached me from this major. The messages, passed on by Clifford and others, were to the effect that as senior officer in our regiment at Padula the major considered my beard and my person a disgrace, and that unless the beard was removed immediately he would write home about it. I would not have minded if the man had given me this message himself. The beard was a mess, for it grew in a black ruff round my throat and in wispy fair straggles on my jaw. I kept it largely because I could not bear to begin borrowing razors and blades again. My first reaction was one of fierce revolt. I simmered on this for two days. Then I shaved off the beard. The major and I never exchanged more than frigid glances. When he left, to go to a more luxurious camp, he did not say good-bye to me.

This incident influenced me more than the other two. Since my imprisonment I had noticed that in most other regiments there was a stiffness between the officers and a rank-consciousness that did not exist in my regiment, where even the second-lieutenant might call the colonel by his Christian name. I loved my regiment. There was a sting in the beard incident.

With me bad feelings often lead to action; kindly feelings may not bear fruit. I watched the senior officers carefully. And I soon saw that they were buying eggs and bread from Gino, the little interpreter, and from odd Italian sentries. I sounded out Gino myself. He did not like to deal with anyone in the wings. They were too public, the wings.

So I at first confined my talks with Gino to making friends, and making an impression.

Gino was a mercurial, fair-haired little ex-head-waiter from Turin. He was the son of an Italian chef who had worked in London and New York. Gino spoke dashing, slightly slipshod American, and much better, slightly Parisian French. He was impressed by my French. And I knew some of the restaurants and hotels where he had worked. I gradually made him believe that I was a rich man, owner of a newspaper in England. (Nothing could have been farther from the truth.)

Then I looked for an opportunity to deal with Gino under cover. I was not going into the camp black market on a small scale. My intention was to corner the market from the senior officers.

Working in the pay office, the place where the Italians calculated what was due to the British officers and arranged about paying them in camp *buone*, was a young British lawyer called Stafford. Stafford was a patently honest and most likeable Englishman, always smiling, laughing, sucking at an old pipe. I made friends with him, borrowed things from him, returned them, and asked him timidly for a job in the pay office "to learn Italian". It worked. Next day I began my new job.

Nobody could be less fitted than I to work in a pay office. I hate having anything to do with money except spending it, and I am extremely clumsy and inaccurate with figures. Furthermore, I write a most unclerkly hand, and the work which Stafford, decent fellow, gave me to do was mainly clerking.

85

The pay was in the charge of a dowdy lieutenant named Ienco. Destiny had made Ienco a builder in Naples, a niche which he was only too happy to fill. Now his main fear was that the Fascists would give destiny a mean twist, and send him to the front either in North Africa or (Oh, Horror!) in Russia. He was no exception. Eighty per cent of the Italian officers and men were only too willing to tell you that this was exactly how they felt. Their hearts were in Italy, certainly not in the war. But then, you would not expect to meet the most bellicose type of young officer in a prison camp.

Ienco was a trial to me. He had an untidy mind and he was a shouter. I detest shouters. He simply could not modulate his voice. But we got along well together. I saw to that. He liked quasi-profound conversations about the future of the world or the necessity for religion. He got them from me. Ienco told me one day that I had brightened the office. That was my chance. I brought in more help. Stafford was a little staggered, but I worked it; I brought in E. J. Y. Dibbs.

Dibbs was my choice for a partner. The dissolution of our original Trig Tarhuna party, with the more senior members going downstairs to the quarters, had thrown us into propinquity. Finding myself in the next bed, I had leisure to observe him, and decided that he was just what was needed.

He had been brought up to believe that if the business men were allowed to handle the country all would be well, that the war-time Army, because filled with business men, was vastly superior to the peace-time Army, and that Wavy Navy officers (many of them, he pointed out, were business men) were, on the whole, superior to officers of the Royal Navy. I held widely divergent views on almost every subject. But E. J. Y. was an ideal partner for the work that lay ahead. Work? It was a battle! Every time that my energies flagged I thought again of the eggs, the queue for boiled sweets, and the beard.

The son of rich parents, E. J. Y. had been at Harrow, then in his father's business, then in the Guards. He was a bald, insistently suave, middle-aged Englishman—a bandit from the City of London, and therefore a die-hard Conservative of the most irrational type. When E. J. Y. faced any problem you might be certain that he would reason it out shrewdly, then make absolutely certain that he did what he wanted, and that he was not "done".

Another character was drawn into our partnership. This was the capitalist, Tony Hay, who at that time was commanding our

86

wing. He came in to look after the distribution end and to finance our early ventures. When the pay got straightened out I knew that I would get plenty of money from the doctors and padres. These people were paid at a much higher rate than the ordinary prisoners, and they were willing to sell camp *buone* in return for cheques paid to their families at home. There would be no need to lose over the deals, I was well aware. The financial point of view did not interest me (or E. J. Y. or Tony). But quite obviously if we got food we could sell it. My main desire was to keep the black market from the senior officers, and I inspired E. J. Y. with the same longing.

We went in with a bang. One night I casually strolled through the Italian part of the building, showing my pass to get to the pay office. E. J. Y., who had been fitted out with a cigar, strutted at my side. When I introduced this bulky, self-assured, and cigar-smoking young man as "one of our English millionaires", Gino was immensely impressed.

E. J. Y. also spoke excellent French. Our well-rehearsed act went over most creditably (remember that Gino was sharp; he had been a *maître d'hôtel*).

"Okay, boys," Gino dismissed us. "Be at the store to-morrow, and I'll see you get a good show."

"A good show!" E. J. Y. complained. "We want everything or nothing."

"What d'you want? Eggs, cheese, butter, fruit?"

"Everything that's good."

"Well," said Gino doubtfully. "I can't give you everything and leave the Indians out."

This was new. There were, it was true, a number of Indian officers who were temporarily in our camp. Very distinguished-looking officers they were too. They had Indian batmen, and they drew special rations since, we understood, their religion forbade them to eat the ordinary food. Every morning, now that I thought of it, I had seen the Indian batmen carrying through cases of stores to the special quarters occupied by their officers.

Next morning, at the agreed time, 10 o'clock, I was waiting in the heart of the Italian quarters. A lieutenant-commander R.N. managed to get past the guards at the entrance to the big court-yard and came up to me shyly.

"Suppose you're hanging about for the black market to open?" he asked. "I don't approve of it, but if there's food to be had one might as well have it."

I said nothing. This was an enemy. Then some Indians arrived, and Gino led us through to the store, a large room adjoining the office where the commandant had sentenced me to imprisonment. All that was visible was a great quantity of vegetables and some oranges. These held no interest for me.

But, diving behind an old counter, Gino began to show some of the produce that this rich, milk-soaked valley could provide. There were, as he had said, eggs, cheeses, and butter. There were wines and vermouths. There were hams.

I let him fill up the Indians' boxes first. He gave them a few eggs and some butter. Then I told him quickly in French to keep them waiting.

"Why?" he asked angrily.

"Then they can carry our stuff through," I said.

"Say, you're smarter than you look, mister. What d'you want?"

"I'll take the lot."

He looked at me and his mouth fell open; then he began feverishly adding up with a pencil, jabbing down waiter's figures on the counter.

"No use," he said. "You ain't got that much money. Twelve hundred lire."

Blessing Tony, who had insisted on my taking all available *buone*, I paid him out as though I were buying a tram-ticket.

"No sales to-day, skipper," Gino was saying to the lieutenant-commander as I left. Later, from our window, Tony, E. J. Y. and I watched the Indians solemnly carry their boxes past the guards and across the court-yard. We went down to count over the spoils. They were enormous. For example, there were four hundred fresh eggs, there were perhaps ten pounds of fresh butter, there were wonderful full-cream local cheeses which we called "Bull's testicles", there was wine, there were biscuits.

Distribution began in Wing 3. We dared not take the whole wing into our confidence. Some of them might run yapping to our enemies, the senior officers. All we could do was organise an underground distribution. E. J. Y. did this with great skill; also the totalling up of each man's bill was in his capable hands.

From then on our organisation steadily built itself up. The Indians went away to another camp. E. J. Y. and I had to organise convoys which ran the food through to Room 6. Tony had moved down to that room, and we sold its occupants a per-centage of all consignments. Often our finances were strained because we made it a point of honour to buy everything good that Gino found for us. If things were bad—for instance, when the quality of the cheese fell off—we threw them back at him. In this way we kept the head-waiter's respect. Soon the convoy system through to Room 6 became difficult, for the boxes had to pass the big doorway into our court-yard, which was always guarded by *carabinieri,* the powerful Italian military police. In the end, after several contretemps (on one occasion the *carabinieri* arrested me and searched me when I was loaded down with chocolate, butter, and white bread), Gino was regretfully forced to give the "Carabs" an enormous rake-off. Prices went up. We went on buying, spreading our purchases more and more over the slums in the wings.

Then trouble developed inside the camp. Leakages were inevitable. Through in the front part of the building the Italian officers began to refer to E. J. Y. and myself as *"I due gangsters"*. The Italian priest, Father Volpi, a delightful person, carried this misnomer into the camp. A counter-organisation was started. It failed. Gino would deal with nobody but "the newspaper magnate and the millionaire". So another organisation started up with the object of seeing that all black market food went into the mess. This organisation formed a corps of vigilantes who trailed us all over the camp. What could they do? We enrolled new helpers, and we walked through "clean" whenever there were vigilantes around.

The vigilantes threatened to break up the cupboards of all officers in our wing, or at any rate at our end of Wing 3. They would have found nothing.

Still the black market grew. Lambs were driven into one of the front court-yards to be slaughtered for us. Peasants asked if we cared for sucking pig. A woman in the village sent a message that she would sell us ice-cream. When the Italian commandant's Saint Day came around he ordered special cakes to be baked for the celebration. E. J. Y. and I picked out the best two of the four huge iced cakes and carried them through to the prison for a tea-party in Wing 3. There were patriotic inscriptions in purple icing on a blue-and-yellow background. Those bakers liked bright colours. We enjoyed the cakes so much that we ordered some to be made every Saturday. Then we began our famous "Sunday afternoon teas".

I sewed some special leg-bags that fitted inside my trousers or the queer, wide-legged shorts that we tailored for ourselves by cutting down Jugoslavian military breeches. On Sunday, after lunch, E. J. Y. and I would stroll through "to the pay office", and stagger back loaded with rich things. Officers would approach us all Sunday morning, asking: "What luck for this afternoon?"

As the weeks wore past I became surfeited with this mundane occupation. Many of the senior officers against whom we had opened the campaign had now been moved to other camps.

E. J. Y. and I sat like fat spiders gorged with flies. The arrival of Red Cross food parcels, an event that galvanised the other prisoners, scarcely caused us to flicker a heavy eyelid. What did we want with tinned margarine? We always had fresh butter, superior to any butter I ever tasted in England. The truth was that we were both eating far too much. One morning I awoke and looked at my body. I had grown fat without realising it. Small wonder. One pound of butter was only lasting me about three days. And yet in ordinary life I am a small eater. It must have been reaction from the starvation period. The black market began to hang around our necks like some vast octopus.

Bit by bit we tried to edge it over to the mess. This was hard. We had given ourselves such a build-up with Gino and the rest of them that they preferred to deal with us. It took some effort to refuse to buy. But gradually the mess, under energetic new managership, began to forge ahead. Then I was expelled as an incompetent from the pay office. To my amusement, E. J. Y. was also expelled, and for the same reason. Nobody could have called *him* incompetent. The food became good all through the camp. We actually got enough to eat, even without our food parcels. And part of the improvement was certainly due to us, we told ourselves sanctimoniously. When the camp as a whole enjoyed a delicious cheese, or rather watery Neapolitan ice-cream, they were enjoying commodities which had originally been ordered by *"I due gangsters"*.

Soon after we had relinquished our underground handling of the black market, there was an explosion of Italian rage and denunciation in the village of Padula. And following the explosion a general of the secret police arrived to conduct a full enquiry. The camp was searched for food. But by that time we were used to hiding things.

Gino and many of my Italian acquaintances and supply agents were arrested, handcuffed and carried off to Naples with threats of capital punishment or imprisonment for life.

The investigating general consulted a huge sheaf of anonymous and signed letters of complaint from Padula and the neighbourhood. The letters had been written by keen Fascists and by peasants who had not been able to profit from the stream of gold which Gino, the mess, Dibbs and I had let loose from the monastery.

One letter (the general showed it to me himself, for he interrogated me personally in French) accused the woman who brought down ice-cream in a barrow of having sexual relations with the prisoners.

This made me laugh immoderately. The woman had no contact with the prisoners, never saw them, in fact. But I saw her one afternoon after lunch as I was going to the pay office to collect some things we had ordered in Naples. The woman, a large, flouncing creature on high heels, walked along the corridor ahead of me and knocked on the door beyond the pay office. Someone replied to her knock and she swayed in.

"Who lives in the next room?" I asked Ienco the following morning.

"It is the bedroom of the colonel commandant."

The storm passed away. The generals, the inquisitors, the black market racketeers and the vigilantes disappeared. The camp settled down to a new peace with new interpreters, a new priest, and a new colonel commandant. I was glad that the black market was ended.

Now that I had been wicked I could be good.

CHAPTER VIII

I SUPPOSE all men blow "now hot, now cold". But it often seems to me that I blow to greater extremes than most.

In prison my blowing took two forms. The first, when I had got my strength back, was longing, both idealistic and practical, for physical freedom, for escape. The second was resignation to my condition as a prisoner, and delight that I now had time, away from routine, hysteria and fleshly attractions, to do so many of the things that I had always been conscious of leaving undone.

I was able, to some extent, to separate the two extremes of my blowing; and often, when my programme for escape was necessarily arrested, though only temporarily, I turned quite happily to the other world. In this, so far as my observation went, I was exceptional. Most escapers, like the Baron, for example, were single-minded fanatics.

In this chapter I blow cold, separating escape from the other interests of my prison life, and dealing with those interests.

*   *   *   *   *

I sought the company of sixteen clergymen and priests who were prisoners at Padula since I wanted to know whether I could find a belief in God or a belief in their religion.

The only time that I went to a religious service at Padula was on Christmas Sunday, when they were producing a Nativity play in which I was interested. What is the use in going to church if you do not believe in the reason for the service, and if you dislike the service? I enjoy sermons when they are theological arguments; I detest them when they are sentimental reiterations that man's hope lies in God. And I notice that the second kind is the more frequent.

There were many in my prison camps who took comfort from religion; about thirty per cent of the officers and four per cent of the batmen. After talking with these prisoners, I decided that half of them, or rather less, went to worship because they believed in God, either consciously or unconsciously; and the other half went because they thought that it did them good or because they liked, whenever possible, to live in the past, and the worship, with its familiar words and music, gave them a sentimental bath.

The foregoing applies only to the non-Catholic officers. There was a small group of Catholics in each camp, and they were naturally fairly well looked after by the Italians. Very often they were allowed to go to Mass in a proper chapel. Sometimes they were even allowed to go to the Mass attended by civilians. They kept silent about their religion, and were, as usual, a little more intense about it (having had much more concentrated and parrot-like doses of it as children); but I never noticed that they were better men, more honest, or happier because of it.

More interesting, and better attended, than the religious ceremonies were a series of lectures or expositions on the Christian religion given by a monk from an Anglican monastery in Yorkshire. He had been sent to the Army by the principal of his monastery. After the war, when we ordinary prisoners (and ordinary parsons) would return to the sensual joys of board and bed, this man would retire again to the life of the spirit.

He was a bony man with vulture-like head. His skin had the hairless and unporous polish, his eyes the far-away, almost vacant, gaze that only seems to be achieved by an

92

ascetic existence and a calm soul. His voice was like filtered, iced water running into a deep basin of purest silver. He was the finest and noblest speaker that I have ever heard. If any man could have shown me the truth that lies in God for some men, I believe that this monk could have done it for me.

His persuasive power was the greater in that his own love, his passionate love, for his God so obviously made him happy and understanding and compassionate.

Religion has always interested me, and I was thoroughly grounded in it as a boy by my mother and my grandmothers. When I began to think for myself, religion ceased to be a creed for me. I thought of it more in terms of architecture, history, and music. I admire the Christian religion for its civilising and elevating influence. I believe in the truth and rightness of many of the Christian teachings, and in the greatness of Christ himself.

I therefore followed the argument of this Anglican monk with eager interest. I followed it to the edge of the gulf which must be jumped if you are to believe in God. And I could not jump because I could see no reason for belief in the Christian God.

The beautiful black Bible with gold-edged pages (which was the first thing that my optimistic mother sent out to me) remained unopened on my shelf.

But I had time for other reading. In the hot summer, when I lay in the sun with the sweat dripping on the pages; in the winter when I sat most of the day huddled, fully dressed, in bed, with a pale fawn-coloured camel-hair blanket, sent from London, around my neck and shoulders, I read and read and read. There were so many books that I had put off reading before because in ordinary life there was too much living to be done.

Music in prison gave another sense, another dimension.

Outside the windows of our wing was the wide cornice topping the architrave of the big Doric order below. The cornice was about three feet wide, formed of fairly massive blocks of stone, but an overhang, nevertheless. Always scared of heights from buildings or mountains, I had some difficulty in forcing myself out on to this high ledge. But it was so convenient, and so pleasant in the sun that I wore down my instinctive fear.

I was sitting on this cornice in the spring sunshine when I heard music for the first time in months—the opening bars of Beethoven's Sixth Symphony. The music came from a worn record and a cheap portable gramophone, but I never was filled with a more intense ecstasy—an ecstasy that was physical

D

as well as mental, for I could distinctly feel the chords drawing a shuddering response from the small muscles running up the centre of my back to my neck. When the first record was finished I realised that I had nearly strangled myself by holding my breath in case the noise of breathing or the muscular effort should interfere with the sounds that came from the gramophone.

At the end I asked several of my friends if they had felt similar sensations, and they agreed that they had. Some of these men were astonished. They protested that they did not care for "classical" music, and thought that they had never heard the "Pastoral" before. The intensity of these musical sensations wore off as we spent our money on subscriptions to buy more records and more gramophones. They showed us, however, to what an extent we had been starved for music, and what an important force it was. Several times a week we were able to listen to gramophone records, occasionally even in the wings, though that became impossible owing to the complaints of young men who were intolerant enough to dislike any but the newest forms of music.

One trouble with prison life was that there was not enough of it for me. I left prison with many things left undone. If it were not for the tugging of the outside, and the annoyance of prison life itself, I think I could have used five years of it. They would have made up for the five years I spent in my public school.

Not that you could learn much in prison. It seemed (for me at any rate) only to be possible to assimilate. And everyone had to fight now and then against the prison disease. It was a mental disease, and we called it "going round the bend". Prisoners of the first world war had a disease which they called "barbed wire disease". It seems to have been the same. When you went round the bend you lay on your bed and wished that you were dead. There was no more to it than that. You lost interest in everything inside the prison and everything outside it. You stifled, you stagnated, you sulked.

In my opinion the disease came from the necessity for hypocrisy, for getting on well with other people. There was an unnaturalness about the smoothness of prison relations that struck the new prisoner very forcibly when he came into an established camp. When you were shut up with all those other people, you developed a safety mechanism which ensured that you "rubbed along" comfortably. If you hated somebody you were ill-advised to say so, for the prison "Bush radio" carried your remark right round the camp within a day. This artificial atmosphere occasionally broke down, and men went round the bend. The disease (or safety-valve?) became more evident in some men the longer they stayed in the bag.

The people who went most easily round the bend were the very young and the over-forties. Both age groups were affected strongly by food shortages and discomforts. The young ones may have had sexual difficulties, and they often found it impossible to get intellectual stimulus from books, music, or work. They played games of course, but in the winter games were often out of the question, since all energy was required to keep the body heated.

We had a great many courses of study at Padula. All the time that I was there I tried to teach French (and learned a good deal by doing so), learned Italian, and attended excellent lectures on history, religion and music. Other lecture courses which I attended embraced: law, wines and spirits, agriculture, German, tactics and military discussions, public speaking, local government, advertising.

Our year was divided up into three terms, with a "holiday" between each term to give both teacher and pupils a rest. But the result was really laughable. Each class began the term with a large attendance. At the end of the first week it was dwindling, at the end of the second it was probably reduced by half, and near the end of the term there were extremely few people in the whole camp doing any work except the teachers. Older prisoners usually claimed that it was impossible to do any work in prison. There was something in the air that killed achievement. Perhaps the killer was doubt—doubt about the future that slyly gnawed at every prisoner.

No prisoner was entitled to have fewer doubts than I. When our mail from home began to arrive, I was almost deluged with letters from Anne. Frequently I received two or three letters at once, and they were almost all from her. I heard from my mother that Anne was discouraging my friends and relatives from writing to me, on the grounds that if they did so she might be obliged to cut down her own output. Her early letters interested and cheered me. She was working now in factories. The first letters told of her driving job at a big factory in Perivale, described the canteen, her car, the long waits for passengers. They were virile letters. Still more virile when she tired of that job and managed to get herself another in a smaller factory in London. True, she knew the factory owner; but she seemed to want to work inside, to get to know the other workers. Soon she told me that she had friends among the girl workers, that she managed to work a 56-hour week. I was proud of her.

Parcels began to arrive. One of mine contained two new pictures of Anne. Strange, dark, over-romantic photographs they were. Her face seemed to have changed, to have filled out. Jimmy le Coq made me frames from *passe-partout,* and later she remembered to send me a double leather frame. It was good to have her photograph beside my bed. People used to look at it and say: "Lucky man."

"Tell me about yourself, everything," she wrote to me. "How many other men are there in your bedroom?"

"One hundred and thirty-two," I wrote back truthfully.

Once she wrote to tell me that the story was current in London that officer prisoners in Italian camps were supplied with women.

"I hope it's true," she wrote, oddly enough. "Because then if you want a woman you can have one, and perhaps you might get ill if you didn't for a long time."

"What a ridiculous rumour," I replied. "Of course no women are supplied, and none are needed."

Before I was a prisoner I had wondered how some men lived a monastic life without any desire for sexual intercourse. Religious fervour might understandably take the place of earthly loves; a religious zealot loves God sometimes to the exclusion of his more ordinary passions. But there were monks and priests who loved the human species rather than God, who yet took their religious vows quite seriously, and had no difficulty in keeping any of them.

Now, as a prisoner, I was astonished to find that I myself had been stripped of thoughts about sex. For twenty months as a prisoner of war I might have been a eunuch. At times I became worried by my sexlessness.

The reasons were probably mechanical. We were on a low and plain diet, and we had very little alcohol. Furthermore, we seldom saw women, and if we did (on occasional walks between guards with fixed bayonets) we could not speak to them.

It is interesting to a normal man to find that he has the power to avoid, without any difficulty or discomfort, that part of man's existence which many consider so essential. I would not be honest, however, if I gave the impression that all prisoners found this avoidance as easy and as comfortable as I did.

This became obvious when a submariner named Mike Caplatt

produced an original musical comedy written by Johnny Johnstone of the Indian Army, with music by Gordon Johnstone. Caplatt had been an actor before the war, and was a wily producer, out to stun his audiences. The title of the thing was *Be Brazen*, and the first scene opened with a female chorus singing languidly in front of the Brazen Buttery, Clover Street ("Side by Side with Dover Street"), Mayfair.

At Padula we were able to buy from Naples such comparatively useless things as material for women's dresses. Among some of the New Zealand officers in the camp Caplatt unearthed two hirsute toughs, who, in private life, had been designers in a big woman's store. The female chorus, chosen for the sinuosity of their figures, their smiles, their eyelashes, were fitted expertly with false breasts, and were so well groomed for their parts that (to prisoners unaccustomed to the real thing) they *were* women. Even better was the young Englishman, a superb actor, who played "Lady Pat", the female lead, one of the love-soured lovelies of Mayfair who (in Act 2) suddenly discovered that she was "in love all over again" and sang "I'll take a risk".

Overnight Caplatt had changed the camp. A tiny spark of sex had electrified the wings, the senior officers' quarters, the batmen's huts. From the church came powerful rumbles as the New Zealand Bishop of Wyapu, an admirably hard-fisted zealot who ran round the cloisters once a day to keep his health, voiced his disapproval of "the tone of the lines and costumes".

The young men who had played the female parts became celebrities overnight, and remained celebrities. Senior officers asked them out to tea. Padres suddenly became interested in their souls. It was all slightly amusing, a little embarrassing, and quite harmless. But it was sex all the same. The camp demanded more meaty entertainment like *Be Brazen*, and got it. Strangely enough the batmen (who drew bigger rations than the officers) caught this craze more strongly. They produced their own revue, a revue which, in some ways, outstripped *Be Brazen*.

Although I approved of batmen in the Army, I could not approve of them in prison camps. The officers were divided up into groups, and each group had its batman, who made their beds, cleaned their room and their shoes, and otherwise did what they told him to do. Like some other officers, I could see no reason for this, no reason why an officer prisoner should not make his own bed and clean his own boots. Furthermore, the majority of the batmen in the prison camps were fighting

97

soldiers, and not men who had volunteered to be servants. They were apt to take unkindly to their menial occupations, and some of us sympathised with them. Both of my men had good jobs. Skinner was an assistant in the mess kitchens, and Jones was batman to the adjutant, Hutcheson, who was a decent person and also a New Zealander. Not all the batmen were so well placed, but then all the men were not of the calibre of Jones and Skinner.

Our prison camp was a muted miniature of the big world outside. When we had been there a few months, even differences of rank had been evened out. Apart from the senior British officer and his small staff who did the routine work, the leading figures in the camp were "self-made"; and, strangely enough (or was it so strange?), they were all comparatively young, and the majority of them were only lieutenants or second-lieutenants. We had our heroes, our outcasts and our social snobs. And our intellectuals, uninterested in anybody outside their cliques, who gave and attended lectures on every subject from Chinese junks to the fermentation of sherry. While the non-intellectual games-playing moustache-cultivators went around saying that all intellectuals should be shot as Communists or Fascists or intellectuals. We had our Communists and our perfectly obvious Fascists too.

Some of our prisoners were rich and others were very poor. Riches consisted in receiving many private parcels. The British prisoner was only supposed to get one personal "next-of-kin" parcel of clothing every three months, and the stock food parcels which of course were distributed equally. But rich relatives at home sometimes were dishonest. Many prisoners frequently received Red Cross "Invalid Parcels", although they were certainly not invalids. "Invalid parcels" were perfectly satisfactory food parcels. Also the same type of officer might get parcels from all over the world as well as from England. They might come from Egypt, Turkey, Portugal, Canada, Switzerland, America (if the prisoner's parents were influential enough to have a pull in foreign countries). At the other end of the scale were officers promoted from the ranks on the desert battle-fields, officers who perhaps had no relatives, or whose wives were barely rich enough to send them duty-free cigarettes.

The lists of names which were posted on the notice-board each day that parcels were received were packed with bitter stabs for many, all the more bitter because the bitterness was veiled.

Beside those long-hand scrawls on the notice-board you would hear the oily chuckle of the rich man who had received a few more parcels, the sycophantic remarks of his admiring friends, and the barely perceptible sigh of the man who never got a parcel, the man who walked three times round the court-yard saying to himself: "I won't look." But in the end he was obliged to look, and he saw the names of the officers who always got parcels, usually two or three at a time. His name was not there, there was nothing to live for. Minor personal tragedies and accidents were exaggerated into disasters.

The war news was either dreadful or wonderful, always extreme. Up to 'Alamein we had an extra cross to bear, since our guards, a degenerate rabble who came mainly from the slums of Naples, were so certain that our countries were beaten and would never recover that they were inspired to insult us. These insults, the price we paid for tens of thousands of haughty British tourists in pre-war Naples, were only the buzzing of blue-bottles, but they still had an effect on our morale. It seemed incredible that the fortunes of war might actually give victory to these creatures. On wet days (so depressing, the rain), you could watch them practising self-abuse in their sentry-boxes.

Then the news of our great desert victory flung the whole camp into a ferment of optimism, and the guards became instantly more friendly.

*   *   *   *   *

All these troubles, problems and nastinesses were easy enough to banish in the summer. Then a man could lie in the sun until he was dizzy. Or walk around the paddock until he was soaked in sweat and tired enough to have a cold shower, sprinkle himself with talcum powder (with which the Italians continued to flood the canteen), then flop on his bed, covering his body with a sheet to keep off the flies. Or he could pass a profitable five minutes killing flies. Then in the evenings there were football games to watch, or to play in. In the summer a man was not so hungry. And parcels arrived well in summer, 1942. It was pleasant to attend an odd lecture out in the court-yard where the sunken stone paths criss-crossed the rectangle in the pattern of the Union Jack, or under the olive-trees in the paddock, or beside the great sunflowers in a garden belonging to one of the quarters.

If I go back to Padula I shall watch the lizards again. They were fascinating, and they were everywhere, sunbathing like me, sometimes ruminant and aloof like me, and sometimes much more social. The swifts too. When we were out on the cornice they dived past us in curves so tight and dangerous that the slightest misjudgment (as Schnoz Campbell and other professional aviators pointed out) would have turned them from something more alive than life into a dead smudge on the old wall. Then I used to think that if you flooded the court-yard to a level, finishing about three feet below our cornice, you would make the most wonderful swimming-pool in all the world.

But I shall not return to Padula in the winter, because winter there is a bitter memory.

Winter is the prisoner of war's most dreaded enemy. It was winter that made most prisoners in Padula hoard food. Partly because they knew that the parcel supply always fell off in winter, due, the Italians claimed, to transport difficulties. Partly because their diet was not sufficiently energy-producing for them to be warm in an ill-heated stone monastery. We hoarded tins through the summer, then, knowing that we should need them to cheer us up in the dark winter evenings, and to provide some calories against the cold. (We talked often, and quite seriously, about calories.)

By the end of the summer Dibbs and I, thanks to our illicit black market activities, had a big accumulation of tins in store. We therefore faced the winter with full confidence as well as with bodies stuffed with butter-fat. It was nearly a year before I lost the forced layers of fat which I had put on in the first mad flush of the black market. Despite our riches, Dibbs was no spendthrift, and we went cannily through the winter using up on principle only one tin of meat or fish each day. On Sundays and on special occasions like Christmas Day we would be reckless and cook a small tin of porridge oats and some tinned sausages for breakfast.

After my exercises at 7 a.m. in the cloisters I made my bed and then worked at something, usually Italian, until the batmen came clattering round the wings carrying buckets of tea. They issued us with one cup each. The arrival of the tea was the signal for everyone else to wake up, and a sticky, grunting awaking it was. Our bread ration was so small (still 100 grams) that I hesitated to waste any of it on such a dismal meal; and I normally ate walnuts instead, and finished off with an apple. Dibbs and I had bought in a great stock of walnuts and hard apples which (stored in big baskets, together with a lot of ancient timber which I had hacked out of forbidden parts of the monastery while doing my reconnaissances for escaping) lay under our beds. Between the two beds stood a deal table, and at the end of the table was the small cupboard in which we kept our spare clothing and our food.

Padula was a "cooking camp". That is to say the mess had not sufficient facilities to be able to cook food from our Red Cross parcels, so they gave us what they could get from the Italians, usually macaroni or rice and some vegetables, and we cooked the food from our parcels individually. We were sometimes able to buy wood for fuel. And thanks to a small, black-bearded genius from the Fleet Air Arm, "Fingers" Lewis, we had plenty of apparatus for cooking.

"Fingers", like Henry Ford or Lord Nuffield, began in a small way when he became disgusted with the early home-made *stufa* (stove), made from a single large tin. He evolved a new system for building "stufas". By beating out Red Cross tins until they were flat, and then joining them together with an air-tight, beaten joint, he obtained large sheets of metal. Then he designed his "stufas" on the drawing-board and built them of shining tin, well-lagged with cement stolen from the Italian workmen.

Without "Fingers's" products I doubt if we could have existed through the cold Padula winter. His "stufas"—and the special pots and pans that went with them—were a joy to handle. He himself had an enormous model with a couple of ovens and several boiling spaces. For Dibbs and me he built a special "quick boiler". Its design was made possible by Skinner, who found me two large flat Italian tins which had contained tunny. These were our pans. The stove was insulated so that you could lay your hand on it while it was going full blast. It had a long chimney and two ways of adjusting the draught. It boiled a can of water in the record time of four minutes and on a handful of twigs, walnut shells, or cardboard fragments. "Fingers" came round inspecting his handiwork while it was in use. He got very angry if the outside of a stove was dirty. He said heat was lost in radiation that way. For our "Fingers Super Cooker" we paid (he had developed a proper business concern with skilled accountants as well as tradesmen and apprentices working under him) 1,000 cigarettes, two tins of porridge oats, a roll of lavatory paper, two razor-blades, and a pair of home-knitted socks. We waited five weeks for delivery.

All prisoners of war seemed to be, like Shaw's sensible Swiss, chocolate-cream soldiers. When we had our quota of parcels, which was rarely enough, we ate more sugar and sweets than normal men, and still we cried for more. Condensed milk, usually called "condensato", became a vice.

Another aspect of the prisoner's appetite was that he craved for "bulk". The mere satisfaction of hunger did not satisfy him; he needed the sensation of a full and warm belly.

We did a good deal of baking for celebrations like birthdays (there were always parties of one sort or another) or Christmas. By grinding down the white biscuits from Canadian parcels we could get flour. Mixing this with pancake mixture, powdered egg, margarine, sugar, and raisins, we made edible and filling cakes, baking them in our own ovens.

All this pottering about passed the time. After breakfast there was roll-call. Then, on winter mornings, I worked at something, it might be at one of my classes or lectures, it might be on a poster for a forthcoming theatrical production, it might be rehearsing, or it might be some more secret occupation.

After lunch, a scrappy meal eaten in greatcoats in the high, draughty dining-hall, we hurried upstairs and went to bed; at least, we sat on our beds and covered ourselves with blankets. Tea was the big meal of the day, and Dibbs and I cooked it alternate days. We usually made a stew, starting from an onion base (we had also laid in a large store of onions), and with a tin or two from the parcels in it. The main object was to have plenty of stew, and to have it boiling hot.

Between tea and dinner there was an endless two hours. This was an exercise period. I knew that feet would be the most important part of the body if I ever managed to shake myself free. For at least an hour each evening I went pounding round and round the cloisters, sometimes accompanied, more often alone. For the longer I stayed at Padula the more I drew myself apart from the others. Some of them thought that I was going round the bend. But I was only drawing away from them so that I could be alone, dissociate myself from them and from their talk.

I adopted a cold attitude towards my companions as the winter days steadily passed. I surrounded myself with this coldness, and practised it until nobody could penetrate it.

CHAPTER IX

I LEARNED by painful experience that the would-be escaper had to be secretive with his friends and fellow-prisoners. All movements leading up to a possible escape had to be camouflaged and concealed.

The British prisoners, pliable men, and often ingenious or a little mad, escaped, it seemed, more frequently than other nationalities. But they were ready, the British, to listen to the conservative type of talker who took the line: "What's the use? Try if you like. It's impossible."

The prisoners at Padula were on the whole far from admirable. It may be that Padula was a particularly bad camp. Perhaps I myself, with the black market, had helped to sap the morale of the place. Others who attempted to escape from that camp can testify that what I say is true. The would-be escaper at Padula was disliked by the majority of his fellow-prisoners. I myself was "cut" by several officers when I came into the great court-yard for the first time after doing thirty days in the punishment cell for attempted escape. The attitude of these persons only amused and interested me. However, I asked one of my friends for an explanation.

"Didn't you hear what happened?" he replied. "The day following your capture at the gate the Eyeties came in and destroyed all the cooking-stoves in the wings. They caught us quite unprepared, nothing was hidden. The only man who thought of an answer was the Bishop. He lit such a fire in his 'stufa' that it became white-hot, and three *carabinieri* burned themselves on it. But you could hardly expect to be *popular*, could you?"

The Baron, who made two brilliant attempts at escape from Padula, was certainly no hero in the camp. He was regarded rather as a nuisance, as someone who interfered with the comfort of others. This was only a general attitude. The officers at the top who ran the escape committee were sometimes helpful and always enthusiastic.

And after all, Padula was a bad prospect for escape. Once out, where were you to go? North? You had the whole length of Italy to cover before you got to the heavily guarded Swiss frontier. South? The nearest British were in Malta. The sea between Malta and the Italian mainland was dominated by Axis airmen who machine-gunned any small boat they sighted. Also there were beach patrols and a stringent curfew for fishing-boats. East? After getting across to the coast somewhere near Bari, a long and difficult trip, the evader might stow away on a ship crossing the Adriatic or attempt the crossing himself in a stolen boat. Once in Jugoslavia he would try to join the guerrillas.

Against the feebleness of the chances was set the Army order that it was the duty of every British prisoner to escape, and to assist others to escape. And stronger than the Army order, at any rate for me, was a longing to escape that sometimes maddened me almost to bursting point; that forced me during twenty months to face rain, snow, and ridicule to keep myself fit. I knew that I was going to escape.

It was the Americans who told me. One day in 1942, with about thirty other officers, I was out on a walk. It was a hot summer afternoon. Our conducting officer, a rather charming Italian who, despite his youth, was struggling to grow a little pointed beard (we called him "the Boy"), sat down to rest in a hollow in the woods well above our monastery.

I lay on my back in the hollow and tried to imagine that I was alone. Suddenly I felt that I was alone, and free, and in France. At that time I had been considering the possibilities of crossing from the north of Italy into France, since I knew the Alps and the coastline there a little. I had even been making maps of that area, tracing them with a mapping-pen on to fine British lavatory paper.

As I lay on my back we heard a powerful drone in the sky, and without hesitation I said to myself: "If those are American aircraft I shall soon be escaping through France." And, of all the strange things, they were American aircraft, silver Flying Fortresses, the first that I had ever seen. After that I knew that I was going to escape. The noise of their bombs did not interest me.

Not long after my time in the punishment cell with the Baron, he and his escaping partner, Jack Pringle, made an attempt. They managed to mix with some Italian masons who were working on the forward part of the monastery, and they actually got out into the roadway in front. There they were arrested and brought back. They had been well-dressed to pass as Italian workmen, and Pringle spoke excellent Italian. With luck they would have got away. The Italian foreman had noticed that their boots were peculiar.

A little later they discovered another way to climb out of the monastery. This time they got clear away. They were caught in a wine-shop, some distance from Padula. Cram managed to tear himself free and there was a chase across country. In the end they caught him too.

The pair were then shipped off, together with all the other prisoners who had attempted escape from this or other camps, to the punishment camp, *Campo* 5, at Gavi, north-east of Genoa. Reports filtered to us (they were perhaps inspired by the Italian authorities) that *Campo* 5 was a hell-camp, a former civilian jail where the commandant carried a great cluster of keys on his belt, and never went through a door without unlocking it and locking it behind him.

From the moment that I began to work in the Padula pay office, which was in the section of the building forbidden to ordinary prisoners, I had searched for a way out. I had discussed my plans with the British authority, walking around the paddock with the pompous officer who was then head of the escaping committee, and I had begun to save food.

The food question was of paramount importance from Padula, whence there were such vast distances to be covered to get clear of Italy, and this barred many people from thinking of escape.

At Capua I had eaten one-third of a bar of Canadian chocolate, because I was ill and needed it. From then on I saved every bit of chocolate that was sent me by the Red Cross or by Anne, and many other things as well. Sometimes this was not easy.

There were other officers who were energetically looking for a way out of the vast maze of buildings which constituted the monastery. Little "Fingers" Lewis caught some disease from crawling about in the sewers. Starting from a man-hole in the small court-yard beside the dining-hall, he and his friends explored all the sewers big enough to take a small man, and made a map of them for the escaping committee.

The Italians were cunning guards. They learned about these explorations. They took speedy measures to block the sewers and to inspect them regularly. Following the attempts of Cram and Pringle, the *carabinieri* carried out regular raids on the wings and the quarters, searching for tunnels, and for escaping gear or clothing. They were first-class policemen, experienced at that type of work through years of enforcing a Fascist régime. If I had something to hide I would rather be searched or questioned by a German, a Britisher, or an American than by a Frenchman, an Italian, or a Spaniard. The Latins have great natural talent for that type of work. When they look at you their eyes bore in.

At one time I had considered myself a reasonably sharp reporter. It was not surprising, then, that in the autumn of 1942 I noted that a tunnel was being worked in Room 6. There were various signs of this which were obvious to me since I was frequently in that room. Mud on a hand. A broken finger-nail.

Some of the Room Sixers changing from the second to the first sittings for meals (obviously so that shifts working on the tunnel could operate a system of staggered hours). I was not surprised, therefore, when the escape committee asked me what plans I had to get out of Italy, and what provisions. I was able to reply that Dibbs, then my partner, and I had everything that was necessary, including food, maps and home-made civilian clothing. We would walk for fifty miles on the North Star, lying hidden by day, walking at night. Then we would jump a northbound freight train. Once up north we would make, according to where the train landed us, either for the Swiss frontier around Chiasso or for the French frontier.

When they had considered our qualifications we were instructed to be ready in two days. E. J. Y. and I got feverishly to work cooking rations for our long trip. We did this to a formula invented by a British doctor. The idea was to concentrate the rations as much as possible, and to make them solid and square (and therefore easily portable in a haversack), and to simplify them down. We made cakes, solid as bricks, rations for at least eighteen days. One cake, type A, was to be eaten before starting to walk at nightfall. It was made on a basis of oatmeal, cheese, margarine, and vitamin foods, and it tasted rather like Scottish "white puddings". Type B, slightly larger and much more palatable, was to be eaten when the walking was over and day was breaking. Type B's main ingredients were chocolate, cocoa, condensed milk, sugar, and oatmeal.

To supplement these hard rations we were prepared to carry a great deal of chocolate and other concentrated foods. In fact, we intended to carry enough food for about three weeks' hard walking.

Our clothing was sketchy, but we thought it was good enough for us to pass as peasants in war-time Italy in the summer. We had obtained civilian shirts and faded blue trousers through friends among the men on the kitchen staff. There was no need to wear a coat of any kind, but E. J. Y. had a leather affair that had been sent from England, and I had a dyed linen coat made for *Be Brazen* and now darkened down with a home-made dye, a mixture of ink, wine, and walnut juice. We had made our own caps to a pattern invented by one of the New Zealand professionals. They were cut from ordinary grey Italian blankets and the scoops were stiffened with cardboard.

On D-Day a meeting was called of all the people who were to go through the tunnel. The committee had decided, fairly enough perhaps, but stupidly in our opinion, that only the officers who had worked the tunnel—there were ten of them—plus another two officers were to go on the first night. Then it was hoped that we could conceal their absence for at least twenty-four hours, and the rest of us would go the following night. The various methods for duping the Italians in the intervening twenty-four hours had been thoroughly worked out, and were reasonably good. Tom Raymond-Barker, of the 60th, make-up and costume genius of the prison theatre and himself one of the second lot for the tunnel, had prepared some very lifelike dummies to put in the beds of the departed. To make the "hair" he nobly sacrificed a fine sheepskin coat. The two officers who were to make numbers eleven and twelve on the first party had been well chosen, and nobody could complain about their selection. They were Jim Craig and John Redfern, both New Zealanders, who had done fine work rescuing British troops from German-occupied Greece and the Ægean. Lots were drawn to determine the order in which our team would go through the tunnel. Dibbs and I drew second position, which we thought was the best. If the Italians happened to be watching the mouth the first pair out would get shot, and lying second there was only one pair in front of us to give the alarm by the noise they made.

The astonishing thing was that out of that large camp the committee had only been able to find thirty officers ready to go out of a hole that had been made for them.

At the entrance to the private lavatory of Room 6 a concrete slab had been cut out, and skilfully fitted with a trap. Underneath the trap the shaft that ran down into a cellar underneath was kept stuffed with damp sacking. Thus when the *carabinieri* came round tapping the walls and floors (they did this meticulously every day) they heard no hollowness. The tunnel began from the cellar, and the cellar had answered one of the most difficult questions in all tunnels, disposal of the spoil. Under Room 6 there had been space to pack all the earth taken out of the tunnel. They had worked fast, and cleverly. It had been tough going in the sixty-foot tunnel that cut through stony ground and hard clay to surface in the maize outside the Italian perimeter wire. Their home-made equipment was superb, including a trolley running on wooden rails, for sending the earth and stones back from the working face, an air-pump that was lubricated with tinfuls of margarine, electric light, and an electric system of warnings worked from the quarter above. The tunnel was a triumph. It was a pity that one hundred officers did not go through it on the first night.

The twelve got through all right, although they found the hole a tight fit, and Richard Carr, whose girth was very considerable, got stuck, and finally managed to burst his way through only after jettisoning his water-bottle.

That night, leaning out of the lavatory windows, which commanded a magnificent view of the valley and the hill behind Padula, Dibbs and I strained our eyes to see into the dim moonlight. We knew that they must all be out. The zero-hour was well past. Then the farm dogs began to bark. First one away to the south, near the banks of the river that ran down the valley. Then another, almost in front of us, to the west, then more up in a northerly direction. It was most dramatic, the barking in the semi-darkness where steam from the warm earth rose between the hills.

I slept beside one of the dummies. At midnight the Italian orderly officer appeared, followed by two *carabinieri*, stumbling with sleep. When I saw the officer's face I knew that we were finished, for he was the most conscientious and the sharpest of all their staff. We called him "The Terrible Turk" because of his permanent serious scowl. Sure enough, he uncovered the poor dummy that lay beside me, and let out a scream that would have sent a million factory workers hurrying home.

Our hopes of escape had fallen, but it was so funny that we had to forget our disappointment. The Italians all ran out of our court-yard, and we heard a yapping that began on their side of the monastery and gradually grew until with a crescendo hundreds of them burst in a flood into the court-yard. We were paraded in our normal roll-call stands for most of that night and the next day.

There were innumerable searches; but so well was the tunnel concealed that neither end was found by the Italians until they discovered that most of the officers missing had been quartered in Room 6. So they tore the place apart until finally, crashing through masonry from the garden, they broke into the cellar which was the real mouth of the tunnel.

Within three weeks all twelve officers who had escaped were back in the punishment cell, awaiting transport to the sinister *Campo* 5. The three youngest, Peter Bateman, a midshipman, Alan Hurst-Brown, of the Rifle Brigade, and Roy Howard, of the King's Dragoon Guards, had got the farthest. They had reached Bari, and were caught while they were searching for a boat. They brought out an interesting point, I thought. They had worn rubber-soled shoes, believing that silence on the way was better than comfort for their feet.

All twelve told us of the difficulties outside. The peasants were shrewd, observant, and, at that time, unfriendly. There were police checks and road blocks everywhere. The terrain around Padula was difficult for walking, in places almost impassable, at any rate in the dark. All of them had had trouble with their feet. Some of them had suffered terribly from thirst.

From then on, through the summer, a few of us looked for a way out, and every way seemed to be blocked. Work was begun on another tunnel, but the Italians watched too closely. The lighting system of the monastery was studied. The Italians got wind of this. The escape committee tightened its security system. They suspected that the Italians had planted a stool-pigeon among us. Summer wore into winter and the general opinion, even among the men who were trying to get out, was that escape was impossible.

A new commandant had arrived following the destruction of the black market. This man was a full colonel of the *carabinieri*. We called him "The Bat" because he always fluttered around in a huge black cloak. He was a hairless man. He reminded me of the hairless Mexican in Maugham's extraordinary story, except that this Italian was plump and short and noisy, a shouter of the worst kind. He wore a reddish wig under his cocked-up round military hat; and, beneath that toppling pile of artificial hair and stiffened blue-grey cloth and silver braid, his face seemed to be made of pinky wax. When he spoke he jerked his mouth so widely that one feared that his waxy cheeks would open in horrid, gaping, bloodless cracks.

"The Bat" had stamped ruthlessly on most of the little privileges that his predecessors had granted us. And he called in ever more sentries to guard us. As winter approached he had more than 1,000 men under his orders, and new apparatus was continually being installed around the barbed-wire perimeter and on the high points of the great buildings—new searchlights, new telephones, new machine-guns, new systems of doing the rounds and changing the guards. By Christmas Day, 1942, all the searchlights had not yet arrived from Milan, but "The Bat" boasted in the excellent Italian officers' mess (they ate well now, since E. J. Y. and I were unable to tap their supplies of food) that the camp was so secure that, if every Italian there did his duty and did not relax for one second, none of these conceited Britishers would get out alive.

Not long before he uttered this boast a party of which I was a member had been on the point of attempting a break. We were to drop out of the window of a lavatory between Wings 4 and 1. From there we got into a deserted part of the monastery and so into the Italian quarters, whence we were to follow rather a complicated route down corridors and across court-yards, finally climbing into a schoolroom window, and out of a window on the other side into the road. For this last climb we required to carry with us a home-made ladder. The plan was cumbersome, but it had been well studied and organised, and it might possibly have worked. Either by accident or design, on the very night that we were ready to leave, and were waiting with all our gear and our ladder in the lavatory, the Italians visited the empty building below our feet, and the following day that route was blocked with a solid wall of concrete which was regularly inspected. This was not the first time since the beginning of the winter that I had been dressed up and ready to go, for I had noticed that when the cold weather began the Italians had slightly, very slightly, relaxed their vigilance, and I had made an unsuccessful attempt to escape with the cook-house rubbish.

After the lavatory window fiasco it became easier to work in secret because there were only four people left in that camp who wanted to get out during the winter and who were fit enough to attempt it. The other three were Gary Cole, a regular R.A.F. pilot, who had once before made a break in the snow, from Sulmona, and Binns and Johnson who arrived at Padula soon after me.

Chief of the escaping committee at that time was Brigadier Stebbins, a grey-haired, active, and approachable little man who had been a dentist in some town on the Channel coast of England. He agreed with the four of us that the only way to work was to hoodwink the rest of the camp. The talking sprang from a species of jealousy. Even your friends talked. They were determined that *they* were not going outside into the great, cold, rough landscape which they tried to ignore as they hurried down the staircase to go to their meals. They thought anyone who did want to go out was mad. And at the same time they were afraid, yes afraid, that he might get back to England. They had to be regarded as enemies.

To avert suspicion I accepted a part in the newest Caplatt

production, the most ambitious of all, *Twelfth Night,* with costumes by Tom Raymond-Barker, and original music by Gordon Johnstone. They had been trying for some time to interest me in female parts because of my girlish face and banana lips. Pretending to fall to the lure of Shakespeare, I accepted the part of the Countess Olivia. Rehearsals began. People ceased to watch me so closely. Who could suspect the Countess?

From then on, when I was not rehearsing, I worked with Binns and Johnson. They were not bothered by outside people. They were so rude to everybody else in the camp that they had gained a special kind of aloneness.

Wally Binns was a strong man. He was not very tall, but was nearly as broad as he was high, with great swelling muscles everywhere, especially around the jaw and throat. He had a Yorkshire accent to go with these muscles, for he had been born and brought up in Harrogate. Before he reached the twenties Wally had joined up as a trooper in one of our best cavalry regiments, and he had done seven years' service with them in India. This service had left its mark on him—although he had left the Army (he hoped for good) when the seven years ended— it showed in his legs, slightly bowed and with varicose veins on the calves. It showed in his wonderful muscular development, in the way he held his head back and calmly looked his own height. In the way he refused to be "put upon", in the way he disciplined himself. In his wonderful cleanliness and neatness. His few clothes were always mended and washed. He could not bear to be unshaven.

Extraordinarily different was Johnny Johnson. Johnny was the son of a Scottish farmer who had moved south to farm in England's Lake District. At first sight, especially when seen with Binns (and the pair were never separated), Johnny was a little runt of a man with a twisted face over which long, rather greasy hair was apt to straggle. While Binns was calm and careful with his speech, Johnny was always shouting and damning this or that. His language was pungent. He seemed to shower electric energy around him.

Johnny had worked himself up to be a pilot officer in the R.A.F. He had been shot down in a Beaufighter. He was probably (because he was vitriolic and outspoken in a broad Scots accent) one of the most feared officers in the camp. His two "normal" prison accomplishments sat oddly on his personality. He was the best footballer among the officers and one of the best card-players. Binns did not bother with such fripperies.

He taught himself German, ploughing through grammar after grammar. Making a thorough Yorkshire job of it.

Gary Cole, the fourth member of our team, kept in the background and counselled caution. By that time we were fairly certain that the Allies would invade Italy; and it never entered our heads that they would do anything so cumbersome as beginning at the bottom end and working up to the top of that long, tortuous and terrible country. We therefore had a special reason for not wanting to be sent to *Campo* 5, which was right up in the north, north even of Genoa. We thought (we prison tacticians) that the landings in Italy would be somewhere round La Spezia or Livorno. In that case we should be in a strong position at Padula. Furthermore, Gary had been out for nine days and nights in the snow on his first escape, and the memory of it still horrified him.

But we had a good plan. The Germans and Italians, preparing rather half-heartedly to face the invasion, had made a great many airfields running down the coast from Naples. With the help of new prisoners, pilots from the Fleet Air Arm and the R.A.F., we plotted these airfields on our maps. The nearest of them was only two to three days' walking from Padula. Once there we thought we stood a good chance of seizing an aircraft, crossing the Mediterranean, and landing in North Africa. Gary would be the pilot, Johnny was a wireless operator, and if Gary got wounded I could probably set the thing down without killing us, since I had once held a civilian pilot's licence. Binns would be useful for killing sentries.

For over a month Wally, Johnny and I crawled about the roofs, cellars, and sewers of forbidden parts of the monastery. It was a puzzle. Sometimes we got lost ourselves in the maze of old buildings that lay between us and freedom. For ten days we crawled beneath the Italian sentry with his searchlight on the tower, and worked with muffled instruments to break a hole in a wall that was over two hundred years old. When we got through we found that we had miscalculated. All the work had been useless. We opened a hole in the building beside the mess kitchen court-yard. Getting through the hole to reconnoitre I slipped off the rope. As I fell into the mysterious darkness I heard a great whistling and I believed that my life was ended. I landed backwards on a stone floor, but fortunately I was relaxed and the blow was taken first by my rump, then by my shoulders, and lastly by my head. I had mild concussion for a few days. And there was no way out by those buildings.

Then Johnny found another way. Johnny was really the mainspring of our determination to get free. He was a wonderful person underneath his violence. Also, despite his flimsy appearance, he was strong, and extremely agile. This time he climbed on to the rotting roofs around the mess court-yard and broke through a window space that had been walled up before our arrival in the prison. After two or three scouting parties through this hole, we found that it provided a good way into the Italian part of the building. More reconnaissance showed that the route through the school was now closed. The Italians had put evacuees from Naples in the schoolroom itself.

One evening when I got back from a reconnaissance through the hole in the wall, I said to them: "There is only one way out. We can get through into the Eyetie buildings, walk down the passage, across the front court-yard, and out of the front gate."

"Huh," said Johnny. "And the guard will let you out?"

"Yes. We can get four Eyetie uniforms."

"But they don't let the Eyeties out of the camp. Not without showing their papers, anyhow."

"Oh yes, they do. At 5.30 the ordinary day shift for the *soldati* is ended. They go and powder and brilliantine themselves, then, around six, they all charge out of the gate to get up to their girls in the village. Also, there are so many new *soldati* now that the guard on the gate cannot know all of them by sight."

As we talked it over it seemed more and more possible. But Gary refused to take the chance. If it had been a certain way out he would have agreed. Now he refused to risk being shot at the gate or being caught and sent to *Campo* 5 when rescue by Allied armies seemed reasonably imminent.

"I'd feel such a damned fool if I had to spend two more years in the bag in Germany just because I went and got myself sent to *Campo cinque* now," he said.

This was a pity, for he was an excellent man in every way. What was essential was a pilot. Two beds down from me was Ian (Schnoz) Campbell, a regular R.A.F. pilot, not a talker, strong physically, and fit; in fact he was ideal. He had not hitherto been one of the escape attempters. But what did that matter? I knew that in his case it was just that he could not see a possible way out. That evening I put it to him, and he eagerly seized the chance. The uniforms presented no difficulty. Prisoners sometimes arrived with odd bits of uniform issued to them by the Italians to cover them until they got British clothing. From these bits and pieces the escape committee fixed us up with four complete uniforms.

I was standing on my last roll-call at Padula. It seemed inconceivable that it should be the last. I had stood on that same spot waiting for the Italians to check my presence, at least 550 times. To-morrow morning on roll-call—provided we got clean away—four men feigning "sick" would take our places, and then, when they had been counted, rush off to get to their beds before the Italians checked the wings and quarters.

Quite a lot of people knew now that we were going. It was too late for loose talk to do any harm. I had been obliged to warn them to rehearse the under-study for my part in *Twelfth Night*. Tom was altering the wonderful black velvet dress he had created for the Countess Olivia, taking in the hips. I still carried a good deal of my black market fat. And I would need it. The weather was terrible. Cold, often wet, but with a good moon. We would want moonlight for our walk south-west over the mountains. It was odd, how excited I felt. Almost hysterical.

Roll-call was at 5. At 6 we should be clear of the front gate.

When roll-call was dismissed we met in the brigadiers' room. The two brigadiers helped us to dress. Somebody had studied the Geneva Convention again; and they said that unless we were wearing at least one article each of British uniform the Italians would be entitled to shoot us as spies. Well, we were wearing our British boots. Three of the uniform coats had grey patches on the sleeves to show that they were for prisoners. The material was cut out underneath, so the best that we could do was to cover them with black material cut from R.A.F. ties. That looked as though we were in mourning. The Italians almost all were.

Ian was as calm as still champagne, I noted. This was the man who had had the worst nightmares at Tarhuna. Now he was the coolest of the four. I was sweating. Partly from excitement and partly because I now had the Italian uniform on under my battle-dress.

"All the luck in the world," said Brigadier Stebbins. "We shall all be praying for you to-night. I've a feeling that you're going to make a success of it."

"We've *got* to," Binns said aggressively.

Now we were climbing on to the rotten roofs. We had to move on hands and knees, distributing the body's weight evenly on four points. Now we were all through the hole in the darkness. Each of us had carried his food and other few necessities this far in a haversack. We emptied the haversacks, stuffed the British uniforms into them, and threw them out of the hole to Gary. We could not walk out carrying haversacks. That would look suspicious, since the Italian soldiery were always suspected of black market activities.

Mussolini before the war had given his approval to the type of bag trousering which some golfers still wear in Britain, only a shade more baggy, coming down well below the knee, and then held by puttees. These enclosed spaces around our thighs and knees made admirable carriers. I filled up both legs with the cakes I had made many months before for the Room 6 tunnel attempt, with eight pounds of chocolate, a water-bottle, a bag of oatmeal, a strong pocket-knife, a safety-razor, a piece of soap, a tooth-brush, two spare handkerchiefs and two pairs of British Army socks (which did not poison you if your feet bled). I was a fat soldier when I had got all these things in. We all were. Binns was fantastic, being naturally such a very broad man.

When we had all made water in the dark, semi-ruined room, we moved off in single file, feeling our way across the room, up a wooden staircase, across an attic, where we had to work our way round the huge chimney-stack that came up from the monks' buttery. Then down a stairway and along an arcaded balcony to a doorway through which a beam of light cut the air in front of us. This doorway was the end of the uninhabited part.

We stopped there in a huddle to listen. We had made some noise on the way along, crunching with our boots on the lumps of old dry plaster covering the floors. Johnny and I, who both knew what lay on the other side, explained to the others just where we were and what there still remained to do. We listened to the noises on the other side. Through the open doorway came a faint smell of bread and garlic and noises of life and movements—very distant movements, they seemed.

"Come on," I said. "It's just on six o'clock. There's nothing to wait for." I was actually thinking: "The longer we wait here the more difficult it will be to move."

We got into our "action stations", Wally and Johnny together in front, Ian and I following. We walked like that because Ian and I were both on the tall side for Italians, and someone might notice our fair hair. The other two made a better shop window.

A slight effort from each one of us, and suddenly there we were launched, clattering round the balcony of the court-yard I knew so well. The pay office was down that corridor, the big door we were passing now was the door of the commandant's offices. What a noise we were making. I hissed to Wally and Johnny in front to shorten their paces and not to walk in step, Italians never did.

I was just beginning to breathe when tragedy happened. I swore to myself, but I refused to think that it was the end.

It was tragedy in the shape of a young Italian lance-corporal who had come out of the commandant's office just as we passed the door. I knew this lance-corporal by sight. He was a Fascist, an officious little beast, and ambitious. A pretty boy with wavy brown hair flowing glossily over his round head.

We all heard the door open and shut behind us, and then the footsteps that followed.

The devil of it was that we now had to walk down an immensely long, dead straight corridor. At the end of it we would descend a few steps, switch right, and we would be beside the great gates of the monastery, the main obstacle. The two in front, spurred on by the footfalls of the little brute behind us, increased their pace a little.

"Who is it?" Binns hissed back out of the side of his mouth.

"The *colonnello's* bum-boy. A shit."

"Shall we knock him off?"

"No." The brigadier had given us precise orders not to use force to get clear. And, anyway, just as I said it two other Italians approached us, walking the other way. They passed without lifting an eyebrow. They had noticed nothing. Now we were half-way down the corridor.

But I heard the little corporal behind us ask the two whom we had passed: "Who are those?"

"Don't know."

The lance-corporal had dropped behind, but now he was half-running to catch up.

"*Eh*," he called to us. "*Eh, eh.*" (This was a kind of goat-like noise that they always made when they wanted to attract your attention.)

We were on the stairs now.

"*Eh . . . Eh . . .*"

At the bottom of the stairs Johnny saw that two *carabinieri* were standing in the passage we had intended to take, swinging right. So instead he turned left. I hoped that this might shake off the lance-corporal behind us. The quarters of the *soldati* lay across this court-yard, and the fact that we had turned towards them might allay his suspicions. We walked across the dark court-yard towards the huts where the soldiers were billeted, then edged round to our left and so entered the main front court-yard. There, dead ahead lay the final obstacle, the huge arched gateway with the new guard-house beside it. A sentry was standing at the gate with fixed bayonet, but the double gates were wide open. I felt like taking a deep breath and rocketing out through them.

But the lance-corporal was at our heels again.

"*Eh.* Who are you? Where are you going?"

Binns now edged near him. There were crowds of soldiers round the side of the court-yard. Some of them were drifting out of the gate.

"*Eh, eh.*" He laid a paw on Binns's sleeve, and the mighty muscles which he felt under it may have startled him, for he suddenly screamed in a high falsetto.

"*Attenzione alla porta! Prigionieri!* Look out at the gate! Prisoners! Prisoners! Prisoners!"

Immediately the great gates clanged shut, and closing in on every side of us came a rush of small, unwashed soldiers. Paws caught hold of us everywhere. Maddeningly. Voices screeched all round us. *Soldati* fought each other to get near us, either to prod us, to touch us, or to pretend to be holding us. We got a little separated. Each of us stood like the centre of a whirlpool, swaying a little here and there, but with most of the activity on the outside of the circle.

Binns was getting angry. His deep voice suddenly boomed out, audible in the uproar because it was on another key.

"Why, you dirty little . . ." he shouted. "I can't stand this. Why, you . . ."

I heard Ian shouting to him not to hit anyone. And I hoped the strong man would keep his temper. They would kill us if he hit one of them.

Now the lance-corporal was shrieking: "*Comandante, comandante, comandante, signor comandante.*"

The lower half of the tall first-floor window directly over the noble fan of steps leading into the monastery proper suddenly shot up, and the commandant pushed his head out with the suddenness of a jack-in-the-box. It took him only a second or two to gather what was afoot; then with a piercing trumpet scream he left the window. We could hear his scream dwindle as he turned his back on the window, pounded across the parquet floor of his great office, turned right, descended the stairs. Then it grew in volume as he negotiated the ground-floor corridors, and suddenly became ear-splitting as he rushed through the doorway and down the steps, his great black cloak flying behind him. Three other officers followed him, but they remained at first standing at the top of the steps, hesitating to thrust themselves into the human tempest below where hundreds of little, grey-clothed, excited *soldati* now thronged the court-yard.

"Back!" shouted the commandant. Gradually the soldiers nearest him pushed back until he stood at the central point of a semicircle of empty court-yard, and the four of us, each held tightly by at least six *soldati*, were on the circumference, opposite him.

The small lance-corporal, insufferable creature, now shouted: "It was I, my colonel, I who saw them. I saw the boots, the English boots."

"Shut your mouth," shouted the colonel. "How many got away?"

"None, Colonel, none, none, none," answered hundreds of screaming voices.

"Lights," shouted the colonel. They put the lights on around the court-yard, but they only lit it with a reddish glow. Now the colonel stood breathing heavily, gasping for breath as though he had a fit. Sometimes his breathing overreached itself so that he gave a sob at the end of a breath. The little men around us were suddenly silent; an awed silence.

The colonel ran across the space that separated him from us.

He swung back his right fist and crashed it as hard as he could into Johnny's face, then he did the same to Ian. I could not believe my eyes. He was shouting again, too. Suddenly I saw a figure in front of me. It was a small Italian second-lieutenant whom I knew quite well by sight.

Suddenly I saw his fist coming at me. The first one took me by surprise. I rode the second by suddenly crushing back on the *soldati* who held me. Both blows landed on my mouth. He wore two rings, and they cut into my thick and vulnerable lips. I could feel a loose tooth and blood spattered everywhere. I struggled to get free. I would have murdered him. The surprise of it maddened me. Two days before, when I was collecting tobacco parcels, we had exchanged a *"buon giorno"*. But I soon cooled off, for things were getting serious.

"*Al muro,* to the wall, to the wall, to the wall with them," shouted the colonel.

But now Boldeschi, an interpreter, an Italian aristocrat and a sensible type of man, came down the steps, and began to reason with the colonel. I caught snatches only of their conversation, although you could hardly call it conversation. The colonel was in the grip of that hysteria common to many of his race in action of any sort.

"Geneva Convention . . ." I heard from Boldeschi.

"But they're wearing our uniforms, the swine, the filth . . ."

"Where . . . get them?"

"Seducers, whoremongers, robbers," now shouted the colonel. "You have been seducing my soldiery with your sordid gold. *Al muro, al muro, al muro.* Death is too good for you, you beasts, you vileness that transcends the uttermost vileness of nature. . . . I who have been so noble, so kind, so Christian, so hundred per cent generous with you filthy bastards. . . . And this is my reward. *Al muro, al muro, al muro. . . .*"

I noticed with relief that wear and tear were weakening his voice.

Boldeschi now came over and looked at all of us.

"Do you know them?" shouted the colonel.

"I know this one," he answered, pointing at me. "He is the one who worked in Paris, the one who spoke about Russia at the debate."

"A dangerous fellow?"

"No, Colonel. I am surprised to see him here." Boldeschi was already adopting the rather tired attitude of a gentleman who would have liked to remind the colonel that he was behaving in a most undignified manner.

Boldeschi said to us: "You have put yourselves in a most serious position. You are liable to be shot since you are wearing Italian uniforms. I hope I shall be able to prevent it."

"I hope so too," said Ian, and we could not help laughing.

"Would you not care to have them searched?" Boldeschi now asked the colonel.

"Yes. Searched, searched, searched. Make haste there, hurry up . . ."

They pushed us into the punishment cell. It was the same place that I had occupied with Cram; but this commandant had ordered the two windows to be bricked up, and the partitioning wall to be knocked down, so that now there was just one bare stone room, twenty feet by ten. The only furniture was a heavy wooden table.

Johnny had carried our only map. As we were hustled inside I had an opportunity to whisper: "Map?" He winked and made a sign showing that he had swallowed it.

A great indignity followed. They stripped us to the skin, and we stood naked in front of them while the senior *carabiniere* sergeant-major had a look to see that there was nothing hidden in our hair or in other parts of our bodies. At least forty Italian other ranks had crowded in to enjoy all this. Apart from Boldeschi, the officers present did not seem to think there was anything improper in their making a peep-show of us. Boldeschi had some sharp words with the colonel, who appeared to tell him to leave the room. That was the last we saw of him that night.

Now the other interpreter came in, a slinking, thin-faced Cassius who had once been a coal-merchant in Cardiff. He claimed also to have a British wife, who had been interned by the Italians when they entered the war to fall like homicidal dustmen on the helpless remains of their great neighbour, France.

Most inappropriately, this interpreter was named Garibaldi. He was a swine. Hurrying in, licking his lips, he shuffled up to the four of us. 'I was the one he singled out.

"You, Millar," he hissed, rather over-playing the stage villain. "You won't see another day."

"What's that?" I had difficulty in speaking, for the cuts on my lips were beginning to stiffen, and my throat was achingly dry. Blood still splashed down over my nakedness. The Italian privates licked me with their eyes. When the stream of blood reached down my body I heard them begin to giggle. Every time I looked at the little man who had hit me I felt my organs dissolve in a boiling, syrupy rage. I tried and tried to catch his eye so that I could bore into it with mine. But Garibaldi was speaking, tugging at my arm.

"Pay attention, Millar. You will not see the light of day. You are going to be shot."

"What for? Doing our duty?"

"You will be shot." He repeated this to the other three. The words obviously pleased him. Perhaps he remembered, as he spoke, some old insult put upon him in far-away Cardiff.

"What are you telling them, Garibaldi?" the colonel interrupted.

"Telling them they will be shot."

"That's right, there's a good fellow. Sometimes I think that Boldeschi's mad. . . ." Then another thought took possession of his poor scattered brain. "Take one of them and make him show you how they got through into our part of the building," he told Garibaldi.

Garibaldi (being Garibaldi) chose the smallest, Johnny. He was also choosing the toughest. Johnny put on a pair of trousers and went off with a wide sneer on his face and an escort of four *carabinieri*, ten *soldati*, and Garibaldi.

The *carabinieri* had now emptied all our pockets—and trouser legs. They had put the contents on the table. It was a very large table, about the size you would find in the kitchen of a big old English country house. But our food was piled high. The Italian officers wandered round, looking at it, staggered by the quantity. Occasionally they could not resist putting a teeny-weeny bit of British chocolate between their lips. The commandant now noticed our audience of *soldati* and ordered them away violently.

"Take all this chocolate and stuff, everything on the table, to the mess," he told the *carabinieri*.

Now the youngest Italian officer, "The Boy", came in. His eyes softened when he saw us standing shivering there. (Boldeschi had privately told some of us that "The Boy" was the only other "gentleman" among the Italian staff.) Now he pointed to my bloodstains and the lesser marks on Ian.

"Has the doctor not been sent for?" he asked indignantly. There was no reply, so he left the room, and a little later he returned with a medical orderly, who sponged my face and chest with cotton-wool soaked in stinging alcohol.

Johnny came back while the orderly was attending to Ian. He was bursting with rage.

"Did you show them?" Ian asked him.

"I did. And that dirty rat Garibaldi pushed me over on my face as we were going down the wooden staircase. He kicked me. Where was he dragged up? His English language is . . . ing terrible."

They brought in battle-dress trousers and khaki shirts. When we had clothed ourselves they took the others away, leaving me alone in the cell. I lay down on the bare table since that was the warmest place. The table smelled faintly of chocolate.

For a long, long time they left me alone.

121

I knew, from my previous sojourn in that cell, that the only lavatory was down the corridor, in another part of the building. To get to it I must be released (temporarily) from the cell. When I had battered on the door and shouted for thirty minutes, I gave up hope and used the corner of the cell. There was not a sound in the great building.

They came for me at two in the morning, three *carabinieri*, and found me sleeping on the bare table. The moment I awoke I began to shiver in violent fits. It was bitterly cold.

The *carabinieri* were half-dead on their feet from sleep; they were quite polite with me. We clattered upstairs to the commandant's office, and the moment I entered the room "The Bat" began his screaming. He was seated behind a large desk, holding in his hand (unfortunately for me) a two-foot-long ruler, square in section, and with brass straight edges. They stood me at one end of the desk, backed so closely by two *carabinieri* that their shoulders touched my arms. Garibaldi, in the quality of interpreter, was at the other end of the desk, but neither he nor "The Bat" could keep in position. As their tempers waxed, they would jab their faces close up to mine, so that I seemed to exist in a whirling kaleidoscope of porcelain teeth, frothing lips, spittle, black ruler, and yellow-and-grey angry eyes. All the other officers of the garrison, with the exception of the friendly Boldeschi, were in the room. But most of them crouched over a fire of big logs in the vast, whitewashed open fireplace. It entered my head that in former days a Lord Abbot had probably done good deeds and succoured the miserable in that room. "The Boy" looked as though he felt sorry for me; the others all shouted at me in chorus when my replies displeased them, and eyed me as though I were carrion. The *sotto-tenente* who had struck me occasionally bounced across the room towards me in his rage, simulated or real. But fortunately for me he kept at a distance. If he had come close to me I should have tried to lay hands on him.

Garibaldi opened the discussion.

"You will be shot at four o'clock." (A glance at his watch.) "In two hours' time. Have you anything to say?"

"I was doing my duty. You have no right to shoot me." Pandemonium followed this, and the colonel whacked me twice with the ruler at the place where my neck and left shoulder meet.

The colonel: "I have behaved like a mother, like a saint, with you disgusting people. With that filthiness of a wooden-faced, red-haired general." (He referred to Brigadier Mountain, the senior British officer.) "Admit it. The odious, red-haired general put you up to this. . . ."

Millar: "Nobody put us up to it."

The colonel: "Lies, the red-haired general has just admitted that he put you up to it. . . ." (Two strokes with the ruler.)

Garibaldi: "You will never see another day."

The colonel: "You speak Italian. Why do you speak Italian? You are a spy. You are the worst of the lot for all your cherub's face."

Garibaldi: "This man was a journalist and a Francophil. He is regarded as highly dangerous. He has three times been suspected of subversive activities and escape attempts. He is an associate of the abominable Cram. He has frequently attempted to seduce Italian soldiery by talking to them of superior living conditions in the capitalistic states. He worked in our pay office in order to spread his propaganda among our officers. He is suspected of being the centre of the appalling black market corruption which brought this camp before the notice of the Fascist Grand Council, the corruption which you, my Colonel, were sent here to stamp out."

The colonel: "Ordure." (Three strokes of the ruler.)

Garibaldi: "I demand this man's life."

Millar: "What are you? Prosecuting counsel, or the interpreter?"

Garibaldi: "Ha! Brave words. But see how he trembles . . ."

All Italian officers: "*Sì, sì.*"

Millar (very angry): "I am shivering with the cold."

The colonel: "Enough of this. Come to the questions, *tenente.*"

Garibaldi: "Where did you get your uniforms?"

Millar: "They are uniforms which were issued to other prisoners in other camps which had no stocks of British clothing. We had collected them over a series of months."

The colonel: "Lies. You bought them from my soldiers. No decent person is safe within miles of an Englishman with money in his pockets. Proceed, Garibaldi."

Garibaldi: "You admit that you put black bands, simulating mourning, over the *Prigionieri di Guerra* signs on the arms of your uniforms?"

Millar: "Yes."

Garibaldi (triumphantly): "Write that down. Accused admits that he mocked at our noble dead."

The colonel: "Where were you going when you left the prison?"

Millar: "To Britain."

The colonel: "How?"

Millar: "On foot and by boat."

The colonel: "Give us the names of your accomplices outside this prison and we may spare your miserable life. I make no promises, mind."

Millar: "We had no accomplices."

The colonel: "Deceitful viper. You shall die at dawn."

After over an hour of this, with the ruler beating on my neck, shoulders, arms, hands and face, they gradually wore themselves out. It was all that I could do to stand upright at the desk, for my shivering was so intense, and my efforts to control and conceal it so exhausting, that I feared I would faint.

Then an extraordinary thing happened. That happy crack which I had previously noticed in the more sinister side of the Italian character suddenly broke the colonel's hatred. We were talking about food when he pitched the ruler to the other end of the room and burst into paroxysms of uncontrollable laughter. He laughed like an opera star, flinging back his pink-and-white, hairless face on its broad neck, and letting it come, peal after peal, from his tight, black-swathed stomach.

"Food," he gasped. "I have never seen so much chocolate. And all carried in the trousers. Oh. Oh! These madmen will be the death of me yet." Then he turned on me again, more seriously.

"Do you realise that you may have cost me my job? It's the uniforms that will worry them in Rome. These accursed uniforms. . . ."

Garibaldi did not like the way things were going.

"Our colonel has too kind a heart," he said to me. "Don't think you are going to get off lightly. You will be shot at dawn."

The colonel interrupted him.

"Admit that you were breaking out in order to have a woman," he said.

"Nothing of the sort," I replied.

"Come, come," he wheedled. "We are all men here, we understand how you must feel. You have been a prisoner for a year now, poor fellow. Come now. Admit it. No? Why, you insolent young dog. Away with him. Fling him into the cell.

No food now, *carabinieri;* no food, no tobacco, no water until he talks. . . ."

Going downstairs I stumbled weakly and the *carabinieri* supported me.

"Poor young officer," one of them said kindly. *"Il colonnello* can be very bad, but now I do not think that he will kill you."

"But he will eat your chocolate," said the other. "Indeed yes, and so will we. The *carabinieri* must have English chocolate. Ah me, there will be much work now, and many roll-calls and searches for many days. A scrap of chocolate will not come amiss."

They pushed me into the cell. But now Wally Binns was there, with two blankets, given him by the *carabinieri.* I was delighted to see him. We compared notes. His interview had been almost identical with mine, ruler treatment and all. He told me that Ian and Johnny were shut up in the men's jail, in the outer court-yard. We laughed a good deal at Garibaldi's dirge-like repetition: "You will be shot at dawn." And we passed the remainder of the night and most of the following day huddled together on the floor asleep or walking briskly up and down the cell, trying to get warm.

Late in the morning the *carabinieri* guarding the door gave us some of our own clothing (which had been sent through by the British) and our toilet things. They permitted us to go singly along the corridor to wash and shave. Binns walked the whole distance (about fifty yards) on his hands with his stocky legs waving in the air.

"What a monster of a man," one of the *carabinieri* said to me. "He is the strongest man in Italy."

"He is the strongest man in the world," I answered. "But his heart is soft and pure—when he receives friendly and just treatment." The Italian considered this.

"Does he like to smoke?" he asked.

"Yes," I lied (Wally was a non-smoker). "And he also likes to eat and drink." He slipped me a packet of Italian cigarettes. Five minutes later he hurriedly unlocked the door.

"For God's sake," he whispered, "hide the cigarettes. *Il colonnello!"*

Unknown to the Italians there was a hiding-place, made at the back of a recess by the tunnellers of Room 6 when they were shut up in that cell. I hastily thrust the cigarettes in there, and Wally and I endeavoured to fan the smoke out of the ventilation-hole with our blankets.

"Ahhh," said the colonel, standing cloaked and sinister in the doorway. "Tobacco! They have been smoking." He screamed and trumpeted: "Garibaldi, Garibaldi, Garibal. . . . Oh, there you are, man. Explain where these prisoners get tobacco."

"Perhaps from the *carabinieri*," suggested Garibaldi stupidly.

The colonel stopped his raging and looked very coldly at the coal merchant from Cardiff.

"Be extremely careful what you say about the Royal *Carabinieri*," he said icily. "I advise you to retract that statement." Garibaldi was an ordinary infantry soldier, and therefore an inferior. "Upon my soul," the colonel now continued quite affably to us. "You English are quite extraordinary. You can make yourselves comfortable, eh? Even here, in my well-regulated prison you have your own little Mafia, your secret service, eh? Just one word of advice, young gentlemen. DON'T SMOKE." The last two words came out in his loudest scream, and he whisked his black cloak out of the door.

Garibaldi paused, like a stage villain, to glower at us from the doorway.

"Swine," he said in English, and spat twice into the cell. Binns sat dourly on his bed, flexing his arm muscles.

We heard later that day that the colonel had been congratulated by Rome for frustrating a "well-planned and desperate attempt at evasion". The Italian theory was that we were helped by Italians working for the British Intelligence Service, both outside the camp and among the soldier guards. Many of the latter were moved to the Russian front. The young corporal who had been instrumental in catching us was given a bonus of 2,500 lire, fifteen days' leave, promotion to sergeant, and an assurance that he would never be needed on the Russian front.

From this moment, except for Garibaldi, who remained sour and spiteful, all the Italians oozed charm, and made us as comfortable as they could within the letter of the law. This unforeseen kindliness was quite a normal thing in their character, following swiftly as it did on bouts of cruelty and brutality. I could give hundreds of instances of the swift change-over which enlivened the lives of their prisoners. Even the second-lieutenant who had hit me came quite frequently to our cell and singled me out for friendly advances. These, however, were unreciprocated.

Ian and Johnny were put in beside us. We had four beds and as many blankets as we needed. We received Red Cross parcels and were fed by the British mess, who naturally sent us more than normal rations. We were allowed out for one hour each day in a small enclosed court-yard with a heavily armed guard. After the first few days we were even allowed tobacco and books.

I remember my thirty days in the cell—days spent entirely in artificial light, since there were no windows—as one of my happiest periods in prison. Johnny and Ian played cards. Wally and I worked at languages and read books.

Binns, remarkably gentle for such a strong man, only used his strength once when he tore one of the bars out of our bricked-up window. The bar was about two inches in diameter and four feet long. He put his feet against the wall and pulled until the metal bent sufficiently for both ends to drag clear of the concrete in which they had been embedded. He wanted this for a crowbar because, during the exercise periods, we had been able to study another part of the monastery, and the four of us had worked out plans for an escape route which we intended to explore whenever we were at large in the camp again.

On the thirtieth day the colonel sent for us, and dismissed us with honeyed speech.

"No hard feelings on either side, eh?" he said graciously. "We were a little mad when we caught you fellows, and maybe we were a tiny bit rough . . ."

Garibaldi, translating this for the others, who did not understand Italian, said: "The colonel says you are swine and are lucky to be alive. Next time you try any tricks you will be shot out of hand."

"I have told Rome," continued the colonel, "that you have behaved decently during your incarceration, and that I do not consider it necessary for you to be sent away from this place to the punishment camp, *Campo* 5."

So, carrying our blankets, and loaded with belongings stuffed into cardboard boxes, we trailed through into the great court-yard. How vast it seemed, and how many prisoners there were, and how coldly (apart from the brigadiers and our own personal friends) they greeted us. We were sorry to be out of the cell.

Next morning Garibaldi approached me furtively outside the orderly-room. We were alone under the great cloisters, and he looked half afraid of me. However, he managed to inject plenty of venom into his voice.

"Be down at the gate here in one hour with all your rubbish," he said.

"What exactly do you mean?"

"I mean that they are sending you four swine where you

belong, to *Campo* 5, a civilian jail for criminals. You are to be ready for searching in one hour."

This was bad news. But I had to hide my chagrin.

"How nice," I said. "And by the way, Garibaldi. We were just saying that we hoped you intended to return to Cardiff after the war. We thought of organising a little Welcome Committee. At any rate, Binns says he will drop in and see you."

"I will be in Cardiff after the war. But you will not be there," he answered angrily. As I walked away across the grass he mumbled insults after me. I wondered what made him dislike me so much, for, although he had been unpleasant to the very limit of his powers to all four of us, it was plain that his major hatred was reserved for me. There is something a little numbing and worrying about such a hatred. While I despised Garibaldi, I scarcely even disliked him.

Binns, whose reactions were more straightforward than my own, thought all Italians were "dirty people", and he could hate Garibaldi with fresh gustiness. If he had had the opportunity he would have strangled both Garibaldi and the colonel, I think. But something seems to be missing from my character. My hatred is a watery thing.

We had exactly one hour in which to say good-bye to everybody in *Campo* 35. I was very sorry to leave it. Nearly one year had passed there, and we left on a wonderful day, the kind of spring day that accidentally gets mixed in with the bitter Italian winter. When it was heard that we were going to the dreaded *Campo* 5 people felt sympathy for us; and some who had been snubbing us because our attempt at escape had cost them "stufas" and other conveniences now came forward with gifts and spontaneous last-minute offers of friendship. Life was so dependent on the characters and talents of the other prisoners that with every departure from the camp those who remained felt that something had been taken out of life.

A crowd of perhaps two hundred officers and batmen gathered to watch us pass for the last time through the doorway marked: "He who enters these portals renounces the world." Both my men, Skinner and Jones, were there to say good-bye, and my heart struck a few doubtful beats as I looked for the last time in Italy at their intelligent and lively faces, the only remaining links between me and the carrier in the Western Desert, and the last days of freedom.

We were searched by Garibaldi and Boldeschi. They performed the inestimable service of abstracting from my belongings every scrap of paper, including a good deal of manuscript for short stories, and the bones of a book about an English village written after and during severe drenchings of Proust.

Our escort consisted of an Italian lieutenant and four *carabinieri*. The lieutenant was a soldierly man, with a rough face pock-marked by disease and scarred by battle. He was a *Genovese,* however; and because of the Italian sailors and especially deep-sea divers whom I had met, I had always considered the men of Genoa to be the finest breed in Italy. He was pleased to be going with us to Gavi, because he would be able to steal two nights with his family on the return journey.

Before we started off he showed me, with charming ingenuousness, his medals for the campaigns of Abyssinia, Spain, France, North Africa, Greece, and Russia.

"You see, I am a professional soldier, it is my life," he said. "I believe in treating prisoners well. I ask for no promises from you. If you try to escape we will shoot you. Otherwise we are friends." And we were.

At Salerno, where we changed trains, he took us into the station restaurant and we drank considerable quantities of strong red wine. We travelled uncomfortably through the night, the four of us squeezed into the middle of a first-class compartment with the officer and the *carabinieri* occupying all the corners and another *carabiniere* in the corridor. Next day in the train we exchanged food, our tinned bacon and jam against their fresh meat, omelette, and farm butter, and they bought us fruit and wine.

It was a happy journey as far as Genoa. Then, at the sight of the bomb damage our escort grew suddenly morose. The officer gripped Ian Campbell by the arm and said: "I cannot blame you personally, young man. But see what your comrades and your countrymen have done. The birthplace of Columbus is in ruins. Ah, I love my city, I love my city." And he burst into tears which persisted as the train slowly puffed along between the sea and the town. Johnny and Ian pointed at each bomb crater with some professional pleasure, and I became angry with them, for my sympathies were with the *Genovese*. Strangely enough, in the main station of Genoa, when we were recognised as British prisoners we were surrounded at once by a large and demonstratively friendly crowd in which there were many women.

Binns tugged at my arm to demand what one ripe young woman was saying of him.

"She says you have beautiful teeth."

"Does she now," he said. "She's a fine-looking lass herself. Ask her if she'd like some bacon."

Several of the crowd wanted to give us presents, but the *carabinieri* forbade this.

"Not that we disapprove," they said. "But there might be Fascists looking on." The *carabinieri* at this stage in the war (North Africa was swiftly disintegrating) were most emphatic that they owed allegiance to the King, and not to Mussolini. Like good policemen all over the world, they were only too willing to turn their coats (to keep law and order, of course).

We arrived at Gavi in the evening. It proved to be small and attractive—too big to be a village and too small to be a town. Our luggage was dumped under guard in the large market-place, and we climbed on foot up a zigzagging path that cut into the hill face rising almost perpendicularly from the town to the fortress above.

A huge, compact mass of blank old stone walls, the fortress seen from below, with the masonry running down in smart diagonals with occasional turrets and bastions to fill in the accidents of the stony ground, fitted the hill like a well-made and well-worn hat. It was strange, though, to think that people actually lived up there. The theatrically-pretty Italian flag floated lazily above the topmost ramparts.

From the bright sunshine of the zigzag path we walked into a forbidding black hole in the fortress wall.

"This cannot be the entrance," said the lieutenant.

"Yes, it is," a *carabiniere* assured him. "Walk with care, for the passage descends brusquely." It twisted under the outer walls of the fortress. Dank, dark and evil-smelling, the floor a succession of ill-made stone steps leading down, it seemed incredible that this should be the entrance to a human habitation. All of us burst out laughing, as Englishmen will at any sudden incongruity.

"I am glad that I am not obliged to live in such a dungeon," said the Italian lieutenant.

CHAPTER X

Two Italian officers, polite but efficient, with four *carabinieri*, subjected us to an incredibly severe search in a cell with stone walls, a barrel-vaulted roof, and heavy bars on a window so small that no ordinary man could have forced his way through it. We were obliged to strip naked and all our clothes were minutely examined. After this they sent us through a heavy grille into the camp itself, where we were pounced upon by former Padula prisoners, including Richard Carr, Tony Hay, and the Baron Cram.

After the immediate first shock of Gavi I realised that it was the best prison camp I had seen. It should have been the worst. The Italian supervision was more ruthless than elsewhere. The quarters were appallingly restricted and unhealthy. (At the time of our arrival questions were being asked in the House of Commons about conditions there.) And for all that it was the best camp.

Two hundred officer prisoners and fifty British batmen were held at Gavi when we arrived. They were rigorously watched and guarded by two Italian colonels, who had under their command twelve officers and 240 other ranks, many of them *carabinieri*.

The senior British officer was a squat and powerful New Zealander, Brigadier Clifton, an indomitable rosy-cheeked little soldier who had been captured at Alamein, and who had arrived shortly before us to take over the command from an old friend of mine, another New Zealander, Colonel Fraser, who had earlier been at Padula. Fraser was tall, sunburned and aquilinely handsome. Long before the war I had formed an exceptionally high opinion of New Zealanders as a race, and everything that I saw of them in the desert and in prison strengthened this impression. Unassuming, intelligent, energetic, and blessed with remarkable physique, it seems to me that they achieve a sturdier form of manhood than any other people on earth to-day.

Since Gavi was a punishment camp, and almost every officer was there because he had attempted to escape, or because he had been a *folboatist* (landed in enemy territory from a submarine) or a parachutist, or had been taken in exceptional circumstances, there were many New Zealanders in the camp. They gave their own flavour of simple decency, bravery and honour to the whole place.

If all citizens of the British Empire were like the New Zealanders, one could have no doubts about the greatness of its destiny. I say nothing against the Australians, who seem to be equally virile and manly, and are often incisively intelligent.

131

But to me the most attractive thing about New Zealand manhood is its simplicity and its modesty. The Australian is usually an aggressive man. There were fine Australians in the fortress, too, and many admirable South Africans; there were English and Scottish officers from all types of environment, arm, and regiment; there were even some Greeks and Jugoslavs. The hardness of life at Gavi bound all these men into a bond of fellowship so deep that it is difficult to write of it. I am proud to have been a prisoner there.

Whereas at Padula I was able to sin against the community by running a black market, I would have died of starvation rather than do such a thing at Gavi. There was no corruption there. The junior officer was protected by his seniors. There was an easy equality and a fairness of outlook that dissolved the worst of prison bonds. Although prison conditions were much more severe than at Padula, I noticed at once that the Gavi officers were better dressed, cleaner, and more upstanding. They had more *amour-propre*. They were a community.

Since the officers were good, the batmen also were on a higher plane. They were better looked after by the officers. They were disciplined, firmly and fairly controlled by a regular soldier of the best type in the world, Major "Tag" Pritchard, of the Royal Welch Fusiliers.

Tag had led the first British parachute descent on Italy. He was a red-haired, white-skinned, man in the early thirties, who had been an Army boxing champion. He again was soft and correct in his speech and behaviour. Among such men, who behaved properly in front of the enemy and among themselves, you could recapture your pride and self-respect. It is impossible for anyone who has not been a prisoner to realise how important such things are in prison. Like any of the other inmates of Gavi, I would have fought and suffered for my fellow-prisoners. It was like having a regiment again. In ourselves we had something worth living and fighting for.

The lay-out of Gavi camp was so complicated that it took the new inmate some days to become accustomed to his surroundings. But when you simplified it to its essentials the prisoners' quarters consisted of two small enclosed and insanitary courtyards. One court-yard was at the top of the fortress and the other in the lowest part. They were joined by "the ramp", a narrow roadway cut out of the living rock, and so steep that it took a healthy and strong man to walk up it at a normal pace. Officers were quartered in large cells in both court-yards, and the cook-house, the batmen's quarters, the infirmary, the parcel store and the mess were all in the lower group.

Richard Carr took me into his room, Number 14 in the upper court-yard. There were seven of us in Room 14, and there was only just room for our beds (which were less comfortable than those at Padula, being of a small, collapsible, canvas-topped variety), two small tables, seven chairs, and seven small wooden cupboards. The room had a low, barrel-vault, and two minute windows. There was one advantage in the thick walls and stone roof; it was comparatively cool in summer, and when I arrived there the back of the Italian winter was already broken.

My cell-mates were: the stout and interesting Richard Carr, with his heavy, bear's head, a cross between a biscuit manufacturer and a poet; Tom Murdoch, of the Warwickshire Yeomanry, saturnine, quick-witted, yet ultra-English; two New Zealanders, Colin Armstrong and Alan Yeoman; and two South Africans, Ronnie Herbert and Robby Mason.

Herbert was an Englishman who had settled and married in South Africa not long before the war. He was a skinny, dancing, kindly, impish person, with a continual stream of banter and cross-talk delivered with a Liverpool accent. Mason, a complete contrast, was a lawyer, solemn and deep and intensely South African in all his opinions and reactions.

Alan and Colin, the New Zealanders, were farmer and lawyer respectively. They were in Gavi because they had been recaptured after one of the most sensational escapes made in Italy. They made it from the first-storey window of a long prison building which paralleled the barbed-wire perimeter. The prisoners in that camp had access to the two storeys above this window. Alan and Colin constructed a kind of trapeze which hung from a boom built up from reinforced cupboard doors. At a given signal one party on the second floor thrust out this boom, a party on the floor above held on to a stay, while on the floor below Alan and Colin, both clinging to their homemade trapeze, launched themselves together into space. Alan cleared the wire beneath. Colin hung on a shade too long, and lost a little of his initial velocity. He fell into the wire, but tore himself free, and the pair made good their escape. They were at liberty for a month in Italy, the longest outing that anyone then at Gavi had enjoyed.

Gavi, in contrast to Padula, was a non-cooking camp. The mess took most of the food from the Red Cross parcels, and cooked it communally. This system worked admirably.

Although the Italians were less rich in local food supplies than at Padula, and less accommodating to our mess, I found the food quite ample; and indeed I continued to save on the considerable accumulation of hoarded tins which had followed me safely from Padula.

Here, too, I continued, and in fact intensified, my keep-fit campaign. In Gavi there was hardly any of the mental opposition to such a campaign that had been noticeable at Padula.

Every morning at six I went out into the narrow upper court-yard. I kept an old blanket to put under my feet on the rickety paving, and I passed a tiring half-hour swaying, jumping, and lying on this blanket. Two Italian sentry posts contemptuously watched all this, and there were usually a few other officers doing the same type of exercises. Then I washed in cold water in the primitive wash-house with several taps trickling into one long trough-shaped basin.

Morning roll-call was at eight, and most of the prisoners paraded in the court-yard, still half-asleep in pyjamas or perhaps naked but for a towel around the middle, ready to queue up for a wash. It was strange to look round at all these faces gummed with sleep and notice how men change when they are awake and have brushed their hair. Roll-call at Gavi was utterly efficient, for the officer taking it and the *carabinieri* with him knew every prisoner by sight, and none of us was allowed to fall out until his name had been called.

After roll-call the Italians unlocked the heavy iron grilles separating the lower from the upper compound, and batmen were able to come up to us carrying hot water for shaving and brushes and polish to clean our boots. Shaving was interesting in one way. Hot water was scarce, and each of us shaved out of a small tin which he kept for that purpose. This was the last remnant of the functional importance of tins which had been so evident when we were new prisoners. Now all of us were fairly old hands, and in the course of our stay in Italy we had each been able to buy a cup, one or two china plates, and a knife, a fork, and a spoon.

I associate Gavi camp with chairs and cardboard boxes. Chairs, because there was no grass in the place. It was all rock, paving, or cobbles, and to make our existence more comfortable the Italians allowed each of us to buy a chair. These were locally made of pale-yellow wicker, and were both attractive and practical. A prisoner, being poor, was very jealous of his belongings, and you often saw officers walking about the camp

134

firmly carrying their chairs. When someone was invited to tea he arrived with his chair. Cardboard boxes were a feature of Gavi, because each officer, from the brigadier down, carried a Red Cross box to meals in the mess. Inside the box would be the officer's personal tins to supplement the mess rations.

So, for breakfast I would put into my box sugar and condensed milk (for the tea or coffee provided by the mess), one or two slices of bread (saved from my 100-gram issue of the previous day), a tin of margarine or butter and a tin of jam and, perhaps most important of all, a book to read. Normally, the breakfast supplied by the mess only consisted of stewed prunes, or perhaps a loathsome, but filling, dish invented by a messing officer there and called "*pasta* porridge". This was made by grinding down macaroni or other *pasta* to a powder, and then boiling it to a porridge-like consistency. Gavi was the only one of my camps where the mess took the trouble to provide breakfast, and it made an enormous difference to the whole day. We sat in the mess at small tables, six to a table. They were heavy deal tables, and they were kept scrubbed white and clean. The mess itself was a long corridor-like place which had once held a large number of small cells for unimportant jail-birds. It was well lit by heavily-barred, square windows on both sides. One set of windows looked into the lower court-yard, the other commanded a magnificent view out over the precipice. We could almost have thrown decanters from the tables into the market-place of Gavi, hundreds of feet below.

Food and routine were prison life. For instance, if I did not go down to breakfast for one reason or another, I "bequeathed" my portion to a friend. The friend would then ask for "Mr. Millar's porridge as well as my own". Then there was no waste. Most people were still hungry. Fortunately for me, I had long been interested in the most important side of eating, fasting, and in the effects of control of appetite on the whole system. It is difficult to fast with a calm mind unless you know that you can get food when you need it. At Gavi the mess was so well run, and our life appeared to be so guaranteed, that I was able to fast for a few days every now and then with great benefit to my body and to my mind. But the ordinary (sane?) prisoner was concerned mainly with stuffing the maximum amount of food into his body.

I have never seen more beautiful mornings than those at Gavi in that spring and summer. After breakfast I would light my pipe and stop on the small level platform at the top of the ramp where it turned at right-angles into a portcullis to enter the tunnel leading to our upper court-yard. There would always be a few prisoners there gazing with dreamy abstraction on the noble scene below, and pretending, as the British will, to be thinking of more prosaic things. A fine river meandered down past Gavi, lapping the walls of the old town. It ran through a greatly accidented valley with rich fields and thin cattle near the river and vine-yards rising to cover the small flanking hills. Standing well out from the huddle of Gavi itself was the octagonal belfry and clock tower of a dignified church. It was good, in all the misty green-and-gold beauty of the valley, to see the people of Gavi going about their daily tasks, to see the convent children playing on the football field, workmen mending a broken water-main, an ice-cream barrow, a woman in a white dress walking out of the lime-trees and crossing the square to do her shopping. I became very fond of Gavi, although I never knew or spoke to a soul there. We heard, though, that some of the women of the town had signed a petition to be allowed to knit "comforts" for the British up there in the fort. The Italian commandant, *il Colonnello* Giuseppe Moscatelli (whom we called Joe Grape), refused.

After breakfast there was a morning queue for the lavatories, and then I sat in the sun till elevenses, for which at this camp the mess supplied boiling water. Then more sitting in the sun, working or reading until 12.55, when everyone assembled in the lower court-yard to hear the Italian news, howled through a loud-speaker fixed over the grille leading to the Italian quarters. Through the spring and early summer the war appeared to us to drag interminably on. The Allies were plainly working their solid way across the Mediterranean. Their orderly progress across the stepping-stones from North Africa was petrifying for the Italians, but too slow for us. Our main "strategical" theme for discussion from the time of 'Alamein to the Italian Armistice in September, 1943, was: "Will the Germans seize British prisoners and take them to Germany?"

The day's second roll-call was at 6 p.m. After that we moved down to the bar in the lower court-yard. Each officer was allowed to buy two glasses of wine when the bar opened, which it did four or five times a week. The wine was young and sour, with a fairly high alcohol content. It cost seven lire a glass. (The Italian rate of exchange was seventy-two lire to the pound. and the 2nd lieutenant's pay was 750 lire a month.) Many officers disliked the *vino* or found it too expensive. They then gave their *vino* tickets to their friends, or bartered them against Red Cross food. So in this camp you saw clearly the different classes of drinker. There was the toper who, regardless of the state of his finances, was always drinking and quite frequently drunk. His emblem was usually a Chianti flash which, in varying degrees of emptiness, he would lug about with him from 6.30 when the bar opened until lights out. There was the heavy drinker, who drank to excess only on occasions, and who drank from habit, or from sociability. In this group the navy were well represented. There was the light or medium drinker who drank only to pass the time, and occasionally to celebrate or to forget. There was the man who scarcely drank because it was too expensive. And there was the pussyfoot who said "poison".

Occasionally individuals gave very splendid "cocktail parties", complete with bar and barman at one end of the mess. I remember one in particular, given by the Lucullan Tony Hay. Sweet red wine ran in fountains all evening and there were many delicious things to eat. (The red wine was made sweet—and sickly—by adding Red Cross jam.)

Another activity, the casino, helped to pass the last hour before dinner. The casino was run by a syndicate of shrewd officers in one of the larger cells in the lower court-yard. It catered for the gambling instincts of the prisoners, and frequently more than satisfied them. Brigadier Clifton at the time that we arrived was beginning to check the gambling, for there was seldom a time when one officer or another was not known to be in serious financial difficulties. Individual debts (or winnings) in the casino often totalled several hundred pounds a month, and the settlements were monthly. Losers were obliged to pay either in camp money or with cheques on their home banks. Since I have no gambling instincts, I kept away from the casino, although I occasionally wandered in with a drink in my hand to watch them playing faro, baccarat, or two more childish games called "Winnie" and "Cars".

During dinner Tommy MacPherson of the Cameron Highlanders read a highly-coloured version of the Italian news in the papers and on the radio. This news was given with a heavy British twist, and heartily pleased all the blimps who lacked the energy or the intelligence to learn to read Italian. And at 8.30 the grille shutting off the news from the ramp was unlocked with an enormous key, an Italian bugle sounded, and all the upper compound officers gathered their cardboard boxes and trooped up the ramp to their rooms.

At this time, in the beautiful Italian evening with searchlights playing on the battlements and on us from different sentry posts, I could imagine that I was cut off not only from home but from Italy and all the world. Once or twice in the moonlight we saw the chilled, gleaming snow of the French Alps, far away to the north-west.

Frequently the night would be hideous with the prisoners' shouts and rowdy songs. After celebrations of Anzac day, Alamein or other comparable festivities, there would be brushes with the Italians, and two or three heated officers would go into the "coolers", little stone cells immediately below Room 14. Steam had to be let off somehow in such a virile camp.

While the others settled down to play bridge or poker I normally read for an hour or so and then went to bed. I slept well at Gavi. It was a non-intellectual life there of discipline and exercise. I was hardening my body every day for the ordeal that surely lay ahead, for I had few illusions that the Germans would easily let us go when Italy gave up the struggle. There were too many strange and important officers in the camp, "*pericolosi*" as the Italians called them—officers such as young Colonel David Stirling of the Scots Guards, the most dashing raider perhaps of all our remarkable officers in the war in the desert.

Also the fact that we were so far north excited me strongly after all those months down near the instep of Italy. Binns and Johnstone felt the same. After all, we were only a few hours in a fast train from Chiasso, a part of the Swiss frontier which was not too hard to cross. At Gavi we could talk to scores of officers who had actually been at large, who had travelled on the Italian railways, who could tell us how to buy a ticket at Milan station without arousing suspicion, who could draw plans of Como, showing where to go past the 'bus terminus to find the road for Chiasso and the frontier.

Not long after our arrival came the first break by officers from Gavi. It was a lower compound escape, so that even if I had been an old Gavi hand I should have had no part in it. It was one of the most remarkable achievements in all the history of escape from prison.

The central figure was a South African Hercules called Buck Palm. Buck was a loose, slouching man, with a lined, rugged, heavy-jawed face and a mane of black hair as long as Samson's. He had been an all-in wrestler, a prospector, and many other things besides. He rolled with long, slanting, hen-toed strides about the prison, talking sensibly and well to his countrymen in Afrikaans and to us in English with a strong Afrikaans accent. He was the teacher at a class which met every day after tea to go through a tremendous series of muscle-building contortions and exercises.

From a cell in the lower court-yard Buck first tunnelled a hole in the wall which led to the cellars and the large reservoir hidden below the court-yard. This hole in itself was a major triumph. Italian supervision was so unremitting and so thorough that it seemed incredible that any hole, no matter how well concealed, could escape their daily, sometimes twice daily searches.

Down below, day after day, and in the icy winter, Buck swam across the reservoir and tunnelled through sixteen feet of solid rock. A man less strong would never have got through. A man who had not mining in his blood and the sting of the fall of Tobruk to avenge would never have got through. To me it is one of the fine pictures of the war; the grim, wintry fortress up above, with lesser mortals shivering in their beds, and down in the bowels Buck, a great, muscled devil, dripping with icy water, *burning* and boring his way through solid rock. Burning in fact, for in order to split the rock he smuggled down quantities of wood and built large fires against the face. Then, when the stone was hot, he flung bucketfuls of cold water against it to crack it. Then he smashed into it with his great crowbar. What a man! What a noble monster of a man!

It was right and just that such efforts should be successful. One night Buck and some of his South African friends went through the hole, swam the reservoir, and crawled through the last tunnel on to the roofs of the Italian troops' triangular compound jutting immediately below our mess windows. They dropped into the compound and let themselves over the edge of it on a rope.

The small South African party got away. They were followed by Jack Pringle and (Baron) Cram. Pringle got down all right. The rope broke with Cram, and he injured his leg in the fall. However, he hobbled off into the darkness.

But at Gavi the sentries were always watchful. The others following on, including the tall David Stirling, found the way barred, and several of them were caught by the Italians when they were actually through the tunnel. This escape, brilliant though it was, taught me another lesson—that spectacular mass escapes are the worst kind, for they draw immediate

139

counter-measures from the enemy. Following this break from Gavi (supposed, the Italians frequently said, to be the most secure jail in the world), two divisions of troops were immediately turned out to scour the country. Cram and the South Africans, including Buck, were still on foot and were quickly rounded up. Jack Pringle, a personable and quick-witted young man who spoke good Italian with an American accent, made a speedy get-away on the train to Milan, and thence to the banks of Lake Maggiore. He found the lake a tough proposition. Escape by water was difficult, since there were no private boats available and the Italian patrol boats were sinister things with silent electric motors and powerful searchlights which snapped suddenly on and off. All the frontier guards were on the look-out, and poor Jack, an escaping genius if ever there was one, was caught within sight of Switzerland.

The next attempt was made by our bold Brigadier Clifton. One night, when I was already in bed and the Room 14 poker game was at its noisy height, there was a sudden burst of firing from three or four different points on the battlements. This was followed by Italian screams at the brigadier, who was perched on top of the roof on the other side of our court-yard.

He had climbed out of his window (disregarding a 100-foot sheer drop), swinging on the shutter until he could scramble on to the steep old roof above. The brigadier had home-made rope wound round him, and he planned to go right along that roof and then somehow descend a couple of large precipices well sprinkled with sentry posts. The noise of his passage on the roof alarmed the sentries, and he found himself up in the sky, dazzled by searchlights, and with bullets whistling past him and chipping the slates. His comment as they led him off to the punishment cell was: "I knew I was all right so long as they were aiming at me. But I was afraid they might be aiming to miss."

Clifton, a bald, lobsterish little man with freckles all over his muscle-rounded back and a devilish twinkle in his forget-me-not-blue eyes, always preferred dash to caution.

Soon after this Johnny, Wally and I got to work on our own escape route. August was beginning, and the heat on the rock was stifling. The summer was slipping away. Six of us formed a team with an ambitious plan to cut through from some cellars under our court-yard to underground passages which we knew existed. We believed that these passages led out of the rock on the far side from Gavi—a side which none of us had ever seen, even on our monthly escorted walks outside the fortress.

Binns, Johnson and I made up one team for the tunnelling. The other team consisted of the two New Zealanders, Jim Craig and John Redpath, and George Duncan, a long-necked Scottish Commando officer, who had been a farmer near Dumfries.

We worked steadily on alternate days. On working days the three of us would slip as soon as possible after morning roll-call into the quartermaster's stores, one of the ground-floor rooms in our court-yard. Once inside we locked the door. Often it was difficult to get in, for there was always at least one *carabiniere* wandering about the court-yard on guard. We had a team of people trained to distract the Italians' attention, talking to them until they turned away from the door so that we could walk in unobserved. There were also two high sentry posts looking down into our court-yard which had to be watched, for the sentries could see the doorway. But the sheer obviousness of the entrance was a good thing. The Italians could never have believed that we were using that room without their knowledge.

Once inside we took our apparatus out of the hole—a square hole cut by Jim and John in the wall between the room and the court-yard. The hole led into a ventilation shaft some fifteen feet deep. We hung a rope made from plaited sheets down the shaft, and it was fairly easy for a supple man to get down and up it. The remainder of the apparatus consisted of a series of iron tools forged in the cook-house fires from old bedsteads, and lamps made from margarine tins, with pyjama-flannel wicks rising out of boiled olive-oil given to us by the mess.

Two of us went down the hole at a time to work a four-hour shift on the face while the third stayed at the top to communicate with the outside world. A line of officers sat reading and sunbathing with their chairs tilted against that wall. The officer sitting against the door was always one of our other team. He passed warnings if the Italians arrived to make a search or if the *carabinieri* in the court-yard wandered so near that they might hear our hammering.

As the tempo of our work increased we were able to ask the British authorities to organise hand-ball, improvised squash-rackets, and other games in the court-yard so that their noise would help to drown our efforts down below.

The air was foul down there. There was a long series of nine large cells, all with low barrel vaults, and communicating with each other by arched openings in the thick dividing walls. The previous entrance to the cells led from number six, counting from the end one in which we worked, and it had been solidly walled-up by the Italians before the first British prisoners of war arrived at Gavi. Austrian prisoners had been incarcerated there in the first World War, and there was still pathetic evidence of their living death—evidence in the shape of old india-rubber children's balls, dates, names and inscriptions in German cut on the massive stonework, and odd rusty mugs and chamber-pots. But all the ventilation holes had been walled in, and most of the shafts had been filled with rubble, which overflowed into the dark cells. It was a sinister place, full of evil memories.

The work was a question of chipping away with chisels and a muffled hammer at the cement, levering with flimsy crow-bars, and gradually, painfully, stone after massive stone, work-ing a small shaft into the end wall. Our eyes became sore, partly from the chips, partly from the lamps; and the foul air pinched at our chests. The hole grew very slowly, every inch representing cramp and sweat and blisters.

We came out of the tunnel at tea-time, carefully cleaned our-selves in the quartermaster's stores, hid the hole in the wall with a packing-case full of spare battle-dress, and slipped out into the dazzling sunshine of the court-yard when the sentry on watch outside gave us the all clear. Then we went down to the cook-house where the cooks had saved a meal for us.

On off days we were employed on watch outside the door, in making and sharpening tools for the work, and in perfecting our clothing for the escape.

This time Wally and I were going together and Johnny was teaming up with the brigadier who, since he was too conspicuous a figure, was not working on our tunnel, but was watching it with closest interest. After talking with almost everyone in the camp who had been out, Wally and I had made a good plan, and a simple one. We were going to catch a train direct from the next station to Gavi, change trains at Milan for Como, walk from Como to Chiasso, where we knew the very spot in the frontier wire that we would cross. We believed that ten hours after escaping we should be on Swiss territory. Everything was worked out, the price of the tickets, the lay-out of the stations, the Italian phrases I should have to use, our behaviour on the crowded trains.

By lashing out liberally with my hoarded tins I had bought article after article of clothing, so that now I could leave the camp quite respectably dressed in a blue, double-breasted suit (mainly adapted from naval uniform). Wally was almost as well equipped. We had forged German papers (made by an expert in the camp). I had prepared a greasy dye for my fair hair by powdering brown chalk into brilliantine (a mixture I had already tried with success at Padula).

Soon after all this work began we were alarmed to see many German troops filtering into our valley. The Sicily campaign had ended with Allied success, the Allies had gained a foothold in southern Italy. It seemed only natural that the Germans should be injecting troops into northern Italy. But what troops they looked to us, who were used all of us to the mechanised warfare of the desert! They had old equipment, and their transport was horse-drawn. There were a great many of them, and they were settling down along the valley as though they intended to stay. Gradually we became accustomed to their presence, and, such is the optimism of man, we decided that Germans of that type would take no action against us.

Then one night as we sat at dinner a great singing shout rose from the Italian quarters below us and from the town of Gavi. We looked out, and the dark material was being torn from the windows of Gavi. Window after window came alive, until the whole singing town was sparkling with light.

The Italian Government had declared an armistice. We thought that we were free.

CHAPTER XI

"THERE is some bother with the Germans," a friendly *carabiniere* said to me as I came out into the misty court-yard early the following morning.

"What sort of bother, *amico mio?*"

"Oh," he answered gaily. "We are going to put them in their place. They cannot push us around as they please."

I had never heard an Italian talking about Germans like that before, and it worried me. I moved vaguely down the court-yard, passed, unmolested by the Italian sentries, to the top of the ramp, and stood there in the deliciously fresh morning sunshine pondering the events of the night before.

It had been the most breathless night since our attempted escape from Padula. I had gone to sleep with the greatest difficulty, for I had been obliged by the movement and optimism around me to allow myself to think of Anne as something now reasonably close and attainable, and to add to the prospect of seeing her again dreams of clean linen sheets, hot water to wash with, music from a full orchestra. . . .

Earlier that night two Italian officers, the only two in the garrison who were friendly to the British, had come into our mess to shake hands with us all. They wept with joy. Our brigadier went straight into the Italian section of the camp to demand of "Joe Grape" that we be immediately released. "Joe" refused, stating that it would be too dangerous for us to be released while the camp was surrounded by Germans. "Joe" said that he would hold us in Gavi by force until he received specific contrary orders from the Badoglio Government. From the windows of the mess we could see the German transport unit camped under the trees of the market-place, stolidly settling down, as though this night were exactly like any other.

Brigadier Clifton, energetic little fire-eater, had prepared an elaborate cloak-and-dagger scheme for breaking out of the camp—a scheme in which, with many other officers, I had been trained to play a minor role. I believe that this scheme would have succeeded, though at the cost of some casualties. But for one reason or another it was not put into operation.

So that Armistice night we had climbed the ramp once more after dinner to be locked into our court-yard as usual by the Italians. There was much excitement and a lot of singing. They sang the "Maori Farewell", and the "Zulu Warrior", which began (phonetically):

"I ziga zoomba . . ." (phonetically from memory)

And a rather charming little song, the chorus of which goes:

"Git away, you bumble-bee,
Git off my nose.
I ain't no prairie flower,
Ain't no bleeding rose . . ."

While the singing was at its height I had walked up and down the court-yard with Colonel Fraser. We agreed that we should have felt more comfortable outside prison and foot-slogging it for the Allied Armies in the south. I had a great opinion of his judgment, and felt as he did that since we had been made prisoners by the Germans, and not by the Italians, it would be extraordinary if the Germans allowed us to walk out. Fraser said that he was sure the Germans would seize us; and that whenever they arrived he intended to have himself walled in at the top of the ramp at a place where John Redpath had pierced a small hole into an ancient passage-way leading through the rock. Redpath and Slater, a third New Zealander, were also going in there. The three of them had prepared a large store of food and water. . . .

* * * * *

Still meditating, I drifted down the ramp. Now I was on the level of the mess; I could see the zigzag path descending towards Gavi, and I stopped thinking back.

Fifteen Italians, led by the familiarly ridiculous figure of a popinjay officer, were cautiously descending the path. As I watched I saw the patrol set out round the last corner before the highest houses of Gavi. They vanished for a moment, but later we were able to reconstruct the events that took place in the minute that they were out of sight.

Two Germans in steel helmets were leaning against the wall of the first house, actually the quarters of the *carabinieri*. One of the Italian soldiers playfully levelled his rifle and said: *"Eh, eh."* Mocking at the Germans in a childish way. In reply one of the Germans shot him with his machine-pistol. The Italians picked up the wounded man and, keening like witches, straggled up the hill.

Eastern cries of grief greeted the bloody body of the dying soldier as he was carried into the fortress. The sentries on the ramp levelled their rifles at me, and ordered me back to my quarters.

All the Italians now took up action stations around the ramparts, with officers crawling from position to position. What had happened was that the Germans had despatched a company of front-line infantry to take over our fortress and assure our capture. While it was on its way they ordered the local troops, sixty men of the Veterinary Corps under a farrier-sergeant, to attack and take the fortress.

Soon after the patrol incident the farrier-sergeant fired a mortar smoke-bomb at the mighty walls. Our brigadier, watching from his room high up under the roof, saw the Italian answer. The Italian vice-commandant, a miserable and decrepit old colonel, stumbled down the slope towards Gavi with ten men and a very large white flag.

An hour later the first German troops, roughly-dressed soldiers, with horse-dung caked on their dusty boots, shambled stolidly on to the battlements. They greeted us with immense curiosity and even a kind of awe as they moved clumsily to take over from the Italians. Gavi fortress had not sullied its centuries-old record of instant surrender. Very soon more lively Germans under a thin and efficient young cavalry captain, troops bristling with automatic weapons, arrived to increase our guard.

The spiritual let-down at seeing these hated and efficient uniforms again at such close quarters, at finding ourselves their prisoners when we had hoped that we were free, was very terrible. Their arrival threw the whole camp into a turmoil.

Everybody rushed round the place looking for a way out on his own. That evening for the first time (since the German sentries did not know where we were not supposed to go) we were able to walk out on to the battlements above our court-yard, on the topmost pinnacle of the fortress. Several of us saw at once that it would be possible with a good rope to get down from one corner, where there was an ancient look-out turret unobserved by any German sentry. With Binns, Johnson and five others I ran down to our rooms below, and by tearing out the cord reinforcements from the canvas covers on the beds we managed in a few hours to make 100 feet of strong pleated rope. Filling our pockets with chocolate and emergency rations, we climbed again to the ramparts. But the game was spoiled at the last moment by a bird-like Italian business man, quite a likeable and decent person, who was interpreter at the camp. He ran out of the Italian officers' mess, far below us, and waved his arms in windmill gesticulations at us, screaming to the Germans: "Don't allow them up there. You don't know them. They are all most dangerous. . . ."

We were never allowed up there again.

When he was later asked why he did this, the interpreter was reported to have replied: "For my wife and children."

Brigadier Clifton now issued clear orders. A swarthy British officer from Alexandria, George Sukas, who spoke, among other languages, fluent Italian, had wheedled from a *carabiniere* the exact whereabouts of the secret passage for which our party had so long been tunnelling.

We soon noticed that the Germans, compared to the Italians, were sluggish guards. This was not indeed to be wondered at, for they were still befuddled in the maze of the fortress. We began to cut a new way out, work which would have been quite impossible under former conditions, with daily searches and all the complications of Italian precautions.

An entrance was to be cut from the end room in our corridor into a disused lavatory, and from the lavatory a way was to be broken to the mouth of the secret passage.

The working of this exit was entrusted to three senior officers, Major "Waddy" Wadeson, of the Royal Engineers, a small, virile, yellow-eyed man who had worked all over the world as a mining engineer; Major Brian Upton, of the Essex Yeomanry, always known as "Hack-in-the-Bush", readily distinguishable by his bowed back and enormous red moustache; and Commander John de Jago.

It was agonising to wait, day after day, while the three men laboriously worked their way through the bowels of the camp. The strain on them was heavy. The strain on us, who waited with freedom in Italy or what looked like permanent incarceration in Germany hanging on their efforts, was even worse. There was discontent among younger tunnellers that the work had been given to these men. But the brigadier could not have chosen more wisely. All three were experienced jail-breakers, and "Hack-in-the-Bush" was the camp's genius at making anything from a skeleton key to an explosive charge.

At the end of the first day they had cut their way into the lavatory, and had chiselled in the thick lavatory wall a hole large enough to see into the passage itself.

Already Colonel Fraser, with his two accomplices, had been walled in at the top of the ramp. A friend among the Italian officers had destroyed the records, so that the Germans were unable to hold accurate roll-calls.

The brigadier launched his alternative scheme, to be put into operation if the secret passage exit failed. All officers who wished to hide were ordered to give particulars of their hiding-places and to work with the authorities to provide and stow food and water. It was felt by some that the Germans either would not have the time or would not bother to search for officers missing when the order to move to Germany was given.

That day another company of German infantry arrived in the camp, and we had the doubtful satisfaction of seeing the entire Italian garrison paraded below us by the Germans. The Italians handed over their arms as though they were glad to be rid of them.

"Waddy", Jago, and "Hack-in-the-Bush" broke into the

passage, only to find that two strong steel grilles barred the way. Also the mouth of the passage opened on to the ramparts near a German sentry post, so that they were obliged to work silently, and therefore slowly. By nightfall they had filed through the first grille.

Binns and I, although fully prepared to leave by the passage, decided that it would be reasonable to prepare for its possible failure. So that day we went down our old hole from the quartermaster's store and, at Wally's clever suggestion, built up a framework of wood, stones and blankets into an extremely solid shelter. We covered this over with big stones and rubble until it looked quite indistinguishable from the other rubble-piles, but it contained a space 6 feet by 4 feet in which we could lie side by side. It was a double-bluff hiding-place.

On Monday, September 13th, everything looked good. "Waddy" and party, now working with several strong helpers, had opened both grilles. The passage had degenerated into a sewer which apparently had been blocked by a land-slide. They were tunnelling now through loose earth; and by breakfast-time they had reached the roots of the grass, and calculated that within a few hours the way would be free.

A movement order for escape by this route had been completed by the British orderly-room. We were all to leave that night in batches of twenty, with half-hourly intervals between batches. There was a little hard feeling about the order of departure, which did not go by seniority. But Wally, Johnny and I, thanks to our escaping proclivities, were well up on the list.

I was sitting with Colin Armstrong and Tom Murdoch in Room 14 at ten o'clock that morning when Richard Carr arrived, breathless from running up the ramp, to tell us that the Germans had given everybody in the camp half an hour's notice to be ready to move to Germany.

After half an hour of pandemonium, with everybody charging in every direction, and the people who were going into hiding getting mixed up with the people who were going away intending to make a break for it en route for Germany, Wally and I stood at the bottom of our little shaft, helping down ten other officers. The ten were all strangers to these cells—Wally and I were the only two of our original tunnelling party who had decided to hide there—and they were understandably surprised by the damp, the darkness, and the stale, clammy smell.

Binns had thoughtfully brought down the last of our oil-lamps, and with this we continued to perfect our camouflaged hut. Other people scrabbled out beds or hiding-places in the rubble, and all were busily at work when the senior officer there, pale-eyed Squadron-Leader Bax, ordered us sternly to stop making a noise and to put out the light.

Our hut was in the cell from which the former entrance to the line of cells had led. The other officers, obeying the nervous herd instinct, eventually all gathered in the end cell of the series, at the other end from our entrance shaft and the tunnel face upon which we had worked for nearly two months. We knew that some fifty or sixty officers at least were in hiding now, and I cannot say that either of us had much confidence in the trick. We were only separated from Colonel Fraser's party by some fifty feet of rock. Tony Hay and some others were flimsily and dangerously hidden under the roof over the corridor outside Room 14. Many others, including the brigadier and Tag Pritchard, were hiding in the mouth of the new escape route, hoping that the Germans would not find them in time to prevent them from digging their way out. David Stirling and Buck Palm were well hidden down a lavatory shaft in the lower court-yard. Tom Murdoch and Richard Carr had been cemented in under the stone staircase leading up from the lower court-yard to the infirmary; and were to be fed through india-rubber tubes with hot Ovaltine and Horlick's poured in by the medical order-lies. They had a similar reverse process for ridding their almost airless hiding-place of waste liquids. Many others were hidden in the camp wood-pile. Altogether there were far too many in hiding. The only hope seemed to be that the brigadier's lot would dig themselves free. The Germans might suppose if they found an empty tunnel that all of us were already outside the fortress walls.

After an hour or two below we heard the Germans begin to loot our quarters. There was the crash of furniture being thrown from the windows of our rooms to the cobbles below, then much singing and shouting as the looters got in amongst our tins of butter and jam. After that we heard retching in the court-yard. They had been eating tinned butter by the handful.

Then the Germans came to hunt us out with picks and hand-grenades. Their search was evidently methodical. Bax's party reported that they had heard the brigadier's voice on the ramp. Almost immediately after this the enemy found Colonel Fraser's party, whom we had considered almost unfindable. The answer to this efficiency (although we did not know it at the time) was that "Joe Grape", who knew the fortress as well as his wife, was telling the methodical Germans which walls to break down. They could not get at Fraser and the two New Zealanders with him, but they fired rifles through a hole which they had hacked into the narrow cleft in the rock. The bullets buzzed around in the confined space until the three came out.

It was clearly only a matter of time until a search-party entered our own cells. Binns and I withdrew into our shelter and closed ourselves in with a large stone blocking the 2 foot by 1 foot 6 inches entrance. At 7 p.m., nine hours after going into hiding, we heard the first pick strike on the walled-up doorway. Binns and I lay touching in the darkness. We counted twenty-three savage strokes, then the brickwork collapsed with a rumble into our cell. Five or six Germans came in at the double. They carried some kind of lantern. Its yellow light flickered through the small interstices of our shelter. They all turned left, and searched first through the empty series of cells there. We heard shouts, probably caused by the sight of the mouth of our old tunnel. Then they came clattering back past us. An instant later they challenged our friends in the end cell. They shouted at them to put their hands up and walk out singly. As they went we heard one German ask Squadron-Leader Bax: "Are there any more British here?"

"You can see for yourselves that there are not," he answered curtly in German.

For two hours we lay there, cold, cramped, but in peace. The Germans seemed to have stopped searching the upper part of the fortress. But soon after nine we heard another party clattering up the ramp. We were not yet accustomed to the thunderous noise of German jack-boots in that rocky place. The search-party came straight into our cell. They searched among some of the rubble-piles in the other cells, then they collected the food store of our fellow-officers and proceeded to divide it out.

This was done in our cell, and two of them actually sat on the upper stones of our hiding-place. The "roof" above me was made of the frames of deck-chairs, and I could see these bend slightly under the Germans' weight. We survived two more desultory searches that night, and I blessed Binns with his heaven-sent idea of the double bluff. It looked as though we were going to get away with it, and that was worth any amount of discomfort. I never remember being more cold and cramped. The cellars ran with dampness.

By eight o'clock the following morning all noise of German

presence had died down. Wally and I crawled out to stretch ourselves, breakfasted off chocolate and water, and decided that we would remain hidden until nightfall, when we would try to climb down the battlements. We knew where to find our rope. However, at ten o'clock we heard a large German search-party march up the ramp and halt at the hole into our cells. This time it was a real search. They tore everything to pieces in the other cells; but because our pile of stones was small, and because it was in the half-light of the entrance cell instead of in the darkness farther inside, they did not suspect it. They were urged on with screaming, angry shouts.

When we thought once more that they had missed us a German bayonet crashed right through the stones and our wooden structure, ending up within two inches of Binns's ear.

A torch beam shone through the hole and a German shouted: *"Mensch!"*

They tore down the structure, half crushing us underneath it, and dragged us out. Two of them had to support me, as I had cramp in both legs. The young German captain, highly pleased that we were found, came bouncing in.

"I allow you as a special favour to collect your belongings from your bedroom," he said. "You will find your things in rather a mess. I had to permit my men to enjoy themselves so that they would not get too angry with you. Apologies."

He turned on his men and shrieked at them: "Only two more to find in the whole camp. What the devil are you waiting for?"

Room 14 was a shambles. Before going into hiding I had optimistically packed a suitcase and a haversack and pushed them under my bed. My suitcase had been ripped open with a knife. Everything worth while had been stolen. One of Anne's pictures lay torn on the floor with a loathsome inscription in German scrawled across it in red pencil. Someone had pissed on my bed-clothes and done worse in the corner of the room, using as paper some pages of manuscript that had been in my suitcase. The rest of the manuscript was scattered over the floor, mixed with the indescribable litter of food the Germans had not wanted and the remains of bedding, clothes, and English books. I visited the other rooms in the court-yard. They were all in the same condition, but, scavenging in them, I managed to equip myself with some warm clothing.

As I arrived in the lower court-yard the last four British officers were discovered. They had been hidden in the wood-pile, probably the most obvious hiding-place in the whole camp.

151

But, when Germans are searching, the most obvious hiding-place is often the best. If these four had been found an hour earlier Wally and I would probably have survived the search, since the Germans had miscounted, and thought that there were two fewer of us than actually were missing.

All of us who had hidden, with the exception of the brigadier, were shut up in the rooms formerly occupied by the British batmen. German sentries, sub-machine-guns on their knees, sat on chairs in the lower court-yard in a stolid row facing the doors of these cells. A Spandau was mounted on the balcony behind them, and another poked its ugly muzzle through the grille beneath the wireless loud-speaker. The rank-conscious Germans had not dared to put a general in such quarters, so the brigadier was imprisoned in the Italian officers' mess. He had to be forcibly kept apart from the Italian commandant, for he had explained to the German captain that if he reached "Joe Grape's" throat he would choke him to death. He was both strong enough and angry enough to have carried out this threat.

Binns and I were lucky. Instead of being pushed into one of the ordinary cells, we were accepted by the senior officers, Colonel Fraser, Wing-Commander Ferrers, a tall, hot-tempered, regular officer, and Tag Pritchard. Tag had established himself as adjutant, and was admirably cheerful and competent. Like Binns, he had taught himself in prison to speak excellent German.

Our cell had been the cook's bedroom, and it had the odd smell of cooks' bedrooms all over the world. Still, there was room for our five beds, and the minute, heavily-barred window commanded a splendid view of the valley. In the foreground, forty feet below, was the Italian troops' compound. There the Italian soldiers were gaily packing and setting off in singing, parcel-laden groups, apparently leaving, with German blessings, for their homes.

Binns, stolid Yorkshireman, remained stoically cheerful, but I fought with a terrible bitterness as I looked out of the window hour after hour, turning my back on my cellmates.

From the day that they arrived in the camp until some ten days later when most of the Gavi inmates arrived in Germany, the Germans themselves provided no food for us. This was the Teutonic method. They saw that there was food, so why should they give us more? The young German captain had allowed his men to guzzle every bit of food that lay about the camp, but he had prevented them from rifling the locked store which held both the mess reserves and those of private individuals. Also in the infirmary Dr. Bill Gray, another fine New Zealander, had saved a number of Red Cross invalid parcels of the type we called "milk parcels". We knew that we should not be able to carry all this food with us, so while we were shut up in the batmen's cells we gorged ourselves on the doctor's parcels, drinking every two hours mixtures of Ovaltine, Horlick's, sugar and condensed milk made by the two medical orderlies, the brothers Fraser. They also were New Zealanders, small, neat, hirsute men who had been fruit farmers before the war.

Before going to bed the Germans kindly told us that since many of us had got very dirty in our hiding-places they had heated up the water by burning a lot of Italian furniture "and other rubbish". We trooped in to bathe, despite the fact that the Germans, many of whom were still desperately ill after their unwonted gorging of rich British tinned food, had defecated on the concrete floor beneath the showers.

It was good to get to bed, but at 1 a.m. 1 climbed out, conscious that I had been atrociously bitten by bed-bugs, and shuffled across the court-yard to the lavatory. Several of the young sentries were asleep, sitting upright on their hard chairs. They looked like grotesque etchings in that dim light; their boots melted into the dirt and rubbish with which they had strewn the once tidy cobbles. The blue muzzle of the machine-gun behind the grille swung slightly with my passage across the yard.

Next morning, September 15th, I burned many bed-bugs out of crevices in the canvas bed-top and out of the woodwork in the walls. Worse was to come, however, for I found to my horror that my phallus, presumably also bitten by a bug or bugs, had swollen to the size of a small melon. Greatly worried, I asked the German officer if I could go immediately to Dr. Gray. A young *Feldwebel* drew his *Luger* ostentatiously from its holster and followed me to the infirmary. When the doctor asked me to show my injury the German shouted something and left the room precipitately. He returned while the doctor was giving me injections. He was accompanied by two other N.C.O.s and the officer who asked: "Are all Englishmen like that?"

The Germans began that day to loot the Italian section of the fortress; and their officer, seeing that we had no means of carrying our clothes (since his own men had stolen or destroyed any haversacks or suitcases that we possessed) issued each of us with a fine big Italian rucksack. All the litter in the lower court-yard was then piled in two enormous heaps in front of our cells to be burned when we had gone. They told Tag that we would leave the following day in buses. Although our scheme for hiding away had cost us most of our prison possessions, we still felt that we had done something worth while. It had given the enemy trouble, it had gained us three days in Italy, and it had cost no casualties.

Next morning we were awakened by the guards who were to escort us to Germany, fierce, clean-looking soldiers wearing on their chests great metal plaques marked *Feldgendarmerie*. Most of them were armed with automatic weapons, and they were clearly ugly customers from the escaper's point of view.

They paraded us with much gruff shouting in a long line, two deep, and we straggled out of the fortress and on to the road in an untidy procession.

Wally and I each carried a rucksack weighed down with clothing and tins, and between us, slung on a broom-handle, we carried a huge salvaged suitcase filled with tins of oatmeal, sugar, cheese and other concentrated foods. We had more than enough in the suitcase to prepare escaping rations for a six weeks' trip. We hoped to escape in Italy and make our way into Jugoslavia.

Leaving the fortress was something of a wrench for me, but many people seemed to be filled with high spirits at the prospect of a change, even though the prospect was Germany and years of extra imprisonment. Wally and I were both serious and occupied with our thoughts of escape.

The valley was looking its very best. Our road twisted down between the vine-yards which were now heavy with grapes nearly ready for the wine-presses. The roads below us were thick with German transport, much of it horse-drawn. Many Italians loitered on the roads too, and others were working normally in the fields.

We stowed ourselves into three big buses, requisitioned in Gavi by our escort. Our Italian driver seemed to be enraged at something.

"What is the matter?" I asked him.

"They are thieves, nothing better, the Germans," he answered. "I own this bus, yet they pay me nothing for the trip, and it will take two days to Mantua, and two back."

"Are we stopping somewhere to-night?" I was not interested in his profits.

"Yes, at Piacenza."

"You hate the Germans?"

"Yes. They will ruin me."

"Then you must do something for us. I shall sit here, in the front seat with my two friends. If I tell you to slow down you must slow to fifteen kilometres an hour. Just for ten seconds, long enough for the three of us to jump from the door. Then drive on fast, so that the guards will not shoot us from the bus. Don't look at the door, then you will not know what has happened."

"I cannot do that. I am a married man."

"So am I."

"But in England you have so much money you buy wives like cattle. I refuse to risk my life for you. If it were worth my while that might be different. Have you any money?"

"We have no money, pig-face," I told him bitterly.

As the buses pulled out into the main roadway I screwed round to look back at the fortress. They were burning the remnants of our former possessions. A huge column of smoke rose from the battlements straight into the golden autumn air, like a picture of a djinn in a German version of the *Arabian Nights* which I had seen as a child. We had no djinn to help us. But we needed one.

CHAPTER XII

WE drove until evening, when we arrived at a large modern barracks in Piacenza. It was stiflingly hot in the buses—so hot and airless that it made you feel like a sick man imprisoned in a Derby-day crowd; it sapped your will and energy until you were only a bag of flesh and acid being carried somewhere.

Three times we halted to relieve ourselves, or, more likely, to permit our guards to do so. They were unsentimental Germans. We noticed one of them when they ringed us round on the halts. He had pale, glass-topped-pin eyes, short ginger hair, a wolfish expression, and a brand-new 9-mm. Italian sub-machine-gun, a pretty weapon. When we halted this creature always slid behind a bush or tree at some strategic point, obviously hoping against hope that one of us would make a run for it to let him try out the new toy. Nobody did.

The Piacenza barracks were really magnificent. Our building had a long succession of high rooms with double-tier wooden bunks. At the far end from the entrance was a splendid wash-room with vast and impractical communal basins carved from marble monoliths. There was enough marble in there to face two London cinemas; and the urinals alone would have made a monument the size of London's Cenotaph. All of us were soon running round the spacious place looking for bolt-holes.

"Waddy" Wadeson and Buck Palm thought that the sewers might be navigable. When they opened the sewer trap in the monumental pee-house great clouds of mosquitoes, like whistling, expanding steam, rose from the opening and filled the whole building. The sewers were too narrow and evil-smelling for anybody to venture inside them. All that night we were devoured by mosquitoes, and we were thankful to get out to the hot buses again for an early morning start.

That evening we arrived at our first German "camp". They called it a camp, but in reality it was only the football ground and cycling track at Mantua. We were in the worst of tempers. Wally and I had sat all day on the front seat beside a brave, but highly strung, South African called Patsy, who had made up his mind to jump for freedom. Patsy had taken the seat nearest the door, and we intended to follow him if he jumped. Several times, however, we were obliged to hold him in his seat, for we were too well watched. We had *Feldgendarmerie* guards in the bus with us, and others patrolling ahead and behind on motor-cycle combinations. Binns and I were boiling up for an escape, but neither of us was prepared to provide some too easy shooting practice for those grimly expectant professional butchers.

So the first sight of the football ground filled us with rage. It was an obvious seat of suffering; and wandering about on it we saw 200 British other ranks in an advanced stage of physical misery.

At this inopportune moment we experienced for the first time the temper of the German second-line troops. No sooner had we left our buses than German privates and corporals who spoke a kind of English shouted at us: "Come on, you. Unload this baggage. Hurry up there." And such phrases. Our time at Gavi had built up our self-respect and reactions to such treatment. The brigadier and all of us woodenly resisted the rudeness of the Germans; and what might have been serious trouble was averted by the arrival of the young cavalry captain who had been in charge of us during the last days at Gavi. Putting on the queer screaming voice that the Germans used, he insisted that we should be treated as officers, and that our brigadier should be allowed the luxury of a seat in the grandstand where the Germans themselves were quartered, and where they had several machine-guns on tripods swivelling down on the field. The brigadier refused, and came on to the field with us.

This little scene had heartened the British troops. It was touching to see their belief that we could help them because we were officers.

The field was half bone-dry and hard, half swamp where the single tap which was the sole water supply for the camp ran into the ground and spread a patch of insanitary mud. The latrines, open pits, were dangerously near the men's sleeping lines, since the Germans had put restrictions on the space, only allowing us to occupy one half of the field. Some of the prisoners, we found, had been there for weeks; and the place had been used as a transit camp for a considerable time. It was suitable from the German point of view, since the large banked cycling track which was "out of bounds" made it easy to guard the field by placing a few machine-gun posts around it. Many of the British soldiers wore civilian clothes. They had been on working parties in the north of Italy, and had been helped by Italian civilians to escape. Wally and I began to circulate among them whenever we arrived, and soon we were bartering, giving here a tin of bully beef and a pair of khaki shorts for a pair of peasant's trousers, there a British Army great-coat for a striped civilian jacket. I noticed (for one grows quick at such things) that other officers who were seriously doing the same thing as ourselves were Buck Palm and the wily George Sukas. Buck spoke good German, and could quickly kill anyone with his bare hands. George spoke perfect Italian and French. They obviously made a formidable escaping combination.

Tag and the brigadier worked on more orthodox and communally helpful lines, opening up the cases of food which we had brought from Gavi to make issues to the British troops, and to provide a solid evening meal for everybody, and organising a draining system for the ground. There was something most admirable about the way these officers went automatically about their business, for the administration side of soldiering is not always easy.

We lay down in a line on the football ground that night, sharing our great-coats and what blankets we possessed. It froze slightly. Some of the British troops had dysentery, and there was a continual coming and going between the sleeping lines and the trench latrines.

Binns wanted to attempt to crawl away during the night, but the concrete circle around us gleamed like glass and I managed to dissuade him. We had three or four long whispered arguments; I awoke in the morning exhausted and drenched with dew.

After another uncomfortable day on the football ground the Germans paraded us and marched us into Mantua. We were already weaker under the fatigue of travelling and the lack of regular rations. My rucksack and the big suitcase on its broomstick became an almost unbearable weight.

As we marched in a draggled and ludicrous procession through the crowded streets we saw the first open signs of Italian friendliness. Civilians, especially women, massed on the pavements and balconies, at first wept and shouted "God bless you," and later threw us apples, oranges and cigarettes. A contrast with my march through the streets of Naples twenty months earlier. Such experiences bring home the damned silliness of the world and the hopefulness of it.

After marching us to the wrong station and then making an agonising detour of at least two miles, the Germans brought us to a siding where a long train of closed trucks waited. A horrid stench rose from part of this train; Italian prisoners had been waiting in it for some considerable time. Their recent allies had refused to allow them the luxury of an occasional sortie.

Binns and I had placed ourselves at the head of the British column, wishing to select strategic positions in the train. As our long line waggled up the platform, a German officer strutted to meet us and held up his hand, at the same time bellowing: "HALT." He then harangued us.

The general would travel with his A.D.C. (Tag) in a third-class carriage out of respect for his rank. We other officers would travel in cattle trucks. But, he pointed out, we would be comfortable. If we examined the trucks we would see that they were French, and that they were marked "40 hommes, 8 chevaux". They were only going to put sixteen British officers in each truck. It displeased the German authorities to be obliged to treat British officers in this way. We should realise that they were doing their best. They had begun to transport all officers in passenger coaches, but so large a proportion had attempted (in vain) to escape that he had been ordered by the high command to expedite us in this manner. He begged that we would give them "maximum co-operation"; any officer attempting to escape would be regarded as a criminal attempting to sabotage the comfort and the security of his fellow-officers, and would be shot out of hand.

We climbed into the truck next to the brigadier's third-class coach. There were three benches inside the truck. Heavy metal mesh covered the four narrow openings high up in the sides which gave light and ventilation. Italian Red Cross workers, charming women, came down the train, giving us water, great bunches of sticky little black grapes and loaves of excellent bread. This was the first we had seen of *their* Red Cross, but we did not know whether that was due to a change of temper in the Italian people or to our now more northerly position in Italy.

When our doors had been closed and sealed by the Germans, all of us began to search round the wagon like terriers after rats, and no sooner did the train move than almost every officer of the sixteen produced an improvised tool and set to work cutting something. John de Jago, the senior officer there, stopped us and called a conference. He then directed the work into two channels. "Waddy" and "Hack-in-the-Bush" were to be responsible for cutting out a panel in the forward end of the truck, while Binns and I, with several helpers, were to continue with our scheme for cutting a hole in the floor.

"Waddy" and "Hack-in-the-Bush" opened a small hole in the outer skin, to find that they were looking at two *Feldgendarmerie* guards each armed with a *Schmeisser* machine-pistol, who sat on a small observation platform in front of the brigadier's carriage and who looked directly down both sides of our truck.

In my spells of rest I kept my nose up against one of the ventilating grilles, watching the peaceful country outside, the small, attractive stations, the lurid Italian sunset, and the Alps, now all too visible.

When we stopped at Verona at 9 p.m. we had already cut a section off one floor-board, and we reckoned that within two hours we should have a big enough space for a man to get through. Jago ordered us all out on to the line to inspect the underside of the train while pretending to defecate. We saw that many of the couplings had not been done up and were hanging down almost to sleeper level. We also saw that in the little cabin at the end of our truck there was an Italian guard. We had been cutting our hole within a few feet of him. He was in railway uniform, and we could not know whether he was friendly or hostile. Jago made up his mind that it would be too dangerous to leave by the hole in the floor unless the train were standing still.

Shortly after leaving Verona some of our party succeeded in opening one of the big sliding doors. They did this by lifting the door from the slide, and at the same time unlatching it and forcing the wire seal with bent wire and some thin metal gadgets. No sooner was the door open than the train stopped at a small village station. There, in bright moonlight, we witnessed a most brutal murder.

The trucks which were filled with Italian prisoners were unguarded, and many of them had large, unobstructed ventilation openings. Two Italians made an effort to escape. They jumped from the train as it stopped, and pattered across the platform, making for the open country. Stentorian German roars of "Halt" drew all of us to our ventilators.

We saw the two stop and slowly turn to face the train. They held up their hands, silhouetted like scarecrows against the frosty countryside. The two Germans behind our truck got down to the platform and fired bursts of five or six rounds into each of the Italians. The machine-pistols rattled dryly, like dice.

One of their victims collapsed as though he had been cut in two. The other clasped his hands to his stomach and shouted hysterically: "*Mama mia. . . . Aiuto. . . . Aiuto. . . ,*"

The Germans fired again. One burst into the body lying in the dust, the other into the swaying, shrieking figure. A silence of horror settled on us in our dark truck. The tall, blond lieutenant in the *Feldgendarmerie* who commanded the train sauntered over to the two bodies, one of which still twitched and yelped, and fired one round with his pistol into each of them. This was supposed to be a formality, the *coup-de-grâce;* but he did not bother to aim, and the twitching and yelping continued as the lieutenant walked away, stretching his long legs in their shorts like a dancing girl walking behind the wings.

When the train moved on we saw that the two guards behind us never relaxed their watch. It would have been suicide to have jumped from the door of our carriage. Jago forbade it. Repeatedly during the night there were fusillades of shots, some from the two guards at the end of our truck, some from other parts of the train. None of us slept, since all of us hoped for some disaster to the train. It was rumoured that large bodies of *Alpini* were operating as partisans in that part of Italy. But dawn found us still in our truck, and still travelling.

It was September 19th, my thirty-third birthday.

At 10 a.m. the German lieutenant acceded to the brigadier's heated requests that the train should stop to allow the prisoners to relieve themselves beside the railway line. Squatting in the sunshine we were able to shout news down the train, and we learned that three trucks away from us the Germans had found nothing but baggage. All the sixteen occupants, led by Major "Stump" Gibbon of the Royal Tank Regiment, had escaped through a hole cut in the back of the truck. They had crawled singly through the hole and leaped from a buffer while the train was moving.

From the back of the train the two small Fraser medical orderlies brought news of the achievement of Bill Gray, the Gavi doctor, and the sick officers in his charge. The sick had been put by the Germans in an unguarded truck which had open ventilation spaces. Even before Verona, one of Gavi's most prominent characters, an extremely voluble and dashing Serb named Maritch, had persuaded the doctor and the others that it was "easy" to climb out of the ventilator, sidle on to one of the buffers, and drop from there to the ground. Immediately after Verona Maritch, who was believed to be suffering from tuberculosis, proved that his contention was right. He left the train, witnesses said, when it was doing twenty-five miles per hour. The next to leave was my room-mate, the volatile Ronnie Herbert. He had his right leg bandaged, and was suffering from a dangerous clot of blood on the thigh. He was followed by Percy Pike, a stocky, red-moustached flight-lieutenant. Percy's broken right leg was in plaster of Paris, and when he had lowered himself out of the window they handed him his crutches. He was seen to pick himself up after his jump from the buffer. Last of all went Dr. Gray, and the two medical orderlies saw him walk back down the line towards his escaped patients, carrying his little black bag.

The Germans did not appear to be greatly put out by these escapes. They claimed that they had shot many of "Stump's" party as they left the train, and that any who had escaped would be killed sooner or later.

We stopped that morning to water the engine at a pretty village called Mezza Corona in the lovely Dolomite country with pale, spiky churches pricking up against the coral mountains. An extremely beautiful young woman came to our door.

"Do you speak French?" she asked me in that language. "Good. For I know that I have seen you before."

"I have seen you also," I lied. For she was as frank and

charming as she was beautiful and her clothes were fresh, well-chosen and well-made. Her mother now approached, an elderly woman, leaning on a long, ebony stick.

"Mama," said the girl. "I met this young man a long time ago in Paris. But then he was much fatter and more beautiful, poor dear. I was just on the point of telling him that if he can escape from the train he must come to our house, and we will shelter him."

"Not so loud," said the old woman. "But indeed, monsieur, I shall be delighted to see you. And we shall talk of Paris. Alas, we are exiles here. And so often we long for Paris."

They pointed at their house, beyond the village on a hillside. It was a clean-looking, square, white house with faded pantiles, and a sloping garden. It looked as though it had a bath-room. I almost fainted at the thought of such luxury. But the train puffed on, the beautiful young woman, waving gracefully, was soon out of sight, and I was alone with my untidy companions.

At the next station, a much less prepossessing one than Mezza Corona, we heard cries of agony from the next truck. These came from Alasdair Cram, the wily Baron, who had decided that he had gone quite far enough towards Germany. He was now claiming in German, interspersed with his cries, that he had acute appendicitis. He managed to convince the attractive German nurse who arrived with a party of medical orderlies that he was a genuine case, and, enviously watched by the rest of us, he was taken away from the train to hospital.

Evening was falling when the long train panted up the last few hundred yards to the summit of the Brenner and stopped in the swagger frontier station.

Here our *Feldgendarmerie* escort left us, and sleepy-looking German infantry, armed only with rifles, took over. They were a hopeful proposition compared to the fiercely efficient military policemen.

In that grotesque station I saw my first American soldiers of the war, apart from a few "observers" whom I had met in Europe and in Libya. These were prisoners from the south of Italy, and they were in a bad way. Their unshaven, tired and bewildered faces stared at us from the openings in the sides of their trucks. Some German humorist had gone down the train with a piece of chalk printing in English on the trucks: "American Pigs".

Although this was my first sight of the American Army in

Europe, it still cheered me. Eventually the men in the stinking prison trucks would be Germans and the guards would be Americans. It was only a matter of time. But time is all-important and never-ending to the prisoner.

It was dark when they moved us into Germany and the train, rocking madly, raced down-hill through forests and along ravines to Innsbruck, where the Germans allowed us to wash at a cold tap on the station platform. Having made this concession, the kindly but stupid Germans who then guarded us decided to move us into cleaner trucks. During this move in the ill-lit station, aided by a downpour of rain, which kept many of the guards in shelter, several of our party slipped away. They included tall David Stirling and Jack Pringle, the Baron's old escaping partner.

When they put us into our new truck we saw that we would probably be able to leave that night. The grille on one of the ventilation spaces opened on hinges. To make things still more easy, they stopped the train for the night a mile or two outside Innsbruck. There were few sentries, and these were armed only with rifles. The rain continued in an almost solid stream.

While Wally Binns and I, in the fiercest discussion of our eventful and productive friendship, decided whether to go or to stay, three of our friends climbed through the ventilator into the rain. They were: hard-bitten "Waddy" Wadeson, who knew the district and spoke German; smooth and intelligent Ian Howie, who knew the district perhaps rather better, and spoke better German; and Bertie Chester-Williams of the 2nd Lancers, who knew neither the district nor German, but who acted always with perfect cavalry dash.

My reasons against going were the following:

We were in bad shape after four days of hard travel on short rations. The weather that prevailed would set a premium on physical endurance and stout clothing; and on the precipitous hill-tops and ridges the mist was so thick that we should be obliged to keep to the low ground. Neither of us knew the area; and our only possible plan would have been to circle the town of Innsbruck and then follow the valley of the River Inn up to the Swiss frontier, crossing that frontier at some mountainous part not far from St. Moritz. I further reasoned that, with the Armistice, many camps in Italy had almost certainly been given their freedom by the Italians, and probably hundreds of British officers had already crossed the frontier into Switzerland. Therefore, if two junior officers did succeed in getting into Switzerland,

163

there would be little chance of their getting out of it before the end of the war.

Against this the stout and earnest Wally, argued that for twenty months we had been working in tunnels, breaking down walls, stealing and plotting and risking our hides, all to get out of prison. And here we had only to go through an opening to be free. It seemed too good to miss.

My arguments for postponement eventually prevailed. Fortunately, I think. But both of us were despondent and bad-tempered when the morning light, entering timidly through that tempting opening, revealed our pale faces smudged with four days' growth of beard. To bolster our spirits, we both shaved forthwith, using the few drops of water that remained in Wally's water-bottle.

That afternoon our train pulled in to our destination, a siding outside Moosburg, a small and muddy Bavarian town some twenty-five miles outside Munich. Soon after we arrived there we saw another train exactly similar to our own which was taking other officer prisoners away from Moosburg. Some of the faces that stared gloomily at us through the openings were Padula faces.

They had not got over the shock and disappointment of being in Germany.

There was a cottage beside the siding and two German women, fantastically blowzy and each wide enough to make two well-shaped women, stood in the garden watching us. Looking at them and at the leaden, soggy landscape, I was thankful that I had so far been a prisoner in beautiful Italy.

A party of Russian prisoners, the first that I had seen, swung past up, shouting defiantly at our guards and giving us the clenched fist salute or an imitation of our own Army salute.

Once more struggling with the rucksacks and taking turns with the suitcase (we had lost the broom handle), Binns and I trudged along in the van of the tired column of British officers which halted at the imposing oak and barbed-wire gateway of Stalag VIIA. All officers of field rank were taken out of our column to go to more comfortable quarters in the hospital buildings. The rest of us shuffled through the gates, into our first real German prison camp.

This was no beautiful monastery like Padula, no historic fortress like Gavi; it was a huge camp of huts and barbed wire, more like Campo 66 at Capua, but, being German, fifty times bigger and much better planned.

164

The first thing we saw—and the spectacle doubled us up with mirth—was a German guard strutting along with a fierce-looking Alsatian police dog held on a long chain.

Stalag VIIA had been built by French prisoner labour. French prisoners of war had been dumped there in 1940, on an exposed flat piece of ground between pine-woods. The Germans had told them: "If you want roofs and walls you must build them yourselves, to our specifications."

The result was a central roadway, one thousand yards along, wide and well-metalled, down each side of which were ranged barbed-wire compounds holding wooden huts. At intervals the central roadway passed through guarded gateways, and the gateway to each compound was also a sentry post. Around the perimeter, where the scrubby pine-woods had been razed for some hundreds of yards to give a field of fire, the German sentry posts were little log cabins raised high on stilts. In fact, at first sight it all looked so efficient that I wondered if Binns had not been right in wanting to get out at Innsbruck.

Near the far end of the central roadway we were halted and then wheeled into a compound. Our small party of officers (the Stalag was a camp for other ranks, and we were only there in transit) was to occupy a corner of one of the wooden huts. Binns and I, opportunists both, were first into the hut, which smelled badly of dirty men. We were met by an unctuous French *sous-officier* with heavily greased hair, who spoke a little English and called us (translating the French *messieurs* too literally), "Sirs". We selected bottom beds, near a window. The beds were three-tiered erections of unseasoned deal fixed together in batches of eighteen; that is, with six people sleeping on each tier, in absolute and revolting propinquity. The "springs" were deal boards, and the "mattresses" were of ordinary sacking stuffed with wood shavings and bed-bugs. Each of us was issued with one tattered and verminous blanket.

There were four or five such huts in each compound and a central latrine building designed to provide manure for the Third Reich's boosted agriculture. Each hut was divided into two parts, with a crude wash-house separating them; and at one end there was a slightly more comfortable room occupied by the French *sous-officiers* who had been there since the camp had opened, and who had been retained to act as interpreters and to explain the running of the camp to new arrivals. They were a cross between guides and what the Germans called "confidence men".

165

The sight of these Frenchmen filled me with delight. They were what we had been praying for. Wally and I decided at once on our plan of action. I would work among the French, trying to obtain German money, maps, papers, and addresses where we might find help outside the camp. He was to go among the British other ranks who had followed us into the compound, and to buy clothing from them until we both had complete civilian outfits.

Life was interesting in the Stalag, an extremely international prison camp. Although our quarters were bad, the rations proved to be much larger than any we had seen in Italy. There were two reasonably bulky meals a day, meals of potatoes, cabbage soup, and extremely sour and indigestible black bread.

Wally and I, determined to escape before we reached a permanent camp, mercilessly attacked our food reserve to build up our strength. For fuel we chopped up our bed boards, and each morning we cooked a great mess of porridge on a fire made between two stones in the compound. At midday and in the evenings, on the Frenchmen's stove in the "private" part of our hut, we cooked greasy dishes of tinned sausages, bully beef, fried bread, meat and vegetables. Between or after meals we drank our reserves of Ovaltine and cocoa, with quantities of condensed milk and sugar. It was both chilly and wet while we were at Moosburg. The weather gave us an appetite and helped us to store food and energy in our bodies. Morning and afternoon we walked quickly for one hour round the compound. So much for our bodies.

On the morning after our arrival, while I was standing by the gateway to our compound, looking rather wistfully at the queer crowd that trooped past in the central roadway, the German sentry, an elderly man, turned to me and asked: "Are you an officer?"

"Yes," I answered.

"Then you have cigarettes?"

"Certainly," I answered, handing him a Chesterfield. We had just been supplied with such luxuries by the American Air Corps prisoners in the Stalag.

"Well, pass out, officer," he said, opening the gate to my disguised, but unbounded, astonishment. "But don't be too long now."

So all that day I was able to mix with the Poles, Serbs, Croats, Frenchmen, Russians, Americans, Italians, Moors, Senegalese, and Indians who populated this strange community behind barbed wire.

From these people I picked up various things. Some Poles gave me a small wood saw. A Russian lieutenant, a pilot, gave me a thin stabbing knife which I sold to an American for thirty marks. A Serb gave me a small bottle of what he claimed were knock-out drops for German sentries which I sold to another American for twenty-five marks. He said they made a good drink.

Best organised of all the prisoners, and rather disdainful of the others, were the French. They even had their own cinema, in which German films were shown. The director of the cinema, taking a fancy to my open face and reasonable French accent, gave me three tickets for the show.

In the most unventilated atmosphere that I have ever attempted to breathe, we saw and heard a crude film about two Luftwaffe friends who fell in love with the same girl, a night-club queen. This was the first film that I had seen in three years, and I was interested to find that my critical faculty persisted. So much so that if I had not found the audience interesting I should have left the hut.

Packed in front of us were the élite members of the audience. Roughly, fifty per cent of these were low-browed and exaggeratedly manly. And the remainder, whom the hairy ones escorted and squabbled over, were girlish types of young men. Two in front of me were heavily perfumed, had pointed, lacquered finger-nails, and affected the coquettish ways of the cruder Frenchwomen. Most of these "girls", so far as I could see, were French, though a few were Polish and one was Indian. That so many of them were French contradicted in some measure the theory that Latins are normally less addicted to homo-sexuality than the Nordic or Aryan types. Perhaps the fact that French homo-sexuals are so much less in evidence in the outside world than British, American, German and Scandinavian ones is another good mark to be chalked up to the Frenchwoman, who is, generally speaking, the most efficiently attractive woman in the world.

It was noticeable that the section of the audience in front of us was sharply separated from the larger section that sat beside and behind us. The section in front brought its sex to the cinema and took it away afterwards. The remainder, on the other hand, were frankly sitting on the hard benches and enduring the vile atmosphere in order to drag a little sex from the screen. If the blowzy German cinema actress showed the tiniest curves of her puffy breasts some of these men howled their approval, while others, more horribly, greeted it with a voluptuous intake of breath. Towards the end of the performance one of the most dashing of the "girls" in front of us had begun to ogle Binns and myself, and we were extremely glad to get into the dazzling freshness outside the hut.

Since most of the kitchens in the camp were run by Frenchmen, I was often asked to take fatigue parties from our compound to get hot water for "brewing-up". The scullions in these kitchens were usually new Italian prisoners, who, poor creatures. were repaying the 1940 treachery of Mussolini—repaying it to irascible French chefs who were obliged to waste their talents boiling potatoes and *würst* all day on patent German pressure-cookers.

I went whenever possible to the Russian kitchens. The head Russian cook was a colossus, a Georgian. When no other cook in the camp would provide hot water, this man often lit a fire specially to oblige us, although we had no language in common. He used to take the great containers of boiling water, one in each hand, and slap them down on the metal counter between us. I would have to get two British soldiers to carry away each container.

The compounds were separated by double fences of long-pronged barbed wire stretched on oak saplings 14 ft. high. Between each double fence was an 8-ft.-wide strip of criss-cross low wire with loose barbed wire laid on the top. Almost every evening a party of Russians, some of them officers, climbed over this formidable obstacle to visit us. Twice when I watched them climbing German sentries fired either at them or in their direction. The Russians had no leather gloves, and some of them were torn about the hands and bodies. They cheerfully settled down in our hut to eat bully beef and bread and jam, and drink tea. They were very professionally-minded, with a great liking for discussions on the design and equipment of tanks and aircraft, or the weaknesses and strengths of their own and the German army. After tea they would ask us, as though to pay for the meal, whether we wanted lonely, sad songs, or joyous ones. The lonely, sad ones were the best.

These were exceptional men. Only the exceptional Russian prisoners had survived the journey from the Eastern front to Moosburg. They had been packed sixty-five to a cattle-truck. The doors had been shut in Russia and opened anything up to

168

three weeks later at Moosburg. Many of them said that they had been obliged to eat their dead comrades. Their hatred and enmity for our common enemy were very terrible to see, particularly as hatred and enmity seemed to sit ill on these humorous men always ready to laugh at themselves or at us. Some of them had faces unimaginably scarred by wounds that had never been dressed or treated. They swaggered about, apparently unconscious of their man-made ugliness, or else supremely conscious of it, flaunting it like a banner.

The French spoke seriously of the Alsatian dogs that were led around by guards. They claimed that they had photographs secretly taken which showed that the dogs had been set on their comrades and had torn them about the throats and arms. But the Russians only laughed at the dogs; and indeed there was something excruciatingly funny about the strutting German with the ultra-fierce animal on a chain or a leather thong. Sometimes when you passed them the dog would spring at you with bared fangs, only to be dragged back by his admiring jack-booted master.

The Russians told us that shortly before we arrived the Germans turned one dog loose in the Russian compound at night. The following day no trace of the dog could be found, not a tooth, not a hair from its coat. That night the Germans left a *Feldwebel* and two dogs in the compound. Next day one dog was found unharmed. "The other dog and the pig will never be found," said my informant.

I saw that George Sukas was working as I did at Moosburg, making friends with the French. Far from worrying me, this put me in good heart. George was a very intelligent customer, and I felt that I must be working on the right lines. After three days of hard work, long talks about France, French guests for meals, I began to strike oil. I struck it in the person of one Robert Cahin, a Lorrain, a young and wealthy grain merchant from Metz. Cahin was an interpreter. He naturally spoke good German. He had been shut up at Moosburg since the fall of France, with two breaks when he had escaped. Each time he had been picked up near his home.

"It is very difficult at my home," he said sadly. "There are so many Boches in Lorraine, and some of our own people are bad too, though not many."

He and I took an instant liking to each other, which made things easy. Nevertheless, Cahin was most cautious. I saw from the first that he was not quite sure of me, and that gave me confidence in him. On the third day, when Wally had already completed our wardrobes of civilian clothes, Cahin began actively to help.

First he found me German money. It was forbidden in the Stalag to have anything but camp money, but the black market was so developed, and so many of the prisoners went outside each day on working parties, that there was no scarcity of ordinary marks. On the other hand, the civilian marks were highly prized, and it was difficult for two newcomers to get hold of them. We had sold a complete Red Cross parcel to some Poles for 100 marks (a ridiculously low price, but we did not know that then). Now I asked Cahin if he could dispose of my watch. That same evening he sold it for 250 marks to a German officer. Next day he sold two pairs of shoes and some clothing and food for us. I then had 500 marks and Wally had 300—quite enough money to get us out of the country, we hoped.

I discussed escape again and again with Cahin until finally he took pity on me and spoke of a party of French *sous-officiers*, all friends of his, who had frequently refused to work on the land or in factories, but who, despite their protests, had been moved to work at a railway siding in Munich. From there they had sent a message to Cahin that if anyone in whom he had absolute confidence wanted to escape he might give that person their address.

Cahin gave me the following instructions:

"When you arrive in Munich, find the main station, the *Hauptbahnhof*. Face the front of the station, then take the road on the left of the façade which follows the lines of the railway. Shortly after the first street crossing you will see a railway yard in which French prisoners in uniform will be working. Approach them most tactfully when no Boches are watching and ask in French: 'Are you *Arbeitskommando* 2903?' If they answer: 'Yes, 2903 from Moosburg,' you must tell them frankly that you are a British officer sent to them by Robert Cahin."

He explained that the plan these *Arbeitskommando* workers usually followed for getting people out of Germany was to stow them secretly in railway wagons which were sealed in the siding, and which then crossed the frontier unexamined as far as Strasbourg, the main city of Alsace. Although Strasbourg was apparently more German than French, and since the battle of France Alsace and Lorraine had been incorporated inside the frontiers of the Reich itself, the population was mainly pro-French, Cahin believed (and so did I).

170

Cahin also gave me excellent Michelin maps of Germany from Munich to the Rhine and of Alsace and Lorraine beyond that river. He would accept nothing in return for all his precious gifts.

Not quite satisfied with Cahin's address, I moved about continually among the French in the time that remained at Stalag VIIA, and I succeeded in getting two other addresses. Both belonged to Paris prostitutes imported by the Germans originally to work in Munich factories. I decided that the railway workers were the better bet, since the women would not necessarily have any means of getting us away from Munich.

We now set ourselves to finding a good way out of the Stalag, but all the ways offered to us either by the French or the Americans (the two richest groups of prisoners and therefore the ones who knew most about the venal German guards) were uncertain, and necessitated a good deal of ground work to build them into sound propositions. Neither of us was prepared to throw away all that we had gained in the Stalag on some attempt that might be expected to fail. We had never been so well equipped in Italy.

American prisoners, who at regular intervals bribed the German sentries with an entire Red Cross parcel to let one of their number out, told us that the recapture system at Moosburg was highly developed. The Stalag sat in the middle of an agricultural plain which offered few facilities for hiding, the peasants were unfriendly, and there existed a special pack of police dogs and human sleuths for trailing escaped prisoners.

On our fifth day there John de Jago, who was living in the hospital, went out of the front gate with a party of French prisoners who were going for their fortnightly walk. The Frenchmen hid him among them until they sat down in a wood to rest. Jago was able to crawl unobserved to the other side of the wood, whence he struck the main Munich road. He was dressed in civilian clothes, but in the first town he came to, Freising, some twelve miles from the Stalag, he was stopped by a plain-clothes policeman and brought back to the Stalag. He was courteously treated by the German commandant, and was given only ten days' cells as punishment.

I had swung more and more to the theory that jumping from a train presented the best method of escape. If you got out of a camp there was an immediate hunt, and the camp had full facilities such as ready constituted and equipped search-parties, telephones, and so on. If you jumped from a train there was bound

to be a delay in beginning the hunt, and they might be uncertain at which point you had begun your escape. Wally and
I decided that we would jump from the train as soon as possible
after leaving Moosburg station. We had been told that we should
be going north, so we presumed that we should have to walk some
distance to get back to Munich. George Sukas and Buck Palm,
I observed (although of course we never discussed the matter
with them), had also succeeded with their new French friends.
George and Buck were living in hiding in the camp. They wore
French uniforms, and they lived in the French compound. They
never attended roll-calls. Among the remainder of our group I
saw no signs of serious preparation or competition.

Early in the morning of Tuesday, September 28th, our party
was told it must move at once to be searched and then to take
the train. Carrying our luggage, we marched in column of
threes to the big searching hut just inside the gates of the Stalag.

Our Italian rucksacks were innocent enough on the surface,
but underneath they contained all our escaping equipment and
clothing.

The searching-shed looked efficient, a long bare room with a
line of tables down one side, and German N.C.O.s, stiff and
smart, standing like *douaniers* behind the tables.

This was a crucial moment for Wally Binns and for me. The
first person to be searched, Tony Hay, had a saw and some
civilian marks taken out of his socks. But we had a plan.

CHAPTER XIII

ACCUSTOMED by this time to bribing German sentries at Stalag
VIIA, I intended to bribe one more German to get my escaping
gear out of the camp. Binns, who had led a more sheltered life
inside the Stalag, and who had more nerve, disliked the idea
of bribing, and determined to slip the search. Neither of us
could have begun to take such liberties in an Italian camp.

There was a general air of polished efficiency about the searching-shed. An officer swaggered up and down the centre of the
floor. Poor officer! Although he shouted and stamped and was
absolutely unafraid of his men, he was quite incompetent. His
mind was sliding about among the surface do's and don'ts. God
bless him!

I was careful to get to the front of the second batch of officers
to be searched. From that position I was able to examine the

faces of the Germans doing the searching, and I soon picked out the one who looked the most dishonest and perfunctory. As soon as this *Feldwebel* had finished with his first officer I seized my greatcoat and rucksack and hurried across the concrete floor to him.

The German undid the lacing at the mouth of my rucksack. A few handkerchiefs were neatly packed on the top. Delicately moving the handkerchiefs, he found a new packet of Camel cigarettes. As soon as he found them I knew that I was all right.

He shot a quick glance round the searching-shed, then his blue eyes came back to flicker into mine. I nodded very, very slightly. His hand flickered as quickly as his eyes, and the packet of Camels was gone. For the next five minutes his hands, buried in my rucksack, turned my camel-hair blanket over and over, pretending to probe the secrets of my wardrobe.

When I joined the group of prisoners who had been searched I found that several, like Tony Hay, had lost escaping equipment. But Wally had managed, unobserved by the cloddish Germans, to change himself over from the group about to be searched to the group of those who had been searched. The searching took a long time. When we were finally marched out I found that I was sweating and shaking with nerves. So very much had depended on the last hour, and all had gone well.

We were halted in column of threes by the main gates. Wally and I occasionally grinned at each other, like small boys about to get into mischief. Jago came past to say good-bye, on his way to the prison jail-house to do time for his escape. Alasdair (Baron) Cram stood in the file ahead of us, his head swathed in bandages. He had managed to escape from the hospital on the way to the Brenner, but he really had been ill. His illness had got worse in the cold and the wet. Then he had been caught by Austrian volunteers with the letters S.O.D. on their arms. These men belonged to one of the angry sections of the Tyrolean population. With the Italian Armistice they had come raiding across the frontier behind the waves of German troops. They had beaten the Baron shamefully, and had nearly murdered him. The greatest thing about Cram (and he was a very exceptional man) was the philosophic way in which he took his failures. He was smiling and enjoying a conversation with one of the German guards who handed us out our travelling rations, sour bread and a kind of sausage.

Far down the central roadway of the camp I could see an

enormous man in extremely tight American overalls. That was Richard Carr, who had changed places with a sergeant in the American Army Air Corps. The sergeant, whose name, funnily enough, was Millar, wanted to see what prison life was like as a British officer. They had completely exchanged identities. The Americans had promised to buy Richard his way out of the camp once our party was well away.

Wally and I ate our bread and *würst* immediately, at the gate and on the way to the station, all of it. We were carrying plenty of food. I saw at once that our time in the Stalag, thanks to Wally's insistence on regular exercise and pressure feeding, had given me back all the feeble strength with which sparing nature endowed me. Wally also felt good. He said that if necessary he would tear the train apart with his hands. But we had all the necessary tools.

When we neared the siding we saw to our disgust that we were to travel in third-class carriages instead of cattle-trucks. Carriages were usually the more difficult proposition for escape, since they always put guards inside them. There were two carriages. The first was divided into small compartments, each capable of holding eight people. The second was divided into two large compartments with a lavatory between them, in the centre of the carriage.

We climbed into one of the small compartments, then, seeing that the brigadier and the more senior officers were doing the same thing, and fearing that the enemy would put a sentry in each eight-seater, we struggled out with our baggage and went to the other carriage. In our compartment there we found three sentries and about eight other officers, all close friends of ours. We immediately saw that the central lavatory might offer good possibilities for a jump.

Before the train started we got down to relieve ourselves on the wheels and to say good-bye to Brigadier Clifton.

"George and I have been trying on and off for twenty months," Wally said. "And this time we'll manage it."

The brigadier gave us a glint from his savage little eye.

"It may not be so easy," he said. "It seldom is."

"The brig. is going to jump for it too," Wally said to me as we climbed back into the train.

"Yes," I answered. "Obviously."

(And he did try, we learned later, but he was shot, wounded, and recaptured.)

This trip went well for us from the beginning.

Our three German guards, instead of distributing their persons about the compartment so that they could control everything that went on, sat together at the end farthest from the lavatory. They were a sleepy trio, and one of them was a weak-chinned Austrian who said that he was very tired indeed of the war and everything else.

Wally and I established immediately with Nugent Cairns, the senior officer in that coach, that we should be allowed to make the first jump. We next examined the window of the lavatory, and found that while it would not willingly open enough to let a man out, Binns, with his great strength, could easily force it when the occasion arose.

Last, and most wonderful of all, the train did not go north, but chugged south towards Munich. We had never expected such a piece of luck. Perhaps we owed it to R.A.F. bombing. It was obvious now that we were going south until we could be shunted on to the main Munich-Kassel line. Our destination, the guards told Wally, was an ancient fortress at Kassel.

"Oh, no, it's not," Wally replied in English. Neither he nor I could keep still. All the way to Munich we were on tenter-hooks. The train ran slowly, at a speed that would have invited jumping had it not been a bright day with good visibility. And there was scarcely a vestige of cover beside the line. At some points, when we ran through beautiful, but thin, pine-woods, the temptation to jump was almost overwhelming. But common sense prevailed, and we made up our minds to wait for darkness.

A strapping German Red Cross nurse gave us scientific card-board cups holding sweet ersatz coffee and barley broth in the marshalling yard south of Munich, where we finally halted. Binns and I drank as much as we could hold, hoping that hot stomachs would make us feel sleepy. The German guards, to their disgust, were taken out of the warm carriages and placed in a ring around them. We were told that any officer who so much as put his head out of the window would be shot, and that we would move on, attached to a goods train, at eight o'clock that evening.

We composed ourselves to try to sleep, but we had little chance of doing so. Other people now approached Cairns for permission to escape whenever we left the marshalling yard. Cairns was firm with all of them when I had told him that we were extremely well equipped, and that, as well as having money and maps, we had an address to go to. It began to rain hard, and a brisk south-west wind drove the raindrops fiercely against our windows.

Many of the occupants of the carriage had influenza or bad colds, results of the long and draughty journey from Italy. None of them had stuffed themselves with food as we had both done at the Stalag, and it seemed that only two of them were really serious about facing the elements. They were South Africans, Karl Koelges and Alec Wuth. The former, who had in a former attempt actually reached the frontier wire at Chiasso, was a friend of mine; and, after fighting hard with my strongly selfish nature, I gave him our address in Munich, pass-word and all. Koelges and Wuth very decently agreed that they had less chance than our pair of getting clear away, and we promised not to lock the lavatory door so that they could follow us whenever we had jumped.

We said good-bye to all the others while the train was still in the siding, and bequeathed our rucksacks and the big food suit-case to Tony Hay and his partner Dudley Schofield. Both of them were fevered and ill. Cairns, generous soul, disposed the others about the compartment to mask as much as possible our entry to the lavatory. No sooner had these preparations been completed than the guards climbed in to take their old seat at the end. The train moved out, gathering speed all too quickly, it seemed to me. The time was 8.52.

Binns walked into the lavatory. I crawled between his feet, so that the guards if they were bothering to look would only see one man go in. I shut the door and locked it while Binns, without apparent effort, tore down part of the wooden window-frame and forced the sliding window wide enough to let even his broad body through. In an instant he had placed his two hands on a ledge above the window and had shot his legs through into the night. When I had unlocked the door no part of Binns was visible. I climbed through more gingerly. It was damnably cold, wet, and noisy outside. When I let myself down to the full extent of my arms my feet found a step. Feeling round with my hands I caught hold of a door-handle, and crouched on the step beside Wally. The train was going too fast to make jumping at all pleasant. At intervals telegraph-poles whisked past our noses with a blowing noise, like seals coming up to breathe on a pitch-dark night. I was shuddering with cold and fear, and was extremely glad that the powerful and strong-minded Wally was beside me. I reminded myself that the essential was to keep loose when I launched myself. Wally handed me the haversack which was our total baggage for that trip.

"Right! Jump!" he shouted. The crash of his landing sounded like tons of coals going down a chute at London Docks. I threw the haversack after him. Then I jumped.

Instead of hitting something very solid, as I had anticipated, I found myself doing neck rolls down a granite chip embankment. I came to rest in a little gully. The wheels of the train rolled past twelve feet above me. And on the other side a high embankment of loose stones mounted steeply. My eyes were getting used to the dark.

It was a long train. I lay still until the last wagon with its red light had rounded a bend, and suddenly the night was silent. Then I heard the crunch of stones and saw Wally's white raincoat approaching. He had found the haversack.

We climbed the embankment and saw on the other side a large area of allotments. Binns stood, a stocky figure peering out into the rain, his torso leaning slightly forward on his steady hips, his big feet making a wide angle.

"Well, damn your eyes," he said. "We made it."

It was stifling, suffocating, wonderful to be free.

CHAPTER XIV

IT seemed a pity that this, of all nights, had to be wet and cold.

"Now, just look what you have done to my nice coat," said Binns, pointing to a dark streak on his shoulder. And I found that my left hand and arm were sticky with blood. There was a fairly deep incision on the wrist, just below the artery. It bled steadily. The hole had probably been made as I jumped by one of the short pointed iron stakes which carried the signal wires alongside the railway. I tied it up with a handkerchief.

"Those allotments are the hell of an obstacle," Binns observed. "And the sooner we are over them the better."

Whereas I was a little light-headed from amazement at finding myself free, he, in his Yorkshire way, was at pains to be more practical and prosaic than ever.

We slithered down a slope and soon were at grips with the allotments, falling into cucumber-frames, climbing absurd fences and trellis-work that broke under us, labouring through sticky, freshly dug earth. The black-out was imperfect, and that helped us to avoid the cottages which were dotted about. At last we were clear of the allotments and in a suburb which reminded me of a quarter of Canterbury where I had once hunted for a murderer. We made our way down a lane, passing a row of bijou residences, and came to a main road. We followed this road for half a mile until we were scared off it by a number of bicycles which flung spray from their tyres as they passed. Then we took to the fields. Away over to our left we could see the lights of the marshalling yard where we had spent the afternoon and evening, and the red glares from the fires of the shunting engines. Now we were travelling on a very small and slippery footpath.

Wally considered spending the night in a large clump of nettles dripping with water. I refused, for the rain-water was already falling down the back of my neck, and I could feel its chill to the base of my spine. We walked on for nearly two hours, searching for some safe place to rest. As we passed a cottage beside a level-crossing a man came out and asked: "Who is that?" We did not answer, but when we were out of his sight we hurried on.

Soon after this we halted under a large tree, an oak, the only natural landmark in that wilderness of railways, bungalows and cabbage-patches. The tree stood beside a lane leading to a small farm. A few yards away was a rusty threshing machine, very ghostly in the darkness and with some small piece of metal on it which swung and clattered dismally in the wind.

Wally, astonishing creature, climbed the fence and, stretching on the mud between the roots of the oak-tree, was soon deeply asleep. Before he allowed himself to sleep, however, he arranged to be called by me at 5 a.m.

There was no chance of my sleeping. If the base of my back is cold and damp, I cannot relax for sleep. And unrelaxed sleep is useless to me.

While Wally slept I walked around the countryside, reconnoitring our route away from that place. Sometimes I walked in fields, sometimes in suburban German roadways with houses and garages and shops on either hand. I moved with extreme circumspection, and in absolute silence. My footgear had come from Harrods in London, a pair of brown half-boots with fleecy linings and crêpe soles. They had arrived at Padula, in my first "next-of-kin" parcel. In prison I had kept them for special occasions, like a first night at the prison theatre, and for escape, because they were at the same time weather-proof and light, and they were silent. I could easily have got more convincingly German shoes or boots at the Stalag, but I had held on to my half-boots (despite Wally's disapproval) on the grounds that in an escape the last reserve lay in one's own powers of running, and I personally cannot run when I am wearing either heavy or uncomfortable shoes.

Now and then during the night I came back to the oak-tree, to look at Wally sleeping stodgily under it. The marshalling yard, some three miles to the south of us, was bright and active all night.

I remember no feeling of fear, only a great exhilaration at being free, and a longing for the dawn and for more positive movement in freedom. In the early morning I saw heavy anti-aircraft shells in the eastern sky, and at intervals German night fighters passed throatily over the Munich defensive area.

Although I walked hard all night in my coat, I was desperately cold, and Wally, when he woke at four o'clock, shivered so strongly that he could scarcely whisper. At five o'clock we breakfasted, eating, for warmth more than any-thing else, slabs of German prison bread and American Red Cross cheese. We drank water from the German water-bottle which I carried in my overcoat pocket.

When we had eaten we set about dressing ourselves to pass into and through Munich. We had jumped in British battle-dress, with coats hiding it and civilian clothes worn beneath it. Our intention had been to bury the battle-dress before going into Munich. But that was now unthinkable. It was much too cold. Instead of discarding it we now changed it round, putting the battle-dress next to our underclothing and hiding it with civilian clothing. I thus had three thicknesses of clothing on my legs. (Long woollen pants, supplied to Padula camp by the British Red Cross, made the third thickness.) But the wind still contrived to cut through the layers of damp cloth and wool.

Waiting for first light, we talked over our movement tactics for the last time. We agreed that we had to forget that we were escaped prisoners; and to try to feel that we were as good as anyone else and had as much right to the pavement as anyone. And that the important impression to give when walking through populated areas was that we knew exactly where we were and where we were going, and that we were in somewhat of a hurry to get there.

Then we set out.

Before we struck the road, Binns, who must still have been

cramped after his night of stiff sleep, tripped and fell full length into a muddy puddle. He rose with mud all over everything, and wiping mud from his eyes and nose. This was too much for me. I sat down and howled with laughter. Five hours later I was still unable to prevent myself from laughing uncontrollably when I remembered him rising from the puddle.

I developed in the age of slapstick comedy. And Wally was feeling so serious, so obsessed with the importance of what lay immediately ahead, that he was the ideal recipient for the custard-pie between the eyes. He looked first astonished, then angry and solemn. My laughter infuriated him.

He spent twenty minutes with handkerchiefs and our clothes-brush attempting to put his ensemble to rights; but the mud had added the last irreparable touches to his appearance. He wore a vociferously checked tweed cap, the white waterproof, now dirtied beyond repair and stained on the shoulder by my blood, and below the waterproof appeared a pair of Italian peasant's trousers, loudly striped and patched in several places. His shoes were very pointed, down at heel, and filthy. His shirt was a grey Italian military affair, and his tie, with plenty of silver in it, was the sort of tie that a Whitechapel Jew would keep for weddings. The tie kept slipping round under his right ear.

My overcoat, an Australian military greatcoat which I had tailored myself to look civilian, was too dirty after my jump from the train and also, we felt, too obviously military to wear through Munich. But my clothes were otherwise passable. I had a tweed coat cut on the American model with a belt and a lot of revolting pleats in the back, reasonably good blue trousers, and my English boots. My shirt was a blue checked one sent to me by Anne, and my tie was a dark blue knitted one (it had been khaki, but I had dyed it in Italy with ink and wine).

The one well-made article of clothing, apart from my boots, was my belt. This was of pigskin with a peculiar type of buckle, and I had bought it in Swaine and Adeney's in 1940. I remembered as I tightened it over the two pairs of trousers that when I had been packing to go to the Middle East Anne and Myrtle (the wife of one of the company commanders in my battalion) had particularly admired it. "A very attractive belt but quite useless," Myrtle had said. Now it was the only thing then in my possession which remained, and it bore a peculiar importance for me.

Both Wally and I had shaved before setting out, and both of us had meticulously brushed our hair, yet there was a certain discrepancy in our appearance. I looked like a slightly seedy and impoverished college boy, but Wally, a tough-looking customer at the best, looked like a professional murderer on his way home from a tiring night's work.

We walked for an hour on small deserted suburban roads. Then we came to a park on the outskirts of Munich. Several imposing buildings stood in and around the park and a thin stream of people, obviously going to work in the town, traversed it on the same road as ourselves. Binns announced that he must respond to the calls of nature, so he left me on the road while he cut across the grass to a clump of ornamental trees. I passed an uncomfortable ten minutes on the road, strolling about and conscious of the glances of the German civilians who passed. On the whole they were well dressed, and I was surprised at the number of young men who wore civilian clothes.

It was raining slightly. Eventually Binns came out of the clump of trees, beaming. He said that he had cleaned his shoes and his coat, and perhaps he looked a little better. He carried our haversack. It improved his appearance, gave him some resemblance to a plumber going to work with his tools. It was filled mainly with food. I carried one chocolate emergency ration and my shaving and toilet things in my overcoat pocket so that, if we were separated, I should be quite independent.

Ten minutes' more walking and we passed a tramway terminus with orderly queues of people waiting. We were obliged to walk past a group of six or seven policemen, and immediately beyond them we had the choice of three streets opening from a star-shaped junction. We chose the biggest and walked on purposefully, as though we were hurrying to work.

My wrist was hurting me, and was again bleeding. I carried my coat folded over that arm to hide the blood-stained handkerchief. Wally stumped steadily along at my side, and occasionally I was caught by paroxysms of laughter caused partly by our presence in that prim dumpling of a town, and partly by Wally's pointed shoes which thumped so definitely on the asphalt. Wally was annoyed by my laughter, but the more it annoyed him, the more it conquered me.

Munich is a big place. We walked for miles. For some distance a black Alsatian dog followed us, licking up the spots of blood which occasionally fell from my wrist.

We were beginning to wonder desperately whether we were

181

going in the right direction, when we saw a group of French prisoners who were building a vehicle park on a piece of waste ground. Leaving Wally at a corner, I strolled down a lane towards the Frenchmen, and as I passed one of them I asked quickly: "Which way to the *Hauptbahnhof?*"

"Take a number nine tramcar," he answered. "Going that way." As he spoke an ugly German came out of a hut and glared at me.

"*Français?*" he asked truculently.

"*Oui, monsieur.*"

"Then clear out. I have too much trouble with you pigs." He bounced back into the hut.

"Don't worry about him," said the Frenchman. "He's sore because one of us has pinched his girl. But move on now, there's a good fellow. We don't want any trouble with the police. See you at Henri's one of these evenings."

"Yes, indeed," I said, wondering what sort of place Henri's was. I picked Wally up at the street corner, and we continued. We had, by some lucky chance, been following the correct streets all the way through Munich, cutting straight across two-thirds of the town towards the *Hauptbahnhof.* Now we were able to direct ourselves by the signs on the sides of the tram-cars. Wally's feet were hurting him, and he was ready to board a tram. But I dissuaded him. I had no confidence in his German accent. The streets were very crowded now. It was still raining, and we were both colder than ever since we had had no opportunity to melt the chill of the night.

The *Hauptbahnhof,* a large, seedy station of Victorian aspect, with its name sprawling across the façade, had six wood-burning taxis in front of it and a police check on all the entrances. The very sight of it warmed me. It seemed to bring Cahin's promises and plans into the light of reality. Without pausing in front of the station, we walked down the street on the left of it, a rather forbidding street lined with poor grey buildings and cheap eating-houses. Like the majority of main-line railway termini, the *Hauptbahnhof* had stained and fouled its surroundings.

After I had first spoken with Cahin of the French workers in the railway yard I had learned in many later conversations all that he knew of the place where they worked, and when we arrived at the first street crossing I stopped uncertainly. I had expected to recognise the place, but I did not. For one thing there was no café on the corner. For another the street running to the right went under, and not over, the railway. Yet Cahin had always been quite definite that it was the first crossing. I stopped a French *sous-officier* who passed. He said that he thought that *Arbeitskommando* 2903 worked in one of the yards some 200 yards farther down the street. Wally and I strolled on, keeping a good watch now for policemen.

We made our way down a lane and into the goods sidings behind the buildings on the street we had just left. There were some Russians working there, but no Frenchmen, and the German guards and railway officials eyed us most offensively.

"If we stay here five minutes we'll be picked up," Wally said. We went back into the street. For over two hours we searched round the first crossing that Cahin had so definitely described. Our spirits had fallen sadly. It was still raining. My legs and ankles were beginning to ache from all our pavement pounding. Wally wanted to go into one of the small eating-houses and order coffee but I was afraid.

"I need a hot drink," he repeated. "Just something to warmy my stomach. You look like death too." He had been long in the British Army, and had great faith in the recuperative powers of hot drinks.

"All right," I said. "We'll just make one more round, and if we strike blank you shall have your hot drink. But this time we'll go under the railway and try the yards on the far side."

"Huh! If you ask me, those Frenchmen were pulling your leg."

However, he stumped along beside me. We went under the bridge and turned left. But now two policemen were walking behind us, so we slightly increased our pace, and did not dare to look at the railway. We turned left some distance along the railway to cross to the other side by a large bridge, and at the far side of that bridge I had the feeling: "I have been here before." After a good look round I said to Wally:

"Cahin made a mistake. He should have said the second street crossing. This is the place."

"Are you sure?"

"Yes. Here is the café with the menu-card in a brass frame on the left of the door. There is the locksmith's and there the little hotel with the bead curtains."

"Where do we go from here?"

"Four hundred yards farther on. Yes, here is the first entrance to the railway yard. Here are the iron railings. There are the Frenchmen, unloading that truck. We've arrived, Wally . . ."

"We'll be there when they agree to take us in. Too many Jerries about here for my liking."

Wally stopped at the wide gateway of the railway yard. I went in, and approached two Frenchmen whose heads alone protruded from the air-raid trench that they were slowly digging.

"Are you *Arbeitskommando* 2903?"

"Yes, 2903, from Moosburg."

The two of them had stopped digging. They leaned, as though frozen on their spades and stripped me with the penetrating and analysing eyes of Latins.

"A droll accent," the smaller of the two remarked to his companion.

"Of course it's droll, my accent," I interrupted. "That man by the gate is with me." Their eyes swivelled round to bear on Wally's square shape. Wally was pointedly looking the other way.

"We are British officers, sent to you by Robert Cahin . . ."

"*Mon cher*, you have come to the right place, fetch your friend at once." They sprang from the trench and violently pump-handled both my hands.

"Supposing they are stool-pigeons?" asked the small one.

"Stool-pigeons," laughed the other, "with a face like this. This is no Boche. Goodness and the light of God shine on his face." (I thought this was going a little too far.)

They led us into a low wooden hut behind a barbed-wire fence at the end of the yard.

"Please be a little quiet in the hut because there is a German in the next room," said the tall man. "Do not fear him, he is a decent sort of German, a *Feldwebel* who is very afraid of us Frenchmen. He will make no trouble so long as he thinks that you are French. Do not speak English, though, at least not above a whisper." The speaker had a thin, intellectual face with soft, calm eyes. His voice was educated and Parisian, his hair, frizzing widely around his high narrow forehead, had a round bald patch on the back of the head.

"Where do you come from, Father?" I asked him.

"From Paris. Yes, I was a priest until the war. Now I am a soldier, a corporal, and I have been a prisoner for three years."

The hut was filled with double-tier bunks. Every inch of

wall space was covered with photographs, shelves, and little cupboards made from Red Cross boxes. These men were old prisoners, skilful at making themselves comfortable. The small man, a birdlike Breton with a strong chin, made us strip down to our underclothing, and he hung our wet things up to dry around the iron stove. Meanwhile the priest boiled some water and skilfully bathed and dressed my strange little wrist wound.

Then the pair of them made us eat the prisoners' delicacies which they heaped before us. There was the dry white bread that France sent to her prisoners, and very fat, salt ham from Brittany, tinned margarine bought from British prisoners and jam made (they told us) by a Munich *Hausfrau*.

When we had finished eating, and were smoking *"Voltigeurs"*, another Frenchman came in, a smooth, tall man with a deep voice. He organised escapes.

"You are my first two Britishers," he said. "We have sent nearly sixty Frenchmen out of Germany, though, and three Poles. All of us in this *Arbeitskommando* are *sous-officiers*. A few months ago it became a question of work for the Boches or starve. So we came here, agreeing among ourselves to pretend to work in order to sabotage the German war effort and to promote escape from Germany. It is a point of honour.

"We shall be very proud to handle you. There are forty-two of us in 2903, and every one of us is for you.

"Now to be practical. Last week we loaded three men into a wagon which was going straight through from here to Paris. Unfortunately that was the last of such wagons. Now the farthest that I can send you is Strasbourg; but as you probably realise the people on the whole would be helpful to you there, and once there you are already across one great barrier between us and France, the Rhine. There is another very difficult barrier, the new Franco-German frontier, that is the old Western boundary of Alsace and Lorraine. You will have to use your own initiative to cross that barrier.

"I can tell you nothing definite about wagons for Strasbourg. There are none to-day, there might be none for fifteen days. You must wait patiently here. If the wait is so long that your presence here becomes dangerous we will send you out to hide with French or German women in the town. You may have to make love to them. That is the only kind of payment they require."

I translated this bit to Binns, who was very shocked.

"Why the damned tarts," he said. "This country is rotten, rotten. And all their men away at the front!"

"In the meantime you should sleep," the Frenchman continued. "Sleep most of to-day. In the evening we shall press your clothes and brush the mud out of them so that you will look a little more respectable in case the Schleuhs visit us. Then I ask that you will do us the honour of dining with the chief and myself."

We went to sleep, well covered with French Army blankets in a two-tier bed under a large framed photograph of Marshal Pétain. We were both dazed by our good fortune and by the blessed warmth and dryness inside the hut. We slept until they shook us and held out clean clothes for us.

Now there were thirty men in the hut to shake hands and slap us on the backs. My eyes refused to remain more than half open and I heard my voice come out gruff and treacly, forcing its way through silencers of sleep.

We ate at a table for four—a table with a white table-cloth. The chief and the escape organiser had cooked an excellent meal. Sardines and tunny-fish, then under-done fillet steak with macaroni cooked in butter, and salad with *croûtons* of bread rubbed in garlic and a dressing of olive oil and vinegar. We drank German beer.

While we ate they pumped me about the British Army and the war in general. Most of their questions concerned "Mont-gom-er-ee" and the Eighth Army. Wally nodded off as I talked.

In the middle of all this the door opened and a German *Feldwebel* came in. He was a tired-looking, elderly man. He mumbled in French the times at which squads must leave the following morning to work in the station. Then he looked at us.

"Who are these two civilians?" he asked.

"Get out, now, and stop asking questions about what is no concern of yours," said the French chief brusquely. "Things will be coming to a pretty pass when we are no longer allowed to have a couple of friends in for dinner. Clear out."

"No offence," said the German cringingly. "You know I am your friend, *les gars*." He walked to the rickety door and then asked pleadingly, holding it open with one gnarled hand: "Nobody has a spare cigarette, I suppose?" There was no answer.

"Ah, well," he said, with a little sigh, and he was gone.

Wally, who had not understood the French exchanges, stared at the door with goggling eyes.

"The nerve of the old rat," exclaimed the chief. "He's had his cigarette ration this week."

"You mean *you* give *him* a cigarette ration?" I asked.

"Yes, the poor old brute only gets two a day from the Wehrmacht, so we make it up to six. The way I look at it, if he is forced to go very short of tobacco he may start shoving his nose in too much, although he would scarcely dare to do anything silly like reporting us."

Two young Frenchmen now came to say good-night. They were dressed from head to foot in black. Black caps, worn rakishly back and on the slant, black jerseys, and black trousers that fitted closely over the haunches and down to the knees, then flared grotesquely.

"Those are their sleeping-suits," the chief explained. "We daren't keep more than our complement in the huts at night in case a German patrol making its rounds calls in to check up on us. All they ever do is count. Just tell your friend to lie still and feign sleep no matter what happens. You will be all right since you talk decent French. Those two boys are leaving you their beds and their identity papers."

"But where are they going?"

"Oh, don't worry about them. They are going out to sleep with their girls."

"With German girls?"

"With Gretchens, yes. The Munich Gretchens like Frenchmen very much indeed. In fact they are apt to be too demonstrative; they make us unpopular with the male population. And you, *messieurs*, how do you find the Gretchens?"

"We have not met any socially since the war. But I find them very ugly to look at, badly dressed, and wide as hippopotami . . ."

A chorus of denials greeted this remark, for Frenchmen all over the hut, perched on the other tables, on the few benches, festooned in loose attitudes over the double-tiered beds, were listening avidly to all that the Englishmen said.

"They are not beautiful like Frenchwomen, nor over-intelligent, but beauty they have, and a great kindliness," said one.

"Indeed but they are beautiful," said another, a hard-bitten sergeant. "They have not the breasts and the behinds of our women in France. But their hair is ravishing, and what appe-

187

tites for love they have, and how they can eat and drink.''

"And how they like foreigners,'' said a third in the strong accents of the Midi. "For me I shall find the women of Toulouse too thin and dried-up when I return.''

"Surely that is the law of supply and demand,'' I suggested. "You take the best that you can get. But tell me. Do you really *like* them?''

"Yes, yes, yes,'' came from all sides of the room. Several watered down their assent, feeling that they should dilute it with patriotism.

"You will understand that these women are not really German,'' said the chief, summing up the watering-down efforts. "They are Bavarian. Elsewhere the Boche women are not like this. But from our point of view the Bavarian women are all right. Although of course we hold most of the cards.''

"*You* hold the cards? You are prisoners.''

"Indeed we are prisoners, but look at our assets. We know that we are going to win the war, and most of the Boche civilians are of the same opinion—asset number one. Just to rub this in with the men, we keep a black list which the Boches know all about. If our *Feldwebel* there, for example, did anything wrong I should drop in to see him, and I should say: 'I am sorry, my German friend, but your case has been considered, and you must go on the black list.' And like most of them he is extremely nervous about the list. He frequently talks to us about it, making efforts to find out exactly which of his friends and enemies are on it.

"Our other assets are more material, though intrinsically less important. In many ways you see we are the richest people in Munich. Look at Gaston there.'' He pointed at the small Breton who had greeted Wally and me that morning. Now the Breton was dressed in his walking-out clothes, a cocky and almost brand-new French uniform covered in badges, good boots and puttees, and a large black beret. He wore this headgear in a manner which seemed peculiar to the prisoners. It was ironed flat, like a huge pancake and creased in the middle so that one half covered his head and the other, making from the front view a sharp angle, fell down over the side of his head. He looked a thoroughly clean and dashing soldier, a contrast to the slovenly French soldiers that I had seen in their millions in the first two years of the war.

"How can the few moth-eaten civilians in Munich compete

188

with such a figure?" continued the chief. "Then the Frenchman has always known how to get along. His are the talents of the *débrouillard*. And now, to help him out, he has commodities sent from our brave people at home which the German civilian population cannot obtain except at enormous expense on their black market. We have chocolate and soap and cigarettes. It is astonishing and terrible what the Gretchens will do for these things, especially for chocolate."

"Ask them what they think of Pétain, and why they have his picture hanging here," Wally said to me. "All this talk about the women gives me the creeps. Does he say they can sleep with German women for a bar of chocolate? I can tell you I'll be glad to get back to Yorkshire."

"I don't think I had better ask that," I said in English.

But the Frenchman who organised escapes evidently understood.

"Father Pétain has been good enough to the prisoners of war," he said. "Many of us still believe in him. Some of the reforms his government has instituted in France have been for the good of France. At such low moments in our history we must never forget the victories and the sacrifices of Verdun. Pétain is the living symbol to many of us of the last victory and the price we paid in blood. On the other hand, many of us are for de Gaulle. He seems to symbolise the real hope, the France that fights on. Sometimes there are sharp schisms on this question. Last week in the other room there a fight began between the Pétainistes and the de Gaullistes. But who can say? You, who are both prisoners, will agree that the prisoner often becomes philosophical, and he sees that there is good and bad in almost everything and almost everyone. This must hold good for generals as well as for privates."

There was an air of success and triumph about that hut. Mixed up with the misery of proud men who for years had been captives and separated from their land and their own people, the triumph came out in the stronger contrast, as a bright red flashes out from a dark background. The men themselves were dashing and brave, radiating confidence. It was the confidence of *débrouillards* who had suffered, who still suffered, though not so much as formerly because of their own character and their own efforts.

Wally and I, still in that half-shivering state that sticks to a man who has been exhausted and exposed, began to nod over our coffee, and they hurried us off to bed. He was in one room,

I in another. The men leaned sideways out of their beds and talked to me when I lay down. One of them pressed an apple on me.

"The English like to eat apples during the night," he said didactically.

"How do you know that?" asked his neighbour.

"I had an English girl friend once. She was a stage star. I met her at Nancy and we fell in love. She used to eat apples all night. Her teeth were like the insides of oyster-shells, and she said that this, and her general good health, were due to the apples eaten at night."

"A star! Whoever heard of a foreign star at Nancy?"

I answered their questions as long as I was able, and then I fell asleep in the middle of an answer, soothed by their friendship and the knowledge that they were risking themselves for us. I awoke once during the night and tasted in my mouth the French cooking, the straw-coloured potatoes, the tang of garlic, the salad dressing, the strong black coffee. It had been coffee supplied (as a present) by Wally and me. Coffee in a tin, from Twinings in the Strand. I had often tasted it before in prison, but never as strong and as good as that. Frenchmen can do things with coffee. . . .

It was 6 a.m. when I awoke, and many of them were getting up to go out to work on the railways. Each of them carried a haversack. They explained that the chief made it a rule that everyone must steal at least one object every day. Hence the haversacks.

"Some of us will have fruit to-night, some vegetables, some meat, some leather or other valuables," they said. "We are pledged to steal every day, not only for ourselves, but to hamper the Boche war effort and to hit at morale. The stealing is a point of honour."

Next time I awoke it was 9 a.m. I was re-awakened by the cries of children. I looked through one of the steamy windows at them, three little boys and a girl standing against the barbed wire, looking towards our hut, and making queer, chirping noises. It was warm in the hut, where the aroma of sleep and French tobacco hung listlessly, yet persistently, in the air. But outside it was a raw morning. The children's hands were blue. Their faces were peaked and their eyes were very large.

The priest went out to them. He had a small slab of chocolate. He put the chocolate on a tree-stump used for cutting kindling, and divided it into four cubes with his knife. The chirping grew in volume and intensity. I turned away, a little horrified. I could not bear to see the children catch hold of the chocolate and devour it.

In the other room the small Breton stood watching.

"That idiot," he said. "Does he not realise that French people are going short in order to provide us prisoners with chocolate. Yet he has to give it away to those little pigs, true Boches, dirty, stinking Boches. Look at them guzzling. I tell you the saliva is gushing from the corners of their mouths. Ugh." He made rude sucking noises with his lips, an exaggerated sound-track for the scene he witnessed through the window. When the priest came in he said good morning to me, then he went through into the little corridor space between the two rooms. In that space he had made an altar. He put on a *soutane* and I could hear him murmuring and chanting for a long time. He had a clean shining skin and bright eyes.

His church had been a fashionable one in Paris. It was near my office. I used to pass it, walking to work from the apartment in the Palais Royal. There were usually big cars, Hispanos, Bugattis, Delages, outside the church, and sometimes the imaginative scent of incense came licking out of the old stone doorway to tickle inside my nose. He was a good priest. Part of me admired him for giving his chocolate to the children of the enemy. His gesture had a shred of the glory of the Master, and the best kind of war-time glory, the most expensive kind. The priest, like all of us, was hungry for chocolate. I was glad that the glory came from such a cultivated man, that it tore itself apart from the Hispanos and Bugattis and Delages—and the narrow racial hatreds of war.

He had painted the background to his little altar. He claimed to me that he was an artist. But he was a bad artist. The background was sugary and sweetly, vulgarly, opulently pretty in magenta shades. As he stood with his breath sighing in front of it he looked deep into the pretty background he had made himself. But the beauty was all in himself.

That morning Wally and I washed and ironed our clothes and trimmed each other's hair. We were feeling human again. Rested and restless to get on. We were alone in the hut much of the time. The priest and the Breton were outside, pretending to dig the air-raid trench in which I had found them the day before.

Wally was full of admiration for the Frenchmen. Honest

admiration for their wit and their manliness and their good manners to us. Wally was a real Yorkshireman, and his admiration was a probe and a scalpel instead of a wash of bright colours. He was a difficult man to impress, but most loyal to his impressions.

They separated us for lunch. Wally went off with the priest to one restaurant and the little Breton took me to another. My clothes were now hanging well on me, and I felt confident. It was the over-confidence of the beginning.

"Très chic," the Breton said of the restaurant. And indeed the place was expensively appointed in a heavy manner, with smooth natural wood panelling and thick refectory tables. The undulating blonde waitress, obviously greatly attracted to her opposite, my small, dark, blade-like companion, gave us the quickest service and the biggest helpings in the restaurant. My companion gave her digging glances in return, glances which reminded me of a fat boy at a garden-party beginning his very last plate of strawberries and cream.

Cahin had told me in the Stalag that you did not need food coupons to eat soup and vegetables in the restaurants. But I noted that this was not the case. They demanded fat coupons for the vegetables. The food was expensive and dull. The beer tasted good in its heavy stone mugs. It was amusing to eat in a restaurant again. The last time had been in Salerno station with the Italian lieutenant on the way from Padula to the punishment camp. And the time before that it had been *langoustines* in the Union Bar at Alexandria with Geoffrey Cox.

The restaurant's clients, mostly family parties, spoke much of the bombing. So did the Frenchmen. After the last raid they had been obliged to go out and help to dig from the crumpled cellars distorted bodies scarred with phosphorous burns.

When we got back to the hut we found the escape organiser waiting to speak to me.

"You are in luck," he said. "You leave to-night. Crowded quarters, I fear. There may be no more transport for Strasbourg for fifteen days. So I am putting eight Frenchmen in with you. It might take you five or six days to get there. The R.A.F. has been knocking hell out of the railways. So provision yourselves accordingly. Just ask for anything that you want.

"All I ask of you is to be careful when you are sealed into the truck. Make no noise at stations or halts. And clean up all the mess before you leave the truck at Strasbourg. Otherwise they may trace it back to us, here in Munich.

"When you get to Strasbourg your best plan will be to go to *Quai* 6 in the port and pick out any French barge which has the markings P.L.M. Tell the bargee frankly who you are, and it is likely that he will help you or put you in touch with somebody who can. Beware firstly of all Belgian barges, secondly of Alsatian ones. If you fail to make contact in the port try first a Catholic priest, secondly a nun, thirdly any woman who speaks a French without too much Alsatian mud in it. Don't trust any of the priests in trousers, the Protestants."

Then he handed me one hundred marks.

"I have money, thank you very much," I said.

"I know," he answered, and suddenly looked embarrassed. "Perhaps I had better explain now why I know. Yesterday, while you slept we went through your pockets. You will understand, we were obliged to do it to safeguard ourselves. I do apologise. Of course we put everything back just as we found it. This will give you a little reserve to get across the frontier. Please take it. Then all of 2903 can feel that they have a part in your escape. To help *la huitième Armée*, that is something to be proud of."

They repacked our haversack, throwing out the prison bread which we had brought along as starch food, and replacing it with the excellent French Army biscuits. They gave us more chocolate, some dried fruit, and four large screw-top beer-bottles full of water. I also filled my water-bottle, and the Breton poured into it a yellowish powder which he called cocoa. He said it was "stimulating". I collected from them some thick, corrugated brown paper to make a hygienic installation in our railway-truck.

At five o'clock a blue-overalled Frenchman whom we had not seen before came to collect us. He was excited and nervous.

"My God," he said. "They look like walking Christmas-trees."

It was true that, added to our other gear, the beer-bottles made us bulge all over.

"Follow me at 100 metres," he said, and walked swiftly out of the hut and the yard. We followed him down the street in which we had searched so long to find 2903 and in at another gate to the railway yards, then, with elaborate unconcern, threaded our way through the sidings. The Frenchmen were loading a train on a siding opposite the main German office buildings. Gretchens typing at the windows of the offices glanced out at us and went on with their work. We both felt jumpy and conspicuous. We were continually swearing to ourselves in whispers. When we got opposite the French working party the escape organiser, who was also foreman of the loading gang, hissed at us: "Clear off. Be back in five minutes."

So we walked out of the yards again, to the street, where we pretended to look in shop windows. I gave him seven minutes by a big clock over a jeweller's shop. It seemed safer to extend his five minutes. This time the escape organiser was making surreptitious signs to us to hurry up.

"*Allo, les gars,*" he yelled at us as soon as we got near, and all at once six or seven Frenchmen were around us, pump-handling our arms, slapping our backs, talking at the top of their voices. A couple of German overseers were watching us. The Frenchmen were pretending that we were a couple of old friends who had come to say good-bye before going off home, repatri-ated. We were now in the narrow space between two trains, and hidden from the office building.

Suddenly we found ourselves hustled, almost carried to the open doors of a truck. The overseers had turned their backs. I found myself flying through space. They had thrown me up into the truck. I landed inside, on all fours. Wally landed on top of me and a case came walloping on top of him.

"*Schnell,*" screamed the escape organiser. "Come on now, get this Strasbourg wagon finished, boys. Two minutes to go. *Schnell.*" Then, aside to us. "Hide, Englishmen, hide."

The merchandise, mainly square packing-cases and motor tyres, was piled neatly at either end of the wagon, sloping down to an empty corridor in the centre. I climbed up to the left, Wally to the right. I hid myself as best I could and was still pulling tyres over my shoulders when the door, which the Frenchmen had banged to, was pulled open and a German over-seer climbed stiffly in. He wore grey overalls and held a tally sheet and a black propelling pencil. He stood there for an age, whispering to himself and stabbing at the paper with his pencil. I was in an agony of fear. There were ten of us there, I knew, within a few feet of him. It seemed too much to hope that none of us would sneeze or say something, or merely rustle a piece of merchandise. I felt the sweat running down the hollow in the middle of my back. Then the German left the wagon, the door slammed to again, and we could hear them sealing it.

"Silence," hissed a French voice behind me. And all of us

were agonisingly silent. I would have paid ten thousand pounds to avoid the chance of the German coming into the truck again. It would put too heavy a strain on our luck.

Our French hosts, before we left the hut, had sent out for beer, and had heartily toasted us in that harmless liquid. Now I realised that I wanted desperately to piss. But I was lying awkwardly, stretched out on the tyres and packing-cases as I had flung myself before the German's entry. And I dared not move. It was torture. I stood it for half an hour. Then I realised that it was only over-civilisation which was making me hurt myself. Looking at it objectively the important thing was not to move. Having thus brought reason to bear, I cheerfully wet myself. But I realised that I expected the ghost of a wrathful nursemaid to descend on the Munich goods yard.

Judging by the atmosphere, Wally and the eight Frenchmen had all reasoned similarly.

About six o'clock, with a cataclysmic thud that turned our neatly packed truck into a dark shambles, the shunting engine ran into our train. Immediately there was a terrible cry from behind me, the cry of a Frenchman in agony.

CHAPTER XV

I BELIEVED that this meant the end, the failure of our escape.

Yells of agony continued from the Frenchman behind me, while from all parts of the wagon came equally strong shouts in French, telling the sufferer to be silent; as those shouts increased in volume the first man raised his pitch and put more wind behind it.

"My leg is broken. Mother of God how I suffer," he cried.

By the grace of an almighty providence the train had begun to move while all this was going on, and the noise from our wagon must have been somewhat drowned in the rattling of the bogies and the thumping of the engine.

As soon as he realised that we were working to help him, the injured Frenchman's yells died down to moans of self-pity. But at short intervals he became angry at the slowness of our efforts to free him, and then he screamed curses. I could have murdered him.

The first Frenchmen to be packed into the truck had been put at either end behind walls of tall packing-cases, and the space had then been roofed in with tyres. One of these walls had collapsed, pinning that man by his ankle.

When we had finally got him free all semblance of order had vanished from the interior of the truck. The merchandise that had not been scattered by the initial shock of the shunting locomotive had been piled up anyhow by the rescue party. The darkness was absolute, and this confusion was something that I only sensed and felt until I struck a match to examine the Frenchman's leg.

Although he had claimed that it was broken, the ankle was no more than badly bruised and cut. I told him so as tactfully as I could, but it was evident that he disliked me heartily for my honesty. He would have preferred compliments, no doubt, on his bravery and his resistance to pain.

The other seven Frenchmen now crawled across the shifting, trembling cargo to shake hands with me. Binns remained stolidly at the far end. He had been disgusted by the noise, and was giving himself time to cool off before opening friendly international relations.

Finding that all the Frenchmen were ordinary *Arbeitskommando* or civilian workers, and that there were no officers among them, I told them that Wally and I were officers, and would be in charge of the party; and that they would take their orders from me.

I then asked them to relieve themselves in one corner only, and on the corrugated paper which Binns and I had brought with us. I explained that there must be absolute silence every time the train stopped, and that if our presence in the truck was discovered Wally and I must be allowed to make the first break for freedom, because, if we were found there, any Frenchmen who were with us might be shot by the Germans.

To my relief they all heartily agreed with this, except for the injured man, who muttered something about officers and Englishmen. I could see that he disliked having us there, and anticipated that he would attempt to form a clique against us in the difficult time that lay ahead.

We made three observation points in the truck by cutting out small knot holes in each of the two main doors and in a small wooden trap in the front end. Beside each of these observation points I had them fix up a comfortable seat, and it was arranged that no man would at any time leave an observation point without first warning another to take his place. Any station names had to be instantly reported to me.

By the time all this had been arranged the train had stopped at a marshalling yard, possibly the one from which Wally and I had escaped only two nights earlier. Wally had now joined me, and we were making the best of an uncomfortable place.

In the marshalling yard we had an unpleasant taste of our travelling companions' sad lack of self-control and discipline. No sooner had the noise of the bogies ceased than a storm of coughing, whispering, and rustling movement filled the dark interior.

Wally and I expostulated in hissing whispers, but in vain. Sometimes the noise died away, but never for long.

There was worse to come. Binns gave me a nudge that nearly broke my arm, and I saw that the man who had hurt his ankle was lighting a cigarette. He had got down behind some packing-cases to work his lighter, but the light must nevertheless have shone into the marshalling yard through the crevices in the sides of the truck.

Binns left me and the glow of the cigarette suddenly went out, followed by angry protests in French. In a whisper potent with suppressed fury Wally said:

"If you damned men think that we escaped to get caught only because you must light fags and keep nattering like a lot of women, you are mistaken. The next man that lights up in a station gets his teeth knocked down his throat."

I translated this fairly freely and with several additions of my own. The noise continued, and was repeated at most subsequent halts, but they confined their smoking to times when the train was moving. If I had not been scared of overstraining our relations with them I should have forbidden all smoking, for it was evident that the smell of tobacco smoke must cling to the truck, and in the day-time it was possible that a German might notice a trickle of smoke oozing out.

"To think that there are some Frenchmen as good as the ones who sheltered us in Munich and who risked their lives to put us in here, and others who are as self-indulgent as these jelly-bellies," Wally said.

That first night we travelled steadily and fast. The rhythmic rattle of the bogies was music. In the morning, when a thick grey light was apparent in the upper part of the truck, one of the better Frenchmen, a small gorilla-like man from the Ménil-montant district of Paris, came crawling over the packing-cases to report that he had seen the name Stuttgart on a station. At that rate we might be across the Rhine within a few hours.

Most of that day, however, was spent in marshalling yards. Nobody who has not travelled under such circumstances could imagine the discomfort.

The main discomfort, to us whose nerves were always tensed, was the noise. The crashing of wagon upon wagon, the clatter of chains, of bogies, of toppling merchandise. The French character is sometimes not very resistant to this type of nerve strain. All that day Wally and I raged and cursed as the behaviour of our companions became more and more undisciplined and dangerous.

Two or three of them went so far as to get a little drunk. They had brought their liquids along in the shape of bottles of beer and wine. To us, who had tried for so long to get out of prison, and to whom freedom was something inexpressibly pure and precious, there was revolting obscenity in the gross attitude of these men who were prepared to risk recapture for the sake of a drink or a cigarette.

We were not surprised in the course of the second night to hear several of the Frenchmen complaining of a great thirst. Wally and I were allowing ourselves only two small meals a day, for we wanted to keep most of our food against possible emergencies when we left the truck, and we drank water fairly often, but very little at a time.

By dawn, our second dim dawn in the truck, most of the Frenchmen were beginning really to suffer from thirst. Yet all of them had been warned to come prepared for a five-day journey. One of our look-outs claimed that we had crossed "An enormous river" in the night, and I thought, from the look of the country, that we might be over the Rhine and heading south now, towards Strasbourg. So Wally and I handed out two-thirds of our remaining stock of water. We had no drinking vessels, and no means of rationing the water. Quarrels broke out among the Frenchmen.

Altogether we spent fifty-four hours and fifty-nine minutes in the truck.

The last twelve hours, the afternoon and evening of Saturday, October 2nd, were sheer agony. I was exhausted from the mere pumping and straining of my hatred and scorn for most of our travelling companions.

At 6 p.m. we drew up in a small station named Strasbourg-Ems and the German customs appeared to make a very thorough examination of the train. The man with the injured ankle said that he had relatives there, and that we were near Strasbourg. After we had waited for about an hour in the station we were shunted off and released at the top of a fairly steep incline, which plainly was at the head of a large marshalling yard. Our truck picked up considerable velocity and rocked and swayed downhill until it smashed, with unbelievable force, into a line of others at the bottom. It took us a good ten minutes to recover from this shock. There was not one of us that had not bruises or cuts to show for it, but fortunately there were no serious injuries.

Most of the Frenchmen decided that they were going to leave the truck as soon as night fell. I was against this, for it seemed to me, after spending some time at the look-out holes, that there were troops in the vicinity. I thought I could hear occasional orders in German, and the stamping of jack-boots. Wally sided with the Frenchmen, however, and I was obliged to fall in with the general wish. We agreed that we would force the door at 9 p.m.

The Frenchmen began to prepare for the sortie. Two or three of them shaved, and most of them put strongly-smelling stuff on their hair or their faces. The atmosphere was indescribable. To make things worse, the last and greatest bump had toppled over all the packing-cases in the corner which Wally and I had made our own, and had thoroughly disorganised us. Among other possessions I had lost our last bottle of water, and although I searched laboriously for it I could not find it. I began to suffer from thirst myself, and now I only had my own water-bottle. The water in this, doctored by our Breton friend at Munich, who had added the yellow powder he called cocoa, was cool and delicious. But the demands on it were very heavy. Wally was also feeling thirsty, and every two minutes a Frenchman would crawl over and ask for a drink. When only a little remained I stopped drinking myself, and said that it was finished.

At ten minutes to nine, when Wally and I were beginning to force the door with the help of the little gorilla from Ménilmontant, a shunting engine approached and pushed us in a series of jerks and bumps further into the marshalling yard.

I fixed my eye to one of the side look-out holes, and saw that only one hundred yards from where our truck had been standing there was a German anti-aircraft post. There were about five soldiers grouped round twin heavy machine-guns or 20-mms.

We moved on slowly through a big marshalling yard where I saw trains loaded with military material, tanks, guns, armoured cars, stores of all kinds. Then we shunted slowly past an enormous munitions dump which was camouflaged with big strips of canvas and a netting roof.

I described all of this in a kind of news-reel commentary for the benefit of my travelling companions. This was a serious mistake.

No sooner had we passed the dump than the sirens went for an air-raid warning. The train stopped at once and we heard men running and shouting. These sounds were closely followed by the noise of British heavy bombers overhead. German anti-aircraft fire, both large- and small-calibre, thundered and spat and whistled around us, but no bombs appeared to be dropped.

It was extremely unpleasant, sitting up there in a high, closed truck. You got at the same time the feeling that you were shut in and suffocating, and that you were perched out in the open waiting to be blown to pieces. The Frenchmen began to show signs of hysteria.

Binns and I held a hurried conference. We prepared what tools we had and laid all our belongings ready to hand for a quick get-away.

Helped by the gorilla, who kept calm in the middle of the hysteria, Binns began to force the door. I took up a strategic position to protect them from interference, for already all the others were beginning to crowd round and claw and shove at us. Hoping to calm them a little I began to make a speech, almost as though I were giving a situation report at a military conference.

"There are many lights outside," I told them. "These have now been put out because of the aeroplanes, but the moment the alert is ended they will probably go on again. There must be a military guard on this marshalling yard, to protect all the valuable material which we passed on the way in. It will be extremely difficult to get out of the yard. It will take much coolness and steady nerves. . . ."

"Let us out," shouted the man with the injured ankle.

"Yes, let us out, *out*," chorused the others.

The door refused to yield to Binns's tools. I could hear him blowing and puffing behind me. Occasionally his crowbar slipped and his muscular body came hurtling back against me.

"If you will only keep quiet there is every chance that we shall arrive soon in Strasbourg goods station. There is no danger now. The bombers have passed. If you will only keep quiet . . ."

"Let us out of here."

"Yes. You English can go first. *But get the door open.*"

At the height of this noise the sirens sounded the All Clear. This did nothing to calm the inside of our truck. If anything, while the marshalling yard outside fell ominously silent the noise inside increased. The shouts rose to screams.

"Let's get out of here."

I put one hand behind me.

"Now or never, Wally," I said. I could feel the muscles on his back heaving and cracking. Suddenly a slit of moonlight appeared.

There was a rush from the crowd pushing against me. I was thrown on my back on top of Binns and three Frenchmen fought their way out of the door, one of them placing his heavy boot on my ear as he went.

The little man from Ménilmontant picked me up and apologised for the others.

"*Au revoir et bonne chance,*" he said thrusting me through the door, and I landed on top of one of his comrades on the ground below.

I saw at once that the situation was most serious.

A line of torch lights was approaching. The marshalling yard was filled with trains, and the Germans, undoubtedly alarmed by the shouts which still came from our truck, were combing the area. The nearest light was less than 100 yards away, and advancing steadily. The only hopeful thing was that the electric lights in the yard had not been turned on; but there was a fair amount of moonlight.

Maddeningly, the next man to come out was another Frenchman. Then Binns thumped down beside me.

He carried our haversack and his white raincoat. I took the latter from him, rolling it into a bundle, and the two of us ran hell-for-leather down the side of the train, away from the lights.

We had not run fifty yards when we saw that the comb-out was a double one. Another row of lights approached us from the opposite direction. We got down on hands and knees and crawled across railway tracks and under trains for some sixty yards. The Germans were uncomfortably close. We climbed up, each of us, on to the axle of a truck. The Germans passed. I saw the light circle from a torch move to within ten inches of my right knee. We waited there for a little, then crawled out.

And now the work became too hot for us to stick together. The Germans had found some of our Frenchmen in the truck, and there seemed to be searchers on all sides. It became a nightmare game of hide-and-seek. I left Wally's raincoat lying under a train. It was too white, and it handicapped me for crawling.

Once I was seen, and escaped only by running all out on my crêpe rubber soles and then doubling back, crawling fast on the sleepers under the whole length of a long goods train.

Finally, I cannot remember how, I reached an empty, accidented space, occasionally crossed by railway lines. At the far edge of this space, perhaps one hundred yards from where I lay, I saw the perimeter fence of the marshalling yard.

Thanks to my khaki coat, I crossed this space without undue risk. But I did the entire crossing crawling on one side as we had been taught to do for stalking deer in the Cairngorms.

As I reached the edge all the sirens began to blow what I supposed to be the alarm to signal our escape, a succession of short, sharp blasts. This went on interminably perhaps for ten minutes.

The boundary fence presented no difficult obstacle. It was seven feet high, made with wire netting and concrete uprights. There was no barbed wire on it. As I lay on the bank below it two German soldiers passed down the lane which ran along the other side of the fence. They were discussing the cinema programmes in Strasbourg. When they had passed I lay watching and listening.

A rustling from my left drew my eyes in that direction, and I saw the dark shape of a man beginning to negotiate the fence about one hundred yards away. Was it Binns? Or one of the Frenchmen? At any rate, this was no moment to investigate. Judging by the torches, the nearest searcher was a good 150 yards away, and a man with a torch has no long vision at night.

Taking a deep breath, I got to my feet and pulled myself quickly over the fence, endeavouring to centre my weight on one of the concrete posts so that the wire creaked as little as possible. I worked my way round some bungalows that lay on the other side of the lane, then found myself on the edge of what was apparently a fairly extensive plateau of agricultural country. I made out woods in the distance, and on my right some hills, fairly well wooded. I had the feeling that Strasbourg lay behind me, on the far side of the marshalling yard.

It seemed best to move straight out into the country, to put a big distance between myself and the marshalling yard, and then to swing round towards the wooded hills.

I was just preparing to move off when I heard shouts from my left and then voices on my right. Looking in the direction of the voices, I saw an orderly group of shadows which could only, I thought, be a German patrol.

Without waiting to think, I ran forward into the fields, at first silently on my blessed rubber soles, and then with a terrible crackling noise as I negotiated some brittle root crop. There were German shouts behind me, followed by stray rifle shots. Then, some distance away to my left, I heard several bursts of sub-machine-gun fire. And I imagined that I heard a scream, as though someone had been hit. The scream reassured me. I could not believe that Binns would scream whatever happened. I felt confident that he had got away, like me, and I expected to meet him again.

I ran on energetically over the fields, breathing deeply, and gulping greedily at the fresh air after so many hours in the fetid atmosphere of the truck.

A visual phenomenon now held me up. Every few yards I strongly had the impression that I was approaching a wall, a hedge, or a fence. But as I advanced the obstacle retreated in front of me. Also when I looked at objects there was often a kind of halo of golden light around them. After a time I became accustomed to these things, deciding that they were probably due to some kind of eye-strain from the days spent in the dark truck.

When I had covered perhaps two miles heavy rain began to fall, and the going became soft, with mud and soft earth in most of the fields. I stopped to relieve myself, and to rearrange my clothes.

I took off my civilian trousers and tied them around my neck in order to keep them as clean as possible. Although I was boiling hot from so much crawling and running, I could feel my legs swiftly chilling under the heavy battle-dress trousers and the long, woollen pants. I checked over the contents of my pockets, for if I could not find Wally, I would be entirely dependent on what I carried myself.

In one pocket of my Australian greatcoat was the German water-bottle. I greedily drank what remained in it, perhaps three mouthfuls. In the other greatcoat pocket were my shaving and washing things. In my inner pockets I had my money and maps, my knife, two handkerchiefs, a pair of socks and the British Army chocolate emergency ration in its gold tin. This last had been in my possession since our convoy had left Glasgow, bound for North Africa.

While checking over these things I looked constantly into the dark country around me. The electric lights had been switched on in the marshalling yard. I noticed that between that strip of light and the place where I was there were two lights which appeared to follow my course directly across the fields. At first I paid little attention to this, and then with the movement of the lights I began to associate the yapping and whining of dogs, a noise which irresistibly reminded me of the melodramatic police dogs at Stalag VIIA.

Keeping the lights of the marshalling yard directly behind me, I ran steadily on into the muddy fields. It was really a lope, something between a run and a walk. I was beginning to get worried again, for I had just realised that, since they had caught some of the Frenchmen, they might know that there had been British officers in the truck. In that case the search would certainly be a serious one. My optical illusions continued, and indeed grew worse. After throwing behind me one of the most intense of these imaginary barriers, a high, cream-coloured wall, I suddenly came upon a man.

He was a small, square man wearing a cap and breeches, rather like an English countryman. He carried a shot-gun under one arm.

"Good evening," he said in German. I repeated his greeting and walked on away from him. As soon as I could not see him I ran for a bit, then stopped to listen for following footsteps. I heard none. But the two lights and the noise of dogs still followed me.

Farther on I made a big circle, trying to remember all that I had read about the wiles of the hunted fox, and then continued on my way. I marked the area where I had made the circle, for there was a well-defined line of dark bushes there. When the two lights reached this line I saw them check and falter, waving slightly from side to side.

I became very nervous, imagining that I heard the patter of dogs' feet, the panting of their breath. I took my knife out and held it open in my hand. Occasionally I jumped at shadows. The dark holds strange, deep, old terrors for me when I am alone in it.

It was a small stream laid there by providence. I stumbled into it and waded up it for about half a mile. The water felt good sucking inside my boots. Sometimes it was below my ankles, sometimes over my knees.

When I left the stream I was drawing near the hills which I had seen from the edge of the marshalling yard. Between me and the hills there was a large house with considerable farm steading. I began to work my way round to the left of the house

204

and found that I must cross a fairly wide, poplar-lined avenue leading to the court-yard of the house.

Darting across the avenue, I fell smack into a deep ditch on the far side. My fall made a considerable noise, and the road-way behind me was instantly illuminated. The light came from the headlights of a car stationed at the far end. I heard boots on the road, and I snaked out of the ditch, crawling away from the road over flat smooth pasture.

After an hour's crawling and walking I found myself in this uncomfortable position: I was in a triangular piece of ground containing some young coverts and bushes. The sides of the triangle were formed by three roads. Its total area was perhaps sixteen acres. The three roads were patrolled by troops in black uniforms with machine-gun posts at four different points. There were also numbers of men in civilian clothes, armed either with long rifles or with shot-guns. These civilians came in bodies into my triangle to beat the patches of wood and scrub. It was easy to avoid their searching so long as it was dark and they remained unintelligent. I lay out in the middle of the fields, among the turnips, trying every now and then to make my way across one or other of the roads. They were too well watched, and I did not know that I should be any better off if I managed to get across.

The fine rain came steadily down, and with all my crawling and my fall into the deep ditch I was in a pitiable state. Despite all this dampness I had a raging thirst—such a thirst that I sucked at the wet turnip tops, and chewed the legs of the soaking blue trousers that were hanging from my neck.

When the first pale light appeared in the east I decided that the time had come to destroy the few papers I carried, and this I did by tearing them into small pieces which I hid as I crawled about the fields. I had written one address and drawn a map on the back of a small photograph of Anne. It was an un-pleasant war-time photograph showing her standing on the roof of a factory drinking a mug of something that steamed. I ate it with great difficulty. Why I ate it I do not know. Something melodramatic about the gesture must have attracted my mind, fuddled with exhaustion. The taste was extremely nasty.

Now that I had prepared myself against capture—I had an idea that I might pass as a Frenchman in order to have more chance of getting another opportunity to escape—I decided to risk something to reach the huge barn behind the big house. Once there I might hide in the hay, the warm, dry hay.

It took me half an hour to crawl and walk to the neighbour-hood of the barn, and when I got there I saw that there were troops sheltering there. Nearer still there was a machine-gun post, situated on the avenue, at a distance of seventy yards from the big house. While I lay there, cold, miserable, and exhausted by my efforts of the past three nights, I listened to the soldiers talking around the machine-gun. I listened because there was nothing else to do, and then something struck me about their talk.

One of them had said something in French.

"Faut en finir," he had said. Or was it my imagination? No more French words occurred, but the German they spoke was completely incomprehensible to me. I decided that they must be Alsatians. Now I lay, and the warmth of my body puddled the ground into soft mud, and I laid my face sideways on the mud and relaxed my body. For some time I thought of digging myself a grave and burying myself, leaving only a breathing hole. But it was too late for that, and too cold. My mind began to play around the Alsatians. Surely they were S.S. troops? And I had heard that many Frenchmen who escaped from German prison camps managed to get themselves enrolled in the S.S. at Strasbourg. The escaping chief at Munich had told me stories to show how disaffected many of the Alsatian troops in the German army had lately become. And anyway I was cold, and so tired that soon I would no longer have the power of movement, but only of sleep.

So I stood up in the mud and shouted in very bad German:

"I am a British officer, an escaped prisoner of war. I am unarmed, tired, hungry and thirsty. I intend to cross the road."

From my first word there had been dead silence around me. I saw the figures on the roadway unnaturally still and bending forward towards me. Otherwise I would not have been certain that I had spoken.

I stumbled across the field towards the road. When I came to it I fell into the deep ditch for the second time. I nearly lay there. But instead I scrambled wildly out. The machine-gun post was twenty yards to my left. The group of soldiers stood around it, silent, watching me. I walked slowly across the road, stepped over the smaller ditch on the far side, and walked, wondering, into the field beyond.

As I moved slowly into the country the men in black uniforms followed me, but at a distance of about 200 yards and on either flank. I orientated myself on the lights of the marshalling yard and moved off to the left of it in a direction which I judged to be north-west.

I expected to be stopped by Germans at any moment, for I thought that the men behind me probably took me for a parachutist and were playing with me, waiting until I should drop into some fool-proof ambush.

After half a mile of slow walking I did run into three Germans. They were in some kind of sentry post, and they shone a large torch or a small searchlight on me. I turned and moved off, and I heard them chattering behind me.

Then I had great difficulty in picking my way through the outbuildings of a large farm, and when I came to the other side I found that I was walking straight into the barbed-wire entanglements of what was apparently a small defensive position of the Siegfried or the Maginot Line. There were three Germans behind the wire in what the British Army calls the kneeling-load position. Again, they did not fire, and I changed direction, walking off into the country, a desolate country rather like the outer holes of a West of Scotland golf-course, Troon, say, or Prestwick, or Western Gailes, but not quite so hilly and accidented.

Soon this country flattened out, but keeping its sandy rushy character and I found myself in an area thickly dotted with army camps. White bell tents, sometimes in groups surrounded by fences, sometimes standing free. I thought I was still being followed.

To pass between the camps I was obliged to walk along a small sunken lane. I had difficulty in sticking to the muddy surface of the lane, for I was now so tired that I swayed alarmingly from side to side. I was only aware of this because I repeatedly bumped into first one bank, then the other, like a child on a pony practising for the bending race.

As I came to a small village, just a row of dirty hovels, I saw another dark-uniformed man approaching me on a bicycle. When he saw me he dismounted, crouched down with his steel-helmeted head low over the handle-bars and his machine-pistol levelled at me under one arm. Holding this attitude he slowly walked to meet me, but some small distance before we met he suddenly turned up a small lane, between two hovels.

I thought again that this was the end, and I felt so weary that I think I would have followed a schoolgirl meekly to jail. But when I passed the end of the lane I saw that the man in uniform had laid his gun along his handle-bars, and held his hands across his eyes in the attitude of the monkey that sees no evil.

A few hundred yards farther down the lane I met a milkboy on an old hulk of a bicycle with rattling cans swinging from the handle-bars. The thought of fresh milk possessed me. I stopped him with outstretched arms and asked him for a drink. But no sooner were the first words out of my mouth than he turned with a scream, leaped on his bicycle, and pedalled furiously away in the direction he had come from. This brought me partially to my senses.

I left the lane and crossed to a large wood on the left. I plunged into the trees and worked quickly through them. On the other side I could see no sign of German pursuit. In the foreground were the railway lines leading out of the marshalling yard bottle-neck. There were two large girder bridges across the railway lines. The nearer of the bridges had a sentry beside it. The sentry was leaning his elbows on the parapet of the road-way viaduct leading to the bridge. His back expressed sleep and boredom.

I walked silently to the entry to the bridge, under cover the whole way. The sentry had not moved. I darted across the road, reached the mouth of the big bridge and walked quite normally across it. There was no shout behind me, and on the other side I saw a peaceful, flat landscape with men of the early morning railway shift beginning to trickle along the road towards me.

My clothes were in an appalling state. I was covered with a thick layer of mud. Even my hair was tangled and matted with mud. My civilian trousers were still knotted round my neck. I wore battle-dress trousers, but these were no longer khaki, they were mud-grey. I took off my overcoat and carried it.

The workers passed me on foot and on bicycles. Some of them gave me *"Guten Tag"*. None of them stared. I began to pick up confidence and strength with each step. The sun was coming up. I opened the brass tin and began surreptitiously to munch a little of the chocolate that I had carried with me through what I had seen of Egypt, Libya, Tripolitania, Italy and Germany.

It tasted musty. Already the night began to seem like a bad dream. Then, I did not question the sequence of events which I have just related. Now, re-writing this from notes I made at the time, two years ago, I wonder if I did not hurt my head when

I first fell into the deep ditch; if from that time until the moment that I crossed the railway bridge I was not suffering from some unpleasant form of hallucination. Sometimes still I dream of the silent men in dark uniforms who watched me cross the avenue, and of the sickly taste of Anne's photograph.

Walking down the road as the early sun began to reach my damp person, I had no time to think back.

I came to a T-junction, and turned left down a main road. What I was looking for was a quiet place, a wood or a copse, in which to change and clean myself. There were plenty of copses and clumps of bushes in that weird, flat landscape. But every single one was marked with a notice-board saying "Property of the Wehrmacht, Entry Forbidden". There were pill-boxes liberally scattered about the place too, and so well hidden that I was certain that I was in the fringes of the Maginot Line.

Rounding a bend, I saw a road block about 400 yards ahead. There were a couple of German sentries guarding it. As I watched, a cyclist passed the block, apparently with only an airy wave of his hand, but it was clearly no place for me. I turned in my tracks and took the first little country road on the left. leading away from the railway. Really I could not have struck a worse bit of country for my purpose. Everywhere, on every bit of cover, I saw the Wehrmacht notices. Although the roads were not busy, it seemed that there was always someone within sight, either walking towards me or following me.

It was nearly eight o'clock when my road ran through a large village. I still had not had an opportunity even to straighten my hair. My heart was in my mouth as I walked steadily through. There were quite a number of people about, and I thought that they looked at me suspiciously. When I passed three people, two elderly men and a woman, standing in the doorway of a house—a doorway from which gushed an entrancing aroma of toasting bread—I heard one of the men say: "What is *he* doing?"

Just after this, to my delight, I saw a canal. I turned down the bank on a tow-path and, taking advantage of the first cover I saw, slithered down into a small coppice concealing a disused machine-gun post at the head of an anti-tank ditch running at right angles to the canal.

There, alongside one of the Wehrmacht notices, I stripped to the skin and cleaned all my clothes with soap, a scrubbing-brush, and water fetched in my water-bottle from the canal. When I had got the mud off them I spread them out and scrubbed myself all over. Then I put my clothes on wet, ate two more cubes of chocolate, and drank canal water strained from my water-bottle through my handkerchief into my hand. Its colour and taste were so utterly repulsive that it killed my thirst.

I was just beginning to shave when a very old man in some sort of semi-nautical uniform passed along the bank above me. He spoke to me with a peculiar accent, but I made out the German word for ships, and gathered that he was asking me if I had come off one of the barges. I replied that I did, and he told me angrily that I was not allowed on that side of the canal. Blessing the few German lessons I had taken in prison, I thanked him briefly in the heaviest French accent that I could muster, and he took his creaking old carcase away.

When I had shaved I buried my battle-dress trousers beside the machine-gun nest and moved off up the canal. My clothes looked surprisingly fresh and good to me, although my boots, criss-crossed with white lines of wetness, could have done with some polish. The sun was shining, and I felt a new man.

I felt that an important phase of my escape was ending, and another was beginning.

But it had not really begun, for I wandered all morning looking in vain for shelter, even the shelter of a quiet wood.

Most of the morning I spent on the other tow-path, the one on which the tractors worked, dragging the barges from lock to lock. I followed one road away from the tow-path for about a mile, looking for woods to rest in. But I saw only small Maginot forts and German troops, and the road led into a village where a youth asked me the way to somewhere. I replied hastily that I did not know since I also was a stranger, a Czech. This incident frightened me, and I hastened back to the canal-bank.

From the tow-path I saw a large black barge on the other side. The barge was named *D'Artagnan*. It was obviously French, and a middle-aged woman sat on deck, peeling potatoes.

"*Bonjour, Madame,*" I said to her across the water.

"*Bonjour, jeune homme.*"

"You are French, Madame?"

"Indeed yes. young man."

"I think I shall cross by the bridge and talk to you for a moment."

But at that moment a tractor came fussing up the tow-path. It was driven by a very Germanic-looking young man with a square face, wide, pale-blue eyes, and flaxen hair. He seized the tow-rope of *D'Artagnan*, made it fast to his tractor, and tugged the barge away. As he did this he cast me what I thought was a sinister and piercing look. I walked up the tow-path for several miles.

At last, when I was feeling very tired, I saw another French barge, the *Sara Bernhardt*. She also was moored on the other side, near a bridge. I crossed and spoke to a tall young man who sat on deck, one thin arm draped around the massive tiller, reading a gaudily-backed novel by Georges Simenon.

"I'd like to help you," said this young man. "But you don't look French, and you speak with a foreign accent."

"I know I do. I am a British officer."

"You don't say. Name of God, I am proud to meet you." He took his arm off the tiller and stretched it limply out to shake my hand. "Good heavens," he continued. "We have never seen any of you people around here before. Ordinary evaders, yes, hundreds. When the Gestapo feel like it they come down that tow-path and pick up a score or so in the afternoon, just like that. . . . *Oi, oi, oi,* life is difficult now for the evaders. There was a time when they just jumped on one of our barges, went to sleep, and next thing they knew they were over the frontier, in France. Not so now. Now the Boches search the barges with dogs. And they have informers all up and down the canals, from here to Paris.

"Two months ago I would have taken you on my ship here, and proud to do it. Now I dare not. The wife is *enceinte*. Six months gone, and a whopper. It's our first, too. Dare not risk it. You just walk down the tow-path again to the Port of Strasbourg. Address yourself to any French bargeman there. You'll be all right. Beware of the Alsatian and the Belgian bargemen. Then you'll be all right."

Feeling very far from all right, I walked wearily back down the tow-path which seemed much less secure now. When I came to the point where I had hailed the first barge I found my way barred by the Germanic-looking young tractor driver.

"Unless I am mistaken you have escaped from Germany," he said in strangely guttural French.

"You are mistaken," I answered mistrustfully.

"Nonsense, my friend. I have seen too many of you poor fellows to be mistaken now. And I have helped too many. One day I will lose my ears or my tongue for it. But I still cannot bear to see you passing, cold and hungry. Listen. I am Dutch, and I like to help the French. I hope that you will come into the café there and have a drink with me. Yes?"

As I followed his squat figure to the dingy, square brick building marked *Hôtel* I did not know whether to feel intensely hopeful or intensely suspicious. I was in his hands, the stumpy, black-grained hands of the tractor driver.

CHAPTER XVI

THE warmth, the human smell of that dingy café room lapped around me like the blandishments, the adoration of an expert courtesan.

My Dutch host led me to a table where three working men already sat. They spoke to each other in the Alsatian dialect, glancing knowingly at me, and offering me cigarettes. I refused, for I was too hungry and thirsty to smoke. So they gave me glass after glass of ersatz coffee. There was no milk in it, but it was boiling hot, with a lump of sugar in each glass. I felt better minute by minute, better, and a little sleepy in the warmth.

"Now you are thawed we shall give you something to strengthen you a little," said the Dutchman. The strengthener was a fairly potent red wine. Each of the four ordered a bottle. Although I drank a considerable amount, it seemed to have no effect on my head. My body took it as nourishment.

"You will eat with me in the restaurant next door," said the Dutchman. "Be careful not to talk French there. It's forbidden by law, you know, although nobody much bothers about that in Alsace. But there are three or four ardent Nazis who always eat there, and I make a point of sitting with them. Just buckle up your lips. By the way, what part of France do you come from?"

"Normandy."

Something about the Dutchman did not please me. I was nervous and ill at ease with him.

"*Oi.* You must dump that thing," he said, pointing at my greatcoat. "*Trop militaire, mon vieux, trop militaire.*"

So I left it in the café. When I got up to go the old woman came out from behind the bar and brushed down my clothes with the kind of stiff, whalebone brush that we use for dogs or horses at home.

The restaurant, which was next door to the café-hotel, was extremely German in tone, with three of the stock portraits of Adolf Hitler on the walls. The clientèle favoured cropped hair and either Hitler or Kaiser Wilhelm moustaches. The Dutchman shared his own lunch with me. It was a sausage stew carried in an aluminium can, and he ordered hot vegetables from the woman who put plates and watery beer in front of us. I still felt mistrustful of the Dutchman, but grateful to him, and very sleepy and dependent on him, like a cat that does not want to be turned out into the cold. I was beginning to wonder if I would find shelter that night.

It was plain that the Dutchman did not intend to do any more for me. I repeatedly led the conversation round to the night, and he skilfully evaded the issue. Finally he advised me to get in touch with one Eugène, another tractor driver, "who sometimes helps evaders".

Accordingly after our meal I said good-bye, feeling forlorn and lonely. I again followed the tow-path, but this time on a part that was new to me. I half expected to be chased, for although the Dutchman had seemed only to be kind and friendly, I could not be sure. When I came to the point where he had advised me to wait for Eugène I stretched out in the long grass beside the tow-path and felt at peace as the food digested noisily in my empty insides, and the good yellow sun played on my face and hands.

A short distance away on the far bank an old man was dismally fishing, as though he hated his rod, the canal, the sun, everything. A small boy, who played near him, asked about me in French.

"Who's that funny man, grandad?"

"How should I know? Looks like a Fritz."

I longed to shout at him: "I am not German."

The tractor came roaring towards me, very fast, unimpeded by trailing barges, and with two plumes of dust fanning out from its huge back wheels. It was a smart grey tractor, with a small awning type of roof on four supports to protect the driver from rain or sun, like the roofs on old British steam-road-rollers.

I stood in the middle of the tow-path and signalled the bounding tractor to a stop. A youngish man climbed down, leaving the engine turning. It turned noisily, for it was a wood-burning *gazogène*. I was obliged to shout:

"Eugène?"

"That's me."

He was a smallish man, but muscular, with a type of good looks in his face that reminded me of Georges Carpentier, or a roughened version of that boxer. He wore a tight-fitting pale-pink jersey with short sleeves clinging to the lines of his biceps. His headgear was an ordinary small French beret to which a patent leather scoop surmounted by a gold cord had been sewn, to give a dashing, slightly comic-opera, nautical touch. His French was throaty and wet. But he spoke well. I could see that he was Alsatian, but I liked and trusted him at once.

"Evader?" he asked.

"Yes."

"What nationality?"

"British."

"Come clean. You speak French with a German accent, and you are too well dressed to be an evader. Who sent you to me?"

"The Dutchman."

"That rat." He spat reflectively into the canal, and eyed me up and down. He was not going to commit himself.

"British or German," he finally said, "I like the look of you. Just give me a hand with those barges waiting by the lock there. Then we'll have a drink and a good talk. Eh?"

I blessed my short experience as a deck-hand. For I was able to help him unclumsily with the towing hawsers. The keynote to his obvious character was a kind of bursting, strong-man vanity. His open smile revealed several gold teeth. He bellowed amicable and amorous jests across the calm canal at the women on the barges. He drove his tractor with frenzied dash, attempting every moment to strain the towing hawser to bursting-point.

While he drove I stood on the back of the tractor, hanging on by the rear uprights of the roof, my feet on either side of the stiff hawser. Now, with Eugène, I felt that I might get somewhere. And the country, which had seemed sinister to me that morning, picked up a cultivated charm. I noticed the trim allotments, the poplars, the rosy children, the placid brown waters of the canal cradling the lovely rounded lines of the French, Dutch and Belgian barges.

Canals have always held great charm for me. Stealing through a country on a canal is the most restful way to move. This was the Seine and Marne Canal. Sliding along its oily waters you could reach Paris—in peace-time.

When we had dealt with all the barges we chugged down to a little shed where we filled up the *gasogène*-burner with white wood chips. After this the tractor refused to start. We went to the inn by the lock to telephone for a mechanic.

"I drive this old nail for the company," he said to me. "I am not paid to be a *mecano*, so why should I do the job of the *mecano?*"

Before we entered the inn he warned me to keep silent.

"Two German sisters run it," he said. "They're fine people. But they'd fry you in oil. They think the British are behind every trouble in the universe."

It was a shining inn kitchen, with a nearly white, stone floor, white walls, and highly polished brass and china everywhere. The younger of the two sisters looked like my flaxen-haired sister. They offered us glasses of greenish-coloured white wine, but Eugène refused for both of us, whispering to me from the telephone: "Never mind. We'll have one elsewhere."

He took me over the bridge and up a long, winding village street to a large and old-fashioned café where we drank many blonde beers. Here Eugène relaxed and trusted in me. Or pretended to.

"Don't attempt to cross into France by barge," he warned me. "It does not work any more. I have a better plan for you. You're a nice-looking lad. When your hair is cut and waved you'll look quite like me. To-morrow I'll take you to the barber's in Strasbourg. The following day early I'll put you, with my papers, on the workers' train to Mulhouse. I'll give you a note to the station-master there. He's Gaulliste to the core. He'll put you in a sealed wagon going to Nancy or some other town. To-night and to-morrow night regard yourself as Eugène's guest, Eugène's honoured guest. By the way, what rank are you? Colonel? Only a lieutenant. Oh well, we can't all be generals, can we? I was a leading seaman. But of course promotion is very slow in our navy."

Every moment his swagger became more exaggerated. I could see that he was thrilled to see himself in the part of rescuer of a British officer. Too thrilled perhaps.

Returning to the canal we stopped to talk to every girl we met in the street. Eugène was a pawer. At the slightest excuse he laid hands on a girl. They seemed to like his blandishments. His gaiety was infectious. He was so sure of himself. Down by the bridge he had half an hour's conversation with some old men and two youngish women who were airing their fat babies in prams. I took no part in this conversation, which was all in the incomprehensible Alsatian dialect, except to smile brightly and nod two or three times.

After this the irrepressibly sociable man led me over to a

party sitting on the bank beside two German barges. These were steel barges, square-shaped and clumsy compared with the graceful ones of other nationalities, but spotlessly clean, shining with paint and metal-polish. Two of the men were in German uniform. They were on leave. With a swaggering rush, the Alsatian introduced me to these people as a Dutch friend, a refugee.

I left him with his German friends, and sat down beside the tractor which waited disconsolately there with its bonnet open. Lulled by the gentle canal noises and the fluty singing of some French children on a near-by barge, I was soon asleep.

The engine was noisily turning and a man was shaking me by the shoulder and talking to me in some unknown language. It was the mechanic, and he was speaking to me in Dutch, since Eugène had told him that that was my nationality. I answered him in French, and he went away sadly shaking his head.

"I thought I spoke Dutch better than that," he said sadly to Eugène. "It must be the accent. It's a long time since I was there."

The day's work was done, and we drove far up the canal to the garage of the tractor company. He drove like a madman through the canal-side evening peace, swirling round the narrow double corners where the tow-path swung towards the water to twist under the bridges. When we had garaged the tractor he produced a dashing silver bicycle which had a carrier over the back wheel.

"You will sit on that, Georges," he said. "And we'll be home in three seconds. It's only about five kilometres."

Eugène did everything with the same furious energy. He pedalled home as though we were competing in a six-day bicycle race. The little electric generator under my right thigh buzzed and throbbed and the light cast a long yellow jet in front of us. It looked beautiful, the country and the solid town. We passed through woods and crossed two fine streams. Soon we were in the middle of Strasbourg.

"If we meet a *flic* I'll try to ride past him," said Eugène. "But if you see that we have not enough velocity you must jump off the carrier and beat it. You are not allowed to double up like this in Germany. It is avoiding road taxes, or bicycle taxes, or something. Life is taxed, death is taxed, wives are taxed, sweat is taxed."

We reached his home without incident. It was in a big tenement building on a corner. Eugène hauled his bicycle up the first flight of stairs and stopped at a doorway on which he beat a resounding tattoo.

A hard-faced young woman with dark hair and glasses opened the door and eyed us both a little sourly. Much less affable with his wife than he had been with the girls on the canal-side, he thrust his bicycle into the narrow passage-way of a hall and surged through into the kitchen, beckoning me to follow.

It was a bare little kitchen with washing hanging in one corner, the minimum of cheap cupboard space, and a small, tiled range. A thin, pale-faced small boy sat at the linoleum-covered table which was laid with three places. The woman arranged a fourth place silently and joylessly while Eugène scoured his oil- and soot-blackened face and hands and washed with a great splashing and spluttering under the single tap.

We ate potatoes with some kind of gravy. After that there was a tiny piece of cheese for the four of us.

"Food is scarce," said Eugène darkly. "Especially in this house, although both of us are working."

The woman said nothing. I saw that she was tired and that she loved him, although he was difficult to live with. Nobody but Eugène had spoken since we arrived. He was what is known as "master in his own house". It was a sad house.

After the meal he dressed me in a pair of black breeches with thick, cable-stitched brown stockings coming up to my knees and a loud coat, too curving about the lapels, with a savage stripe in the material, much padding in the shoulders, and a pinch waist. He disliked my plain blue tie, and gave me a louder one which he said was "more swing". On my head he fixed a rakish black cap, saying: "Now, Georges, don't take that off wherever you go. Your hair is too long for all these nice clothes. I must say," he ended appreciatively, "you now look a real *seigneur*."

He himself put on a white cap, a dark, waisted coat (like mine, but newer), black breeches and tall, patent leather riding-boots which he claimed had been captured by the Germans on the Russian front. He became a cross between a French apache and a roystering German.

"These boots and breeches are useful to me," he said half-apologetically. "The Germans are stupid enough to think that any Alsatian is a Nazi who wears the breeches and boots which they admire so much."

His wife had also dressed up to go out, but more ordinarily, in a black coat with a small fur, and a high black hat.

The three of us walked into the centre of Strasbourg. The black-out was very thorough, and my eyes still played me tricks.

We stopped at a café called Grinzing. Eugène flung back the green baize curtains masking the door, and we were enveloped in a wave of noise and smoke, rude German laughter, and the fumes of beer and wine. It was an L-shaped room with a bar in the short leg of the L and small tables down the other walls. Behind the bar was a stock picture of Hitler, and the radio greeted our arrival with the latest German waltz. The place was packed to suffocation point.

But the energetic Eugène, nipping the behinds off the two stout waitresses, managed to have one end of a table cleared to permit us to squeeze ourselves in. The rest of the table was occupied by three young German naval officers, very shy and clean and polite, and one blonde Alsatian prostitute who was evidently bored by her too correct companions, and was casting a roving eye around her for more calloused and profitable game.

Some of the German officers were openly lecherous with the girls at their tables. The women appeared to accept this treatment as normal, although some of them looked as though they came from respectable families. There was drunkenness even among the women. One young woman, fattish but pretty enough, climbed on a table and did a loose imitation of a fandango, clacking her flaccid fingers and lifting her skirts above her knees.

The young Germans at my table could not take their eyes off those knees.

"The fräulein is very, very pretty," my neighbour observed to me. I replied coldly in French that I did not speak German. Eugène kicked me below the table.

"He must learn our beautiful German, must he not?" he said oilily to the young officer. "After all, it is still an offence to speak French here."

But the German, annoyed perhaps by his accent and his familiarity, looked at him coldly as though he were some animal crawling out from under a stone, and made no reply. To me he politely smiled.

We drank red wine out of half-pint glasses. I noticed with some concern that Eugène drank quickly, and became quickly affected by the alcohol. I was thankful when, after two rounds of drinks, he hissed into my ear: "Here are our friends. The organisation."

My heart sank when I looked at the "organisation". There were five of them, two women and three men, and there was no room for such a large party at Grinzing, so we moved to another café. All of them were elevated by alcohol, and they all wanted to talk at once.

Milo, a little round-faced man in a handsome spotted bow tie, was there with his wife, tiny, auburn-haired, with soft brown eyes. Dédé, a man in the fifties, cadaverous and grey-haired, with a loud voice and a ranting manner, was there with a faded and puffy blonde, a girl friend for the night. The only one of them who interested me was Alban, a small pig-faced Frenchman from the Dordogne who spoke with a delightful Southern accent. While the others vinously talked and argued among themselves Alban sat with me in a corner. He told me that he had been sent by the Germans as a civilian worker to Vienna. He had "escaped" from there by enrolling in the S.S., knowing that when he had done this the German authorities would give him money, railway tickets, and passes, to get to Strasbourg, where he was supposed to report for enlistment. Instead of reporting he had thrown his German papers into the river, and had been living off his wits in the town for six weeks before my arrival.

"Don't pay any attention to these people," he warned me. "They are a useless lot except for Dédé, and he might be dangerous. He was in Vienna too, and he got away the same way that I did. But he went the length of enlisting in the S.S. here. He even has his uniform. I've seen it. The advantage about him is that he's got plenty of money. He makes it by painting views of the town, and they pay him several hundred marks a time for them at the art-shop near the cathedral. I know that's the truth, because I've taken canvases there for him, and they've actually paid me the money. Dédé likes to have a crowd of admirers around him, so he tolerates these others. Milo works in a factory outside Strasbourg, and he's a decent little *père-de-famille* with three brats, nice ones too. But he's too soft for Dédé, and he's a fool. Soon he'll be worse. . . ."

"What exactly do you mean?"

"I mean that he'll soon be a cuckold. Look at the way his wife puts fire into her eyes when they rest on Dédé. Poor old

Milo. And he thinks she dotes on him. Like cuckolds all the world over.''

"How am I to get out of here and into France?''

"We'll think up a way. Just take it easy, and watch Dédé.''

"What about Eugène?''

"Him! He imagines he's Jean Gabin, or one of the gangster parts that Gabin plays. He's wax in Dédé's hands. But Dédé wouldn't dare to cuckold *him*. That Eugène is reputed to be an artist with the knife. . . .''

There was something perversely attractive in the cold immorality of Alban, in his slightly-protruding, shrewd brown eyes and the loose lips, always hanging open, over which an immense tongue often played. He wore a bright blue jacket, gathered at the back in an American fashion, long bag-shaped nether garments, of the type the French call *golfs* and the English used to call "plus-fours", and below these things a length of dirty white stocking appeared.

After a long discussion with Eugène, Dédé turned his attention to me. First he uttered several phrases which I could not understand, but which were evidently supposed to be in English. He looked mistrustful and disappointed, and I heard him whisper to the others: "This is no Englishman.''

He pooh-poohed Eugène's scheme to get me away by Mulhouse.

"Absolutely absurd, absolute lunacy,'' he said. "Eugène, *mon cher*, you are always in too much of a hurry. You are a big strong baby, good with his knife, who wants to butt everything over at once with his own animal strength. For this case of the British officer we must have brains. We must have a PLAN.''

Soon the café shut, and we were turned out into the street. It was arranged that we would meet the following morning in a café by the river to discuss plans for getting me away. Before following Dédé into the darkness his blonde girl friend, to my astonishment, leaped upon little Alban, kissed him passionately, and exclaimed in her husky voice: "That pig has money, but you know how to love.''

"That is the truth,'' agreed Alban frankly in his broad accent.

Eugène seemed to be a little embarrassed on the walk home.

"Never mind, Georges,'' he said. "I'll see that you get away somehow, even if Dédé forbids it.''

"Why should he forbid it?''

"He's the chief, and he must be satisfied that you're not a

German spy. I work with my heart. I know, I just feel that you're all right. Dédé is a thinker. He works with his brain. But once he makes a plan for you it will be good. By the way, our house is no palace. You won't mind sleeping with us, will you?"

"My dear fellow, not in the least."

There were two double beds in their bedroom. Eugène and his wife occupied one, myself and the small boy the other. Eugène's wife, a taciturn creature, explained to me that the boy was not hers but was the son of one of her husband's former mistresses. Further, she warned me that he was a piss-a-bed. My bed had a rubber sheet, and smelled strongly of both rubber and urine. However, the cotton sheets and the pillow-case were clean.

I lay awake listening to the heavy breathing of Eugène and his wife. The sleeping child put his arm around my neck. To my surprise I felt bed-bugs biting me. The place had seemed too clean for that. But in a tenement they can circulate by the chimneys, or so they told me later.

The others were nearly an hour late at our rendezvous the following morning. It was Eugène's day off, and he was annoyed at being obliged to waste it in this dull, if patriotic, manner. However, Dédé at once put us all in a good humour by standing us an excellent lunch, washed down with both wine and kirsch.

Dédé was much more affable to me than he had been on the previous evening. Seen in the bright daylight he had a horribly sharp, foxy face. His hands were in an advanced state of shakiness, and, like his teeth, were heavily stained with nicotine. He was a neurotic, and his conceit obliged him to seize the centre of the stage at all times. If anybody else began to venture an opinion he interrupted with a merciless: "You permit me, *mon cher.*"

Over the coffee and the kirsch he said to me: "Gee, baby, but you're swell," or words to that effect. Fortunately I replied without thinking: "Gee, baby, so are you." Whereupon he turned to the others and said: "All right, boys, the chief is satisfied. I knew Georges was neither English nor German. The answer is simple. He is American." My assent to his statement was not demanded.

They discussed plans then. All that emerged from some hours of talking was that Milo was eventually to make a trip to Mulhouse to try out the land there.

H

Already I was disgusted with these drink shop-plotters. I could see that the others, even to some extent the shrewd Alban, were obsessed with Dédé, his lightning speech, his bad manners, and above all his wealth. He claimed to have been a captain in the French Air Force (although he kept his soft hat on all through lunch) and admitted that he was in the German S.S.— "But only to learn their military secrets, *mon cher*. The Intelligence Service, hein? You understand?"

I could have kicked him. It is insulting when such people are convinced that their shallow lies and extravagances take you in.

Milo took me to his flat, two bedrooms and a tiny kitchen on the sixth floor of a rickety building behind the cathedral, and gave me a pair of *golfs*—an enormous pair that hung nearly to my ankles. Then I had my hair cut short in the German manner. The shop was crowded. Milo took the barber aside and whispered (I shuddered to think what) into his ear. So the operation passed without conversation on either side. Dressed in the *golfs*, I felt entirely un-British. But the moment Dédé saw me he exclaimed: *"Très chic,* but much too English."

Eugène and his family came as my guests to the circus that night. We dined early, off potatoes as usual, and the four of us left on two bicycles. The circus was a small French one in a tent on the outskirts of the town. Half-way through an indifferent performance the sirens sounded an alert and the audience stampeded for the doors. Eugène was very nervous.

Before we went to bed he said that we had been taking too many risks.

"I was crazy to allow you to go out like that to-night," he exclaimed. "And henceforward I beg that you will remain indoors through the day, and only go out at nights when accompanied by me. I don't fear for myself, but for my home and my family. My wife leaves this place at 4 a.m. to queue for potatoes. At seven she comes back to take the child to school and go to her work. She comes home to eat at midday. To-morrow, if you would be good enough to boil the potatoes, you can spend a nice quiet day arranging your clothes and resting."

The following morning I took advantage of the empty flat to wash myself and my spare socks and handkerchiefs. It was lonely in the flat, with the bustling noises of the tenement all round me. I had to keep the shutters half-closed because people might see in from the street.

When Eugène's wife came in at midday she attempted to be

normal, picking with a rusty fork at the potatoes which I had over-boiled. Then she thrust her plate away and burst into tears. A long story came tumbling out. She was overworked. Eugène no longer paid any attention to her. He kept running the most appalling risks. Her mother had heard the children talking in the tenement yard, saying that there was a strange man in Eugène's place. Her mother was very angry. She did not know if it would be safe for me to stay there.

That evening, when Eugène returned, grimy and bad-tempered, I told him that I must leave his place at once.

"Where else could you go?" he asked non-committally.

Later, in Grinzing, we sat down beside a strange Frenchman who had already made the acquaintance of Dédé.

"How the devil do I know you are genuine?" I heard Eugène ask the stranger; and forthwith the Frenchman produced two enormous pocket-books stuffed with papers and photographs. For some time we examined these. He was a French N.C.O., a regular in a cavalry regiment. His name was Ramon Delgado, for he was of Spanish ancestry and his father was a wine-grower in North Africa. He also was an escaped prisoner of war, and he claimed that he wanted to continue his journey to North Africa to fight for de Gaulle.

My first impression of Ramon was good. He had dark, greasy hair, and rather ridiculous little side-whiskers, grown long and curving to the finest of points near the bottom of his ears. But to offset the whiskers he had a steady, olive-skinned Spanish face, a slightly sinister face, with rocky brown eyes under strong brows. He was well-built, and big for a Frenchman.

When we had repaired to the quieter café he took me by the hand, and said with numerous effulgent words and gestures that we would get out of Nazi-occupied Europe together, that we would be brothers, and that we would never part. I thought that his intentions were good and his sentiments honest.

Ramon said that he must find somewhere to sleep, and I explained that I would like to go with him, whereupon Dédé exclaimed: "I have just the place for you. The criminals' hide-out, *chez* Lucien." Ramon carefully took down the address, and we agreed to go there after we had paid a call on a friend of Alban's.

Alban pointed out that for nearly two months he had managed to live quite well in Strasbourg on what he called *combines* or *Système D*. Now he proposed to introduce us to one of his *combines*.

There is a street of brothels in the garrison town of Stras-ɔourg, a narrow, shadowy street in which the houses are all numbered more plainly than is normal. Alban took us to the parlour of Number Six, where he was affectionately greeted by the *sous-maîtresse,* a stout and kindly Czech lady. She had been evacuated from Strasbourg in 1939 when the French cleared all civilians from the Maginot area. Like many other inhabitants of that city, she had been sent to Alban's home country, the Dordogne. Their reception had been good there, much better than in many other parts of France where the evacuees became known as *les Boches de l'Est.* So the Dordogne had a good reputation in Strasbourg. Alban was cashing in on this reputa-tion, turning it into food and money and wine and beds.

٭ Now the Czech set drinks in front of us (*crèmes-de-menthe frappées*), and went off to see what she could find for Alban. Three of the other tables in the room were occupied by German soldiers in different stages of wooden embarrassment. The girls, Alban told us, were all German. None of them, apart from the *sous-maîtresse,* even spoke French or knew how to make love with French refinements. Ramon said that it was disgraceful that all the whores should be German in a French town. I thought that if it were a disgrace then the shame could be laid on Germany rather than on France.

"I forgot that you were British," Ramon apologised. "You all have such sentimental ideas about love." The *sous-maîtresse* arrived with some very splendid gifts "for that sweet lad, Alban, and his friends". There were cigarettes, German ones which at that time and place cost the equivalent of two pounds for a packet of twenty on the black market, and some tins of genuine Strasbourg *pâté de foie gras.* Ramon, a very heavy smoker, kept the cigarettes. Otherwise we handed everything over to Alban to help him operate his bartering *Système D.*

The criminals' hide-out proved to be a place of such utter filth that at first I refused to enter, let alone sleep there. This Lucien lived in two rooms in an old half-timbered building. The first room was a small kitchen crawling with cockroaches and smelling strongly of mice and decaying food. The second room was a revolting bedroom.

Lucien vacated the double bed, to let us sleep in it for the sum of ten marks a night (a high rent). He himself would sleep in the cot with his baby son. He proceeded to get in alongside the protesting infant, showing large and filthy bare feet as he did so.

Ramon whisked into the double bed as though this were Claridge's Hotel, and pronounced it "most yielding and comfortable". The sight and smell of the bed filled me with quaking nausea. But, since I did not want to make a bad impression, I managed to force myself to climb in, and I lay holding my breath while Ramon, in low swift sentences accompanied by the snores of Lucien, told me of his escape from Germany.

He had been working in a garage at Nuremberg, where he had a German mistress. He made a habit of spending one or two nights a week with this woman. One morning he was returning to the *Kommando* when a French friend stopped him. The Germans had held a roll-call that night. Ramon would be sent to a punishment camp if they caught him, perhaps to the salt-mines in Poland. Thereupon he returned to his lady friend. He spent eight more days with her, collecting from her and from his different friends sufficient money, clothing, and food to help him to escape. He also managed to buy forged papers showing that he was a civilian worker returning to France for medical treatment.

From Nuremberg station he took a third-class ticket to Strasbourg, a town which he had known as a soldier, and where he thought he would find old friends. The German police twice controlled the train on which he travelled. Each time he avoided the control by slipping unobserved into the lavatory, wedging himself behind the door, and holding the door *open*. If you locked yourself into the lavatory the police would knock on the door and demand your papers. Arrived in Strasbourg, Ramon had not been able to trace his former friends, except for one man who had put him in touch with "the chief of an organisation". In other words, Dédé. Ramon shared my low opinion of Dédé and his café accomplices.

"They are a lot of useless drunks," he said. "Except for Alban. That little boy is smart. We must work in with him."

I awoke at 4 a.m., and my squeamishness, if anything, had increased. I got out of bed, washed completely in the kitchen, hurried on my clothes, and sat in the cold on a hard wooden chair. There was a basket chair too, with a soft seat, but in that place the wooden one appealed to me more. At 7 a.m. Lucien got up and dragged off to work. Ramon slept on. There was one book in the place, a translation of a Wild West penny novelette. I read through to the happy ending. It was 11 a.m. I awoke Ramon, and told him that unless we left immediately I should be ill.

The child attracted my attention. It was crying and pointing down at the chamber-pot. I lifted it down, ashamed of my nausea at having to touch such repulsive living flesh. There were sores on its face, and one eye was askew. When it had finished on the chamber-pot it asked to be put back in bed, instead of running about the floor as a normal child would have done.

Ramon carried with him a cheap despatch-case which he called affectionately *la valise diplomatique*. From this he produced a large amount of food, including bread and butter and condensed milk. We gave some of this to the child. Shortly afterwards it began to cry. It had eaten ravenously and its stomach, unaccustomed to food of that nature, and probably to food of any kind, had become distended. Even Ramon's untender mind was horrified by Lucien's treatment of the child.

Lucien had told me that morning that his wife had left him for another man. He had divorced her, and had obtained the custody of the child. While relating this story Lucien wept, and protested that the child was all that mattered to him in life, and that although his wife had asked several times to have her child back, he would die rather than give it up.

We were delighted when young Alban arrived. Only for geniuses like Alban, with his thick accent and his southern tendency to break into falsetto song, was it possible to eat in Strasbourg without food coupons.

He took us into a small café near-by, and we ordered coffee while he went to talk to the proprietress. Soon he came back with a loaf of bread, and this we ate with some of the butter Ramon had brought from Nuremberg. The café had been a haunt of Ramon's when he was soldiering in that town. The proprietress, a knowing-looking, heavily-bosomed creature, cast us several long looks, and as we left the place she said in her throaty voice: "Be careful, *les gars*. Don't do anything I wouldn't do. And if you're desperate with hunger you can always come back to mother." After that we called her place "Mother's".

Ramon and I spent that day nosing round the town and the "port" where all the barges lay. I was still hoping against hope that the barge route would prove to be possible. To Ramon this route was distasteful.

"Stinking old tubs," he called the beautiful barges.

There was a scene at our table in Grinzing that evening. Little Milo was there alone, and in tears when Ramon and I arrived.

"The bottom has fallen out of my life," he told me, buying us drinks. Grinzing was the only café where one could always get wine.

"Explain yourself," Ramon said.

"My wife has run away with that swine Dédé. She is living with him. I do not know where she is. I cannot find him and kill him. Already it may be too late. . . ."

Ramon was strongly affected by this.

"Only find him, and I will kill him for you," he offered, flicking open his knife and testing the edge on the hairs of his hand. "That will leave you free to leather your wife."

"You do not understand," said Milo. "I love my wife. I would never hurt her."

"Then you deserve to lose her. . . ."

"What is all this?" asked Eugène, who joined us at that moment. He then vied with Ramon in threats as to what he would do to Dédé. Milo seemed to take heart from these threats, and from the strong moral support of his friends.

"All drinks are on me to-night," he said, ordering another round.

When Alban came in Milo jumped up from his seat, took three little steps across the floor of the café, and slapped Alban's face in front of an amused German audience. Ramon was greatly incensed at this. (After all, Alban had provided us with both breakfast and lunch that day.)

"Snake, Judas, betrayer," exclaimed Milo to the red-faced Alban. "You work hand in glove with the reptile Dédé. All the time you receive money from him. He was too stupid to see that my dear wife fancied him. It was you who put the idea into his head. Now I do not know where this man is seducing my beloved. But *you* know. Pimp, leech, back-stabber. . . ."

"Calm yourself, calm yourself, your wife is not worth all this emotion," Alban replied, licking his lips, and stealing a quick glance round our circle. "Yes, I know where they are. And I will take you there alone, you, but nobody else."

This was agreed to. An hour later Milo returned alone, and again in tears.

"I went to the room, a sordid hotel bedroom," he told us between sobs. "She was in bed, and Dédé was walking about the room in full S.S. uniform. He said to me: 'I am S.S., and I remain S.S. Do you understand exactly what I mean? And tell your friends, especially the American, or Englishman, or whatever he is, that they must clear out of this town before I get angry with them.' Then," ended Milo pathetically, "he ordered me to leave the room."

From this moment Ramon and Eugène despised Milo and called him *le cocu*.

While Milo attempted to drown his grief in red wine we were joined by a friend of his, a tall, very drunk man who, when we left, followed us out of the café and reeled with us round to the street where Milo lived. Milo and Eugène had asked us to accompany them there in case Dédé had sent a gang of thugs to Milo's house to murder him or to beat him up. Eugène vanished upstairs with Milo, leaving the two of us in the empty, dark street after curfew and with this annoyingly drunk Frenchman.

"Leave Strasbourg immediately, leave Strasbourg immediately," the drunk repeated incessantly. "I have done eight years as a fighter pilot. I speak therefore as a brave man. And I say, leave Strasbourg immediately."

After standing this monologue for a short time, we went back to Lucien's, where Ramon occupied the bed alone and I slept sitting upright on the wooden chair. My body now smarted and itched from a thousand bites.

Next morning Ramon and I were about to enter a café where we found that we could get good strong *apéritifs* of the fortified wine variety, when we ran into Milo. He looked like a maniac. His normally immaculate bow tie was hanging down, tears still streamed from his eyes, his hair was all over the place, and he was followed by his three children whom he said he was sending with their godmother to stay with his parents at Mulhouse. They were pretty children, fair-haired and brown-eyed and neat, like their mother. The oldest, a boy of seven, was openly scornful of his little father.

Poor Milo left the children with us in the café. He was going again to the hotel bedroom to give his wife "one final chance of forgiveness". He returned, in floods of tears, and repeated a jumble of threats which Dédé appeared to have uttered against all of us. It seemed likely to me that Dédé was getting tired of the whole business, and of Madame Milo into the bargain.

"If you keep on worrying at Dédé like this I think you will get your wife back," I told him.

"If you still want her," put in Ramon.

"You cannot understand," Milo countered angrily. "I love her. And whatever her failings, nobody could call her a bad mother. Yet now she is bewitched. She is determined to stay with her lover. What is that man's satanic power? She told me that she would rather be made love to once by him than one million times by me. Yet he is revoltingly ugly. What has he that I have not got? She says that she is determined to go back with him to Vienna, where he claims he can make a living by his painting."

He took the three nice children away to their godmother. Ramon and I went on drinking *apéritifs* and discussing the comedy in this tragi-comedy. We were joined by the sly Alban, who drank at our expense and poked fun at *le cocu.*

At midday *le cocu* returned alone.

"I am liquidating everything," he announced. "Maybe myself, unhappy wretch that I am, into the bargain. All is ended. I dare not be alone. Come back to my place and eat with me and live with me."

Such invitations were uncommon in the Strasbourg we knew. We caught him by both arms and hurried him to his home. Upstairs in the kitchen he waved his arms around the place.

"Eat everything here. Eat it up. Finish it. I have not eaten for three days. But I never want to see food again. I regret that I have no wine. Now I go to find my children. Be sure to eat everything. . . ."

The three of us were half-starved, ravenous. We found food all over the place. Sausages, noodles, several pounds of margarine, bread, tomatoes, onions, garlic. Everything went into three large frying-pans, and Ramon, who had constituted himself the cook, ladled in the fat.

Anybody living in Germany or France at that time would understand what it meant to have almost unlimited fat, probably a fortnight's rations for the family, to eat at one go.

We stuffed ourselves, and stuffed again. A mountainous pile of dirty dishes rose in the kitchen.

Milo came back with the godmother and his three children. He was very fond of them. He dressed them in their best clothes, weeping copiously over the little flannel suits, the artificial silk shirts, the shining button shoes. Now the three children also cried in a bewildered way, as though they cried in sympathy with their father. Even the godmother, a hard-faced pastry-cook, snivelled occasionally and wrinkled her long nose, and dabbed at her deep-set eyes with a nice lace handkerchief. When the woman and the children had departed Alban, who had gone out after lunch, returned greatly excited.

"Never say Alban is not your best friend," he said to Milo.

"I saw your wife at the hotel. She told me she wanted to return home to collect some clothes. I advised her to do so, telling her that the door was open and that nobody was here. She asked particularly if you were around, and I said you had left for Mulhouse. Now just keep quiet. She should be here any minute."

Five minutes later we heard doubtful footsteps climbing the long wooden staircase. There was intense drama in the sound.

When she saw us all her eyes gleamed with fury. She was not bad-looking; small, thin and well-made, but with a dry little face and a mean mouth. The last type of face one would expect to find in a woman who exchanges a husband with a good job and three children for a most dubious lover.

Le cocu jumped at her at once and slapped her heavily on the face. But Ramon darted in and separated them.

"You miserable rat," she cried at her husband. "That is just what I would expect from you when you are supported by your own thugs and I am here alone. You only sniffed and cried when you found me in bed with him in the hotel. I have had one night of utter happiness," she continued vindictively. "Seven hours with him have blotted out the memory of seven horrible years with you. In seven years not one moment of peace and understanding. Seven years of a husband who continually came home drunk. I am sick of you. I love the children. But I need romance in my life, and now, thank God, I have found it."

Milo replied with vigorous words upon mother love. He described how he had wept as he had dressed the little ones for their journey. He said that they would learn to detest the memory of their mother, that soon they would regard her as a harlot.

Ramon could not keep out of such a resounding scene. He told her that in seizing love with both hands she was obeying the primeval instinct of all beautiful women, but that she must weigh her passion against her permanent love for her children. And she must examine also her love for Dédé, who was a traitor, and a man who would never offer her any permanent kind of love.

I could see that the last part of this speech impressed the little woman, especially as the theatrically good-looking Ramon put both hands on her shoulders while he spoke, and gazed earnestly into her eyes. I saw, too, that she was thrilled to have four men in her flat emotionally discussing her life, and that she was beginning to enjoy her love-affair, not directly as a love-affair, but because it put her in the centre of a brightly lit stage.

She seemed to be sorry to leave to rejoin her lover. As she passed through the kitchen she gave a scream of horror at our mounds of dirty dishes which overflowed from the table to every flat space and in places were piled knee-high on the floor.

When she had gone Milo produced a bottle of brandy.

"Let us drown our sorrows, and listen to the British Broadcasting Corporation," he said hopefully. He turned on a programme from London called *"Les Français parlent aux Français"*, but we soon tired of that. Milo left untouched his own small glass of brandy. He could not concentrate on anything, poor soul. The three of us polished off the bottle. Then, replete and satisfied as starving boa-constrictors that have spent a warm evening, let loose among a flock of fat sheep, we flung ourselves on sofas and beds and slept through the afternoon.

That evening in "Mother's" café a tall and youngish blonde woman stood with the heavy proprietress behind the stainless-steel top of the bar. Occasionally the blonde bent forward to arrange her piled Edwardian coiffure reflected in this shining surface. Finally, after watching Ramon and myself for some time, she nudged the proprietress, who beckoned us over.

"Drinks on the house, *les gars*," she said, adding hastily: "But there's only beer."

"Where do you come from, Monsieur?" the blonde asked me. "Paris."

"Truthfully?"

"Paris, but I lived a lot of time in Holland."

"No need to play games with me. Not that sort, anyway. And it was not Holland. You are a Tommy. Tell me you are a Tommy."

"No, Madame." (I had noticed her wedding-ring.)

"But your little friend from the Dordogne said that you were a Tommy," she said. "He told us the first morning you came here. That was why we gave you bread without coupons."

The café was packed with Germans and their girl friends— quieter Germans than we usually saw at Grinzing. The blonde told me that her name was Greta, and that she was in Strasbourg to recover from a terrible loss. I asked for details, since that was plainly what she wanted.

"I have lost my lover," she said, and two big tears formed in her grey eyes. "He was young, but already the finest man

231

that ever lived. He was killed on the French frontier."

"Where?" I asked, for this interested me.

"Near Hayange, or Hayingen as the Boches now call it, in Lorraine. He was a Communist, and he worked to get people out of Germany. They tortured him for a fortnight before they shot him."

I noticed that she spoke French without accent.

"You are not German, Madame Greta?"

"Are you trying to insult me? No, I am a Lorraine, and one hundred per cent French. But my husband is a Boche and a Nazi. I loathe him. He is an officer now. A gunner on the Eastern front. I hope he gets killed.

"Do you want to get into France, my Tommy?" she asked, lowering her voice and putting her head close to mine. "If so, I think I can help you. I have a house at Hayange, and you could have a room. You could wait there until I got a passage fixed up for you."

"I'll think it over, we have so many plans," I told her, for I was a little nervous. I noticed that she wore beneath the filmy silk scarf around her throat a small round enamel button with the Nazi swastika on it.

"Pay no attention to that," she said quickly, for she was extremely sharp, and quick at following thoughts and glances. "I have to wear that because I have an important job with the Nazis up at Hayange."

"What kind of job?"

"I am a chemist."

"Why are you here then?"

"Isn't my Tommy suspicious? I have six weeks' sick leave. Besides, the boss is a friend of mine."

We returned to Milo's place, and got ourselves the evening meal by heating up what we had omitted to eat at midday.

Ramon was most enthusiastic about the blonde, whereas I had put all thoughts of using her help right out of my head. The husband and the swastika button were too much for me.

"Just leave the *gonzesse* to me, Georges," Ramon said. "I know how to handle that type. Besides, she pleases me."

"We must not mix business with pleasure."

"No, but I thought she seemed a sensible kind of woman. I believe she meant what she said. Maybe she's fallen for me. Blondes often do. She talked to you all the time, but she was throwing me such looks. Think I'll call round again to-morrow."

"You be careful."

Ramon was satisfied, for he was filling the whole flat with tobacco fumes. When he had no tobacco he was a desperate character, quite impossible to live with. Now he had found our host's store of dried tobacco leaves. He had cut them into shreds with Madame Milo's herb-chopper. The fumes made me glad that I had stopped smoking. Cigarettes had never interested me, anyway.

Eugène came in with his wife and Milo.

"I am going to leave *my* wife here with you two boys," he announced recklessly, "while I go out with my knife to get Milo's wife back for him. Unless Dédé hands her over with good grace he can taste my steel for supper; and he will need no champagne to wash it down."

As he slouched from the room he gave a forward tweak at his white cap, turned to me with his most toothy smile, and said: "Wouldn't Jean Gabin give his eyes to play this role, eh, Georges?"

In a cupboard which we had earlier overlooked Ramon found a bottle of heavy red wine, and he and I and the woman sat around the kitchen range discussing the awful effect that the advent of a ghoul like Dédé could have on a basically solid family life.

Eugène's wife, somewhat surprisingly, disclosed after her second glass that she too had often felt an urge to have affairs with young men, but that hitherto she had never succumbed. Ramon, who could scarcely have been more susceptible to women, began to shoot her boiling glances from beneath his heavy brows. But at that moment the door was flung open and Eugène strode in, followed by Milo's wife and finally by Milo himself. Milo was beaming, radiant with joy.

"She has come back to me," he cried. "I must have wine. What, there is none left? I must go out and find some. My darling wife is back again."

"Don't be an idiot," said his darling wife. "I have returned this time because Dédé is a swine, but I assure you that there will be other men, and I have not been drawn back by any love for you. On the contrary, I despise you."

No amount of acid could dissolve the husband's joy. He embraced his unwilling wife several times, and urged us all to do likewise.

Alban, who had slunk in just in time to avail himself lavishly of Milo's last invitation, told us without shame and in front of the protagonists, the story of the dénouement in the hotel bed-room.

He said that Eugène and Milo had burst into the bedroom while he was sitting there chatting to the couple in bed. Eugène said to Milo's wife: "Come on, get your clothes on. You are coming home with Milo and me."

Dédé lay in bed, smoking, and flinging ash with studied non-chalance over himself, the woman, and the bed.

"I advise you both to get out," he had said to them. "Other-wise I will report you to the S.S. and the Gestapo for sheltering the Englishman."

Eugène thereupon extracted his knife from his pocket, jerked it open, and said: "Any more of such talk and I will let this little beauty make love to your jugular." Dédé making no reply to this, Eugène continued: "Madame here does not love you. She loves her children. She is in bed with you to recover from a fit of ennui. She knows that you have often had other women, that even now, here in Strasbourg, you have five or six strumpets. She knows in her heart that soon you will throw her over.

"Tell me," he went on, stealing a little closer to the bed. "Is it not true that after a night and a day in bed with her you are already sickened? You want to get up, to go out and find other, more exotic women, to get drunk again as usual."

Dédé looked from the strained little woman beside him to Eugène in his white cap. He looked around the room with his hard, lizard-like eyes and then said slowly: "I am an artist. I am sick of all this. No woman has ever caused me so much bother with husbands and things running in and out of the bed-room. For goodness' sake get out and take her with you if you want her. I have had all that I needed of her."

"And you would let me go?" shouted the woman.

His answer was to turn his back upon her in the bed, and feign sleep. She slowly left the bed, dressed herself before them without shame in her blue costume and her hard hat, and followed them out of the hotel.

Alban, the jackal, had waited to talk to Dédé.

That night Alban slept on the couch at the foot of their double bed, while Ramon and I squeezed ourselves into the children's bed in the inner room.

When the lights went out we heard her say to Milo: "Now listen, you. If you lay one finger on me I will kick you out of bed."

"My darling," he replied in a voice strangled with happy emotion.

Next morning she smilingly brought us coffee in bed, and settled down cheerfully to the appalling job of cleaning the flat and washing our dirty dishes. She told us that Milo had gone back to drive his crane after five days of unexplained absence. And that morning while I was shaving, there was a knock on the door, three feet from my ear, and a deep voice said: *"Police."*

She shut me in the bedroom and spoke to the Gestapo man in the kitchen. He presented her with a summons directing her husband to report immediately at Gestapo headquarters.

Did she know why her husband had been absent from work for five days?

"Anyone would have been absent in my husband's place," she told him frankly. "I had run away with another man."

"Your husband will be required to explain that himself, Madame."

When Ramon awoke I told him that we must clear out of Strasbourg. I was afraid of Dédé, and of Milo too. *Le cocu* did not seem quite sane to me; and I feared that he would now begin serious drinking, or would be goaded by his wife to some stupidity. I said to Ramon that if we could find no better escape route during that day I would be prepared to take a risk and accept the offer of the blonde in the café. But how were we to get to Hayange?

Ramon and Milo's wife said that they thought we might manage by taking small "omnibus" trains on Saturday, the following day. The express trains were all controlled by the German police, and in one of them we would probably be asked for our identity papers twice or three times on the journey. But the Germans, particularly on Saturdays, when all trains were crowded to bursting-point, rarely bothered about the "omnibus" trains, which dithered along, stopping at every small station.

I asked Madame Milo to go that morning and buy two tickets for us. While we talked little Alban came in. He asked if he might come along, telling me that if we succeeded in reaching France we might hide with him in the Dordogne, and that he knew some people who might be able to get us across the Spanish frontier. Alban amused me, and I had been impressed by his *combines* and *Système D*. I decided to take him, and gave the woman money to buy three tickets.

Then, on Ramon's very sensible suggestion, he and I went to have our photographs taken. There was a small shop across

the river which advertised: "Passport Photos While You Wait."
We waited for nearly an hour in the queue that wormed out of
the door and along the dingy pavement. A youth immediately
in front of us in the queue had "O" on the left sleeve of his
blue reefer coat. He was a huge, spotty-faced lad with a shaven
head. When he climbed into the photographing machine the old
man who pressed the button and took the money began to shout
something at him that I could not understand. Then he ran the
youth out into the street and called a policeman. Another policeman soon arrived, and they marched spotty-face away. Ramon
whispered to me that the lad was Ukrainian, deported from his
home to be "saved from the Russians".

We were both badly scared by this business, and indeed a
shudder seemed to run through the whole queue. Probably ours
were not the only outlawed bodies standing there. The only
thing to do was to keep our places and chance our luck. And the
old man rushed us both through the machine. The photographs
were quite good.

Alban invited us to lunch (although he permitted us to pay
for it) in a small French restaurant belonging to a woman who
was in love with him. Responding to his impassioned entreaties,
she unearthed two bottles of wine, and the meal passed off well.
That afternoon we went to a cinema. The German film was so
bad that, although it was only the second film that I had seen in
three years, I went to sleep.

When we arrived that evening in the *apéritifs* café we found
Eugène and his wife celebrating what everybody hoped
was our last night in Strasbourg with a bottle of Nuits St.
Georges. Eugène was already half-seas over. We had four
bottles of this reasonable wine (reasonable in quality that is,
for the price was the equivalent of 35s. a bottle) before we all
said good night.

Ramon and Alban went off to sleep on the couch at the foot of
Milo's bed. As Milo's children had by now returned to the love-
nest, there was no space except the floor left for me, so, for the
last time, I climbed into the double bed with the rubber sheet
chez Eugène. I was wakened at 1 a.m. by the boy's howls.
Eugène had torn him from the bed and was slapping his bare
behind. "Dirty little piss-a-bed," Eugène said. He asked me if
I wanted the sheet changed, but I declined and moved nearer
the wall.

There were only potatoes for lunch at Milo's. Madame explained that we had left nothing in the larder, and she did not

know how the family was going to eat for the rest of the month. She was still living in the golden haze of her strange love-affair.

Alban, with many sly grins, kept admiring the pink carnations which stood by the bed in an ornate crystal vase. Milo had bought them, one dozen of them, at the price of five marks a bloom, and had presented them to her that morning. All that he got in the way of thanks was a gale of hysterical laughter, followed by the promise that she intended to be unfaithful to him with the first man who pleased her.

They were both very kind to us. They gave me a little brown attaché-case with rounded corners to carry my things in, and to help me to look respectable on the train. I left the Australian overcoat with Eugène, since I feared that it was too military for the journey and for the highly dangerous frontier area to which we were travelling.

On the way to the station we called at "Mother's" to see the blonde. She seemed to be delighted that we were taking her at her word.

"Go to 10 Hermanngoeringstrasse in Hayange and ask my *locataire*, Madame Hess, to lodge you in the small room under the mansard," she said. "Let's see, to-day's Saturday. I'll be there on Tuesday, and we'll soon arrange your passage, for I know all the *passeurs*. You, Ramon, could slip along to the Café de Paris at Hayange one morning and ask to see Monsieur Bébert. He is head of the main *passeur* organisation. They make ordinary people, Jews, etcetera, pay well to be taken into France, but escaped prisoners like you they take for nothing."

Milo and his wife walked with us to the station. Both of them were bad walkers, taking mincing steps on their small, coarse legs. Alban and Ramon too, like most Latins, dawdled from preference rather than walked. It seemed to me, heartily anxious to be away from Strasbourg, that we would never reach the station. But we did.

We had one "workers' ticket" for the three of us. The station loud-speakers were playing the *Valse des Fleurs* between railway announcements, and the big place wore a Saturday afternoon holiday aspect. Ramon pushed first through the barrier, I followed, and Alban brought up the rear. Every now and then I got fits of laughter, just as I had when Wally Binns fell into the puddle outside Munich. We looked a comic trio. All of us hatless. Alban and I in our ridiculous, long *golfs* and Ramon clacking along in his dismal, dark German civilian clothes, his boots making a terrible noise. They were German military boots which he had stolen at Nuremberg.

"All will be well," Milo announced importantly as we approached our train, the most old-fashioned and dilapidated little train in all the station. "I know your *Chefesse*."

Our *Chefesse* turned out to be a heavily painted and mascaraed young woman in railway uniform with wide-bottomed trousers. Milo took her away for a little walk up the platform, then came back to say: "All is arranged. The *Chefesse* will look after you."

He and his wife stood hand in hand, both laughing and crying as our train pulled slowly out of the station. I was thankful to see the last houses of Strasbourg passing our windows, then allotments, and at last the green fields.

CHAPTER XVII

THE *Chefesse* wore a perfume so heavy with sweetness and musk that it half suffocated me, and it drove Alban and Ramon, those torrid Southerners, to extravagant heights of competitive charm.

For the first three stations we were obliged to travel standing in the corridor, but after that the train was nearly empty and the lady was able to ride with us, and talk frankly.

Milo had not exaggerated when he told us that the *Chefesse* would see us through. She was supposed to function as a combined ticket-collector, guard, and police spy; and she was in a position to warn us if any Germans or policemen began to search the train.

Ramon got off to a flying start, for he and she decided that they had known each other four years earlier in Strasbourg, when he had been a recruit, and she a dance hostess. There was so much blacking on her eyelashes that when she closed her eyes, as she frequently did when abashed by the sallies of one or other of my two companions, the lashes became entwined, and she was obliged to disentangle them with her scarlet-nailed fingers.

They told her that I was an officer of *la Huitième Armée*, a British Army which, despite German counter-propaganda, then had a fantastic reputation among French people. She looked at me very closely, as though she expected to see in me some resemblance to the hard features of General Montgomery, and finally, after weighing things up, pronounced me *"très swing"*.

After two hours of slow travelling we were obliged to change trains, and our friend handed us over to the care of the new *Chefesse,* an Alsatian this time, and a much older woman. This train was busy, and, beyond winking at us each time she passed, the *Chefesse* could not pay us any special attention. We sat in a wooden-benched third-class compartment exactly the same as the one from which Wally and I had escaped.

Immediately behind my head, scratched upon the surface of the cheap mirror, were the words: *"Vive la France",* and on the other side of the compartment somebody had deeply carved the cross of Lorraine, at that time known as the Gaulliste emblem.

Our fellow-travellers were at first chiefly peasants. As we neared the important town of Metz, however, more townsfolk boarded the train, and these were talkative, and daring. There was a good deal of fairly open talk against the Germans, and the French language was used almost exclusively. It was delightful, to be at home in the language, and to hear French people who spoke out flashingly and colourfully. All three of us cheered up considerably, although by that time the journey was becoming wearisome.

We changed trains again at Metz, and then rumbled up through the industrial belt of ironworks and blast furnaces which I remembered well from visits to "that fortified smell" (as Tom Delmer called it), the Maginot Line, in 1938, '39 and '40. The ironworks were still going full blast. There were no lights on the train, but a constant red light from the furnaces flickered into our compartment. It was a moment when I felt small, shivering, defenceless, and far, so far, from home.

This train was filled with business people or factory workers returning to Thionville after spending Saturday in Metz. One of them, a German, told Ramon that he would show us the only way to get on the tram to Hayange that night. (Ramon spoke the strangest prison-learned pidgin-German that I ever heard, but he managed to get along surprisingly well with it.)

So, as our train was slowing up in Thionville station, we leaped out and dashed for two hundred yards after our German guide, to leap panting into a tram-car that was already more than full.

The imagination usually creates simplified pictures. I had imagined Hayange as an old fortified town standing alone in a bare, open country, with the frontier, clearly marked out, running past its walls. Instead of this it was busy and industrial, and we arrived there only after rattling through a built-up factory area that reminded me of the cobbled streets of Glasgow running past the backs of the shipyards on the north bank of the Clyde.

On the journey we had all lost confidence in Greta. I cannot say why. Even Ramon now thought that it would be better to try to get in touch directly with the *passeurs*. So at Hayange we went to the Café de Paris.

Here Ramon committed a grave error. Instead of sitting down quietly and ordering a drink, he walked straight up to the fat *patron* and said to him: "Is Monsieur Bébert here?"

"Never heard of him," promptly replied the *patron*.

"Oh, but you must know him," insisted Ramon. "We were told to come here. My friend here is . . ." At this point I gave him such a savage sideways kick on the ankle that he relapsed into heavy-breathing silence.

"And who sent you here to ask for this man?" demanded the *patron*.

"Madame . . ." began Ramon, and moaned as Alban kicked him on one side while I kicked the other.

We consumed drink after drink in the café, but could get no further. So at length we saw that it was useless, and decided to find Greta's house. I was depressed about things, for I could not see why she had directed Ramon to go to such a place as the café without giving him a password.

It was a long walk to Hermanngoeringstrasse. Number 10 was a narrow, red-brick house, with a little garden in front and an iron gate which could be opened by a device inside the house, like many of the garden gates in Edinburgh.

The house looked dead, and there was no response to our ringing at the electric bell beside the gate. After a while Alban and I climbed over the railings, leaving Ramon on guard in the empty street. A light drizzle began to fall. This was quite usual on such occasions. I now expected rain whenever things began to go wrong. The fields beyond the house looked damp and horrible.

To our surprise the front door was unlocked. I borrowed Alban's lighter and tiptoed in, shutting the door silently behind me, and then lighting up. I found myself in a bare hall with four doors in it. All the doors were locked. I went upstairs. There was a landing with two doors, both locked. It looked as though the house was empty and the tenant had lost the front-door key and therefore had locked all the other doors. I descended to report this grim news. The drizzle was becoming more intense.

Down at the bottom of the street we saw a café. After making Ramon promise to ask no questions there, we went in and ordered coffee and brandies. The place was run by Germans, and three German fräuleins, fat and greasy, made sheep's eyes at us from the next table and finally plucked up courage to ask Ramon if we liked dancing.

"*Jawohl,*" he replied enthusiastically, before I could kick him. But they only wanted us to take them out to a local dance the following night. Noticing my black looks, Ramon said that we would dearly love to do that, but that we might have to leave for Strasbourg the following morning.

Outside in the cold the rain was coming down like machine-gun fire. The only thing left to do was to go back to Number 10 and sleep on the landing.

I curled up on a small deal table alongside a tin of boot blacking and a brush. Alban and Ramon sat on the floor below me smoking expensive and evil-smelling German cigarettes. It was bitterly cold. The cold came nipping through my "golfs", particularly around the seat. I thought a lot during the night about the people whom I had left behind in prison, and wondered if they were thinking about me. By now, too, Anne should know that I had broken out by the code post-card that I had written her from Stalag VIIA.

We all three awoke at dawn, and even Ramon, usually so sluggish in the morning, felt that the only thing to do was to get out and walk fast. We were chilled to the bone. Fortunately the rain had stopped, but an icy wind bit through our poor clothing and under-nourished flesh.

More to get out of the wind than anything else, we boarded a tram and took tickets to the terminus, which was the station at Thionville. There, in the large, high-ceilinged buffet, we bought coffee and bread (the latter with some coupons that Milo and his wife had given us in Strasbourg). The bread here was in long loaves of the French type, and although it was made with the same, or even inferior, flour, it already seemed to be lighter and better than the heavy, sour bread of Germany proper.

After breakfast, because there did not seem to be anything else to do, and because it was so bitterly cold, we took the tram back to Hermanngoeringstrasse. We did not expect to find anybody there. And we were so depressed by that miserable, murky place that we could make no plans for the future.

However, we saw from the front door that somebody had entered that morning after our departure. And when we knocked at a door on the first-floor landing a stout, cheerful-looking woman opened it with a jerk, and answered our queries in voluble French. This was Madame Hess.

She had spent the night with her sister, who was expecting a baby, and she had been worried when she returned to find many cigarette-ends strewn about her landing.

"Come in, come in," she urged us. "You look famished."

She had a comfortable kitchen with a brightly-tiled range and prosperous fittings and crockery. An open door revealed glimpses of a pompous bedroom with a vast, four-poster bed in it, and from the window you looked into the muddy yard behind the house and the long strip of back garden in which there was an imposing collection of live stock: hens, geese, ducks, rabbits, and even a big porker. I saw Ramon bare his long pointed teeth like a hungry fox as he considered the significance of all these edible animals.

Madame Hess was a Lorraine, and "absolutely French", she claimed.

"My husband, Hans, is a Lorrain, but a Boche for all that," she told us. "I should not call him a Boche, really, for he is a darling and a good husband who works hard at the factory. He hates the Nazis too, although he can scarcely speak a word of French. Nobody could be more unlike Greta's husband than my Hans. You will forgive me. I am a bore when I talk about the Germans, I hate them so. . . .

"I don't like the British either," she said, when she had learned my nationality. "But it is a duty to pass you on since your country is now fighting a bit better than it did in '39 and '40. Running away like that at Dunkirk! However, we must let bygones be bygones."

Although it was only ten o'clock, she said that we must have "a mouthful of food". She produced bread, butter, beer, and an enormous jar of some kind of pork *pâté*, which she insisted on our finishing between the three of us.

Unable to believe that such food could be true, we sat around the table, gorging. Madame Hess rattled on all the time. She soon told us a lot about Greta, whom she evidently disliked.

Greta's family had been turned out of their comfortable house in the neighbourhood because the Germans considered them "too francophil". They were now penniless refugees near Lyons. Greta had returned from a holiday in Paris to find that

242

her parents had vanished. Because of her husband, a leading Nazi, she had been able to protect her own property, and had remained on good terms with the German authorities.

"When she arrives you will see her flat below, which is very much more splendid than this," said Madame Hess spitefully. "But it is plastered over with things that you won't find here, no matter how you search—Hitlers and swastikas and such like. And pictures of her lover too. I thought she'd go mad when he died. She got his body from the communal grave in which the Boches deposited it, and she bought the best lot in the cemetery for him. Now she visits the grave every two or three days, and the flowers she leaves there are a sight worth seeing. But soon she'll forget him. She is the kind that must have men and excitement. Too highly strung."

Our bedroom under the mansard was a double room, entered through a dressing-room-cum-kitchen. The place had been rented from Greta by a German *Feldwebel* stationed at Thionville. Whenever he got a long-promised promotion this *Feldwebel* intended to marry his fiancée and move into Hermanngoeringstrasse 10.

"He calls those sticks of furniture his luxury bedroom suite," said Madame Hess scornfully. "It was all sent from Berlin under Hitler's scheme for producing more babies. You will find that the luxury beds have mattresses stuffed with sawdust. But they should be clean, since they've never been occupied."

"Supposing the *Feldwebel* comes round to have a look at his place?" I asked.

"Don't worry. He is a meek young man. I can easily tell him that the door is locked, and that Madame Greta has the key."

Ramon and I occupied the twin beds, and Alban settled down on the sofa in the dressing-room. For two days we ate and slept enormously, gathering our forces and resting away the tiredness resulting from the jerky, nervous life we had led in Strasbourg.

At midnight on the second day, although we had not been expecting her for another day or two, Greta arrived. She dragged us down from the homely kitchen of Madame Hess to her more bourgeois apartment below, and the more bourgeois delights of black coffee in small cups and sweet biscuits bought on the black market in Strasbourg.

Her rooms were well furnished, though without any talent for choosing or mixing furniture. There was a strangely feminine air about them. The sitting-room had all the adjuncts of

243

Madame Hess's room above, the cooking range, the battery of pans, the dish-rack. But whereas in the room above these things dominated and were the central, functional features, irresistibly attracting the eye, down here they seemed to be coyly hiding themselves for all their solidity. You noticed much more than the white-tiled range (neater, and of a more expensive type than Madame Hess's), the six coquettish hats that hung from long, padded pegs behind the door, the silver-framed photograph of her cadaverously romantic lover, the frothing pink eiderdown through the bedroom door that was usually open.

Greta made us sit with her until 2 a.m. But little compulsion was needed. She was very gay, and obviously thoroughly accustomed to dealing with men. She sat there, at the head of her little table, playing with the three of us as though we were billiard balls which she manœuvred in gentle cannons.

Obvious sirens, no matter how charming, make me shy. Although she was very nice to me and continually asked: "Is our Tommy always so tongue-tied?", I remained diffidently silent.

Alban and Ramon paid her marked attention. Before we went to bed she asked the latter: "Why are you staring at me so?"

"Because I admire you," he answered boldly. "And I never know when my admiration might not turn into love."

"Don't let it change, *mon ami*," she said. "Although you are handsome in a dark way, your love is too easy for me."

In the intervals of all this more or less sensual badinage she had given us bad news. That week the Germans guarding the frontier had arrested in a sensational ambush no fewer than forty *passeurs*, including one woman. The woman and several of the men were known to be under torture (or "friction", as she put it).

All illegal activity on the frontier was at a standstill. The gang that had been arrested was that with which her lover had worked. She believed that there were other gangs, but it might take time to get in touch with them. In the meantime we must lie low. Hayange was a dangerous place at all times, and now, with forty prisoners who might be forced to talk, it was doubly so.

"I don't think they will bother me, the Boches," she said. "I stand in too well with them."

When we had said good night Ramon hovered behind in her rooms, but she sent him packing after us with a sharp: "And what do you think *you* are waiting for, my boy?''

Then the days passed slowly.

Sex thrust a new complication into our triumvirate. Even when the woman was not there, my companions' talk about her was so gross and so direct that I was nauseated, and I was obliged to withdraw from the conversation to avoid being rude to them. Greta herself did nothing to help, but seemed to enjoy heating up the atmosphere, swelling the little jealousies and rivalries.

With her we did not eat so well as with Madame Hess, for Greta's talents were not culinary. Alban took over the cooking, and was expert at it since he had been a pastry-cook at the beginning of the war and a cook in his regiment. Greta bought lavishly on the black market, but the goods she bought were necessarily inferior to those grown by the Hess family.

I tried to spend most of my days up in our bedroom, trying to sleep, or just looking out of the window at the dirty fields between the stains of the great factories. But Greta would not have that. We must all be there, around here at all times.

A new danger flowered in that over-effeminate, hot-house atmosphere—a danger that came not from the Germans but from the temperaments and the jealousies of my companions, particularly of Ramon, who began to fret over the woman until he was ill.

His eyes took on a yellowish look, and his lips became dry and burning. Although he spent hours washing, powdering, and brushing himself, he looked more savage and unkempt each day. Sometimes when I woke at night I would hear him muttering or tossing feverishly in his sleep.

On the second day of this situation, a Wednesday, a figure straight out of the theatre or the wildest of fiction walked into Greta's room, and laid on the table a string bag in which was a brown-paper parcel containing a fat chicken, a bottle of Burgundy, and a Münster cheese "For the Englishman". The bearer of these welcome gifts was a little old woman who introduced herself as *Grand' mère*.

She was a puny, bent old woman with thin grey hair hanging down the sides of her bony face and a black feather bonnet toppling over it. Her shoulders were so narrow that her much-darned brown shawl kept slipping down. Every five minutes, with an annoyed exclamation, she wrapped the shawl tightly around herself until her shoulders looked like the tapering neck

245

of a bottle of Rhine wine, and her wizened old face the half-drawn cork.

To Ramon's annoyance, she insisted on all the others leaving the room while she talked to me alone. She asked first for proof that I was an escaped prisoner of war, and examined my feeble proofs with quick intelligence. I could only show her the remains of my British emergency ration, some camp money from Italy and Germany, five Egyptian pounds hidden in my belt, the belt itself (which was obviously neither French nor German), my boots, and my English accent and appearance. She took the camp money and one of the Egyptian notes away with her, hiding them inside her nodding hat.

She told me that she was the "under cover woman" for an organisation of *passeurs* which worked to the north of Hayange.

"We are Italians," she told me. "But don't worry. We are communists. We know plenty about the lady with whom you are staying. She has a good and generous heart, but we consider her dangerous. She is under observation. If anything fishy happens to you she will be killed. We are greatly pleased with the possibility of being able to pass a British officer. We hope to be able to take you from here within eight days. . . ."

"Impossible," I interrupted. "We cannot last here eight days."

"What do you mean?"

"A very impassioned domestic situation is growing up in the house. . . ."

"Oh, I know all about that. Madame Greta is indiscreet. Every time she goes to have a fitting for a dress, which is very frequently, she talks to her seamstress. And the seamstress is Italian. I know the situation. The North African is most passionate, and desires Greta. Greta has the *goût de l'étranger* and desires you, or so she says."

She hobbled off, saying that she would do her best. A most disconcerting old woman.

The following night the three of us had to go out into the darkness to dine with a sister of Madame Hess, who lived a mile away. We returned about midnight, having dined extremely well, to find that Greta had prepared a party. It was to be a party in the Teutonic style. She had laid out on the kitchen table four small glasses and three bottles of cognac. She was obviously playing for a flare-up. I could think of no way to stop it. We settled down to several hours of serious drinking.

Alban and I became pop-eyed, flushed, and drowsy, leaving the conversation entirely to Greta and Ramon.

Towards the end of the second bottle Ramon lost all control. After telling Greta that she was the most wonderful woman he had ever laid eyes on, and that she loved him madly although she did not know it, and that in the more technical aspects of love-making he would certainly surprise her with his Moorish passion, his skill, and his stamina, he thrust the table aside and flung himself upon her.

Greta took this in bad part.

"Salaud, salopard," she hissed at him. "Is this any way to repay my kindness and my hospitality? The vanity of some men. Ugh, you disgust me. Get away from me, you beast. Georges. Alban, make him sit down. . . ."

Ramon paid no attention to her entreaties. Finally, Alban and I were obliged to seize him by the shoulders and pull him away. I replaced him as gently as I could in his chair. He slumped there with his bitter eyes swivelling like twin anti-tank guns. We dumbly awaited the stream of invective that inevitably followed.

He told Greta that she was a whore. She had led him on, and he would stand it no longer. He would leave her house first thing in the morning. She had invited him to embrace her and then had repulsed him just to put an insult on him in front of the Englishman. If she wanted the Englishman she could have him. If the Englishman thought that he was a better man than a mere North African, then the said North African, a *Français* to the core, would fight it out there and then; first *la boxe*, since that was the English habit, and then with knives.

I hurriedly explained that I never boxed, that I still regarded him as my friend, that it was only the alcohol in his veins that made him talk of knives, that we had sworn to escape together; that, great as was my regard for our charming and intelligent hostess, no woman could be allowed to harm our friendship. Then I gave him a lot more cognac, quickly. He savagely downed three or four little glasses like a Russian drinking vodka to recover his appetite. We were obliged to open the third bottle.

Gradually the tenseness eased off in an alcoholic fuzz. Dawn was creeping dirtily through the windows of our bedroom when Greta and I helped Ramon up to his bed. Alban followed, pulling himself upstairs hand over hand on the banister-rail. Ramon collapsed fully dressed on his bed, came to for an instant to pull the sheets over his boots and trousers, and collapsed again. Alban was already unconscious on his sofa.

"Give me your hand, Tommy," Greta said, swaying in front of me. "You can drink like a Boche, and for once I mean that as a compliment."

I had hoped that the outbursts of the night would ease Ramon's pains, but next morning towards eleven o'clock, when Greta and I were struggling with strong coffee, he burst in, dishevelled and almost raving.

"I cannot stand it, I tell you," he shouted at both of us. "This woman is torturing me. Does she not realise that I have done forty months in prison? Forty long months of spiritual, mental and physical agony, and this woman treats me like a spoiled lap-dog. I am a *man*, and I will not stand it. I shall kill you. I shall shout to the neighbours that we are here. Let the Gestapo take us and torture us. . . ."

Greta was beginning to see that he was dangerous. She unearthed a small bottle containing more cognac, and gave him this in his coffee, talking to him softly and charming him round. At best I saw that she could only gain us a short respite. As she left to take flowers to the grave of her lover, I told her that she must ask the organisation to take Ramon off to another house that day, and to prepare to muzzle him or to intimidate him into silence.

She agreed to do this, but she said with most sinister composure that she intended to keep me in the house for at least another eight days and then to leave with me herself for France. She would travel with me down to the south, where we would stay either at Cannes or Biarritz.

"I have plenty of money," she explained. "For I have the power to draw all that my husband possesses from the bank. As for Alban, I shall allow him to stay on here with us provided he does not annoy my Tommy. He is so useful, since he does all the cooking and the housework."

Things were going much too fast for me, and I spent one of the most worrying days of my life. In the afternoon Greta displayed all the contents of her husband's wardrobe. After trying several shirts, suits, and ties on me (there was no sense in denying the headstrong creature, and besides, I was sharp enough to see that I needed new clothes badly, particularly since the seat of my "golfs" had given way during the struggles of the previous night), she decked me out in a white shirt with crisscrossing lines on it, a dark grey suit of hard and durable serge, and a rich red tie. The last-named article had been the property of her dead lover. Her husband was evidently a much smaller and more portly man than I. His suit was short and loose everywhere for me. The trousers were so wide that they flapped, and they had no turn-ups.

Those lavish gifts did not help to soothe the jangling nerves of Ramon. He was obviously on his best behaviour as we sat down to an early dinner, but, glancing at his bloodshot eyes and twisting, nicotine-stained fingers, I had no confidence in his self-control. We were saved by the Italians.

After a frenzied banging on the door, two small people ran in, spouting agitated French with strong Italian accents.

"You must fly, fly at once," said the man.

"Madame, these *messieurs* must leave your house, you are in the greatest danger," said the woman. Their hard boot-button black eyes stared at Greta, and remembering the old grandmother's words, I was sure that they were lying. They only wanted to get us away from Greta.

Scarcely pausing to take breath, the little Italian told us that both he and the woman were members of the *passeurs* organisation. They had been sent to take us away immediately to a "safe house" on the other side of Hayange. Soon, they hoped, we would be out of German territory. The reason for this swift move was, they said, that Germans had been overheard talking on the Thionville-Hayange tram-car. From their talk the organisation had learned that the Gestapo knew that a British officer was hidden somewhere in a small area which included the Hermanngoeringstrasse, and that a house-to-house search was imminent.

Within twenty minutes we were walking up the road to Hayange. It seemed that when we got out into the dark street most of the fumes of jealousy passed away. Alban and Ramon began to talk almost normally. Greta caught hold of me and obliged me to walk arm-in-arm with her.

"Would you like to see the château?" she asked me suddenly.

"If it's interesting, yes," I replied unwittingly.

"If we hurry we can do it," she said, and dragged me at an accelerated pace down a side street. I was astonished to see our small guide turn round and shout, with great waving of the arms: "No, no. Come back here at once. What are you doing with him?"

Greta hurried on, and I could not be so impolite as to refuse

249

to follow. We went through a small side gate into the grounds of a colossal house. She explained that this belonged to one of the richest manufacturing families of Lorraine, and that the factory where she worked was in its grounds. The windows of the château itself were brilliantly illuminated, and the sound of music came out to us as we negotiated the lake of gravel in front of it.

"Yes," Greta agreed. "A splendid house. It is the German general's mess at the moment. If we meet anyone," she continued softly, "just say that you are with me, and I will get you through. Perhaps it was foolish of me to bring you here. I never could resist a 'dare', and as we were coming along here I said to myself, 'You wouldn't dare to take Georges in there.' So, I ask you, what was a poor girl to do? Yes, it was mad. But now I shall have the memory of your presence here to cheer me through the long, grey months that lie ahead. . . ."

Memory or no memory, I heartily agreed with that part of her which thought that it was mad.

By this time we had left the château well behind, and were walking down a magnificent avenue lined with tall beeches. At the far end she led me through the outskirts of a factory. Going out of the factory we walked past a glass box of a room where a doorkeeper sat like a hooded crow, while two German soldiers lounged behind him, warming their legs at an electric fire.

"*Heil Hitler*," shouted Greta to the men in the office, flinging up her arm in the salute.

"*Heil Hitler*," I shouted, copying her gesture.

The Italians and my two French companions were waiting in an anxious huddle farther down the road.

"If you had lost the lieutenant I would have killed you," the little Italian told Greta. She made no reply, and I was sorry for her. A bus came down the street going in the opposite direction. The Italian stopped it.

"I go on with them alone, from here. Kindly board the bus," he said to the two women. Greta obediently followed the Italian girl into the crowded vehicle after taking affectionate leave of all of us, including, I was glad to see, Ramon. I am afraid that I was relieved to see her go. She was too volatile a companion for men in our position.

Twisting and turning, repeatedly stopping to make certain that we were not followed, the Italian led us to a small house on the northern side of Hayange. On the steps of this house, sheltered by the heavy portico, we stopped for at least ten minutes, listening to the muted noises of the town. Then he pressed an electric bell, sounding the letter L in short jabs and a long buzz. Instantly the door swung open, and we were pushed up uncarpeted stairs to a glittering place that reminded me irresistibly of gangsters' apartments in American films.

Here was everything that small-town money could buy and everything that small-town tastes could devise in the way of luxury. The furniture was new, and in ultra-shining woods and metals and glasses. There were stiff crystal vases holding artificial flowers, and small, fussy bowls holding real ones. There were silver and ivory crucifixes hanging on the walls alongside sugary texts, pictures of half-naked film stars, and signed photographs of wrestlers and racing cyclists. There was a large radio in every room, and a harmonium in the kitchen.

Our new host bustled and roared about among this pink, silver and gold finery like a grizzly bear that had dropped in to have tea with Mae West.

Enrico was dark, with low-growing, close-cropped wiry hair, a blue jowl, a mouth that opened abruptly and snapped shut before the words were properly out, and the deepest, most virile voice that I ever heard from a man. His wife fitted in with his furniture. She was a blonde, fluffily pretty in grotesquely high wooden-soled shoes. She had a blonde, fluffy baby which slept under a frothy white coverlet in a silver-gilt cot shaped like a swan.

After letting us hear the B.B.C. news on a battery of radios, Enrico gave us *foie gras* sandwiches washed down with Cointreau, and told us that we would certainly be passed across the frontier the following day.

"Only my organisation now remains in this area to pass people," he growled at us. "The reason for our survival is that we are more cautious than the others. More cautious in choosing our contacts and in conducting them to the frontier, and quicker to fight, to use our guns, if anything goes wrong. To-morrow all the people will be armed who, seen and unseen by you, will shepherd you to the frontier. They will not hesitate to fight for you, and if they find that you are a traitor they will not hesitate to kill you. All of us are Italian. We ask of a British officer that he will say when he returns to his own country that some Italians are men and not all Italians were Fascists.

"I am not saying that we do this for fun. I am a business man. All my employees are well paid, and I still make enough to keep my little home together. But we will run you lads across

251

for nothing, and proud to do it. All I ask of each of you is to sit down now, take a sheet of this notepaper, and write me out a nice certificate. The Frenchmen will put at the top: "To whom it may concern." The British officer will put: "To all British, American, French, or Allied Officers and Other Ranks." Then just tell in simple, straight language how Enrico has helped you. . . ."

When we had done this he added our certificates to a great pile of others which he took from a secret drawer in the marble and rosewood altar which stood beside his bed.

The three of us slept in the double bed in Enrico's spare bedroom. Alban slept in the middle—an unpleasant bedfellow, restless and smelly.

Enrico came in next morning while the others slept and I was doing my exercises.

"Why, you are a fanatic!" he exclaimed.

"Oh, no, I'm not."

"Yes, you are. You're one of those Britishers I've read about. A bit cracked, but always willing to have a try. How I hope you get across! We lost two yesterday. The party were surprised by a German patrol. Two of them, both Jews and elderly. They just lay down and waited to be taken. They were. The others split and ran into the darkness. They all got away. I think you would be a runner."

"Yes, I would be a runner. I would do more than run to avoid going back to prison."

"Would you kill to avoid it?"

"No, I don't think so. I don't like the idea very much."

"Nor do I. I only allow my boys to kill when it's absolutely unavoidable. And then I always tell somebody else to do it. Well, Georges, you are leaving to-day. It's all fixed. Now wait, don't thank me until you arrive."

Before I left he arranged a little brown beret on my head. His wife had tears in her soft eyes. "Poor boy," she said. "So young, and obliged to run such risks. This unspeakable war. . . ."

I followed one hundred yards behind Enrico. He strolled along chewing a stick of cinnamon. When he bent down to fix his shoe-lace I knew that he was in front of the café where I had to meet the others. He never even glanced at me as I passed by him. His caution communicated itself to me and made me nervous.

Ramon and Alban sat inside, drinking marc. We shook hands

as though we were old friends who had not met for some time. Ramon ordered three more marcs. We had scarcely lifted the glasses to our lips when our next guide arrived in the crowded, long café.

We knew him because he carried under his left arm a copy of the newspaper *La Liberté* folded in a peculiar manner. He was accompanied by a woman, tall, broad-shouldered, hideously ugly.

They had one drink standing at the bar. We paid our bill. When they left the café we strolled out, following them through the town to the station. We were followed too. The whole town seemed to be strolling nonchalantly to Hayange station that fine afternoon. Enrico had told me earlier that there were sixteen people responsible for our protection on the journey.

We had half an hour's wait at the station. If the Gestapo had arrived what a gun-battle there would have been! When I saw these people strolling about with their hands in their pockets and their cold, calculating, desperate eyes, their efficient clothes, their shoes with good, solid leather soles, I felt a great wave of gratitude for the little old *grand'mère* and for Enrico and all his satellites.

Maybe these were criminals. But they were people who did things, people who had the power and the will and the guts, to implement their promises. How much better these people with their cold, daring power, than the hot-tongued café plotters of Strasbourg; yes, and than the emotional woman of the Hermanngoeringstrasse!

When I went into the "mixed" lavatory I found the tall, ugly woman there. She zipped open the large handbag she carried to show me a well-oiled German machine-pistol, a *Schmeisser*. I could have kissed her.

God, how I wanted to get home to England!

Only two of our discreet escort got into our carriage—the man whom we had followed and another, a thin young Italian with two fingers missing from his right hand. They told us that we were going to the terminus station of the line—a station then called Deutschhof in the corner of the right angle where the Luxembourg-Lorraine frontier meets the frontier of France proper.

They were extremely nervous, our escort. They told us that a control was not expected, but that it was always a possibility. At each station they sat looking back down the train through tiny mirrors which they held next to the window in their out-

I

stretched hands. There were a great many German police and frontier guards in the little stations at which we halted. I saw some more of the *Feldgendarmerie* with the metal plaques hanging from their necks.

At Deutschhof we left the station with the two men from our carriage, and the five of us, having passed the barrier together, walked in a bunch out of the village, down a dusty twisting road to the next village, where they told us we were to wait in a cottage until nightfall. But the cottage was shut, and there was no reply to their knocking.

They took us into the café next door—a dark-panelled room with the usual picture of Hitler, a small zinc bar, and an elderly landlady who sat knitting beside the blue-and-white china stove and raved to us about the cream-cakes, the lemonade and the ice-cream in Luxembourg.

We drank beer, a watery, frothy mixture with a pleasant taste, for two hours and fifty-two minutes by the clock. After the first hour we were obliged to make constant excursions to the yard at the back, and we made bets as to who would make the fewest excursions. This caused some amusement. Otherwise we were a sombre, a strung-up party. The Italians were most nervous.

They told us that the crossing of the frontier was "a bagatelle", but that there were always liable to be accidents, since the German guards had been doubled, and at most places there were sentry posts at 300-yard intervals. There was no frontier wire, but the sentry posts were all supposed to have police dogs. Here, as in other places, the German police dog was held to be a very much overrated animal; but nevertheless the casualties on this part of the frontier had been heavy. They advised us to take our direction by the stars when we set out, and in the event of any trouble to run off singly into the darkness. Our immediate destination would be the French village of Villerupt where the organisation had asked its contact (whose name would be given to us if we crossed safely) to procure false papers and money for us.

All this sounded fairly good. But I was beginning to be sceptical about all plans and promises, even ones that emanated from this organisation which so far had fulfilled every promise.

Greta and other people, including Enrico, had advised us to make Nancy our first stop, telling us that we should go to the *Bureau des Réfugiés* there and ask to be put in touch with any of the organisations which helped French evaders. Enrico had told me that from Nancy we would be passed on to Dijon, thence to Lyons and Spain by the Pyrenees, or alternatively to the Swiss frontier somewhere near Geneva. Now, however, our two guides told us dark stories of Nancy, where they said there had been a Gestapo drive with many arrests. We had an alternative plan of our own, which was to take the train directly from the frontier to Paris. I believed that I could find friends and money there, and so did Ramon. Although Ramon and I still had a considerable amount of German money, French francs were hard to find. Greta had given me 200. The Italians advised us strongly against going to Paris.

"Too dangerous, too dangerous," they kept repeating. "All the evaders under the sun pass through Paris, so it is the centre of the Boche counter-organisation. You will risk capture every minute there, especially the Englishman with his accent."

As darkness began to fall, and the woman set an oil-lamp on the china stove, we left the inn, and walked off into pretty, hilly country. We had taken the minimum of luggage for the crossing, since we had heard that we must be prepared to crawl or run. Ramon only had his *valise diplomatique*, I had my little attaché-case, and Alban had nothing.

We arrived after thirty minutes of brisk walking at a game-keeper's cottage in the wilds. Inside, packed into a smoky, lamp-lit atmosphere beside what appeared to be a peat fire, were the gamekeeper, his wife and children and a Jewish family, father, mother and son, who evidently intended to make the crossing with us.

The Jews leaped upon me; and, although I let them see that I spoke fluent French, they insisted upon talking to me in extremely bad English. They were sweating and jumpy, and all three of them, even the son, who was more like a girl than a boy, exuded the sharp smell of fear. The father told me rapidly that he was a rich business man from Strasbourg. He had decided to hide in France because his son had just received his papers to join a German anti-aircraft unit. All three of them were well, though unsuitably dressed. The woman wore a mink coat, a large, floppy hat, and shoes with fairly high heels. Looking at her middle-aged figure, I was fairly certain that she also wore stays, no suitable garment for an unhealthy person who proposed to crawl and run if need be and to climb and descend hills. Her husband wore a fur-lined overcoat, a stiff hat and a town suit. When we rose to go they produced (with meaning looks at us strong young men) two large leather suitcases.

Our *passeurs* were the gamekeeper himself, a huge, thin, active-looking Alsatian, and his eleven-year-old son, a fair-haired, slender boy with wild eyes of the palest blue imaginable. This boy was already famous in all the clandestine organisations on that frontier.

"If the guides are obliged to split, follow the boy in preference to his father," one of the Italians whispered to me.

We set off up a steep hill. Our guide had told us that the frontier lay at the top of the ridge which faced us, that he would tell us when we had passed it, and that we must keep together and must copy all his movements, lying down when he lay down, stopping when he stopped, running if he ran.

It was obvious that the Jews could not carry their suit-cases. Ramon took one and I took the other. Alban carried our own light luggage. After the first few yards we were also obliged to help both the woman and her husband. Even the son seemed to expect help, but I fixed that half-way up the hill by planting my boot smartly on his tail. The resulting yelp was dangerous, but it was music in my ears. The *passeurs* treated them with royal indifference. As we neared the top of the hill the poor woman could not walk ten steps without stopping, heaving and panting. Her breathing sounded like a flight of bombers in the still darkness.

Near the ridge we halted, lying down, while the gamekeeper's small son, running and weaving backwards and forwards like a gun dog, smelt out the situation ahead. When he came back we went on, bearing now more to the right and making a tremendous noise negotiating some low thorn bushes, which had little respect for the mink coat.

The big *passeur* turned to us on the other side of the bushes and whispered: "You are in France, but you are not yet safe."

We all shook hands, and I was filled with a deep and wonderful joy. Perhaps this was partly communicated to me by the emotions of my comrades. But I myself had always been deeply attached to France; and now that the soil under my feet was no longer in any way German I felt that I had reached half-way in the journey to freedom, and had achieved half of the objects which Wally and I had formulated in prison. I thought of Wally too, and wished that he were with me, brave soul.

At the bottom of the hill there were lights. They came from a large hospital. Our guide led us to the back quarters of the hospital and a young French doctor came running to meet us, shook hands warmly, and invited us to follow him. He put us in an old building which was used as a barn. Most of the rooms were half-filled with hay. The Jewish family talked incessantly, as people do who have been through an ordeal, real or imaginary —this despite the warnings of both the *passeur* and the doctor that there were Germans in the hospital only a few yards from our cobwebbed windows, and that we must be absolutely silent.

At last to our relief the guide came back and said to the Jews: "I will take you three to Madame Philomène at Villerupt. There are false papers and beds waiting for you there.

"You, *messieurs*," he continued, turning to us, "will be obliged to stay the night here. There are no papers for you because you were not expected for another week, and it was only the urgent need to get you clear of Germany that made the chief decide to push you across to-night."

"But they promised that we should get both papers and money," said Ramon.

"*Démerdez-vous, je m'en fiche,*" replied the *passeur* rudely.

"But at least you are going to put us in touch with your organisation in Villerupt?" I said.

"Yes, I may as well," he replied. "I'll ask the young doctor to take you over there in the morning. Madame Philomène is the name. But there's not much that she can do for you, poor soul."

"Do you sleep all to-morrow?" I asked the young son when he prepared to follow his father into the darkness. It was after 3 a.m., and he had to cross the German lines again to get back to his bed.

"No, *messiers*," he answered. "I go to school at eight in the morning."

The doctor brought us a little food and wine, and told us we should sleep in the hay. He was a thin youth, short-sighted and round-shouldered, with a harsh angry voice. He talked to us while we ate cheese and meat, cut very thinly, inside cylinders of French bread.

"Don't think you have come to the land of plenty, my friends. France is suffering, suffering. Food is very difficult. Even the peasants are starving round here. The Boche takes so much. The workers are well paid. But what is there to eat? We lack fats. Fats! In peace-time we never thought of them except as things you put in soap and face-cream and explosives. Now we think of nothing else.

"That cheese you are eating is miserable. Yet the factory that

257

made it turned out fine cheese until 1940. The only difference is that the cheese you are eating has no fats in it.

"Revolting, is it not? Men dying for lack of fats. Gross fats, horrible fats, necessary fats, *wonderful* fats. Before the débâcle we wallowed in them, and we never knew it, never realised it. My friends, it is a sobering thing to realise that fats are as important as a soul. If the soul exists. At any rate nothing is more certain than this. The soul may exist when the body has a sufficiency of fats. The soul ceases to exist when the supply of fats ceases. . . ."

"Completely mad," was Ramon's verdict on the doctor. But I was not so sure.

Next morning, in the main street of the half-mining, half-agricultural village of Villerupt, we met Philomène. She was middle-aged and gipsy-looking. With her well-cut, Roman features, she could have passed for an older and swarthier version of Marianne, the girl on the French currency notes. Her cottage was in the main street. It was clean, and very poor. Her son was there, a fine young man called Raoul, in the breeches and heavy boots of a land worker.

The three Jews sat around Philomène's kitchen table, eating their breakfast. I felt the spittle rush to my mouth as I carefully positioned myself in the rocking-chair, discreetly away from their family circle, yet close enough to politely embarrass them. They ate good bread, and covered it thickly with fresh butter. These delicacies came from the suitcases which we had carried across the frontier. After we had sat there for ten minutes we were each given a slice of bread with some butter on it.

But nothing was offered either to Philomène or to her son. The pair of them could not tear their eyes from the sight of such unusual food. I felt a beast as I ate in front of them. The Jewess wrapped up what was left in grease-proof paper. It was time for the three of them to catch the bus for the station.

Philomène shook her head when we asked her about papers.

"The mayor here will give no more," she said. "In fact I dare not ask him for another false identity-card. I am in trouble with him myself. Last week the Germans asked for another blanket levy from our village. The mayor sent a note round, apologising, but requiring me to deliver two blankets at the *Mairie* immediately. I only took one, and I told him to his face that he was too soft with the Boches. Maybe he is a good man, but he should stand up to them. More than half my blankets and sheets have gone that way already. No, I could not ask the mayor here in Villerupt. But I tell you what. The mayor at Tiercelet is a good man. You might try him yourselves. Spin a hard-luck story. He is decent, really decent. . . ."

The mayor of Tiercelet did not look like a hopeful proposition. Ramon and I had called first at the *Mairie* and had seen his son and daughter-in-law. They had snubbed us, and they did not know the worst; they did not know that I was British.

He was a big peasant, the mayor, broad-shouldered and as weathered as a man could look after some sixty years of work in the fields. I did not let Ramon talk. I told the mayor my story, beginning from the desert and telling it quite slowly, as though I were a little simple and very earnest. I have never been more earnest in all my life. I was pleading for my life.

The mayor sat at one side of his kitchen, leaning his battered face on one hard hand. I sat at the other side, my brown beret held in my two hands, and my hands wedged between my knees. I wanted to flutter my hands about, but I remembered Henry Snell teaching us in our public-speaking classes in Padula prison that immobility helped the speaker.

When I had finished the mayor thought for a time, breathing a little noisily, and turning his big head like a worried dog. Then he lifted his head and spoke sadly, speaking his mind and giving his considered judgment.

"I am sorry, young man. You have got the right to ask me what you ask, because you are fighting against our enemies, the Germans. But I have not got the right to do it. I am a father and a grandfather; I have a duty to my family. I am mayor of this village; I have a duty to my people.

"You speak French well for a foreigner, but with an accent. If I give you an identity-card I shall have to stamp it as coming from the *commune* of Tiercelet. You say that you intend to travel right through France to the Pyrenees. Man, I have never travelled all that way even in peace-time. What chance have you with your accent? And your appearance? Maybe the Germans are already trailing you. Perhaps you will get through to Spain. I hope so, indeed, I hope so. But we must say that the odds are strongly against you, or seem to be. I have not the right to give you an identity-card."

"Will you give my friends identity-cards, my two friends? They are both Frenchmen who have escaped from Germany."

"Yes, I will give them cards."

He sent to the *Mairie* for his son-in-law and forms for identity-cards and fifteen-franc stamps. I sat there in his small kitchen. I twisted my brown beret until the blood ceased to flow in the fingers of my right hand. I knew that so long as we remained in the room there was some hope. The mayor wanted to give me an identity-card. But his reason had the upper hand of his desire. I knew that the French peasant is slow to change his mind. I felt embarrassed there—embarrassed that I had made the mayor uncomfortable.

But this was no moment for diffidence. I made my seat into a sucker that gripped my kitchen chair. My two feet were two iron pegs driven into the red cement floor. I was a fixture in his kitchen. I was sitting there for my life, for freedom, for a sight of Britain again.

His wife came in. I told the whole story again. This time I made it longer, slower. I dared to put in some flowery touches. They were not bored. The son-in-law, the forms, the fifteen-franc stamps had all arrived from the *Mairie*. But the mayor listened to me all over again. He did one thing at a time. He was not going to give out false papers for Alban and Ramon while he was listening to me. When I had finished he began to breathe deeply again, and his head wagged slowly from side to side.

"At least you will drink some coffee," said his wife. It took a long time to get the coffee, but at length it was boiling and we drank it with noisy sucking noises. Ramon offered cigarettes. The mayor and his son each took one. I nearly gasped with hope. We had been in the room over two hours.

The son wrote out identity-cards for Alban and Ramon. They fixed the photographs on them and stamped them in two places. I sat at the other end of the room, talking politely to the mayor's wife and the daughter-in-law. Ramon picked up the two cards and put them in one of his pocket-books. There was a silence.

"Jean-Jacques," said the mayor's wife suddenly. "You will give this young man his identity-card, or I will never speak to you again."

He looked at her, and I wondered to see gratitude to her in his face.

"I said that I had not the right to give him the card, Marie, because of the family and because of the *commune*."

"I will answer to the family if anything goes wrong, and you have always been man enough to answer for any of your actions to the *commune*. Give him his papers."

"I could not do it without the sanction and backing of the *Gendarmerie*."

"All right, then," she agreed. "Anne-Marie, ring the *Gendarmerie* at once, and tell the lieutenant that the mayor has something to discuss with him, if he is not too occupied—something urgent."

We waited for another twenty minutes. The mayor looked happier now. He had passed his reason over to his wife and to the *gendarmes*. Now, unless the *gendarmes* interfered, he could give way to his desire, he could be a *bon Français* and a patriot. If there is one thing that a *bon Français* likes it is being a patriot, especially when some risk to himself is entailed.

"Will you promise one thing?" said the mayor to me. "If the Germans or the Militia catch you, will you immediately take all possible measures to destroy your identity-card?"

"I promise."

The lieutenant and a *brigadier* arrived in their smart blue uniforms. The lieutenant saluted me and then kissed me on both cheeks when the astute Ramon said that I was one of the famous *Huitième Armée*. The mayor explained about the identity-card.

"What are you waiting for?" exclaimed the lieutenant. "Give it to him at once. I personally will guarantee it."

On his advice I gave my correct date of birth for the false papers and only slightly changed my name. . . .

"MILLARD, Georges," the mayor's son wrote on my card in spidery, decorative copper-plate. My picture looked cadaverous and timid beside the name. They described me as a house-painter, *peintre en bâtiments*. Ramon and Alban were both given their real names, and were described as an engineer and a cook respectively.

When we got outside the mayor's cottage I felt as though I had come through a long ordeal. When we left I had said: "I will never forget what you have done for me." It was neither the first nor the last time that I used those words to a Frenchman. But I could not have meant it more.

Now I was carrying the mayor's life and the lieutenant's life and a part of the *commune* of Tiercelet in my inside pocket.

The energetic Philomène had been working for us in our absence. She sent us straight off to see another man, an employee in the big steel works of Micheville, near Villerupt. This young man forged certificates showing that each of us was a full-time employee at the Micheville steelworks, and gave us individual forged letters from the manager of the steelworks stating that the bearers were leaving Micheville on fifteen days' leave, beginning the following day.

Now the only thing we needed was money. A single railway ticket to Paris cost 300 francs. All that we had in French money amounted to 350 francs. Ramon went to the director of the prisoners of war organisation with an introduction from Philomène. He asked for 1,000 francs to help him and two other *French* evaders to get to Paris. And he got it. That evening we sat down to dinner knowing that all was ready. We could leave for Paris next morning.

Philomène was a fine, lusty woman. Her husband, a handsome Italian metal-worker, was fifteen years her junior. But you would not have guessed it then, in 1943. He was stringy about the neck and jaw, and he had blue pouches beneath his eyes.

He talked all the time of *"La graisse, la graisse, la graisse"*, as though the word for fats were the equivalent of "Love" or "Heaven" or "Joy". Every time that he opened his mouth *"la graisse"* or *"matières graisses"* seemed to force their way out along with the other words, as though a long queue of the words for fats was waiting always just under his tongue.

Although Philomène must have earned considerable sums from the *passeurs,* and her husband and son both had good jobs, we had only potatoes for dinner, boiled potatoes. She told us that even the potatoes had not been bought. She had stolen them from a silo "belonging" to the Germans. Most mornings before the dawn Philomène went out with other women of Villerupt to steal what they could from the black winter countryside. Sometimes they found nothing better than the leaves of root vegetables.

Philomène talked a lot about rations. I was to get used to this in France. The meat ration was 88 grams per week, but it was a gala week, she said, when they could get their ration from the butcher.

"We can buy nothing here, absolutely nothing. Even salt lacks."

"Salt! Who wants salt if he can get fats?" said the husband. "I tell you, men, I dream about *la graisse.*"

I stopped listening to their talk, and looked around me at the French kitchen, so practical and efficient. I wondered when peace and plenty would come again to this strong woman and her kitchen on the edge of France.

262

French housewives are conservative creatures. In Philomène's kitchen I saw the things that I was to see in so many other kitchens in France. Then they were newer to me, and I noted their efficiency or inefficiency, although I did not fully realise their national character until I had lived in many more French kitchens.

Up to my escape I had never had the good fortune to live in kitchens. While the others talked, then, I looked at the range, much more like a table than an English range, like a big solid rectangular table standing a foot out from the wall on four short curly legs, with two ovens, and a hot-water-tank with a bright brass tap, and a fat chimney-pipe sticking straight out of the top and then curling into the wall through a brass ring. Handily fixed behind the range hung the enamelled rack for holding a battery of ladles and other cooking utensils with a small trough over which their working ends could drip. I saw the sloping, shallow sink with a single "cold" tap high above it, the bead curtains over the window, the little deal cupboard holding shoe-cleaning things, the dresser well filled with plates and glass (much better filled with such things than most English kitchen dressers), the well-worn board for chopping herbs and vegetables and for cutting meat, a seed catalogue, a picture of the Virgin, two or three crumpled illustrated histories of the 1914-18 war. . . .

Alban, being the smallest, was put to sleep that night on the rocking-chair. Ramon and I had a bedroom immediately behind the kitchen, and beyond us was the room of Philomène and her young husband. There were fierce yellowish photographs of men posed in *poilu* uniform all round the walls of her room. Just over the bed was the picture of a *chasseur alpin* whose eyes spat brimstone, and whose moustaches even in the photograph looked as though they would twang like tuning-forks if you touched the waxed tips.

"That was my first husband," said Philomène when she saw me tremble before this picture. "I keep him over the bed to remind my second that there is a tradition to follow. There were few men like my first husband. Except in the autumn. He never could stand the autumn. It made him go soft and weepy to see the leaves fall."

Behind Philomène's bedroom was the garden, and the earth lavatory was at the far end of the garden. You could either get to it by traversing all the rooms or by a corridor that ran past the kitchen. In the early hours of the morning I was returning to the kitchen by this corridor when I heard the heavy tramp of German boots in the street outside. This disquieted me considerably. The door leading from my corridor into the street was not locked, was not even closed. Philomène regarded her kitchen door as the front door, and left the other open. As silently as I could I slipped into the kitchen. The lock turned with a slight creak.

After a little I moved to the window and peered out. There were a few lights in the narrow, bending street. Seven Germans stood outside Philomène's cottage.

My heart jumped furiously, ran away from me, and came back with a thud. I felt like the rifleman I had seen hit in the chest by a 20-mm. shell. For a small fraction of time he had looked shocked. Then he was dead. But once I had my heart back I felt better. The Germans were men of the *Feldgendarmerie*. They were not looking at our cottage. They were standing looking down the street, their machine-pistols ready, pointing where they looked.

"What are you doing here?" one of the Germans asked in French. His words just reached the kitchen, through the cloudy glass of the window. I could hear no reply.

"*Venez avec nous*," the German said.

"*Je viens*," answered a French voice.

The big grey figures moved back up the street with a smaller black figure in the middle of their group. I took a long deep breath and went happily back to the thick feather-bed where Ramon lay half-dressed and half-buried in the spongy softness of the *plumard*.

It had been a good day. We had papers and money, and with luck by that time next morning I would be in Paris. Paris. I went to sleep again, thinking of the serious, beautiful Paris that I had left in June, 1940. Paris. I would take a taxi to Le Bourget, and in an hour and a quarter I would be at Croydon. Pity Croydon airport was so far from the centre of London. The journey in was so annoying, so annoying. . . .

CHAPTER XVIII

"PARIS, three singles," said Ramon to the man behind the ticket office grille at Longwy station.

"Your papers, please."

"What's the idea? Want to see the papers of my *copains* too?"

"New regulations. No. Yours will do. O.K."

I was standing watching this, and fuming with concealed rage. For on the journey from Villerupt to Longwy, a 30-minute journey in a crowded bus, Ramon and Alban had struck up a warm friendship, full of banter and easy-come-easy-go phrases, with two young women of the shop-girl type.

Now Ramon was collecting the change and the tickets while I stood impotently with the girls and Alban, who was continuing the banter. Because of my English accent, I scarcely dared to open my mouth.

"Come on," Ramon now exclaimed. "We have twenty minutes before the train arrives. Let's all go and have a glass of something in the buffet."

"How lovely!" chorused the girls.

"*Salaud!*" I hissed at Ramon, pulling him back by his coat.

"Don't look so glum, man," he whispered back. "Don't you see? They are our best disguise. They make us look respectable, or at any rate normal. Just smile at them—and pretend to have laryngitis."

Soon we were seated round a wet table-top with five tiny glasses of brandy on it. I fixed my eyes and my mind on nonessentials like the extremely dirty neck of the white blouse of one of the girls. Occasionally I smiled and moved my lips when none of our own party were looking, to give outsiders the idea that I was inside the conversation. Sometimes they asked me a question and I answered: *"Oui,"* or *"Non,"* or *"Pensez-vous!"* in a husky voice.

Ramon was showing all his signs of tobacco famine. He kept taking out his empty cigarette-case, a bluish tin affair, and slapping it open and shut, then replacing it with a sigh in his waistcoat pocket. He restlessly fluttered his hands, and asked several people if cigarettes were plentiful in the region. At length he went off, after a discussion with the woman behind the bar, to return beaming with a packet of *Gauloises Bleues*.

He announced loudly and proudly that they had asked 100 francs for the packet, but when he had told them that he had escaped from Germany they had taken only 80 francs. To add to the 80 francs I had been obliged to pay the bill for the brandies, which came to 100 francs. I was not yet accustomed to the occupation prices in France, and our financial resources were so slender that this extravagance infuriated me. The young women departed with effusive thanks, and when these were done I turned on Ramon and told him that unless he were more discreet and sensible I would quit his company.

"And yours too," I told the gaping Alban. "Kindly remember, the next time you feel inclined to pick up a couple of *gonzesses*, that I am with you, and that you have some responsibility to me."

They were not accustomed to frankness or criticism from me, and they replied with profuse apologies, although Ramon looked a shade rebellious; and at the rate he was smoking he would require another packet of cigarettes at 80 francs before we left the station. (I learned a little later that he had actually bought two.)

Just before we caught the bus from Villerupt young Raoul had come up to me, and, with becoming embarrassment, had slipped 200 francs from his own savings into my pocket. He had also given me one of his own ties, a blue one with pale blue diagonal stripes. He said that the one Greta had given me was too red and communistic, and might attract the Germans' angry glances. It looked as though his 200 francs would be more than useful.

We could only find one empty third-class seat in the whole long train. As we had previously arranged, I sat down, while Ramon and Alban stood in the corridor outside my compartment. There were four women and three other men in the compartment. They all seemed to be decent, ordinary people, and none of them paid much attention to me. Indeed, thanks to Greta, I was now dressed rather better than the average Frenchman, yet my clothes were so obviously provincial that I could not have looked less like my real identity.

Ramon and Alban turned frequently to grin at me through the corridor windows. The train rattled and bounced along at a good pace, a refreshing speed after our previous journey in the "omnibus". I began to feel that I was getting somewhere, but the idea of a German control was always uppermost in my mind, and too imminent to allow me to relax.

We had not been travelling for an hour when I saw Ramon put his index finger to his nose, our agreed signal to indicate that the control was coming. Ramon moved down the corridor to the left, while Alban slid off to the right.

It seemed to us that since we all had identical papers it would be better if the Germans did not examine them all at once. The controlling was being done by a steel-helmeted *Feldgendarmerie*

266

N.C.O. accompanied by a French interpreter in German uniform. They came to Ramon a few yards before my compartment. Ramon handed over his identity-card. The photograph, insecurely fixed with gum the day before at Tiercelet, fell off.

"*Papiers, s'il-fous-blaît*," the German said from the doorway of our compartment. He wanted our workers' certificates as well as our identity-cards. When it was my turn to hand mine over the photograph fell off my identity-card. I picked the photograph off the floor, and he fixed it back on the card, asking no questions.

At the far end of the carriage Alban showed his papers, and the photograph fell off his identity-card. The German called up the interpreter, who asked Alban why there were two other men in that carriage with exactly similar papers.

Alban replied indignantly that so far as he knew there might be twenty with similar papers. He produced the letter from the director of the Aciéries de Micheville stating that he, Alban, was released that day for a fifteen-day holiday.

"They seem to be quite all right," said the interpreter, turning to the German. "Their papers are quite in order. I do not think there is anything to be suspicious about."

Philomène had given us food that she could ill spare, brave woman. We had bread and sausage, in long, scrappy brown-paper parcels. When the control had passed I felt a spring of relief gush inside me. And I was hungry. I ate shyly, listening to the simple talk of the friendly people around me. They got packages out too, bigger ones than mine. And when I had finished one of the women gave me a hard-boiled egg, and a man gave me a tumbler of red wine. Then another woman gave me more bread and cream cheese "to finish your wine with", and another man gave me a small glass of prune brandy "to help digestion", and a third woman gave me some coffee from a thermos-flask. They thought that I looked thin and delicate. I contrived to keep within the warmth of their conversation with an occasional "*oui*" or "*non*". When one of the men asked me where I had come from I thought the best thing to do was to put a finger to my lips and give a long and meaningful (or meaningless) wink. This worked admirably.

When the eating was finished I pretended to go to sleep. As though I could sleep! The rhythm of the bogies sang: "Paris, Paris, Paris this evening. Paris, Paris, Paris this evening."

In the evening the Germans dragged six young Frenchmen

off the train and down the platform past our window. If we had not been given workers' certificates by the young man from the steel-works, we should have been there too. They were what my French companions called *réfractaires*, young Frenchmen who had hidden from the Germans' labour call-up.

Even in peace-time, with money in my pocket, with friends and acquaintances to go to, with some kind of assured position however feeble, I was always nervous when approaching in a train at night a great city like Paris or London. Now we were running through the suburbs, the grey and dark-grey-with-pale-blue-splashed suburbs, and we had no idea where to go or what to do in Paris. We were extremely short of money. The train was two hours late.

I knew the Gare de l'Est well, and had always found it one of the least sympathetic of Paris stations, like London's Gare de l'Est, Liverpool Street. Now we plunged into its darkness and its coldness. I felt the weight of the trio upon me. Up to then I had left the lead to Ramon, I had let him be spokesman. He had more of a presence than Alban. But now, strangely enough, I was more at home in Paris than either of the two Frenchmen, for they were both provincials, and had only passed through the capital at best. They regarded Paris, as provincials will, with awed wonder. I had less awe for her than I had for my own capital, London.

We felt our way across the wide space of darkness in front of the terminus, and I led them into the big Café de l'Est. We sat down at a little shiny red-and-black table, overcrowded with the three of us, a typically Parisian table. Ramon wanted "three blows of white", but there was no wine, so the waiter brought us little frosted-glass bottles of highly-coloured synthetic fruit juice. The radio blared in the bizarre chromium and dark red interior. The last time I had been there I had been doing the strangely tragic, the deeply moving story of French soldiers leaving civilian life in September, 1939, and going off in hundreds of thousands from the big station across the open space outside that café. They had been a little drunk, some of the soldiers there. But I had not put that in my story. Because on the whole they had been so silent and resigned about that strange disruption. Geoffrey Cox had asked me to go out and do the story. And it had depressed me. Was France facing Germany with these amateur brave (but unenthusiastic) hearts and their rifles, carbines, light machine-guns and 75s? Tom Delmer was sitting squashed in the big leather arm-chair when

I returned to the office, like some dark, digesting Buddha.

"Do you think now that the Germans will win?" he asked.

"Very likely," I answered honestly and wearily.

Then, when I was doing the story, I had had some power behind me, some status. I had had a home in Paris, and Anne. I had been independent. Now I was dependent on Paris.

Now that I was clear of the train and the station, I liked being dependent on Paris. Taking a chance with her. Facing her with next to no money, and with my life dependent on her whim and the whims of fortune. It was fine to be in Paris again, and to hear the quick, neat French being clipped out all around me.

Ramon, urged by me, asked the waiter to recommend a cheap hotel. The man wrote an address on the back of one of the café's florid cards: "Hôtel d'Angleterre et des États-Unis." The name made us smile; there are probably many hotels with that name in Paris. This one was within half a mile of the station.

We climbed a narrow staircase to the office. The proprietor, eyeing us shrewdly, said that if we paid in advance he could give us a room for three—one double and one single bed—for 80 francs a night. There was a basin in the bedroom, with running water and hot water that was hot. Leaving our scanty belongings there, we went down to the café on the corner.

While the others drank their pale onion beers I went into the telephone-booth and dialled Cécile's number. I heard the ringing tone, and imagined the bell shrilling in her comfortable Passy flat. Cécile was a Jewess, it was true. But a very unobvious one, and I did not think that the Germans would have touched her. She was a charming person, an old friend of my family. She had been a good Frenchwoman, working herself nearly to death among the wounded and the refugees in the reception centre at the Gare de l'Est right up to the end in Paris. Perhaps it was the Gare de l'Est that had reminded me of her. She had been rich, and I knew that she would help me. What I needed was money.

Now, with rising excitement, I heard the receiver being lifted at the other end of the line. I asked for Cécile, and a voice which I recognised as that of her maid answered: *"De la part de qui, Monsieur?"*

"De la part de Georges Millar."

There was a gulp, then a hissing noise over the telephone.

"Madame is not here," she cried. "She is not here, do you understand? You have no right to telephone. Ring off, I beg of you, for all our sakes. . . ." She had slammed the receiver down.

I stood alone in the dark, damp-smelling booth, as though I had just realised that there was a war on: that behind the Paris that I had glimpsed only in the garish café there was vileness and fear, and perhaps death.

I had last seen Cécile only two days before the fall of Paris. I had driven her to dinner at Maxime's. We had not eaten much, and we had drunk pink champagne. I had advised her to clear out of Paris, to go to her villa in the Midi. Poor Cécile!

This attempt at making contact had disgusted me with the telephone. It was only, probably, that Cécile was a Jewess, and therefore her home might be presumed to be under constant Gestapo surveillance. But perhaps the whole telephone system of Paris was tapped and watched by the Germans. And any of my former friends might be under surveillance as people who had been associated with the British.

Ramon and Alban saw that I had had a shock, but I refused to tell them anything about it. Alban said that he had an aching emptiness in him. So we went off to the buffet at the big station, a place where I had frequently eaten before, and eaten reasonably. Now all we could have, at an enormous price, was stale bread, apricot jam, and beer. Back in the hotel, we drew lots for the single bed. Alban won as usual, and I had to sleep with Ramon.

Early in the morning I rose, washed and shaved. The room smelled badly, and Alban and Ramon were swathed in thickly unpleasant sleep. The roofs of Paris were glowing in a cold dawn, those friendly roofs that always seem to pair off like lovers. I was filled with nostalgia for Paris, and desire to get out into the streets alone. While I cleaned the shaving soap off my face I glanced down into the narrow canyon of a street below.

A reasonably well-dressed man of the clerk type, wearing a correct white collar and a black tie, was moving down the street in a peculiarly furtive manner. I soon saw why. He often stopped in doorways to examine the contents of the ash-cans. Immediately below me he stuffed into the pocket of his dark overcoat something that looked like potato-peelings.

I was already half-dressed when Ramon awoke and asked me (a shade suspiciously, I thought) what plans I had for the day. I told him I intended to try to find my former secretary, and asked him his plans. He had had a rich friend in his regiment. This man was now running a postage stamp business in Montmartre. Ramon thought he would look him up to ask for money.

"How much will we need to take the three of us to the Pyrenees?" I asked.

"At least 10,000 francs," he said. "Think you can get that?"

"Yes, if I can find this secretary."

"Think you can find your way alone to her place?"

"Of course I can. I'll take the *Métro*."

"O.K., Georges. We'll meet again this evening."

But a little later he changed his mind and said that it would be lunacy on his part to allow me to go out into the streets of Paris alone: that he would never forgive himself if anything happened to me, and so on. I saw he was determined to accompany me wherever I went, so I put as good a face as possible on it. I did not quite like the idea of introducing Ramon to Scherb. I was not yet absolutely sure of Ramon. I did not believe he had recovered from the rancour which had grown in him in the Hayange hot-house. But if he suspected that I wanted to shake him off he would undoubtedly become doubly dangerous. Alban was going off to see the wife of a man who had been in Vienna with him.

Ramon and I went to the big café by the station. The black coffee was made from roasted wheat seeds, and you were required to sweeten it by sprinkling in liquid saccharine from a sprinkler designed to throw more interesting drops, like those of angostura bitters. The waiter asked us to try their patent breakfast cakes, "Madeleines". These sold for five francs each without coupons. But we found that they were made of sawdust.

Outside in the morning air I stood sniffing.

"What's the matter?" asked Ramon.

"Paris has lost some of her personality, she has lost the morning smells of coffee and fresh bread and water sprinkled on the dusty streets."

But the *Métro* smelled the same. I remembered that smell from my school-days. It smelled of tarry hemp rope. The stations had not changed, except that they were four times more crowded, and you often had to queue up in the tortuous tunnel approaches before the scarlet automatic gates. And there were many Germans, or *"Verdegris"* as the Parisians called them, among the crowds.

Inside the carriages there was an intense politeness. An unnatural veneer of good manners sat on the French *Métro*-users as awkwardly as a shiny top-hat on a naked cannibal chief. They were shamed into these good manners by the impeccable politeness of the Germans. If the Boches gave up their seats to Frenchmen, then Frenchmen were obliged to do the same thing, only to do it better, with more dash. Now, for the first time, I saw Jewesses with the persecuted air of persons under the shadow of official race hatred, and wearing on their breasts as concrete evidence of the persecution bright badges showing the letter J. Everybody, including the Germans, looked rather annoyed and bored by the general atmosphere of politeness. It was all as forced as the German orders to the *Wehrmacht* to "make a good impression in Paris".

We went up five flights of handsome staircase to Scherb's flat. Ramon had whistled as we swung in at the solid doorway.

"This is class," he said, as we went upstairs. "These people must have plenty of *ronds* (dough). Ten *billets* (10,000 francs) will be a bagatelle to them."

"Ten *billets* are ten *billets*," I replied politely. "I don't know yet that my friends are here."

Ramon, as I had instructed him to do, rang the door-bell. The door was opened by the charming Swiss, *Mademoiselle* Guex, who had been with Scherb's family since they came out of Russia and before.

"*Mademoiselle* Mara, please," said Ramon.

Mademoiselle looked at him a little doubtfully, and at my dark shape on the landing behind. Ramon carried his *valise diplomatique,* and she took us for commercial travellers or black marketeers.

"*Entrez, messieurs,*" she said politely. "I will tell *Mademoiselle* Mara that you are here. What name shall I say?"

She had shut the door behind us. Now she suddenly threw her hand up to her mouth and let out a strangled: "Ah, *Monsieur* Millar. . . ."

We heard noises of upheaval from the back parts of the flat where Scherb and her sisters were still in bed (it was only ten o'clock). I led Ramon into the salon. I was delighted and greatly touched to see that it had not changed. Many, many a time in England, in the desert, and in prison, I had wondered about this family and about this correct, prim, little room in Passy. There was such family solidity expressed in the room with its pictures of Russian royalty and relatives and houses, with its flowers and its *bric-à-brac*. Nothing had changed. The family had held solid. Now I knew that I should be looked after. I should be able to move on from Paris.

Scherb came in first of all. Very tall in a long dressing-gown, beautiful in her strange, remote way, and with her strange way of moving as though her feet were always a little in front of her body, as though her body were a reed being blown back from her smoothly moving feet. I thought she looked better, stronger than the last time I had seen her, near Tours in the terrible, dissolving days. She shook hands with me, and then ran back to tell her sisters that it was "really Millar".

Ramon was loud in his praises. According to his expert judgment, she was really a *belle gonzesse,* and I suppose that it was the first time that Scherb had been described in those exact terms.

Scherb had been the centre of the *Daily Express* Paris office for some years before the war: in fact she had really *been* the Paris office. Ramon could only ask what she had been to me. And I could only explain to him that she had been a superior kind of secretary. He could not get the thing properly arranged in his mind.

Now she came back with two of her sisters. The third, the extremely beautiful one, was married, and lived elsewhere, but not too far away. They all wore long flared dressing-gowns, and their faces were correctly made up, and their hair was smooth and black with brown lights in it. They all talked quickly to me in the English they had learned at their English nanny's knee. None of them had ever been to England, but Scherb at any rate spoke much better English than most Englishwomen. It was wonderful to be among people who behaved in an ancient and correct manner. I had to pinch myself. These were women who did not make noises like fire-hydrants when they drank coffee.

They gave us breakfast—real coffee, bread, butter and homemade jam.

White Russians are notoriously expert at *combines.* I was glad to see that Scherb and her family evidently had the ability to survive despite the Germans.

I mentioned to Scherb the names of several wealthy acquaintances. They were all in the south, or they had disappeared, or they were believed to have left for Britain.

"Do you want money?" Scherb asked.

"Yes, I do."

"How much do you need?"

"Ten thousand francs." (Then worth £60.)

"I can get you that by this evening." She went to the telephone and spoke to her brother-in-law.

"I want 10,000 francs for something important. I shall explain when I see you."

"Come to lunch and I will give you the money," he answered at once. Ramon rubbed his hands in delight as we left.

"That was too easy," he said as we went downstairs. I could have kicked him.

He took me to lunch with friends of his who lived in a Grenelle tenement. The husband had been in Ramon's regiment. Now he had a good job in a Paris garage. It was not difficult to see the signs of starvation both in him and in his wife. They had been stout Parisians before the occupation. Now the skin hung emptily from their jaws and their wrists. They were hospitable, like all good French people. They insisted that we must lunch with them.

I could have wept with compassion as I saw the woman rifling her precious and pathetic little stocks to give us something worth eating.

She produced radishes with butter, then two eggs between the four of us followed by a dandelion salad. Instead of olive oil and vinegar dressing, she poured upon the salad a little precious melted and seasoned butter. The bowl had been rubbed with garlic. The salad, like the whole meal, was one of the most delicious that I had ever eaten. I picture them sitting the following day at the table beside the big brass double bed and wondering what they were going to eat. They pressed on us, too, their weekly ration of a litre of red wine. We could not refuse. They would have been offended.

With food coupons, the wife told me, she could buy wine for 9 francs a litre. Without coupons it cost between 45 and 100 francs a litre. I talked to her a lot about the black market. I offered her the meat coupons that I had been given in Villerupt.

"You could give me one hundred meat coupons without its making the slightest difference to my larder," she said. "There is never any meat in the butchers' shops. You can only find it in the restaurants, and ordinary people like us cannot afford that."

The German rations were starvation rations. Even so, the Parisians could not find the rations in the shops. It was a question of buy on the black market or die.

But how could you buy on the black market unless you were

274

a millionaire? this poor housekeeper asked me. She took a little book from her apron pocket, and showed me the prices she had been obliged to pay for commodities which had always been cheap necessities in every French household.

Butter was 500 francs a kilo. (Before the war it had been about 20 francs.) Coffee, which had been as cheap as butter, now cost 3,000 francs a kilo. Oil, not olive oil, for that was absolutely unobtainable in the north of France, but oil of the colza bean, was 1,000 francs a litre. A chicken cost between 300 and 500 francs, and lucky indeed you would be to find one. Sugar was easier to get and comparatively cheap, thanks to the advanced French sugar-beet industry. It only cost 200 francs a kilo. Bread was 2 francs 75 centimes a kilo with coupons and 38 francs a kilo without coupons. A kilo of pork cost 350 francs.

Tears ran out of her honest eyes as she went over these figures. Ramon was talking to the husband of war-time experiences in which Ramon, according to himself, figured usually as a tough, but modest, hero. They arranged to go out "to do a round of the best places" that night. I told Ramon that I would not accompany them, since I had arranged to meet Alban that evening (and I suspected that their ideas of enjoyment might not tally with mine).

The stamp-shop in Montmartre was closed when we arrived there. So I left Ramon waiting there for his friend to arrive and open up the shop while I wandered off alone into Paris.

I had never imagined in peace-time, when I passed through *les Halles*, the great markets of Paris, to eat *tripes à la mode de Caen*, or perhaps *soupe à l'oignon* in the early hours of the morning—I had never imagined that I would see suffering in that fat and efficient and prosperous square. But suffering was there as I walked through in 1943. No more wonderful stalls, no more fierce porters breathing wine and garlic over everybody, no more bursting shopping-bags of string and oilskin. Now the cafés and restaurants around the great square were shut or depopulated, and here and there thin women were searching for cabbage outsides or turnip-tops to take home for dinner.

The women of Paris looked fantastically heavily made-up. But then I had not seen women of that type for three years. The shops, from the outsides anyway, still had their Parisian polish and air of richness. I noticed, too, with amusement and without shame that the Germans were thickly clustered in the places where British and American people had gathered until the *Wehrmacht* cleaned them out of France in 1940.

In one such area, in the Place Vendôme, I saw my first *Zazou*. He was a slender youth who swung a heavy umbrella from one languid chamois-leather-gloved hand. He wore a brown hat with turned-up sides of the type that the French called "Anthony Eden". His coat was long, with a slit in the back. His trousers were narrow, almost fitting the leg, and his shoes were heavy. In fact, the clothes seemed to be modelled on an exaggerated idea of an English "gentleman's" clothes.

There were *Zazou* women too. Women in tweed costumes, also with long, slitted coats. They had heavy handbags swinging on straps from their shoulders, and they often led big dogs, Airedales, Setters, Great Danes.

The *Zazous* seemed to be as unpopular with the Germans at that time as they were with the majority of French people. Another odd group of personalities was pointed out to me. These were the *Swings*.

The *Swings* (as their name implied) appeared to me to follow a slightly more American model. The *swing* young man wore a coat with pleats in the back, wide trousers, and co-respondent shoes if he could get them. The *swing* young woman wore long hair hanging over her shoulders. She affected short, wide skirts.

Both the *Zazous* and the *Swings* were made up of young people exclusively. There seemed to be something unhealthy in their existence, as though the youth of France, or a part of it at any rate, cheated of self-respect by the defeat of France, had turned enthusiastically to stupid, ugly, decadent fopperies.

When I bought an evening paper I saw this in the correspondence columns:

Odette (the correspondent): "I picture you of medium height, with dark hair, about 30 years old, a shade *swing*. . . ."

Roger (replying): "Permit me to tell you in my turn that I picture you, Odette, charming, petite, blonde, and less *zazou* than *swing*. . . ."

I found that it was impossible for me to enter the Ritz by the entrance in the Place Vendôme. That was reserved for German officers and their friends. But the back entrance by the Rue Cambon was free to French people (and so-called French people). The place temporarily had a new "morality" rule. No woman was allowed in unaccompanied by a man. The people inside it were all French, and the bar had not changed, except that the drinks were less varied and much more expensive.

The women were very smart. But I felt that I noticed in their clothes, too, particularly in the towering hats, a hint of decadence, something *fin-de-siècle*. Something that fitted in with the *Zazous* and the *Swings,* and the general atmosphere of Paris. I had the impression that Paris was emptily sad, and that Parisians had lost their vitality. The women's breasts were no longer aggressive. The men's eyes were not daggers that stabbed into you, or claws that stripped you from your neck to your ankles with one raking slash.

I collected Alban at the Gare de l'Est, and took him down to Passy. Scherb gave me the 10,000 francs, and asked us to dinner. But there I could refuse without offending them. I was not going to eat *their* food, so I said that we had a previous engagement.

"Where is our previous engagement?" Alban asked dully in the street.

"We will ask the girl in the *Métro*," I answered. "You will tell her that we have full note-cases and empty stomachs."

"O.K."

"Go to Grenelle, get out at La Motte Piquet," advised the girl. "You will easily find black market *bistros* there."

It still made my heart turn over when the *Métro* train ran out from the tunnelled darkness under Paris. It ran out from the Passy station into the evening sunshine over the Seine. The air of Paris was clear, and the distances lovely.

Beside the *Métro* station we found a *bistro* that showed plenty of signs of life. The place was full of tarts. After two glasses of an agreeable white burgundy, Alban began to arrange to go up-stairs with one of these women. Their noises grated on my ears like the screeching of wounded men. Their vulgar perfumes fizzing inside my nostrils were more unwelcome than the odours of the latrine in the murderous fort at Trig Tarhuna. I do not normally detest such women. When I was escaping I was afraid of them, and I hated them because I believed that they might be dangerous.

I dragged Alban off before he could vanish with the girl he liked. She was at least useful in that she directed us to an excellent little restaurant which had a menu over the door marked *Prix Fixe Frs.* 40—a menu which mentioned only soup and vegetables.

But when the proprietor saw me drag out a roll of notes to pay for the *apéritifs* he asked me in a whisper if we would like some nice fillet steaks, and any other delicacies. We ate well then; and my only annoyances were caused by Alban, who made advances to some of the tarts from the *bistro* opposite who had come in with three dubious-looking Frenchmen.

After dinner Alban apologised for his behaviour, and then proceeded to repeat it in the *bistro*, where we drank coffee and cognac. The place had filled up with German soldiers, and the women with whom Alban had considered mounting the stairs were now obviously preparing to do precisely the same thing with the enemy.

Alban knew he had misbehaved in my eyes. He sat watching me sadly in the *Métro*, and finally said: "I did not think that I was doing any wrong, Georges."

"You can commit every sin known and unknown so far as I am concerned. But not when you are with me. I cannot afford to have such people find out that I am British. It would be preposterous to take such a risk."

"I will not do it again. You promise, Georges, that you will not hold it against me."

"Of course not," I replied, softening my voice. But I lied, for I had determined to ditch him at the earliest possible opportunity. His blubber lips with the avid, darting tongue were beginning to get on my nerves, and in his craving for women I saw danger.

Next morning I went to the Palais Royal gardens and looked up from them at the windows of our old apartment in the Rue Montpensier. The big rectangle I stood in looked just the same as in 1940. Perhaps the pollarded trees had grown a shade stumpier and more attractive in my memory than in fact they were. But the statue of a female whom I had always vaguely considered to be Aphrodite rose just as coyly and as whitely from the white stone foam. The grass was the same brilliant yellow-green. The children chirped in the same way as they played in the empty fountain basin. I could project myself back into the past, when I often sat there, among the children, reading on my day off, or when I walked down to the Tuileries gardens with Vicky, our huge chestnut Poodle, jumping at me from all angles. I was happy, projecting myself back, back through the past to the delightful days (for me) of the "phoney war". It was like lying in a warm bath. I always found it easy to think in the dusty, time-drenched grey bath of the Palais Royal.

My escape plans had got no more precise in Paris. I had tried through Scherb to touch the channels of the underground organisations, the secret "railways" that everybody knew existed to get Allied airmen away to Britain. But it was difficult to touch them. Each of those "railways" was obviously wrapped around in protecting cotton-wool of disguise and secrecy. Well, now I had money, and I was confident (though not too confident) that I could get along without organised help. I had made up my mind to leave that evening for Lyons. If there was no organisation to help, Ramon and I would still muddle through. There was just one more chance—a risk, but still a chance. I left my Palais Royal and walked quickly over to the Rive Gauche.

The dirty hotel not far from the Luxembourg had not changed. The staircase still smelled of cats. I opened the door and stood just inside.

Max was clipping his moustache. Infinitesimal points of grey hair were falling on the dressing-table in front of him. (He clipped it every morning.) He was watching me in the mirror.

I saw his eyes flow, rippling down my person. He was making up his mind whether this visit was good or bad for him. Max was always like that. If a horse slipped and fell in the street he wondered: "Is this good or bad for me, Max?" If Britain and France declared war on Germany he wondered: "What is there in this situation for Max?" He was probably looking to see if I had a gun.

He was older, I saw when he stood up. No thinner, that was impossible, but certainly no fatter. You wondered how his spine held him together. He gripped my hand with his firm skeleton's hand.

"Mr. Millar, what are you doing here?"

"Better talk French. The walls must be thin."

"You have money?"

"Why?"

"Give me 200 francs to buy cigarettes. I am too *énervé* to talk to you without cigarettes."

"All right, Max. But I can give you no more. I am poor, and I need all my money now. . . ."

I went to the window and peered down into the street from behind the heavy and dirty lace curtains. I saw him cross the street and enter the *tabac* opposite. Soon he was back. There was a telephone in the *tabac*, but I had decided that the risk was worth it. When he had filled his empty, bony insides with smoke—I half expected to see whiffs of it oozing out through his flies and the ends of his sleeves and trousers—he spoke. (Note that he asked no questions. Max never liked being questioned, and he never questioned.)

"You are stronger and thinner, Mr. Millar."

"I have been a soldier."

"Ah, you have been a soldier, like me; long ago."

"You are still a patriot, Max."

"Of course. Poland will arise. But even patriots must eat."

"We shall eat, and drink, after the war."

"No, you will never come back to Paris after the war. She is degraded now. Only men like me who must be in Paris to live, men who die outside Paris, who can breathe only the cultured air of Paris, will live here after the war."

"We will have many drinks in the Boulevard St. Germain after the war."

"Do you remember when I won the bets over the *formidables* and the *distingués* of beer in the Brasserie Lipp?"

"Could I ever forget?"

Now there was a silence. He would not ask me what I wanted. I must tell him. But Max found silences awkward.

"Would you consider selling your droll English boots, Mr. Millar?"

"No, I need them too badly."

"Ah, you need them too badly. Pity, I know somebody who would give 5,000 francs for them. You do not buy stories now?"

"No, I am not interested in stories."

"Pity, I have a wonderful story. Maybe there would be too much sex and colour in it for your paper."

"Such baits have no interest for me now, Max."

"No interest. What a pity. I wish I could help you."

"You can. Tell me the name and address of a patriot who would help me to find my feet in Lyons."

"Lyons, to find your feet now in Lyons? Ah, Mr. Millar, Lyons is most temperamental at this moment. Too many communists in Lyons."

"But the communists, they say, are doing a wonderful work in Lyons."

"If I could only get straight in my poor head what the communists will do with my Poland. Yes, you could possibly go and see my friend Barbarossa in Lyons."

"Which Barbarossa—the emperor, or the pirate?"

"I do not know whether you are laughing at me now, or just talking nonsense Barbarossa is a patriot and a *débrouillard.*"

"Both interesting qualities. Well, good-bye, Max, see you after the war."

"Good-bye, Mr. Millar. Yes, indeed, if you can face the decadence of Paris. But I warn you I may no longer be here. My tuberculosis grows daily worse. My lungs lack the disinfecting influence of tobacco."

"My poor Max. Here is another 200 francs to buy cigarettes. You *must* live to the end of the war, and I shall see you again at Longchamps."

"Ah, at Longchamps. Remember the day I said to you: 'Mr. Millar,' I said, 'that was a lovely red-headed *poule* I saw you with at Longchamps the other day.' And you replied: 'That was no *poule*, that was my wife.' "

"And you said: 'That was no wife, for I could see that you loved her.' "

"Now one has not enough heart and enough stomach for such feeble witticisms, Mr. Millar. See, I have jotted down Barbarossa's Lyons address. Well, remember, I accept the second 200 francs, but only as a loan. I shall write it down. Yes, I insist. Give me that small pleasure. Good-bye, good-bye, *à bientôt.* . . ."

When I had memorised Barbarossa's address and torn the paper up and scattered the fragments, I took the *Métro* west, for I had a luncheon engagement with the parents of Ramon's rich friend. They lived in the Avenue de Versailles. In front of the building I stood and wondered. Everything in Paris seemed to conspire to fling me back to my past there. I well remembered the front of this very building.

It had been a glorious spring day in 1940. I was lunching with Anne and some other people in our apartment. By an odd coincidence, Geoffrey was also lunching in the Palais Royal, but two or three houses farther up, nearer the theatre.

While we ate there was the usual alert and the clattering of anti-aircraft fire. Anne said once: "That really sounded like a bomb." Everybody laughed at her in a very superior manner. In fact, it was rather bad form to mention such things.

But five minutes later I heard Geoffrey's urgent, high voice on the telephone.

"Got the car there?"

"Yes."

"Well, collect me at once from Number 33. Did you hear those bangs?"

"Yes, the usual ack-ack."

"Those were bombs on the Citroën factory."

"Bombs! My God!"

How fantastic our existence had been, then, in 1940! In 1940 I had said: "Bombs! My God!"

Geoffrey and I had stood near the bridge next to the Citroën factory. The enemy aircraft were so high that they were only traceable by the white lines of vapour. But the bombs crashed well into the target. What a lovely clear Parisian day it was!

One of the American newspaper-men near the bridge said that the Germans *must* have stolen the secret of the American Sperry bomb-sight.

Geoffrey and I had done a tour of the wreckage. First of all the poor district where the bombs that had overshot had fallen. Then up on the other side to the rich area near the Bois. We had looked at the crater of one that had narrowly missed the empty bijou residence of the Duke of Windsor, and at some gory ruins in Passy; and last of all we had come to this very building in the Avenue de Versailles, where there had been a big hole in the ground-floor walling, broken glass in the hallway, and a dead *concierge*.

The damage had been skilfully repaired. But I could still see the outline of the hole in the wall.

Ramon's friends were prosperous middle-class people. The women were carefully dressed, and their faces were as hard and as careful as their over-elaborate hair. They gave us a very splendid meal, with oysters and other delicious things, and they asked me again and again if the British would bomb Paris. I did not find these people sympathetic, and I was thinking of the great delight that was to follow.

As soon as I could with decency escape, I took my leave and walked in the windy sunshine down the quays.

"It is ready," said Scherb in an excited voice when I entered the flat. And she took me to that temple of luxury and of sensuous pleasure, the bathroom. The family had sacrificed and scraped all day to get enough of the closely-rationed Paris gas to heat the bath water.

I never remember feeling a more harmless, a more delightful, a less exhausting, a less complicated physical pleasure than that which possessed every nerve in my body as I lowered myself slowly into the clean hot water. In prison I had had hot showers, but this was the first hot bath since Alexandria in June, 1941, the first hot bath in 29 months. It was a delightful bathroom, with every sign in it of a well-run household, with clean towels and soap and bath essence.

After the bath they gave me a clean, beautiful shirt, made for Scherb's brother-in-law and generously sent to me by him. A most superior shirt. Her married sister, the beautiful one, was there, and the three of us had tea which was brought in cup by cup by the charming Swiss, *Mademoiselle* Guex.

They watched me put on my brown beret in the hall, and they all laughed a little in a slightly sentimental way at my funny clothes and the brown beret. Scherb leaned over the banisters saying, most dangerously, in English: "Good-bye, good-bye, good luck."

The bath had filled me with energy. I felt like pushing the train over or tunnelling out of the *Métro*, instead of taking the ordinary pedestrian route, by the stairs. Alban was waiting for me in the big café by the Gare de l'Est. I was prepared to be politely hard with him, but he saved me the trouble.

He told me that he had been invited to stay with a woman who greatly attracted him. He really wanted, he desired very much, to spend that night with her. But he was, he protested, fully prepared to make a sacrifice and travel down to Lyons with us, or alternatively to take me to his home in the Dordogne, since Ramon was anxious to go to Lyons.

Or, suggested Alban, would we consider putting off our trip to Lyons for one more day?

I regretted that that was impossible, and I gave him a 1,000-franc note, saying that we would meet again in Lyons. He had the address in that town of Greta's exiled parents. I gave him the money partly out of gratitude for the amusement and the help that he had given to me in Strasbourg, and also to salve my conscience, which told me that I would hurt him by letting him drop. But I had made up my mind that his weakness for women made him too dangerous a friend. And he appeared to have outlived his usefulness. In Paris he had done nothing at all in the way of *Système D*.

At the Gare de Lyon Ramon bought our tickets. Now that I had money he seemed to have big ideas. I had difficulty in persuading him that, dressed as we were, we should be safest travelling third class. He wanted to go first or second.

We dined in the *Buffet de la Gare,* a place in which I, like thousands of other Britons who travelled to the south of France, had often eaten before. A pleasant place with shiny black seats dotted over it in orderly islands. For some reason I wanted the best meal possible. Perhaps to drown my reluctance to leave Paris. There was little to eat, and it was expensive. But we managed to get a bottle of indifferent Bordeaux for 250 francs and two infinitesimal glasses of Armagnac, which cost me another 150.

Inspired perhaps by the meal, Ramon made me a present of one of the several note-cases which he carried in his pockets. It was a plain one of black leather, and it had been made by friends of his who worked in the upholstery department of an automobile factory in Nuremberg. The black leather, therefore, was stolen German property, which gave it a sentimental value in our eyes.

Into the case I stuffed what papers and money I had, and also a photograph which Greta had given me. I had noticed by now that Alban, Ramon, and other young Frenchmen of that type always carried a sheaf of photographs with them, and I felt that my lack of them might look suspicious if I were searched. But the note-case definitely made me look more respectable, and the gift warmed me towards Ramon. It also helped me to push into the almost unvisited store-room at the back of my head the knowledge that his rich friend had given him some money. I had learned about this by accident at the luncheon in the Avenue de Versailles. But Ramon, who was not aware that I knew of his small windfall, was pretending to me that we must both live and work with the funds which Scherb had given to me.

My position with Ramon was now like that of a man who rides a very spirited and determined horse—a horse which has definite ideas and fancies of its own, but which knows nevertheless that, once arrived at the end of the long journey, the rider will be able to get him a mangerful of oats. If sufficiently goaded or annoyed, however, the horse might attempt to throw the rider, and even to kick him to death.

I had agreed to go to Lyons at Ramon's suggestion because Lyons, a big city with a much stronger Resistance in it than Paris, was a good half-way house for the south and the Pyrenees. Ramon, on the other hand, wanted to go there because of a girl. This girl was his *marraine-de-guerre*, his war godmother. She appeared as a fine-looking wench in the photographs he showed me, and I could well understand his longing to see her again. Yet his longing annoyed me because, like Alban, he was always trying to make our escape flow along personal channels. He wanted to escape, but he also wanted to have a good time. I

284

just wanted to escape, wanted it so badly that I had no patience for having a good time.

There were no novels on the station bookstall. From the bookstall alone I could have told that Germany and her satellites were losing the war. There was nothing to read there, no sparkle, no new ideas. Only the old Nazi foghorn wailing out the dusty ideas of Hitler and Goebbels in a few badly-produced books, and the smaller, in some ways cleverer, but none the less moth-eaten, Vichy foghorn wailing out of key with the Germans, so timidly and so tactfully out of key. I bought one of the Vichy wails. A book written against England by a French naval officer. Not a genuine naval officer, I noted. He had been a newspaperman, like me.

This time we separated on the train. Ramon went to the front and I stopped in the rear carriage. We were afraid that there would be a severe control when we crossed the Line of Demarcation between occupied and unoccupied France. But, at any rate, on this train, we should pass it at 4 a.m. I found that the *Feldgendarmerie* lieutenant who was in charge of the train was asleep in the rear compartment of my carriage. I thought it might be a disarming thing to be next door to him. The only other occupant of that compartment was a monk in white robes. He was already stretched out on the seat, and sound asleep. I lay opposite him, and listened to his smooth, untroubled breath·· ing. The train pulled out of the great station and raced through the town until I could hear by the reflected noises of our passage that we had flung Paris behind us.

CHAPTER XIX

PERHAPS this time I was helped by bombers of the Royal Air Force. There was a heavy bombardment of the line somewhere between Paris and Lyons.

Dimly in the night, for I slept well after our meal in the Gare de Lyon, I heard shuntings and imprecations. Dimly—for I was determined that my white-robed companion should believe me to be asleep, and that the Germans, if they came, should find me tranquilly sleeping—dimly I heard that the train had been obliged to make a long and time-devouring détour by Dijon. We arrived at Lyons two and a half hours late, at 9 a.m. The *Feldgendarmerie* lieutenant was still asleep when I passed his compartment to leave the train. There had not been any control. Lazy lieutenant!

We went first to the address of Ramon's *marraine* in Villeurbanne, the communist subuib, the quarter which was giving the Germans a great deal of trouble even at that time. When I was there the curfew in Villeurbanne was fixed by the enemy at 6 p.m., two hours earlier than in other parts of the great town.

Ramon's *marraine* and her mother were both out at the factory. The young sister took us round to see them. I thought that the *marraine* was a shade doubtful in her welcome of Ramon, although it was a welcome full of the ordinary platitudes and felicitations. We left the women at their factory, and went to their house to wash away some of the stains of travel.

Ramon found a bottle of bean-oil in the corner of one of the food cupboards. He rubbed this generously over his black hair from the thick dome down to the points of the stalactitic side-whiskers. He gave his face a bit of a wash, shaved for the first time in four days with my razor and soap, and finally told me that he was confident of sweeping all before him.

"Provided you can see your way to giving me a clear field," he said frankly. "It's not that you in yourself would interfere, or would have the faintest chance of supplanting me in the affections of my *marraine*. But look around yourself. Regard the thing practically. The place is small. Into it must fit my *marraine*, her mother, her young sister, and Ramon, the hero. With you here as well, the thing would be impossible. I leave the situation in your hands, knowing that your friendship, your tact and your discretion will find a solution."

I weighed up my friendship, tact and discretion. While I desperately craved in Lyons some safe place to lay my head, I told him immediately, if a shade huffily, that I would see Barbarossa.

When I first entered the machine-shop I could not see anybody, although I could hear a blow-lamp somewhere. It was an unusual machine-shop. For one thing, it had a black marble façade. For another it seemed to have a most peculiar mixture of "machines" in it. I recognised a printing press, a perambulator, an enormous generator (in six or seven pieces), a small motor-cycle and sidecar, and many other machines which I failed to identify.

"Who is that?" demanded a polished voice.

I followed the sound into one corner of the shop, and saw a

vast, red-bearded man who lay on his stomach mending a frying-pan with a blow-lamp. He twisted round his head to look at me. He wore glasses tinted to a deep pink. I could see through them sufficiently to distinguish eyes which moved restlessly behind the glass.

"Who are you?"

"*Monsieur* Barbarossa?"

"Some people call me that."

"My friend Max, for example, who was at the Sorbonne with you."

"That skeleton. Yes, maybe. Who are you?"

"I am a British officer."

"Can you mend pots and pans?"

"No, I don't think so."

"Damnation, I want to go out and dance. There's a new tango band at a hotel not far from here, and I promised them I'd go to try them out. I am a tango champion. Most French bands play tangos too fast—German style. But on the other hand I promised Bloch across the road that I would mend a couple of pans for him, and the old beast brought in eight. I have already done four. Look here, see what you can do with the others, and earn my undying gratitude."

"I am most sorry, but I have to go out to Paryllis."

"Oh, don't go there. You won't like it there."

"But I must. I have an address there of people with whom I can hide."

"Hide? Oh, yes. You say you are British. Well, you could not have come to a better man. I am a British agent. Give me your name, regiment and number and so on, also the address of your next-of-kin. If you are genuine I may get you away within a week."

This took my breath away.

"Surely that would be impossible," I said tremulously.

"Impossible, my dear fellow! Why, have you never heard of little things that go BRRR BRRR BRRR in the sky, and then swoop down ZEEE-EE-EE to land at Croydon? Have you never heard of our underground railways? Why, soon we shall have more Britishers than Frenchmen in Lyons. . . ."

"What kind of Britishers?"

"What kind? Why, parachutists, agents, saboteurs. My dear friend, in Lyons something is blown up every night. Really it's too wonderful. And three nights ago I had a British general to dinner. My wife would never have guessed, except that he had an English accent you could have cut with a knife, and he demanded, yes, demanded *rosbif.*"

I saw with disgust that I had fallen on another liar; but perhaps he was just putting it on.

"How did he arrive, your general?" I asked politely.

"He just dropped in. Ha! That's a good one See it? He just dropped in. You know. *Tombé du ciel.* Ha!"

Barbarossa took my name and the address at Paryllis. He scratched them on the green-painted surface of one of his lathes.

"Is that not a little dangerous?"

"Dangerous, my dear friend? Only writing things on paper is dangerous. Shall I show you how easy it is to rub this out?" He seized a brush heavy with green paint and splashed it over his scratches. "Now just repeat the name and address." He caught hold of my arm. "Who is that, waiting in the street?"

"That is a friend of mine who has come with me from Germany."

"Hm. Don't like his looks. I am allergic to dark people. Fortunately you are fair. Never fear. Barbarossa will keep in constant touch with you. And don't tell the darkie there that I am a British agent. Never a word about the *Intelligence Service.*"

"Of course not. Au revoir." I was very angry with Max. He had sent me to a madman. But I said nothing to Ramon.

Ten minutes later I had my mind changed, or almost changed, for me in a most dramatic fashion. In Paris at that time you were obliged to go everywhere in the *Métro.* In Lyons you were obliged to go by tram. Ramon and I were standing in one of the small beetle-like tram-cars. Looking vaguely back, I saw a pair of dark glasses and a red beard, partially hidden in a silk scarf. It was Barbarossa. He was trailing us on his motorcycle. He wore a black leather three-quarter-length coat, a *canadienne,* and he really looked most dashing. Too dashing for a British agent.

It was obvious to Ramon and to me that Lyons was a dangerous place. In Paris there had been a non-resistant atmosphere, the people gave the impression, perhaps falsely, that they were accepting the defeat and the presence of the conqueror. In Paris the conqueror himself gave an almost gentle impression, as though he politely took for granted the acknowledgements of the conquered. But Lyons was different, ugly, rich, provincial, heavy, and with a sturdy people to match. There was no abasement in Lyons. It seemed to me that there was hatred and revenge and battle in the air. The Germans were different too. More soldierly, more wary, more observant. By this time I was beginning to imagine that I knew a plain-clothes Gestapo man when I saw him. I imagined that I saw many of them in Lyons.

Paryllis was a miserable new suburb, right outside the town. We had a long walk from the tramway terminus. We found the house where Greta's parents lived, and my heart bled for them when I saw the outside of that house, broken-down, dirty, a hovel standing on mud and offal. I remembered their beautiful and solid farm in Lorraine, the farm with its huge *fumier*, its heavy orchards, its piggeries, its barns, its acres and acres of wheatfields.

An old woman opened the door to us. I did not recognise in her sad and shrivelled face the buxom mother whom I had seen in Greta's photographs. When we had told her whence we came, and that we had recently seen her daughter, tears rolled slowly out of her wide-open eyes. There was something terrible about this way of weeping. She had wept so much that now she did not know when she wept. The tears came out to show that something had touched more than usual a heart that steadily suffered.

This was a family that had been torn from its riches because it was considered to be "too French" for German ideas. Here it was, suffering, and starving, and dirty, in France.

Surely these were the depths of martyrdom and disillusionment. The country for whom they had been martyrised recognised them only sufficiently to put them in this hovel; to give them cooking utensils, but insufficient cooking utensils, so that they were obliged to make soup in a tomato purée tin; to give them sheets, but only one pair of sheets for each of the two beds, so that they were obliged to sleep in dirty beds, the people who had never lacked for anything, the people from whom the Germans had carried off a whole lorry-load of priceless old family linen.

Ramon was so anxious to get rid of me that he at once asked the old lady if I might stay, and she said that I *must* stay—if I would not mind sharing a bed with her son Louis. I dared not refuse for fear of hurting her inflamed, her wonderful pride. She got out a paper bag and put the old chipped enamel coffee-pot on the fire. Then I knew that she was a great woman. Her home, her civilisation, her family, her love and admiration for France had all toppled. But she could still make the big gesture to a hungry and unexpected guest. She was making *real* coffee.

I looked at her and I could have kissed her feet in their home-made slippers of dirty felt. I looked at the old lady and I tried to put into my face and my eyes the love and the admiration that burned in me for her. Into the trembling well of her soul she took my look and my admiration, and there was not room for that in the well. The tears overflowed from her eyes.

Louis the son arrived, and I was afraid of him until the mother thought to explain that this was her son. For he was dressed in the blue uniform of the Pétain police.

"Greta told me that he was working for a butcher," I said.

"So he was, but he had no clothes, poor lad. When we were expelled from our home he was still only a boy. He has grown to be a man in these surroundings. How could we get him clothes? This was the only way. Now at least his body is covered, he is protected from the wind and the rain, and the shame of being half-naked."

"It's not so bad as Mother thinks," said Louis, who looked like a coarse, masculine version of Greta. "We have a Resistance movement among us *flics*. Some of the members are officers. We take the British radio regularly at the station.

"And not all the work we do is dirty. To-morrow we leave for fifteen days. We are going to Grenoble first thing in the morning with an interesting job on hand."

"Who would have thought that I would ever have a *flic* for a son?" said his father, a small bent old man who spoke bitterly between bouts of terrible coughing. "What dirty job can they give you that is interesting?"

"We are to round up all the Italians in Grenoble and pack them into railway wagons. They are to be taken to Germany. Is that not interesting? Is that not good?"

"Yes, that is good," said the father.

But the mother asked: "Ah, son, have we not already had enough suffering in this war?"

Louis was already engrossed in packing his suitcase for Grenoble, putting in three spare clips for his automatic and swishing his white truncheon joyfully about the kitchen.

The old lady gave Louis and myself the best dinner she could make. There were two boiled potatoes for each of us, followed by a kind of pancake with sugar sprinkled on it and the remains of the coffee she had made for us earlier. Neither she nor her husband ate. I realised that I was eating their rations. But I was giving them pleasure in depriving them of their dinner.

Life was not so hard for the men, I saw. The father was

290

able to run away from the shabby home that so ill-befitted his former dignity and wealth. He could leave the sordid problems and the ultimately degrading things to his wife. Were these not purely domestic problems, things in the woman's province? He could go out to the café on the outskirts of Lyons and play billiards and talk of the life he had led as a prosperous farmer. And the son had been torn from the other life when he was still unformed. Now he was almost happy, as boys can be. He was becoming formed in his new environment. But his forming alone was agony to his mother, because she feared the soil into which his roots were pushing.

"His language is terrible," she said to me. "I have spoken to his father, but his father has his own troubles and he is very bitter. And now Louis is always with other young men who have no respect for their fathers, no respect for religion, no respect for the army or for their country—young men who have been raised in city slums, who say that the men who work on the land are slow. In the last two years, here in this hovel I have watched my only son coarsening in front of me. I still love him. Perhaps I love him more now that he is coarse, but something has gone out of my life all the same. Are all these years of decency and labour in building up the home and the family in Lorraine, are all these years to go for nothing? I had hoped that my son would be a preacher or a great lawyer or an architect or a doctor or a politician who would bring honour to his country and our name. Were those hopes just vanity? Surely not. My home was a good home, a cheerful and a happy home, but now it is pillaged and soulless, and the things that it held are degraded."

"Surely you will have your home back after the war."

"Perhaps we will get the land, and that will already be much. But none of us will be fit for the land. We have grown bitter and cruel in our disappointments. I suppose that I should be proud to have suffered so for France. I suppose that the sacrifice of my son's coarsening is something that I should give cheerfully to France. But I have passed that stage of easy patriotism. We gave plenty to France on the last war, my family, and what are we now, the remnants? We are beggars, *les Boches de l'Est.*"

It was terrible in the bed beside Louis. But I suffered the bites and the odours willingly, almost as though I were offering my body to such petty annoyances. A feeling of guilt possessed me that I should be so fortunate, strong and young and escaping to a secure and happy home while this fine family struggled under such a load of bitterness.

After drinking some coffee in the morning, I said good-bye alone to Greta's mother, for the two men had departed to their separate employments. I gave her the shirt that Scherb's brother-in-law had sent to me. It was a lovely shirt, well cut and well sewn, of fine, soft linen. I had to give it to her for her son. What would I do with two shirts? I still possessed the old blue one that I had worn for special occasions in the prison camps. The blue one was more suitable for me. It did not show the dirt.

And with great diffidence I offered her a 1,000-franc note.

"Please do not be too proud to accept this," I begged her. "Your daughter saved my life, and my life is worth more to me than any money."

To my surprise and delight she took the money without embarrassment.

"I am not money-proud," she said. "I was money-proud when we had everything. But now we are starving, and with this I can buy food for some weeks for my men."

I returned to the centre of Lyons by tram, a nerve-racking journey for me, for the tram-cars were filled to bursting-point, and in such close proximity it was difficult to avoid talking to people.

"Paryllis not good enough for you?" asked Barbarossa coolly. He was cutting out a large sheet of tin in some special shape.

"The family are starving. I cannot burden them with my presence. I should be so grateful if you could find me somewhere to live."

"Certainly, certainly, my dear friend. I shall put you in a small *bistro* round the corner. It won't be too comfortable, but I think you will be safe. In the meantime, just pretend to be working about the *atelier*. You don't know how to mend pots and pans, you say? Pity. Well, anyway, just look busy."

When Barbarossa led me into the *bistro* I sensed that there was a strained situation. Nobody looked comfortable, and everybody seemed glad to have me, a stranger, there. Barbarossa took me through into the kitchen to introduce me with copious asides hissed into my ear.

"Madame Henri, or Dolores, whichever way you like it," he said, presenting a buxom woman in the early thirties. ("She runs the place and is an angel, unless you fall foul of her. I've fallen foul, but that will pass.")

"Monsieur Henri, a good friend of mine," he continued, and I shook hands with a lean, yellow-toothed man with quick nervous movements and reactions. ("Pretends to be married to Dolores, and has financed the *bistro*. Has a wife and family in a more respectable part of the town, but never visits them. Infatuated with Dolores and with her cooking. Desperately jealous of me. Would murder me if he could.")

"And lastly, Claudette, the apple of Lyons," he cried pinching the rosy cheek and the voluminous behind of a very-much-bleached young blonde. ("She's the maid. Did you ever see such buttocks? But don't make eyes at her while Dolores is around or you'll go out on your ear.")

These unusually thorough introductions completed, we went into the *bistro* where Henri, Barbarossa and I sat down at a marble-topped table and played a very complicated game with dice. Henri played superlatively well, and soon had taken 300 francs off me and 100 off Barbarossa.

Barbarossa paid up with extremely bad grace.

"I only lost to put you in a good temper, Henri," he said. "Your temper has been vile lately."

"Splendid, then let us play again," said Henri, laughing boisterously, and showing many sharp, yellow teeth.

"No, seriously," said Barbarossa, changing his tone and turning to me. "Did you ever see such luck? The man is bewitched. He is certainly a cuckold to have such an amazing streak of luck."

Henri again laughed loudly, but I noticed that his face went purple with rage and his foot drummed on the tiled floor. He did not dare to allow himself to look higher than the red beard across the table.

The women called us to table, and the situation eased slightly.

I was surprised at the air of richness that pervaded the small restaurant. It was little more than a tunnel running from the street to the kitchen. As you came in there were four marble-topped tables with bronze legs along the wall on your right. On your left there was the usual zinc bar and then another two tables. Behind the bar there were bottles of brandy, Kümmel, and Cointreau (all then supposed to be unprocurable in Lyons) and different types of *apéritifs*.

The lunch was tremendous. I had not seen such food since before the fall of France in 1940. There could not have been a greater (or grosser) contrast with the poverty and starvation of Greta's parents.

Henri was what Barbarossa (who spoke a slangy type of English) described as a "rabbits" or in more direct French as a *"froussard"*. During the meal he talked to me for some time, then said to the table at large: "This Barbarossa will be the end of our house and everyone in it."

"Explain yourself," challenged Barbarossa haughtily.

"The Englishman, Georges, speaks with an accent. We cannot hide him entirely from everyone who comes here. That would be stupidity, it would be asking for suspicion. We must present him to people, but how?"

"Simple," said Barbarossa. "Georges, it is formally forbidden that you open your mouth inside this room or in the kitchen when there are strangers present. Officially you are a cousin of Dolores, come down to visit her from her people in Savoie (that explains the blonde hair) and you are, poor boy, deaf and dumb."

"Fantastic," Henri grumbled. "But I can see no other way out. That's fixed then."

After the meal Dolores led me upstairs to the bedroom over the *bistro,* and told me to go to sleep on the huge double bed in which the maid usually slept. The place was clean. The ceiling of the room was criss-crossed with clothes-lines, and hanging from the lines were hundreds of tobacco-leaves. Some of the newer leaves which still retained humidity were brilliantly green, and spear-shaped. Others were wizened and shrunken into fantastically solid-looking forms.

I went to sleep. And thus began a shut-in life of sybaritic luxury, of over-eating and over-sleeping. If I had fasted too much and suffered from malnutrition in prison, all minus feeding must have been more than counterbalanced by my nine days of plus feeding in the Lyons *bistro*.

Dolores and Henri had no bath, no central heating, no running hot water, no water closet. But for all that they lived like nabobs.

There was a regular clientele, about a dozen wealthy people who came often to eat copiously at the *bistro* either at midday or in the evening. Dolores never bothered with coupons. It was entirely a black market restaurant and the prices were extremely high. Clients paid for a meal from 400 to 1,500 francs per head. I, of course, paid nothing. Like the owners and the maid, I was fed from the profits.

After the first day, when I found my complete understanding of the French language a handicap for a deaf-mute, I had difficulty only with one client. This was a nymphomaniac, a great friend of Dolores. When she heard that I was deaf and dumb this woman became greatly excited. She used to expatiate on the extraordinary convenience that it would be to have a deaf-mute for a lover, and sometimes at table she described my charms in gross detail and with imaginary flourishes, or even described imaginary nights spent with me, and fictitious tussles on the dark staircase. Fortunately, her talk usually so enraged me that I forgot to blush.

The upstairs plan of the *bistro* was simple. When from the kitchen you had mounted the narrow, steep staircase—it was really more of a ladder—the door of the small dining-room was on your left and the door of Dolores' and Henri's bedroom straight ahead. A third room, the one with the tobacco-hung ceiling, opened off the dining-room. The dining-room itself was used only for most important and most secret of clients, gangsters, black market kings, ministers.

On my first evening they carried a settee out of Dolores' bedroom, a big room with many frothing white curtains and elongated French dolls in it, and placed it in the dining-room. The bed was well fitted up with clean sheets and blankets, and I slept admirably. But the following day Dolores, who believed in discipline, said that it was ridiculous that I should sleep on the settee while the domestic help occupied a double bed. Henceforward I had to sleep in Claudette's bed while she used the settee in the dining-room.

Claudette was a strong, broad, and healthy young woman. A real peasant, as earthy as a field of yellow waving corn.

She often came into my room while I lay in bed in the afternoons, or even at night, to talk as a child might of her day, or of greater periods of time in her simple life. The day's reports usually dealt with the amount of money which clients had disbursed in the shape of tips. Claudette was frankly a mercenary character, and she did not disguise, at any rate from me, the fact that she was working in the *bistro* for a limited time and purely to make money. Since the meals were expensive, and the clients usually gave ten per cent tips, she normally made over 1,000 francs a week, and sometimes it was nearer 5,000 francs (then £30).

Otherwise she would talk to me of her fiancé, a prisoner in Germany, and "such a lovely boy, so beautiful", of her home, a farm near Lyons, of her aged parents, of the priest who had helped her so sagely through her difficult adolescence.

There was other talk of a more dangerous nature from my point of view. Claudette and Dolores were not friendly, although they worked well together. Claudette would frequently slide into her artless conversation barbed references to Dolores, and would ask me to agree. But I avoided such obvious pitfalls. Dealing with Ramon had made me careful and circumspect in my personal relations with people, and the storm over Greta had made me wary of women.

I was careful to show the maximum of politeness and the minimum of interest towards both Dolores and Claudette. I did this also with one eye upon Henri, who regarded himself rather as a cock regards himself in a run full of plump and desirable hens, and with the other eye upon Barbarossa, who frequently made the most searching inquiries into my relations with both women.

Lyons is a fantastic town. A dull town if you like. A stodgy town with its fat and ugly inhabitants. A town with rich streets, with large shops, fine stations, big houses, expensive flats, re-nowned gastronomic centres. Yet there appears to be no sanitation in the place. All the lavatories that I encountered there were no more than holes in the ground. And in the warm evenings and the muggy nights of that late autumn the mosquitos came out in mass sorties.

Every evening before turning on the lights I would shut my windows and search the ceiling and the walls with a long mop, destroying hundreds of mosquitos. But no sooner was I in bed with the light out than I would hear them cruising around, waiting to dart in for the attack. Persecuted by them, I seldom slept until 4.30 a.m. when they all seemed, by common consent, to cease their activities.

From 4.30 I dropped into a sleep like death. And I was always awakened by Dolores, who seemed to make that her prerogative. She awakened me with two slices of pure white bread (bought on the black market at the astounding price of 600 francs—over £3—for a small loaf) spread with delicious butter, and a cup of real black coffee sweetened with sugar. Her coffee bill alone amounted to 4,000 francs—then £24—in a normal week.

After breakfast I would get up lazily and slowly, put on my grey trousers from Germany and my blue shirt from Harrods', London, and stroll downstairs to toy with an *apéritif* before lunch.

I could feel my body softening and growing more supple like

that of a cat; my hair began to shine and bend more pliantly, under this forced absorption of rich food. I felt like some prize bullock that was being fattened up for a show. Or like a White Russian in one of the plays that once were fashionable in Paris, London and New York—a Russian in high-necked silk pyjamas who lay always on a bed and was ministered to by a woman or women. Sometimes (since I had been brought up to consider such a state of affairs unhealthy) the idea that I was "living off" women would occur to me and would operate with the surfeit of rich food in me to build up a state of boredom and disgust.

Sometimes, to pass the time, I attempted to wash some of my clothes or to wash the dishes. But on these occasions Dolores and Claudette became very angry, and explained to me that my conduct was a deliberate insult. It was woman's place to do such things. They insisted on doing everything for me. My clothes were washed and scented twice a week, my trousers were pressed with the electric iron in the kitchen every second day, Claudette cleaned my long-suffering boots every morning. Dolores even offered to wash and "set" my hair.

Each morning Dolores put on what I called her "battle-dress", which consisted of a towering velvet hat, a pale fawn coat with a great fluffy fuzz of pale fur around the collar and on the hips, and high wooden-soled shoes open in the fronts to show two or three of her painted toe-nails. Thus attired, she went out to the markets or to the large dealers. And for the next hour or two her orders would come pouring back into the *bistro*. As well as selling meals in her restaurant, she also dealt as a "between woman" for the black market. People often asked her to get them delicacies such as a duckling, a sucking pig, some asparagus out of season, or a dozen peaches.

Often black marketeers would come into the kitchen, would drink a glass or two of her fine Chablis—which was reserved for them and for us—eat a few oysters, and then produce their wares which varied from champagne through salmon to fresh lemons.

Dolores was a slashing business woman. She never seemed to care what she paid for all these things. And it was seldom that she rejected, since the sellers knew that she would accept only the best, and that she was a competent judge.

"It costs about 1,000 francs a day for us to live as we live," she said. At the astronomical sound of all those figures I began to worry about the financial aspect of things. I now had about

3,000 francs in my note-case, and they were spending 1,000 francs a day on me. They were essentially hard business people and once I overheard Henri asking Dolores what she was going to charge me for my keep.

"He must have plenty of *ronds,*" continued Henri. "And I should think he would be soft enough about money. He would pay you anything you asked."

I did not catch her reply, but to counter Henri's arguments I must confess that I laid myself out to be particularly pleasant to Dolores and to arouse all the motherly sympathy that was in her. As the days passed I became increasingly certain that she would not expect me to pay money to her when I left. Such an attitude was foreign, I believe, both to my upbringing and to my nature, but any fastidious scruples were easily subjugated to my need for freedom.

In the afternoons and evenings, when the back of the day's work was broken, Dolores would turn her busy mind to the things of the spirit and the things of the flesh. Often, when I slept upstairs after lunch, she awoke me with a cup of tea or coffee. She wanted a listener.

At such times she talked of the slyness, the unattractiveness, the double-facedness of Barbarossa. She would recount all that had passed between them that morning (for if Barbarossa did not call Dolores always sent round Claudette to demand his presence so that she could upbraid him). She would tell me how good she had been to him, how she had supplied him with money and clothes, how she had helped him to set up his shaky business, and how bored he was with his aristocratic wife. In fact, although she would have scratched my eyes out if I had voiced this conclusion, she seemed to me to love Barbarossa, and he seemed to be trying to ease himself out of their association as tactfully (and as cheaply) as possible.

From snatches of such conversations, from odd remarks of the iniquitous Barbarossa ("Dolores—it would take seven or eight to satisfy her.") and from Claudette, who disliked Dolores and liked Barbarossa, I pieced together the main thread of their affair.

Henri had selected Dolores for a mistress partly as an investment, as one of the ablest business women in the town. In spite of the fact that they were living together as lovers, there was every sign that they disliked each other, and they bickered whenever they met whether in private or in public.

Some months before I arrived Dolores had fallen in love with

Barbarossa. The affair had been hectic. She had fallen in love with his red beard, his polished voice, his sophisticated love-making, his great size. He had been attracted by her coarse vitality and by her divine cooking.

She was an attractive woman in a plump, sensuous way. Particularly attractive when she cooked, for then she was completely at home. Claudette had to do most of the preparing of the food, the cleaning and washing and peeling. But Claudette was never allowed to do the actual cooking. Then, with perhaps fifteen people all anxiously waiting for a wonderful meal and prepared to pay for it like millionaires, Dolores would bang about her spotless pots and pans, cooking with lightning speed and no fuss, throwing things in here and there with apparent slap-dash haste, tasting, adding, sending the finished product rushing through into the restaurant. The results showed that one of the golden rules of good cooking is "prepare slowly and cook fast".

When I arrived Barbarossa had already turned from Dolores to Claudette.

On Sunday, October 24th, 1943, my third day in the *bistro*, Henri decided that he would take me with him to the races, as he thought that my presence might bring him luck. The whole place was thrown into a turmoil, since Dolores decided that I must be a credit to the house.

She fitted me out in a stiff starched shirt belonging to Henri, a very loud tie with a Paisley shawl pattern in red and yellow, one of his suits, brown, pinched at the waist and wide in the trousers, and a pair of long, narrow, pointed shoes. I was permitted to wear the large blue beret which Greta's father had given me (apparently my brown beret was too conspicuous for Lyons), and even this Dolores ironed so stiffly that it looked like a scone on top of my head.

We went to the races on bicycles, and Henri took tickets for the cheap enclosure. I was glad of this, for I knew that many of the better French journalists were working in Lyons then in preference to Paris, and I was afraid that I might bump into an acquaintance.

The course looked attractive enough, squatting at the foot of a forest of great radio pylons, and the meeting reminded me of every other French meeting I had attended, except that now my life was less busy and my reactions consequently were brighter. Henri was an interesting companion. Sour, jealous and boring in the house, he flowered at the races. Gambling, in a small way, was his passion, whereas I normally abhor it.

Immediately after the first race, when I had won 1,000 francs on a ten-to-one shot, I met in the bar a young woman whom I had known when I worked in the *Paris Soir* building at the beginning of the war. She looked at me hard, slowly put down the glass of champagne she was drinking, then looked at my clothes and my companion and as slowly raised the glass to her lips again.

She had not recognised me, and I had looked straight through her.

For the first time in my life I could do nothing wrong with my betting. When the fourth race was over I was 5,000 francs up, while Henri, the expert, was 3,000 francs down. When the favourite was blatantly pulled in the fifth race, and an outsider which I had backed came romping home, Henri could contain himself no longer.

"Vous êtes certainement cocu, mon cher Georges," he said.

This made me smile in a superior manner. But, naturally, since I was in France where the marital relations are always discussed with light badinage, I replied that he was probably quite right.

The race meeting was to be my only outing in Lyons. For Henri, a highly-strung person, became from then on increasingly nervous about my presence in the *bistro*. His fear of the Gestapo gnawed at him and grew so obvious that I saw something must quickly be done about my future.

Henri's nerves were not improved by Ramon, to whom he took an instant dislike. Ramon claimed that he was having a wonderful time with his *marraine;* but, although he had been only too eager to throw me out of his love-nest, when he discovered how well I had settled myself with the aid of Barbarossa, he made a habit of popping in to see me (usually round meal-times) with protestations of undying friendship. For my sake Dolores was always charming to him, although, like Henri, she disliked him. Ramon never failed to get a wonderful meal, and of course, he never offered (and was never asked) to pay.

Henri was afraid that Ramon might be followed, and might lead the Gestapo to the *bistro*. He kept asking me to tell Ramon to cease his visits, and he showed me several times an alternative exit in case the Germans should arrive to search the place. This exit entailed jumping from my bedroom window, crossing a couple of roofs, then burrowing through a coal-heap to find a hole in the wall and thence a disused sewer which led into the street. If I had been obliged to use it I should have broken at least a leg, since both of the roofs were completely rotten—so rotten that when I dropped stones on them the stones fell straight through to the ground twenty feet below.

Every evening in Lyons we seemed to hear bangs and explosions as the Resistance played around with the German overlords. These noises stirred me vastly, and I asked Barbarossa if he would not put me in touch with the Resistance so that I might do some work for them as a sniper or saboteur.

But Barbarossa was no longer the man who had boasted so airily to me in the *atelier*. He was no longer even hopeful. He said that he had sent the message to England about me, but that it might be a long time, weeks even, before he received instructions. When there were instructions, he claimed, I should have to await my turn—for there were, according to him, so many British officers hiding in Lyons at that time that there was "a long waiting-list"—to go to "a camp in the Charente" where again I should have to wait "possibly for months" until I was sent in convoy across the Pyrenees. None of this sounded true to me. I believed that he was a man who lived boastfully in the clouds and that now he was cooling me off, giving the same kind of treatment to me as to Dolores.

One day Barbarossa brought another supposed British agent to see me. This was a small, miserable-looking man whom Henri and Dolores called "the lion-tamer". This man appeared to pay more attention to the Chablis and the oysters than to me, but at his request I wrote a letter to Anne (which never arrived).

The pampered, cosseted existence began to get on my nerves, and for the first time since I had escaped I became jumpy, waking up occasionally sweating with fear and imagining that I heard the Gestapo at the front door.

When I had been there five days Dolores's cousin, a farmer from the Swiss frontier near St. Julien, in Haute Savoie, spent one night in the *bistro*. He offered two or three times to take me across the frontier into Switzerland. He and I got on well together, and I enjoyed talking to him, for he seemed with his rosy face and his mountaineer's clothes to bring a needed freshness into the over-nourished *bistro* air. I did not take his offer seriously.

But next day, just as a feeler, I told Barbarossa of the offer, and to my surprise he said at once: "A most excellent idea from every point of view. Once across the Swiss frontier you will be safe, and you will have a pleasant time until the end of the war."

"You are trying to get rid of me, Barbarossa."

"*Mon cher Georges!* How can you say such a thing? All I think of is the danger for you here. The urgent danger. You have already been here several days too long."

Something in his tone frightened me. I wondered if he might be capable of getting rid of Dolores and me with a profitable denunciation. I talked the Swiss proposition over with Dolores. It was not the idea of Switzerland that appealed to me, but the idea of going to Haute Savoie. I had heard the Resistance was well organised there; and it seemed to me that if I could once get into the Resistance I should inevitably find a real British agent.

Dolores said that if I wanted to go up there to the mountains she could put me on to a man who really was a man, and not a bag of stale wind (like Barbarossa). But before she produced this man I had to promise not to mention his name, or his visit, to Henri. I promised.

The man who was a man was dark and silent. He stood just inside the kitchen door and looked me up and down with friendly brown eyes. He did not take his hat off. His hands were long and very, very white. His name was Pascal, and he was a Corsican. If his eyes were soft, his mouth was hard and firm. He moved delicately and smoothly. He scarcely talked. He did not boast. I had confidence in him. There was something in him that reminded me of Enrico. Something hard and dangerous perhaps in the centre of the man.

"I would take Georges away on Saturday, the day after to-morrow," he said. He had a trick when he spoke of taking a coin or his knife from his trouser pocket and regarding it fixedly, as though he were able better to consider his words when he addressed them to a familiar and inanimate object. "I would not take him to St. Julien. That is too near the frontier. But I would take him as far as Annecy by train. The frontier controls usually take place after Annecy station."

"And from Annecy?" asked Dolores.

"I would take him to a friend of mine."

"What friend?"

"Since, being a woman, you are obliged to ask so many questions, I would take him to La Pepette."

"You should go, Georges," counselled Dolores.

"All right, I'll go. But what about Ramon?"

Pascal had heard of Ramon.

"It would be inadvisable to leave Ramon in Lyons," he said. "If he thought you had run from him he might make trouble. I don't think so, but it would be a stupid risk to take. I think we should take him along."

"Agreed."

"Right," said Pascal, staring rigidly at the coin. "Just one thing. Not one word to Henri, here, either about me or about Pepette, or even about Annecy. Not one word about any of them to Ramon. And most important of all, not one word to Barbarossa. I shall meet you at 10.30 on Saturday morning on the train to Annecy from the big station. It is too late to book seats. You must be there the moment the train gets to the platform."

When he had gone, when I had lost a little of the confidence that his face and purposeful bearing gave me, I began to wonder whether there was not something a little suspicious in the promises of secrecy which he had imposed.

Barbarossa came into the kitchen an hour after Pascal had left.

"Have you decided anything?" he asked.

"Yes, Ramon and I are going up to St. Julien on Sunday."

"Alone?"

"Why, yes, the two of us."

"You are lying," he suddenly burst out, putting his face close to mine so that his fetid breath sprayed over me. "You do not trust me and I can see your plan. When you return to Britain you will go to the Intelligence Service and you will seek to damage my reputation there. Well, Barbarossa has thought all that out. I also have lodged a complaint against you. I have told all to my friends in London—and believe me, I have important friends there—I have given instructions for my complaint to be held. But if yours is lodged mine will be released, and then, ha ha, you will languish in a stone cell in the Tower of London for the rest of the war."

"That arrangement is fully agreeable to me," I told him gently, "I assure you that I feel only gratitude towards you, and I have no intention of lodging a complaint."

"Then why do you lie to me? Dolores," he bellowed, going to the foot of the staircase. "Dolores, Dolores, drat the woman. . . ."

"Coming, coming."

"I followed him; I saw him and I followed him to his home,"

303

he shrieked at her as soon as she entered. She was barefoot. She had nice little bare feet and thick legs tapering to delicate ankles. There was a slight ring of flesh immediately above the ankle. They were legs that reminded me at once of John Leech's drawing of the woman of the illicit distiller with whom Mr. Jorrocks passed an evening in a cave.

"I don't know who or what you are talking about," she said to gain time.

"Oh yes, you do. A thin dark man. He was here for thirty minutes. What devilish games are you up to with Georges? I would remind you that he is a British officer. I brought him here. He is mine."

"No, he is mine. Have I not nourished him and cherished him? What have you done for him, you empty bag of stale wind?"

"He is mine, I repeat."

"He is mine." She softened her tone as somebody came into the café. "As a matter of fact, the person you saw is a railway employee. He was here to advise Georges and Ramon how to get to St. Julien."

"You lie. Whoever saw a railway's employee in silk socks? I shall speak to Henri of him."

"If you speak to Henri I shall do three things. I shall get rid of Claudette, and you will be obliged to keep her, I shall tell Henri of the money you owe me, and I shall never let you eat here again. Hein? You hear? Never again."

Barbarossa weighed up these threats for a moment.

"I shall still tell Henri," he decided and left, banging the kitchen door.

"Don't worry," Dolores said to me. "Unless that Claudette stirs him up he will say nothing. Phew! Now I must wash my feet, for they are extremely dirty. And these arguments always bring on my stomach trouble."

While she washed her feet in an enamel basin I considered the move to Haute Savoie.

"What sort of a woman is La Pepette?" I asked.

"As hard as nails. As good a cook as I am. She was a business woman in Lyons. Now she is getting on, and she started up this restaurant not far from Annecy about the beginning of the war. She charges heavily for meals, just like here, but perhaps more heavily. She has a good deal to do with the Maquis. Her house bristles with sub-machine-guns and revolvers. I would say that she had a heart of gold. But unless she takes a fancy to you she might have her eyes on your wallet. You must make certain from the start that you make friends with her. As you did with me," she added, with a sharp but friendly look. It would have taken a more cunning and expert man than I to fool Dolores.

The atmosphere in the *bistro* grew electric as the hour of my departure approached. Dolores had to wash all my things all over again, since everything must be spotless for the move.

"What would La Pepette think if you arrived in a dirty shirt?"

Henri, secretly pleased that I was leaving, pretended to be sad. I think that in a way he was sorry to be on the point of losing his authority to tell me to be careful ten times a day.

Dolores and Claudette became openly tearful as the hour approached.

Barbarossa's visits grew more frequent and more oily.

On the last morning Dolores fried two young pike in butter for me. She followed this with kidneys and a Madeira sauce, then a salad of cress, then Gruyère cheese. There was Chablis with the fish, a half-bottle of Macon with the kidneys and the Gruyère, and Armagnac with the coffee. All this at 9.30 a.m. While I struggled with the food and drink, for I was too excited to want to eat, Dolores worked with the electric iron on the kitchen table, pressing all my clothes and my beret for the last time.

She had told me that although she knew it was indiscreet, and Henri would never forgive her if he found out, she intended to accompany me herself to the station, but "in disguise" (she meant in quieter clothes than her "battle-dress").

When the time came, however, she could not bear to dress quietly, and she put on the high hat and the coat with the fluffy fur on it that she liked so well.

Travelling through the stodgy, hard streets of Lyons in the tram-car, she suddenly caught hold of my hand.

"I know that you love your wife," she said. "And I hope, I pray God that you will get back safely to her, and that she will be glad to see you."

The tram-car was full of Germans and hard-eyed French civilians. I dared not reply.

Ramon and his *marraine* were waiting for us in the big ticket-hall. The *marraine* was dry-eyed, and did not seem unduly put out by Ramon's imminent departure. Ramon himself was pleased, I could see, at the prospect of movement and change.

Like me, he had taken a great fancy to Pascal, who had been to Villeurbanne to see him.

To get into the station we had to show both our tickets and our identity-cards, running the gauntlet of two Pétain policemen and two Germans of the *Feldgendarmerie*. However, Ramon and I, with our women friends hanging tenderly from our arms, went sailing past this reception committee. They only appeared to be stopping passengers who were catching the *rapide* for Marseilles and the south.

We arrived at our train one hour and a half before it was due to leave, and the only unbooked compartments were still empty. Dolores said good-bye in the compartment. Ramon was walking his *marraine* up and down the platform outside. I gave Dolores all the money I thought I could spare, 3,000 francs, asking her to buy a present for herself and one for Claudette. She refused to touch the money. Then the habits of a lifetime were too strong for her. She took 1,500 francs, and said she would pay it as a gift into the Prisoners of War Fund. I believed her.

Her eyes filled with tears.

"It's nothing sentimental, I assure you," she said to me. "But it's just the feeling that we have worked for you and sheltered you, and now you must go out alone into a world that is looking for you, hunting you, seeking to kill you. Is it not a queer thing, Georges? But when you depart like this I wish I had always been a good woman, that I had a husband and three or four children. Seeing your insecurity makes me wish that I myself were secure. I shall pray for you. Au revoir."

"Au revoir," I said. "I shall be back in a couple of months."

I saw her over-dressed figure stumbling down the steps to the underground passage that connected the platforms.

When I said that I should be back in two months I was only repeating something that I had said before. For now a longing was growing in me to work against the Germans in France.

CHAPTER XX

It was October 30, and there was a sharp nip in the air. The first passengers to arrive and crowd in beside us wore ski-ing clothes and left their black skis in the corridor. Those who followed wore Sunday best and carried flowers to lay in the little graveyards in the mountain villages. Some carried fresh flowers and others degenerate waxen posies covered over with glass cases.

Pascal, brown hat tipped jauntily over one eye and a dark leather *canadienne* swinging from his shoulders, slid into the compartment. He looked as though he were prepared to enjoy the journey. He and Ramon began well by giving their seats to two young women and holding them firmly in conversation until Aix-les-Bains. There I produced the sandwiches which Dolores had made me. They were *foie gras* sandwiches, but it was not this that drew sightseeing crowds to our compartment. They were made with pure white bread. None of the people in the train had seen such bread for two years.

The train carried many professional black marketeers, people who left Lyons every few days with empty suitcases, and returned with loads of cheese, eggs and sausage; colza oil, and flour; butter, wine and ham. I noticed that Pascal knew several of these people. The Germans did not control the train: and we should have had ample warning of any control, since many of the railway employees, said Pascal, were his friends. Possibly they were in his pay. I noticed that they treated him with respect.

It was dark when we arrived at Annecy station, dark and much colder than it had been in low-lying Lyons. We saw at once that there was a German control, a serious-looking one with two officers and several steel-helmeted soldiers, on the single exit.

But Pascal had an easy answer to this. He led the two of us into the station buffet, which had a brightly-lit entrance from the platform. We walked straight through the buffet and out into the street. There was no German control on that door.

Leaving the station square, we walked briskly past the Carlton Hotel, which was evidently a German headquarters, for it was surrounded with a barbed-wire entanglement. I saw a place called "English tea-room". Pascal led us into a very different type of place—a long, narrow wine-shop full of smoke and the sour smell of alcohol. Two friends were waiting for us there. Both had hard, bold features and gruff voices. One was called Angelo, the other Tintin.

They both looked on me with stern approval, and ordered round after round of strong red wine. These were Savoyards. Now I was in the mountain region. They were no longer like French people; they spoke less easily and more fiercely than the people of the plains.

We went outside to a one-ton *gazogène* truck. Since I had no coat and I was the guest of honour, I was put in front beside Tintin, the driver. During the short drive to the village of Chaumontet, Tintin pointed out a white mound of flowers in a graveyard on the right of the road. This covered the grave of British airmen who had been killed when a four-engined aircraft parachuting supplies to the Resistance had recently crashed.

Tintin swung the *camionette* into a small garage. A faintly-illuminated sign outside La Pepette's place said: *"Ma Baraque".*

Inside the double doors beneath the sign there was a splendid bar with space to dance (then filled with a ping-pong table), and a chromium-fitted bar with concealed lighting over it and a signed picture of Charles Trenet, the singer, standing among many opulent (but empty) bottles on shelves behind it. Paul cut through this empty bar, and led us into the kitchen immediately beyond.

A small, and at first sight insignificant, woman sat disconsolately at the kitchen table. I could not believe that this was the famous Pepette. She held out a hand which shook lamentably, for she had some kind of nervous illness in her small body.

"Enchanté, Madame," I said, laying on the charm, and remembering Dolores's injunctions.

There was little room in the kitchen for anything more than the table, a large range, an enormous dresser and two dogs, one of them nearly as big as the dresser.

We went into the small dining-room which led off the kitchen. This was a depressing, dark blue room, with thickly painted mountain scenes hanging on the walls and a couple of huge and bloody carcases (one had been a bullock and the other a pig) hanging in the window, inside the closed shutters.

All the Frenchmen now bought bottles of red wine. Another man, much of the stamp of Angelo and Tintin, had come in. The newcomer's name was Edouard. Dogs and cats wandered all over the scene, and La Pepette, who had a particularly loud, but not a grating voice, alternately scolded or mothered them. She and a young man who had the face and bearing of a pimp, and who called himself Tino, produced a tremendous meal. We drank a sharp cider with the food.

After dinner there was more eating and drinking to be done. The Savoyards are huge eaters. Angelo made *la fondue.*

First he cut up a few cloves of garlic and heated them with a little butter in the bottom of a huge iron saucepan. Heated the garlic until it was golden brown. Then poured in a litre and a half of good dry white wine. When the wine was nearly boiling he stirred in 3 lbs. of cheese, beautiful mountain Gruyère, cut into slender shavings. The pot now had to be continually stirred until the contents became one viscous, bubbling, yellow semifluid. Meanwhile Edouard had gone off to a baker and had returned with a loaf of near-white bread. The bread was cut with sharp knives into little triangles. The pot was set on a slowly burning spirit-stove in the centre of a table. We stood round in a circle. Each person took a triangle of bread, fixed it on his fork and swirled it in the mixture. When the bread was withdrawn it was soaked in, and covered with, the *fondue*. There are few things more delicious.

If any guest dropped his bread into the pot, he was obliged to pay for a bottle of wine. With the *fondue* we drank *Roussette,* an excellent local white wine which was then new to me. In this pleasant manner we consumed several bottles.

I discovered two things about Pascal when Angelo playfully pushed him over as he sat balanced on the back legs of his chair. Firstly the brown hat—always cocked over one eye, even in Pepette's familiar and friendly house—fell off, and I saw that he was bald; he only had fringes of black hair on either side of his young-old face. Secondly, I have never seen a man bring out a knife more quickly or more adroitly. Before he had touched the ground the long blade had sprung from his pocket to his hand. He was only play-acting, of course, but he gave us a dissertation on the beauties of the knife as a weapon, and the cleanliness and fairness of knife-fighting as opposed to other methods of settling differences. His knife was a curving one with a black wooden handle and a *cran d'arrêt,* a ringed device for holding the blade open. I agreed with all that he said. I would have agreed with anything that he said, for while he talked he made swishing gestures with his blade, and the blade was sharp enough to cut air.

I was obliged to share a bedroom with Ramon, a pleasant bedroom with shaded lights and flowered wall-paper. The linen was fresh and smooth, and there was a clean towel for each of us. When I opened the window a rush of pure, cold mountain air came in, entirely different from the muggy, mosquito-infested atmosphere of Lyons. You could smell the pine forests on Chaumontet's air.

In the morning I awoke to find that Ramon had felt cold

during the night, had shut all the windows and had smoked a cigarette to send himself to sleep.

I was the earliest riser in *"Ma Baraque"* that morning, and indeed from that day until my departure, twenty-three days later. But as I tiptoed down the corridor, with bedrooms on either hand, I heard Pepette taking the B.B.C.'s seven o'clock news in French.

She listened to this every morning, for she was an ardent supporter of de Gaulle. In fact, I used to believe that she was more than half in love with the General. She had two photographs of him in her bedroom. One of them shared a double frame with the photograph of a blonde young woman friend of La Pepette's, La Fifine.

I went out. The place was pervaded, dominated, by the noise of running water. It had been a mill of some sort, and one-third of the house was built over a narrow, but potent, mountain stream of clear, icy water. It was a most disciplined stream. A shade untidy where it ran out from under Pepette's house, rushing over three bottomless buckets, an old chamber-pot, a pile of broken china and a few once aristocratic bottles. But from that point it ran free and straight for two miles alongside the road to Annecy. As straight as though it had been drawn in with a heavenly ruler.

Hard-faced Angelo, who owned the neat little garage across the road, left the tractor which he was repairing to say good morning and to tell me proudly that the somewhat mechanical-looking stream was "full of beautiful trout and even fuller of *écrevisses*".

Bustling up to the right of the stream was Pepette's vegetable garden, a large one, well cared for and stocked with everything that really mattered.

"Ma Baraque" was a fragile house at a fork of the road from Frangy to Annecy. The signpost said that the smaller road bearing left led to Metz (another, much smaller Metz). The longish front of the house facing the road was painted white, and looked opulent. But Pepette, caught by the war's labour and material shortages, had not had time to decorate the whole place, with the result that it gave a mixed impression. It was part prosperous, part dilapidated.

At one end there was a huge shed which held the hutches for her hens and rabbits, an ancient Citroën car, and an enormous caterpillar tractor which belonged, oddly enough, to the State Railways. Behind this shed I found Pepette's big wood-pile, with an axe and a French saw with thin blade and wooden frame.

Across the road from the house a sky-backed hill rose with startling abruptness. Two-thirds of the way up its precipitous side there was a big cave. From the top windows of Pepette's place, and from the hills on the other side, you would have sworn that there were packing-cases piled in that cave, and a man standing beside the packing-cases. Several times I tried to climb to it, but to reach it would have taken the efforts of a skilful and daring climber, and I am neither, being cowardly on heights. The hill on the other side was heavily wooded, and the woods ran right down to the house in that dense form of scrub known in Corsica and later in France as *maquis*.

Between the hills a plain snaked through to the town of Annecy at the end of its glorious lake. From Pepette's place this plain petered out, the road rising through the hamlet of Chaumontet, a hamlet which consisted chiefly of Pepette's and three other establishments of the same type, places where you could eat and dance and amuse yourself (in more normal times).

It was fine country, between the wooded hills, with many fruit-trees, deep pastures, and milk cows in warm browns and pale beige.

Pottering about below the house, I came upon the cellar, kept cool by the stream and sunk in the earth. There was a fair amount of wine there, properly binned, several barrels of cider, and big stores of potatoes and coal.

The music of the stream, the dogs, the hills, the clean pine-scented air, were a combination that was almost too much for me. I realised what a nostalgia I had for open country after two years of imprisonment.

Bobby, the big dog, was a cross between a great-dane and a *loup*, a French wolf-hound. He was a fine beast, intelligent, stately, and fierce with strangers. Pompom, a son of Bobby by a spaniel mother, was silly and cowardly, but a good hunter.

Pascal took me that morning to inspect the Maquis site which had functioned immediately behind La Pepette's house that summer, and where they had hidden Griffiths, the British pilot who was the sole survivor of the aircraft which had crashed between Annecy and Chaumontet.

Griffiths had evidently behaved well, for his name, shortened to "Griff", had become a legend in that valley. The bed made of wire-netting in which he had lain wounded in the Maquis was kept as a kind of shrine.

"How did he get away from here?" I asked Pascal as we stood beside the bed.

"Pat, whom you should see to-day or to-morrow, fixed it up. He was taken in a car with an armed bodyguard to the Swiss frontier, which he crossed in broad daylight."

"How are the Swiss?" I asked.

"*Très chic.*"

"Griffiths was lucky."

"Immensely so. At that time La Pepette had a *corps franc* of the Resistance quartered here. When it was fine they occupied the place where you now stand. When it was wet they were in her attic. Most nights they went out on patrol, and they were employed also to execute collaborators. Pat was the chief, although he is very young. La Pepette fed them. They lived like kings. It was a good *corps franc*. Now most of them are dead.

"Well, one night, when I happened to be in the village (for I have property here, and often come up from Lyons for the summer week-ends) we heard a big aircraft circling, circling round the valley. Soon we realised that all was not well with the motors. Griff was trying to bring it down on the flat ground alongside the road there, but the night was pitch dark and it struck too soon, among the houses. It exploded and burst into flames and they were all killed except Griff, who was miraculously flung clear and became entangled in some telephone wires. All the occupants of the house it hit were killed too, but they were Italians, so nothing but good was done, except for the poor airmen.

"We managed to get Griff back here, and next day we got a doctor to him. He had not fully recovered from his wounds when he crossed the frontier.

"There was a man, that Griff. He did not speak French like you. The accent was strong and the vocabulary limited. For some days all he said was: '*Je suis veinard.*' And he was right, he could not have prayed for such luck."

That afternoon we watched the village football game. Two teams of callow and effeminate youths played in front of perhaps one hundred peasants. They played in a bad-tempered, self-conscious and pomaded manner, and you could not help contrasting the players unfavourably with their more sturdy and masculine elders.

There could be no doubt that the young men of France were degenerate in the period immediately preceding the second World

War. I often wondered why this should have been. Perhaps the trouble usually began in the schools, where it was not uncommon for a French boy to begin to have sexual relations from the age of eleven or twelve. This leads me to believe that chastity in boys is a good thing up to the age of, say, eighteen.

Pat, a tall and supercilious young man, arrived to see me the following day when Pascal had returned to Lyons. Pat wore a little moustache, handsome clothes, and an air of aristocratic disdain. Although he was at least twelve years my junior, he spoke to me as a field-marshal might speak to a lance-corporal.

Having taken my particulars, he said that he thought he could get me across the Swiss frontier within a week. But he would not be able to help Ramon, whom he advised either to go into the Maquis in Haute Savoie or to make his own way down to the Pyrenees and attempt alone the dangerous crossing into Spain. I told him that I did not feel inclined to go into Switzerland since, as a junior Army officer, I should have little chance once I was interned there of getting back to Britain.

This argument only appeared to make Pat suspicious. He offered to deliver a letter which would eventually reach my wife. I knew that his offer was probably designed to furnish an additional check upon my story. However, I wrote one willingly enough, and he stuffed it into the top of his stocking before setting off on his bicycle. I realised that Pat was an intelligent young man, but I could not bring myself to like him. He left with our arrangements still at a deadlock, but I thought that in him I had planted a seed which might lead me to better things. And I was right. I never thought, when I watched Pat's cycling figure growing small on the long straight road to Annecy, that my future would be bound up with his, and in a most dramatic manner. But that was to come much later, when he had been to England and had changed his name to Albert.

He had warned both Ramon and myself that we should be under rigorous, though unseen, supervision by the Resistance while we were at La Pepette's, and that any breach of faith on our part would mean instant death. We were not unduly impressed by such talk.

The following evening, as I returned from a walk in gathering darkness, a long black car swished up behind Pepette's house. Four men with their hands in their pockets walked quickly into the narrow passage-way beside the refrigerator, and one of them asked sharply: *"C'est vous l'officier anglais?"*

They were either Gestapo or they were Resistance. But all of them looked obviously French, and they were hardly well enough dressed to be Gestapo.

"Oui, c'est moi," I replied.

The speaker asked if I would mind stepping upstairs with him for a moment. Turning into the first bedroom, he closed the door, looked me carefully up and down, and said in English: "I am a British officer."

He was a man who called himself Xavier, and who became famous in all that part of France. A short, square man with a powerful though nondescript face. There were tired lines around his eyes, and a livid bruise showed on one cheek. His hands were big for his size, big and rounded with muscle. He wore poorish clothes, no better than my own—a grey suit which might have been made either for town or country, a dirty shirt, a frayed tie, worn black shoes.

Here at last was the real thing. I felt a surge of pride and patriotism, yes, patriotism, as I looked at him. For this was a workman. A British officer doing a hard job, and doing it without bogus theatricals and paradings. He knew that I was genuine. He congratulated me on escaping, and he took my name, rank, number and regiment and Anne's London address as though he knew that I was telling the truth.

"I shall send a message about you to London to-morrow," he said. "I am a soldier, and it is not normally part of my job to pass escaped prisoners. However, I cannot let you drop, and I will help you. As a matter of fact, I am arranging to pass some British airmen down through France into Spain, and I hope I shall receive instructions to send you along with them.

"It would be utter nonsense to send you into Switzerland. I could do it. And I might do it if you were wounded. But the only way for you to get back where you can be useful again is to go down through Spain. The way will be long and hard.

"In the meantime, you must wait quietly here. You should hear from me within the next week."

"Is there no chance of doing some work while I wait?"

"What kind of work?"

"Helping you."

"No chance at all,' he replied, so firmly that I dared not press the matter.

I told him about Ramon.

"Call him up," he said. He spoke to Ramon in perfect French, without the faintest trace of accent. His French in fact was too perfect for that part of the world. It was the cultured

French of Touraine. He told Ramon that he would like to help him because of the assistance that he, Ramon, had given to me, but that the only Frenchmen whom he was allowed to help to leave the country were trained airmen. He would see what he could do.

"Are you sure of him?" he asked me in English when Ramon had gone.

"Not absolutely. I *think* he's all right."

"Watch him carefully. If he is at all dangerous, we can always get rid of him. . . ."

"Oh, I don't think he's dangerous in that way."

"Warn him to keep his mouth shut, and to keep out of the *bistros.*"

After the first two nights Pepette, who saw that I disliked sharing a room with Ramon, moved me into a small single room called *la chambre bleue.* The vivid blue walls were hung with gaudy prints of the Savoie landscape in spring. There was a wash-basin with running water and a *bidet* discreetly hidden behind a screen.

It was very cold there at nights and in the mornings, so Pepette put a huge electric heater in the room. The heater hissed and spluttered and fizzed with a smell of burning rubber. Once it blew up when I plugged it in. *La chambre bleue* smelled usually, though, of roasted chestnuts. Since it was the warmest room in the house, the whole household frequently retired there last thing at night to eat hot chestnuts roasted on the mammoth heater. I slept well. The air suited me.

I took myself physically in hand at La Pepette's, for now that I had seen the British officer I knew that the mountains in winter-time lay ahead of me, and I am scared of mountains in any climate. Every morning I returned to my prison routine, waking at 7 a.m. and doing half an hour of exercises on my bedroom floor, followed by a run with the barking dogs outside, and then a complete wash down in cold water. The Frenchmen made merry at my expense over *la culture physique,* but I think that they liked me for doing it, since it fell in with their ideas about mad Englishmen.

Pepette was a wonderful hostess. I never saw such a woman for work. When my exercises began to shake the flimsy structure of the house she would leave her B.B.C. morning programme and go down to the kitchen to light the fire and give the place, often disorganised from the celebrations of the previous night, a swift clean out.

315

For breakfast she gave me a huge bowl of milk, just browned with the excellent "coffee" which she made from roasted wheat grains, with long slices cut from the great brown loaves, beautiful white butter, and honey or peach jam.

After breakfast Tino and I would do the vegetables for the day, preparing large quantities of potatoes and sometimes chestnuts, carrots, turnips, French beans, leeks, or onions. Then we cut wood.

Tino claimed to have been a butcher and an expert in the refrigeration of meat, and he made himself very useful by cutting up the carcases which Pepette bought from the local farmers. His real trade, however, had been a more sinister one. *"Maquereau"* was written all over his broken-up face, and sounded in his husky voice, which broke into a fluty falsetto when he sang.

He admitted that he had lived off the earnings of harlots, and I knew that he was hiding up at Pepette's because he had killed a policeman. (I found this out by accident, and Pepette herself did not know it, and thought that she was sheltering Tino as a *réfractaire* who should have been working in Germany.) Despite his unsavoury profession, I liked the man. I liked him, and I was sorry for him, for I have a sixth sense about some people, and I knew that Tino had not long to live. When he was near I could sometimes smell death.

He acted as Pepette's general helper and factotum, and he was a good and conscientious worker. His main trouble was cigarettes.

"Without cigarettes I die," he said to me once. "Joséphine is not sending me enough. I shall have to get her to move in here. She must be smoking them all herself, for she has plenty of money to buy all the luxuries of life."

"Who is Joséphine?"

"She is my wife. A good little wife. Most faithful, and with a fine job in Lyons."

"Have you any children?"

"Yes, one. A boy."

"Why don't you have him here? La Pepette was saying that she would like to have a child around the house."

"Merde," he answered roughly. "The child is ugly. It squints, and I do not think it can be mine. It stays with the parents of Joséphine in Annemasse."

One day Joséphine arrived at La Pepette's. No woman could have less resembled Napoleon's Joséphine. This one was small, bony, with a raucous laugh that sounded like the chuckles of a grey parrot. But she was well, and even quietly, dressed. I soon perceived that she was a good and loving wife, and a nice girl, though colourless and unattractive. It was as though a steam-roller had passed over her personality and a gramophone record of patterned reflexes played always beneath the flattened remains. So that everything that she said or did was done with the dull geisha tactic of pleasing men. That *chez* Pepette this tactic was employed only to please her own husband, whom clearly she dearly loved, did not enliven her personality, at any rate to the casual watcher like myself. I was interested in their marriage.

Surely she had a great love, Joséphine, who worked in a brothel to keep Tino, and to buy cigarettes for him (and for herself—since her employment "fatigued the nerves," she said).

At lunch, after her arrival, she and Pepette discussed the work in "the house". Joséphine said that the German customers were "supportable". But since the Germans had fixed the curfew at six in the evening because of acts of sabotage there was no work worth doing. Madame Eugénie had found herself over-staffed, and had told the girls that if any of them wanted a holiday without pay they could go right ahead.

Pepette took her on at a high wage as domestic help.

"If you work half as well as your husband you will doubly earn the pay," she said. "It's a lot of money for a maid, but then you are used to something better—and you smoke like a chimney. What's money anyway, when so many are killed, and are going to be killed?"

Joséphine was slow, weak, and inexpert about the house. She spent much of her time "fixing" a perfectly good, healthy-looking bedroom until the bones of the room had disappeared in swathes of glittering artificial silk, the pillows were disguised as heavily-ruched cushions, and three languid dolls that looked like tapeworms in apache clothing lay on the shining bedspread.

At the end of every meal at La Pepette's there was a moan about the enormous pile of dirty dishes. Often Pepette would say: "If I am ever rich I shall never wash another plate. I shall fling the whole damn lot out of the window when the meal is ended." Occasionally she was as good as her word; hence the pile of broken dishes in the stream, twenty feet below.

To Ramon's horror, I frequently washed the dishes. He had been brought up to believe that it was undignified, indeed disgraceful, for a man to "meddle in woman's sphere" by helping

L

with the housework. The only French people, I found, who held
views on this subject that differed from Ramon's were women,
and many Frenchwomen agreed with him. However, through
this, and my other small and mostly pleasant labours, I became the blue-eyed boy of the house. Poor Pepette was so
over-worked that she was glad of every little bit of help. She
became embarrassingly proud of my eccentricities.

"Look at him," she was capable of shouting to a large gathering of sternly disapproving mountaineers. "He is a British
officer, but he always makes his own bed."

And Ramon once answered: "I would die rather than make
my bed while there are women there to do it for me. That is
why Frenchwomen are the best women on earth. They are never
spoiled by their men."

Perhaps Ramon was right. At least he did everything in his
power to live up to his maxims. He never, if he could possibly
avoid it, helped Tino and me with the vegetables or the wood
or the wine and cider fatigues. Occasionally, like all the rest of
us, he would take a turn at being barman, but beyond that he
refused to go.

Tino could not bear Ramon, and Ramon hated Tino. One
afternoon I thought that they would fight. I had been called up
to the attic by Ramon, whom I found standing, lost in admiration in front of Pepette's five fur coats which were hanging up,
each one encased in a cellophane cover. Ramon was running
his long, dirty hands up beneath the covers, stroking the fur
and loudly, with many exclamations of wonder, assessing the
values.

"Take your filthy hands and eyes off those coats," rasped
Tino, who had come quietly up the ladder behind me. "You
heard me, Ramon Delgado. Just step away from those furs."

"Listen to who's talking," said Ramon, but he stepped away
all the same. "One would think that the thrice-defiled coats
belonged to you."

"They belong to me before they belong to you, idler," Tino
replied hotly. "What do you do in this house but sleep and
eat?"

Something about this talk made me feel ill at ease. Tino was
a strange trusty to have about the house. But Pepette was incapable apparently of doubting anybody, and good workers like
Tino were certainly scarce.

Day after day I walked with Bobby and Pompom in the thick
woods above *"Ma Baraque"*, until I knew the woods as well as

I knew the streets running off Fleet Street or Piccadilly. Until I knew every glade and clearing where the Maquis had stayed in the summer. For the Maquis, like any soldiers, left obvious traces of their presence. They marked routes to the places where they squatted by cutting zigzag paths through the scrub.

Usually they had built rough shelters against the sun and the rain. The roofs of the shelters had been broken down by the weight of the winter snows. Beside the ruins I would find perhaps a few rusty rounds of ammunition, a few old letters, a pile of whitened snail-shells, and the old droppings of men. In one such clearing there were rusted tins that I recognised well from my prison days, tins which had held British "Meat Roll", margarine and bacon, tins which had been parachuted.

When I was there the *maquisards* had been driven by the winter to camouflage themselves in the remoter villages, to work mainly as wood-cutters. A few of the hardier outlaws still occupied chalets in the high mountains, and against these men the Austrian mountain troops quartered in Annecy made sporadic sorties.

I found more profitable things than the stains of man during my walks in the wood. Sometimes, for example, we had expeditions to find the shy little autumnal mushrooms, the black *trompettes de mort* which grew under the wet leaf-mould and looked somehow so chic and Parisian, and the *chantrelles d'automne,* more ordinary to look at but better to eat, which grew at the roots of trees and bushes in the most inaccessible parts of the woods. And sometimes I would go out at first or last light to the other side of the hill to find hard yellow apples. They tasted like British pippins, and Pepette was fond of them.

When it was too wet for the woods—I had no change of clothing—I occasionally offered to work in the garden, though my amateur efforts in that direction were most sneeringly and angrily received by Pepette's gardener, the Baron Pépé.

Pépé was a man of seventy-one, who was a baron in his own right, senior representative of one of the old and noble families of France, a family which had been great in the days of William the Conqueror; which had owned much of the land that we could see around us; which had continuously through the centuries and the generations overspent its income.

The baron had nothing but the money he earned as a part-time gardener and his pension as a private soldier from the first world war. He lived, unmarried, in a one-room cottage not far from Chaumontet. He was the logical conclusion to his family.

Baron Pépé had always lived as a poor man. He jealously guarded his family tree, but only as a curiosity. In upbringing and mentality he was completely the jobbing gardener. I was interested to see that his hands were genuine peasant's hands, wide and rough, with wrinkled pads of flesh on the back. But I thought that I detected a few signs of breeding in him.

He was irascible to a degree, and always a little off-hand, even with Pepette, who paid him, and whom he greatly admired. His was a dried-up head with finely-chiselled cheek-bones and a small, ragged goatee beard. He was a fussy eater too, and anything but a drinker. He would refuse any red wines and all strong alcohols. He disliked eating meat and fish, although occasionally the motherly Pepette would manage to hide a little of one or other of these protein foods (which she considered most necessary to health) among his vegetables. His favourite food appeared to be potatoes, but these he only liked in the *purée* form, a form which La Pepette turned out to perfection. Often she grated the potatoes and fried them into a huge pancake, which she turned by tossing ceiling-high. But the old man turned his nose up at that.

Pepette treated Baron Pépé with an unexaggerated and natural courtesy, almost as though he were the rich employer and she the impoverished employee.

Lunch at Pepette's was an enjoyable meal. She was a great cook, but an extremely temperamental one, and the clock meant nothing to her. We might sit down to lunch at 12.30 or we might sit down at 4.30 in the afternoon. She was a believer in a few good dishes. The food was simpler than that which I had eaten *chez* Dolores. In its own way it was as good.

When Pepette announced that the meal was nearly ready, Tino and I would drag the kitchen table over to the window, set it, and cut the bread and fetch drinks from the cellar. Often I helped Pepette with little details in the preparation, mixing the salad-dressing or the cream for the chestnuts, picking herbs in the garden and chopping them.

Eight days after his first visit the British agent, Xavier, appeared again. He arrived this time on a bicycle, and he was greatly amused to find me working in the kitchen. I was cooking a roast and preparing the herbs and garlic for the morning's dandelion salad. Xavier was genial that morning, particularly when Pepette had insisted upon cooking him a meal all for himself. She also gave him a glass of King George IV whisky to begin with and a glass of 1892 brandy to end the meal.

320

He was optimistic about my chance of leaving fairly soon for the Pyrenees.

"I am expecting the airmen evaders any day now," he told me. "When they arrive the following plan has been evolved for getting you down to the *Midi*. You will all travel in a light lorry, shut in the back. The lorry will have a police *laisser-passer*, and a *gendarme* will act as scout, riding ahead on a motor-cycle. If the scout strikes a German control he will signal a warning back to the lorry. If he strikes a French control he will arrange that the lorry passes straight through without stopping. But the whole route has been reconnoitred, and we find that by taking the secondary roads it is almost always possible to entirely avoid controls.

"Now here is the point," Xavier continued. "You are quite capable of travelling down in the train, and that might be safer for you than travelling in the lorry with five companions who will not speak any French. On the other hand I should like to think that you would be in the lorry to help the airmen, and to act as interpreter. All right? Good.

"The final stage of your journey will be more exciting. You will leave a town near the Pyrenees in a party of eight, all armed with Stens, and will drive hell-for-leather right through the forbidden zone to the mountains, shooting up anything that tries to stop you. I take it," he concluded dryly, "that this method will not be distasteful to you?"

"What about Ramon?" I asked him.

"He is dragging himself too much around the *bistros*. He is associating with several doubtful women. I cannot waste space and government money in helping him through to North Africa. He can easily fend for himself from now on. Or if you think he is dangerous he will be killed."

I said hastily that he was not dangerous.

Xavier charmingly thanked La Pepette for all that she had done for me, and promised that he would give her more work to do later. He peeled a 5,000-franc note off his bank-roll and handed it to her, saying that it was a token payment on account. He then asked me how much money I had.

"About 8,000 francs," I said, too honestly.

"That is quite sufficient," he said, and put his money away.

Pepette was radiant, more on account of the thanks than the money. (Compared with her expenses on the black market, 5,000 francs was the smallest of drops in the bucket.) At that time there were German-inserted advertisements in all the papers saying that a reward of 100,000 francs in cash would be paid immediately for a true denunciation of any person who hid or sheltered a British or American evader. Pepette was well aware that if I had been caught in her house she, Tino, Maggie and the Baron Pépé would be killed, and possibly tortured, by the Germans. She laughed at that risk. Still, it was agreeable to be thanked and appreciated.

I followed Xavier out into the dark corridor by the refrigerator. Big Bobby had my right hand in his teeth, and he was pulling me towards the door, towards the path cork-screwing up into the woods. But I was tired of walking with dogs.

"Was it you who blew up the transformers at the ball-bearing works?" I asked him as he opened the door.

"How did you know about that?" He shut the door and we stood in the darkness. The refrigerator ticked beside us.

"The village people are all talking about it."

"Yes, it was our people. A good job. But it'll have to be done again soon."

"Let me help you."

"How could you help?"

"Let me come with you when you work at nights."

"You are not trained for sabotage or guerrilla work."

"I can learn. I'm a good shot. Don't you see? I want to do this work. I would rather do it than anything. I would rather do it than return to England."

"You're crazy. Why would you rather do this?"

"For many reasons. The idea appeals to me. Then I want to help the French. And I think I am a coward as an ordinary soldier. Please let me help you. Take me on as a man, not as an officer."

"But you would be of no use to me. You are too spectacular in appearance, and although you speak fairly correct French you have an undeniable accent."

"I want to work."

"Funny, isn't it?" he smiled bitterly. "I am sick of this work and nervous about it. I want to give it up, but I cannot because I know it well, and nobody could take it over. Now I am bound to go on until they catch me again or until they are beaten."

"Catch you *again?*"

"Yes, they caught me not long ago, and let me go. My cover story was so good that they could not break it down. I couldn't expect such luck again, touch wood. I am very superstitious. It's the life that makes one that way. Another thing that is odd is your desire to work for the French. I'm sick of them. I want to work with people who act without talking; I want to work with people who have some idea of punctuality and who always keep appointments. No, George, there is only one country that is worth a damn."

"Which one is that?"

"Britain. Our country."

This sounded like sacrilege to me. But if anyone had ever made me proud to be British it was Xavier. I told myself that he was just over-tired.

"So you won't give me anything to do?"

"Out of the question. Just stay quietly here, then do your damnedest to get across the Pyrenees, and pay me back by doing a good job in the Army once you get back."

"But I don't want to go back to the Army. I want to work like you."

"That is impossible."

"Surely you could do this much for me? In your next report to your people in England will you tell them that I am coming back, and that you consider me suitable to do your kind of work? They can train me for it if I get back."

"All right," he said. Nothing more than that. But I knew that he meant it, and that he would do it. Otherwise he would have refused without compunction.

Ramon had been in Annecy, "having a hair-cut". He returned in time for lunch, and we had a stormy interview. At first he was angry.

"Up to now the difficulties were all because of you. I did not allow you to drop. Now the difficulties are because of me, because you are British and I am from North Africa. You should not allow me to drop."

"But these things cannot be arranged on a sentimental basis. Xavier is not allowed to use the mechanism to send you. Perhaps if you had been an airman, or British or American. Although it is not certain that he would have sent a British or American Army man of your rank."

"I *am* North African. But now North Africa is occupied by the Americans. Therefore I am American."

"Shame on you," cried Pepette and Tino.

"Oh, I know I am French. But I claim American citizenship too. Well, if you will not help me, to hell with you. I have a good mind to try this prisoners' organisation in Annecy."

La Pepette had been trying to make him do that for over a

week. This organisation helped escaped French prisoners by giving them money and clothing and, if they so desired, hiding them in good positions with false papers so that the Germans could not find them or ship them back to Germany as civilian workers. Many of them were put in the police. Such organisations were apparently encouraged, though not openly, by the Vichy government.

There was another reason for Ramon's decision. This was washing day, and when there was manual work of any kind to be done he usually had a ready excuse for being far away. Pepette, as well as running the bar, cooking two enormous meals, and cleaning out the place (with Joséphine's feeble help), once a week did a washing that would have chilled the heart and taxed the muscles of the stoutest British washerwoman. And Pepette had no luxuries like running hot water. She put the sheets and towels in huge cauldrons, folding them carefully around metal mushrooms which were supposed to help the water to circulate; the cauldrons were fixed upon improvised fireplaces outside the cellar door, and one of us lit big fires beneath them.

Although La Pepette was a woman whom some might describe as coarse, or mercenary, or hard (she was none of these things; she was an angel, even if she did let go an occasional naughty word), she was a woman with a genuine passion for cleanliness. Her own clothes were often ragged, but they were always spotless. Every laundry day she did all the household linen and the clothes of Ramon, Tino, Joséphine, Pépe and myself as well as her own. My sheets and towels were changed every five days.

Yes, she was an angel. She even had to make her own soap, and what British washerwoman would do that? She made it by boiling up a mixture of fats (bought on the black market), caustic soda and resin. She had a little *savon de Marseille* too, the splendid olive-oil soap which had once been so plentiful and so cheap in France. Now it was more precious than gold. Pepette used to lend me a cake when I wanted to wash my hair.

La Pepette had a genius for laughter. Her jokes were not stock ones, she made them up as she went along. They bubbled out spontaneously, mixed in with her high, helpless laughter.

I thought that she would throttle herself with laughter the time that she and I sent those townees, Ramon, Tino and Joséphine, out to search for snails. It had been a wet morning and they went off, ploughing through the long grass, baskets in their hands. We watched them from the kitchen windows for about two hours, laughing all the time. It was five months too early for snails.

She would laugh and laugh and laugh until the laughter turned into paroxysms of screams and helpless tears.

She was fond of me with the love of an angelic, unpossessive and unselfish mother. When I remember her I think of the smell of good food, the words *"mangez, il faut manger"*, the tappety-tap of ping-pong balls, and beautiful singing. Pepette might have been a famous singer of the night-club genre. She had a voice full of purity and warmth, and all the artistry of production to draw sophisticated and knowledgeable crowds like those which thronged the *boîte* of Suzy Solidor. Pepette had even some talent for rhyming, and she made her own words to sing to the exploits of Tintin or other *maquisards,* and to sing of the infamy of Laval, Mussolini, Hitler or Philippe Henriot.

After dinner she was disappointed if I did not play a game of ping-pong with her. She played well for a woman, and beat the others in the place with their stiff wrists and clumsy eyes. She went on trying to beat me, but I saw that she would be disappointed if this happened, so I strained to keep my unbeaten record and was just able to do so.

With all her other virtues and qualities, La Pepette, this elderly business woman from Lyons, who could show five fur coats and a café-restaurant as fruits of her life's labours, was as sensitive to mood and atmosphere as any scholar or mystic. She understood me too, because sometimes when England and Anne seemed impossibly far away I would come down in the morning unfit for anything but work, and Pepette would tell people before I opened my mouth: "Leave Georges alone this morning. He has the *cafard.*"

On Saturday, November 13th, Xavier rode up to the house on his bicycle.

"You will go south next Wednesday, I hope," he told me. "Five airmen should arrive in this area before Wednesday. If they arrive, you go."

La Pepette said that she had heard that there were many R.A.F. pilots hiding up in Lyons, to say nothing of parachutists, saboteurs, and such Britons. At the time I did not associate Pepette's remark with Barbarossa's nonsense, pumped into Madame Dolores, and passed on by her to La Pepette at their last meeting.

Accordingly I listened without protest when Xavier agreed to let Pepette produce five airmen from Lyons. She said she would send Tino by train with a verbal message for Pascal to find five bodies, and pass them up to Chaumontet immediately.

Tino dressed up in his full *maquereau* rig for the first time since my arrival—the narrow-brimmed felt hat pulled tightly down over the right eye, the waisted blue coat, the bell-bottomed trousers, the long, slender black shoes, the button-hole, the lavender gloves. Xavier and I looked at him with concealed horror. It seemed to me that he carried a wreath for himself in one lavender hand.

"I almost wish that I could look like that," whispered Xavier. "What a cover story; one could pass anywhere."

Then we discussed Ramon. I had discovered that the North African had searched through the pockets of my jacket while it was hanging upstairs in the empty *chambre bleue*. Pepette had seen him searching in her bedroom, where we were allowed to go as a special concession to listen to the wireless news from London.

"I don't like it," Xavier said to me. "I can understand that you feel grateful to him, but we dare not risk too much for a man of that type. He has been making love to two women at the German-Swiss place near here, and in order to get somewhere with them he boasted that he had escaped from Germany and that he had 'somebody important' with him. Perhaps we should warn him that if he persists in such practices he becomes a danger to the decent section of the community—and that we might have to kill him."

"It's only that he does not fully understand the risk. I tell him nothing, and Pepette mistrusts him since she caught him in her cupboards. I am sure that he has a good heart."

"From our point of view, indiscretion is worse than a bad heart. Warn him soundly, and say nothing to him, nothing."

"He is getting money and clothes from the escape organisation in Annecy. Then he will go down to Perpignan, he told me . . ."

"Why Perpignan?" he said sharply.

"Another North African here told him that was the best place."

"Which other North African?"

"Aha," I thought. "So it's Perpignan that we are going to. That's why he's worried; he thinks there has been a leakage . . ."

Before Xavier left that morning, he said to La Pepette:

326

"Have you got room for another person, a woman, in your house?"

"Room for six, if they are not too fussy."

"Good. A young woman will arrive on Tuesday. A tall woman with reddish hair. Usually wears a *tailleur*. *Un peu le type Croix Rouge.*"

From three miles away with the naked eye I picked out Xavier's *type Croix Rouge*. I was lying up in the woods with Bobby's huge head on my knee and I saw her striding down the road from the bus stop. She looked enormous alongside the smaller French people who had got off the bus. When her figure was no taller than the foresight of a service rifle, she turned into the doorway of Pepette's place. I hurried down from the hills.

"*C'est vous, Georges?*"

"*Oui, Mademoiselle, c'est moi.*"

"Then for God's sake get me a drink and a bicycle." Her English came out with a slight American intonation. And the note of command in her voice was all-American-womanhood ordering the subject male. It took me aback, but I obediently found her some whisky and borrowed a bicycle from Angelo.

She had draped her body over a kitchen chair. It was an awkward enough body, with big, though well-formed, hands and feet. It reminded me of English girls' bodies, thrusting about in a sexless way. Small wonder. I soon discovered that the poor thing had been sent to a girls' boarding-school in the South of England. She had pale reddish hair with pale eyebrows and eyelashes. Increasing the paleness were the spectacles she wore, with thick lenses and transparent amber mounts. She wore a handsome costume, of brown tweed, extremely well cut, with a divided skirt. Otherwise her luggage consisted of a small hide suitcase with a cover over the leather, and a large rucksack.

"Carry my things upstairs for me," she said, or rather ordered. "Where are *Les Waters?*"

When she unpacked the rucksack, talking to me the while about arrangements for my departure, she uncovered a dressing-case of such obvious costliness that it made me gasp with wonder.

"You don't intend to leave that thing lying around?"

"Why not? I always carry it with me. It's my face. Stop fussing. Aren't we among friends here? It is rather lovely, is it not? Keller made it for me just before the war."

"Yes, we are among friends. But some of the friends might be tempted by such an object. All those solid gold tops and brushes and everything. It must be worth a million francs."

"More than that now, I should say."

"Some people would murder for that."

"Nonsense; you just don't know the French as well as I do. I shall leave it here in my room, perfectly openly. If you trust people, they behave."

With that, she departed on Angelo's bicycle. When she returned some hours later, she was very tired. Her long body was limp, and her pale eyes dropped with fatigue behind the lenses.

"Champagne, Pepette," she cried mannishly. "Champagne is the only thing that will buck me up. I am so infernally tired, and the news is bad. The five airmen will not arrive this week."

"But name of a dog," shouted Pepette, bustling herself into one of her fits of energy. "Tino will arrive to-night from Lyons. If he has not succeeded I shall leave first thing to-morrow morning in Tintin's *camionette*."

I did my best to dissuade her, for I knew that she would seek out Dolores and Barbarossa, and I was afraid of scenes.

Late that night Tino returned. When Joséphine, who had given him a rapturous reception, left the room, he described to Ramon his amorous conquests, which appeared to have been so numerous that I did not see how he had fitted in his visit to Pascal. But he had brought back a note for Pepette which said:

"Nothing doing. Regards to G. from P."

Next morning Pepette left in Tintin's dirty old lorry. A metamorphosed Pepette wearing one of the fur coats, an absurd little biscuit of a hat, and a costume with a tight, short skirt. She was slightly hen-toed when she walked in high heels. As she tittuped out, she called: "Look after yourselves, my children." And I felt as though my mother had gone.

Joséphine at once approached me in great distress.

"What is to become of us, Monsieur Georges?" she asked in her cracked and squeaky voice.

"Why?"

She stammered and stuttered for a few seconds, then brought out a dreadful sentence.

"I do not know how to cook."

But Tino had more courage, and soon they were sitting down with the cookery book, working out a menu for lunch. The big woman, *la grande* as they called her, was still in bed, and had shouted a few minutes earlier for her breakfast. She had ordered coffee, toast, honey and butter, and a jug of hot water for washing. Tino and Joséphine both breathed heavily at such hoity-toity ways. But they did not dare to criticise her in front of me.

"After all, it's something, *l'Intelligence Service*," said Tino.

While they struggled with the lunch, a small Italian arrived with a ladder and paint buckets and brushes. He announced that he had come to paint the kitchen.

"When do we eat?" he demanded.

"What's that to you, Coco?" asked Tino, breathing most loudly through his angry nose. "I thought you came here to paint."

"Name of God! I only said I would do the kitchen as a special favour to Pepette and because she promised me my meals as well as the contract."

"You are out of luck, Coco," said Tino grimly. "There will be quantity to eat. If you are hungry you will not starve. As to quality, I smell burning from every oven and every pot."

The house was agitated that morning. Tino and Joséphine managed to produce a meal that tasted of sweat and tears. The painter ate with us. He was naturally greatly intrigued by *la grande*, with her mannerisms, and by my accent, which I aired easily in front of him. I was becoming too confident. Elizabeth (for that was the name that *la grande* gave herself) spoke perfect French, with the slightest trace of an English or American intonation.

La Pepette was only absent for three days. But they were days of agony and accident. On the second day the first major tragedy occurred when that stupid dog, le Pompom, jumped into the biggest rabbit-hutch, frightened the occupants so much that they all jumped out. Tino discovered this some hours later, and came to Elizabeth and myself for counsel.

We scoured the countryside for several hours. We found five of them, two dead, and some hours later, when darkness had settled in, the sixth and last, a large white buck, came limping home. The two corpses were obviously the work of Pompom, to whom Tino administered a terrible leathering. Just as this was going on, La Pepette telephoned from Lyons to ask if all was going well in her house. Tino put his hand over the mouthpiece to muffle the dreadful howls of Pompom, gulped down three-quarters of a tumblerful of marc, and—fortified by this fiery spirit—told her of the day's accident. However, Pepette said philosophically that she herself was too tender-hearted to kill the rabbits, so perhaps her little Pompom had done a useful thing.

"Just put the two rabbits in a *marinade*," she added. "We shall have *civet de lapin* when I return." Tino and I skinned and gutted the rabbits that evening, and put them in a bath of red wine with a little vinegar, some bay leaves, tarragon, pepper, salt, and other ingredients which I have forgotten.

Next day, a Saturday, I found that there were many *gendarmes* around the place. The Annecy *gendarmes* made a practice every once in a while of stopping all traffic on the road outside La Pepette's, searching the vehicles and pedestrians for black market goods, and at the same time checking their papers. Just as English policemen would drop into the nearest inn or tea-room, the *gendarmes* always called once or twice on La Pepette in the course of the day's work. Pepette had a good deal of confidence in them, and she was generous with her red wine and coffee. One of the younger *gendarmes* was an escaped prisoner who had been found this job by the Annecy organisation that was helping Ramon. At the same time, Pepette knew that the police were seldom models of discretion, and she did not want them to know that she had a British officer or even a stranger, in the house. Accordingly, when they were there, controlling the road, I would spend the day hidden upstairs or in the woods.

This particular day there was a double control, and some six *gendarmes* prowled around the place. It was an extremely cold day. I found it difficult to keep warm in the woods. The smell of burning drew me towards home, and when I came into the low scrub, with only 100 yards of precipitous pathway between me and the house, I saw the chimney was on fire; in fact, flames were shooting out to a height of fifteen feet above the ridge of the roof.

Forgetting the *gendarmes*, I ran down the hill, flung open the kitchen door, and shouted: "The chimney is on fire."

I found myself looking into a roomful of policemen; so, without waiting to see the effect of my words, I turned sharply on my heel and darted out again into the woods. The whole lot came streaming out after me, but not quickly enough to see where I had gone.

One of the *gendarmes* said to Tino: "Who is the stranger with the fair hair?"

"Some loony that hangs around the villages and the woods.

330

An evacuee of some sort. You never know what he'll be up to next."

"Funny I've never seen him before. What's his name?"

"How should I know?"

It took them an hour to extinguish the fire, and when it was out the house was a shambles. They had been obliged to tear down the chimney pipes of the kitchen range and the big blue and silver china stove in the bar. Clouds of sooty smoke had filled the house. The kitchen, in which the Italian had only finished work the day before, was dirtier than any other room.

Tino and Joséphine were hysterical. They came to me in tears, Joséphine jabbering in her high parrot squeal and Tino protesting, protesting in his deep underworld croak. I soothed them and promised to defend them in front of Pepette, should any defence be necessary. Joséphine said too much:

"If Pepette throws Tino out he is finished, finished. If it were only the Boches that he had to fear . . ." Tino hit her with the side of his hand just over her hip, a savage, jolting blow. The breath left her stomach in a rush, and she began to sob and cry. Tino locked her up in the room with the dolls.

I offered to help him with the cleaning operations. We went first to La Pepette's bedroom.

What a bedroom! An enormous, pale yellow, shiny bed and a wardrobe to match, with chromium fittings on the jaundiced wood. A fine radio on a tassel-hung table beside the bed. On the other side, the heavy twin frame with General de Gaulle looking coldly at the warmly smiling Fifine. There were two arch pictures of kittens playing beneath monumental oaks and beside romantic meres. The window was obscured with fish-net curtains in mixed colours.

The bed had been left unmade and rumpled since the morning of Pepette's departure. We made it quickly. Tino washed the yellow linoleum floor. I opened the window looking out over the straight stream and the valley. Mont Blanc was a whiteness in the sun and mist away to the left.

"There's a duster, if you feel like helping," said Tino from the linoleum. "Ah, Georges. What a splendid room this is. If things go well for Joséphine and myself maybe we'll have a room like this."

"You have plans for quick success?"

"Yes," he said, and shut his mouth tightly, as though he had said too much.

Pepette and Pascal were thoroughly depressed and bad-tempered when they arrived from Lyons that evening. They had had one or two scenes with Barbarossa; and were so incensed against him that they strove to make Elizabeth believe that he was a dangerous masquerader who should be exterminated by the Resistance or by British agents. Barbarossa, of course, had continued to claim that he knew of several British officers in hiding in Lyons, but he had refused to deliver up these hypothetical officers to "such persons" as Pepette and Pascal. Elizabeth, who was tired and a little overstrained, went early to bed.

The rest of us stayed up late, discussing the difficulties of the situation and the dilapidations of the house, over bottle after bottle of Pepette's strongest red wine (fourteen degrees). I woke up next morning to find myself sleeping beside Pascal in Pepette's big bed, with my head full of resounding phrases and inspiring music.

Xavier arrived to see Elizabeth. We had a meeting in her bedroom. She sat up in bed with the magnificent dressing-case open on one side of her and her breakfast-tray on the other. Xavier was tired. He had spent the night before at a "reception committee", a parachutage of arms for the Resistance. He did not tell me this, but I knew from his description of the place where he had spent the night that he had been on a plateau where such events took place.

Neither he nor Elizabeth ever told me anything. This was a matter of policy, I fully appreciated. In such work it was a mistake to tell anything unless the telling were absolutely necessary. The obvious reason for this was that the Germans were in the habit of torturing or otherwise intimidating their prisoners, and the less the prisoner knew the safer were his former comrades who were still at large.

I often thought that this wall of silence was a good thing, a thing that might with profit be carried into the ordinary world at peace, when we should have defeated Germany. And yet it was unnatural.

Xavier was an unnatural figure to me, and big Elizabeth too, with her strong reticences. With Xavier the silence was so disciplined, so ingrained, that he carried it out with no effort. But the woman found it more difficult. Her little walls of silence never broke down so far as I was concerned. She never told me anything that mattered. But I often sensed that the walls were bulging and trembling with the effort of keeping the silence. They would never have given way, for she was loyal to her training, and in most ways was a strong character. Often, though she would soliloquise to me about the oddness of her life and her job—and her future if she were caught.

From such talk (for I had been a trained listener, and was able to keep useful bits aside so that I could add them to other useful bits) I slowly learned, or thought that I learned, that she had an American mother and a French or English father. She had left France after the occupation, and had crossed the Pyrenees to be trained in England for her present employment.

Xavier did not wait long on this occasion. He told us that there had been an accident. Now the five R.A.F. people might not arrive for some time. We must wait. Elizabeth would wait with me. He thought that I had been too long with La Pepette. It was dangerous to stay as long as three weeks in the same place.

"Shall I take him away?" asked Elizabeth.

"Where to?"

"To Mégève, perhaps. We could stay in one of the hotels, and do some ski-ing."

"No. Mégève is packed with Jews and *réfractaires*. One day the Boches are going to tear it apart."

"To the farm then?"

"You mean the farm where Jean stayed?"

"Yes."

"We must keep the farm out of it as much as possible. But if it blows up here, touch wood" (he *was* superstitious), "you might take him there. Well, *à bientôt*." And he was gone.

"What do you think of him?" Elizabeth asked.

"I have never been more impressed by anyone in my life."

"Nor have I. He is so hard and self-sufficient."

"He has a sensitive, almost a sensual, face."

"Yes, but his self-discipline is so good that he never relaxes, so far as I know."

The talk was going the way I wanted it; the only way I could learn things about the work I wanted to do was by making Elizabeth talk.

"Self-discipline. That must be the terrible thing about your work. To fear, and never to have the safety-valve of companionship. To desire, and never to have the safety-valve of release, of accomplishment. To hate, and never to dare to voice one's hatred."

"Yes, indeed," said Elizabeth. "And to live like a pig. I, who have always been spoiled—I frankly admit it—who have always had everything that money could buy. To live in such

333

places. To be dirty. I only have half a dozen shirts, and often I am obliged to wash them myself. Look at my hair, my nails, my shoes. That is why I cling to my big ring, to my gold-backed hair-brushes. I know as well as you do that it is dangerous to do so in this *milieu*. Well, maybe I wasn't cut out to be an agent. I am not strong like Xavier. And then he is so unfeeling . . ."

"Indeed?"

"Not cruel, mind you. I say nothing against him. Except . . ."

"Except?"

"Except that he keeps me idle."

"Idle!" I exclaimed with a politely incredulous laugh.

"Yes, you can laugh. I know lots of people would give their ears for my type of work. It is romantic. I have money to spend. But there is damn-all to do. Listen. I was trained for a life of action. I was trained to blow things up, to fight, to shoot straight. But Xavier has other ideas. He likes me, I know. But I don't think he trusts me. Either that or he is old-fashioned. He does not think that I am capable of doing such work. But I am, I am. Why, at the schools in England I was one of the best of them, women or men. I worked, I tell you. I had the best reports of almost any of them. I want to work, I want to work. Without work this life is the devil. You can't get away from your nerves. I can do nothing but smoke and drink and wait for the Gestapo. For the knock on the door and the words, *Police allemande*.

"The other day I was in Paris and something took me to the *Rue de la* . . . Well, anyway, something forced me to walk past my mother's house. The Germans put her in a camp when America entered the war, but she was ill, so they let her go home. The butler was at the door with one of the dogs. I had to whisk down a side street. I adore my mother. She does not know whether I am alive or dead. And I used to think that this job would be romantic, wonderful. Hell, that's what it is. Plenty of discomfort and dirt, plenty of unhappiness and fear, and a lack of work. There you have my life."

"Poor Elizabeth! But I still want to do your kind of work."

"*You* do it! You'll get back to your ever-loving wife and you'll go back into your regiment. By the way, I know several people in your regiment. A very nice regiment. I must say it *is* rather nice to have somebody like you to save, rather than all those others."

"What do you mean exactly?"

334

"I mean a gentleman. I have never been so deceived as when I picked up my first R.A.F. and American pilots. I had been expecting something romantic in the Leslie Howard line, you know. And then they turned out to be so common."

"Elizabeth, really! A 'secret' agent who remembers to be a snob!"

"Beast! Of course I'm a snob, and unashamed of it. I was brought up to be a snob. I cannot help it, can I? Do you think Xavier's a gentleman?"

"What do you mean by a gentleman? I am not a snob."

"You know perfectly well. Sometimes I think you are nearly as foxy as Xavier. And he is much too foxy to let a poor girl even smell at his antecedents. He is so clever that he speaks even his native language without accent. A fascinating man."

"I think that you are in love with him."

"Rubbish! If he would take me into his confidence a little. If only he would give me some work to do!"

"He has. You are to save me."

"Huh! I mean real work, you ass. Military work, like we were taught in the schools."

"They must have been fun, the schools."

"Yes, they were wonderful. Busy all day long. Military problems, and being treated exactly like a man. 'Forget my sex,' I used to say to the major. 'I can do anything that a man can do.'"

"Where were the schools?"

"Aha! You've been leading up to that. Well, I'll tell you where they were not—Aldershot." That was the end.

There was a luncheon party that day, with our amateur *civet de lapin* to eat, and Pascal there and another man, a business man who spoke English. The table was set in the big café, and we played ping-pong before the meal and drank cocktails which Elizabeth had made with Armagnac. The business man had brought me some papers. I had been angling for these for some time, for now my worker's certificate and the letter from the manager of the Micheville steel works were out-dated and useless. The business man had procured me false papers which stated that I worked for the huge Renault firm in Paris, and that I was an inspector entitled to travel all over France, looking at Renault agencies and garages.

When I had got hold of the papers I looked around me and saw that Pepette was quite green about the face. She could not eat, and she kept sending Tino out on messages. The messages

335

were not given out openly, but with whispered instructions. I asked her what was the matter, and she repeated again and again that all was well. But finally she broke down and explained that Tino had discovered that there was much talk in the village of Chaumontet and even in Annecy.

"What sort of talk?" asked Elizabeth sharply.

"That there is an English officer hidden in my house."

Tino told us that the thing had begun two days before when I was accompanying Elizabeth as far as the bus stop. Walking behind us up the road were two men, one of whom was the little Italian who had painted the kitchen.

"Who is that man in front?" asked the other man. "He has a queer head (*Il a une drôle de tête*)." This was too much for the Italian.

"Don't you know?" he exclaimed. "That is the British officer who has escaped from Germany and who is staying with La Pepette."

Pepette had always insisted that she had complete control of the French police in Annecy, and that she had even a friend who worked in Gestapo headquarters who would inform her if there was any danger from that quarter. But she was worried at the rapidity with which the news had spread. She admitted this.

At the same time she was angry, extremely angry, when Elizabeth decided: "This is no place for us. I will take Georges away immediately."

"Don't do that. There is really no danger."

"Yes. Pepette. There is danger. You only say that because you desire to keep him. Examine your conscience. Georges is my responsibility. He will stay no longer. Tino kindly step across the road and ask Angelo to be at the door with a car in ten minutes."

"How far will you be going?" asked Tino, and I thought that he seemed to be pleased about something. "Angelo will have to know how much petrol will be needed."

"One hundred kilometres," said Elizabeth after thinking a little.

"Where are you taking him?" Pepette asked.

"To a farm. I will not tell you where. It is better for you that you do not know. He will not be so comfortable there."

"Will he have enough to eat?"

"Probably not."

"Then I shall give you a parcel."

The grim-faced Angelo was hanging over the wheel of the old

Citroën. Elizabeth got in behind. Pepette kissed me on both cheeks. She was too worried to feel very sorry that I was departing. The parcel that she gave me was heavy and bulky. Tino gave my hand a hearty squeeze. He was smiling, and I wondered why he was glad to see me go. I left a letter for Ramon, who was away visiting his organisation in Annecy.

Angelo whirled us away. It was strange to be in a car again. I was nervous of the roads. We were climbing most of the way, climbing into the Alps. I asked Elizabeth in English where we were going. She replied that Angelo would leave us in the village of Chaumont, above Frangy, and that we would have a long walk from there to the farm.

"Oh, George, I hate the place, I hate it, hate it, hate it."

"Why?" It was growing dark, and Angelo had turned on the flickering old headlights. I wanted her to explain away my nervousness. Xavier was right. I had stayed too long with the kind Pepette. In the woods and the work I had grown harder physically, but in her never-failing kindness and courtesy I had grown soft. Soft and frightened of the big, hungry world.

"I once had to spend three weeks there, and I nearly went mad. Talk about discomfort. But now it's better. I think it has a roof now."

"A roof? I hope so. It's raining."

"It is always raining where we are going. . . . Turn to the left and stop the car," she said in French to Angelo.

We stopped in a lane on the outskirts of the village, a lane with a huddle of dark cottages and a strong odour of steaming manure. I put her heavy rucksack on my back and tucked the bottoms of my German trousers into my socks.

"Have you no overcoat?"

"No."

"My poor George, we must get you one."

We walked on into the darkness, walking north, I could see by the Pole Star, which appeared now and then through the rain and mist. There were high banks on either side of the lane, which was very muddy. It was so dark that we could not distinguish puddles. Soon my feet were as wet as the back of my neck. A cold finger of wetness reached down my spine.

Elizabeth caught hold of my arm and held it. Perhaps she was scared of the dark.

"Oh, my God, isn't this miserable?" she exclaimed. "It's the *bled* all right. A wilderness of rain and mud and discomfort. Discomfort is the worst of all pains. The blow with a cudgel

337

is easier to bear than feathers on the soles of the feet."

"Pampered Elizabeth."

"Speak French. Sound carries, and the mountain peasants are suspicious. Damnation. . . . My feet are beginning to hurt."

CHAPTER XXI

THE lane ran out of its enclosing banks and along the side of a dark hill-side. A cutting wind swept the rain at us, and despite my load and the exercise I was numb with cold, for my German city clothes offered no protection against such weather.

Elizabeth strode out as energetically as any man, and her ski-ing boots bit into the mud, whereas my English crêpe rubber soles slithered back and made it an effort to keep pace with her and to avoid falling. There was something bleak and terrible about this landscape, and something in Elizabeth's attitude also which helped to drag my spirits down.

"What's the matter with you?" I finally asked her.

"Speak French or I will not answer you."

"Nom de Dieu! Must we be unfriendly just because it is cold and wet."

She burst out laughing.

"What odd expressions you are picking up, *mon cher Georges.* And if I seem a little odd it is only because I so dislike the immediate prospect. I do like comfort, and I loathe this place that we are going to. I loathe the place, yet I love and admire the people in it. Just one thing, though. I must warn you that they are very anti-British."

"Anti-British! Then why are we going there?"

"They are French patriots, and they do splendid work. They work for France, and therefore they are obliged at this moment to work also for Britain. Politically they are against Britain. The man, Clément, was a famous guide in the Alps. His wife ran a small hotel near St. Gervais, under Mont Blanc. During this war they have lost everything, their home, their hotel, his photographic business, his work as a guide. They have moved to this farm, Les Daines, and they are hiding here, that's what it amounts to, while Clément carries on working for us. He is a difficult man. But I am certain that once you know him you will admire him as much as I do. Only he is a hard character and self-opinionated. Please be tactful with them. As for the hardship of living there—I know you will find it unpleasant, but I am sure that you will be polite about it. When they arrived not so long ago the place was quite derelict. They have done a good deal of patching up to the structure of the house, and now I think it is at least weatherproof. The last man that was hidden there was an American, and when he was there the place was without certain roofs, walls and windows. You know how difficult it is to find building materials in France."

Every now and then Elizabeth stopped and peered into the darkness. Once we heard the creaking of a farm cart's wheels, and she became excited at the sound.

"Don't tell me you are expecting a parachutage here to-night," I said. "It would be a good place for it, I imagine, except for the high hill on our right. But surely the weather is too bad?"

"The place is all right for it," she answered. "One thing, we are unlikely to meet any Boches in such a deserted spot. This is the only road to Les Daines, and as you see, at this time of year it is quite impassable for cars. If the Gestapo ever raid the place they will do it at dawn."

"Might they know about it?"

"Yes, they might. Although this farm is tactically much safer than La Pepette's place, Clément does a tremendous amount of work outside, all over France, and the family are strangers in this part of the country. Therefore there is danger. They are something of a mystery to the surrounding peasantry. There might be talk, even denunciations. The jealousy of the French peasant is unbelievable. Or Clément might be trailed back to the neighbourhood. I would advise you all the time that you are here to keep your eyes open, to keep yourself hidden, and to be ready to run for it at any time, especially at dawn I expect that you will be here about eight days."

"As long as that?"

"I once stayed here for three weeks. You'll manage eight days, though I expect you to get the *cafard* pretty badly. There is no privacy. You will have to sleep in one room with everyone else. You will be cold, and you will eat badly.

"I must warn you too that what lies beyond this for you is quite terrible. I crossed the Pyrenees in spring, when the weather was perfect, and it was the most awful experience of my life. It is a long, hard walk with plenty of scrambling climbing. In winter it will be hellish. Be prepared for that."

It was after eight o'clock when we came to a raging burn

which had been bridged by the simple expedient of laying a flat boulder across it. The burn was greatly swollen with rain, and it topped the bridge by a good three inches. She took my hand to guide me over since neither of us had a torch. We found ourselves in a farm-yard so soft underfoot that I thought in the darkness that we were walking in a midden. I skated and slithered after her to a yellow light that came boldly out from the glazed upper half of a rough doorway.

Elizabeth flung open the door and we pushed into a dimly-lit kitchen with a puff of rain and wind which ceased when I closed the door. She put on her most hearty, mannish front, and strode up to a group of three men who were hammering and banging away at a some large metal object in the centre of the kitchen floor.

She slapped their backs and talked to them loudly for a moment. None of them offered to shake hands with me, and they reacted quietly, almost sourly it seemed, to the boisterousness of Elizabeth. Two of the men were young and the third, Clément, was middle-aged. All were strapping creatures of the mountain breed, and all wore small berets and rough ski-ing clothes which made my own muddy town suit look silly and effeminate. They were repairing an old kitchen range, and very intent on their work.

"I have brought Georges to stay with you," Elizabeth said.

"Don't know whether you can stay here," Clément answered slowly. He had a wide-browed face with steady eyes and a great gathering of muscle around the jaw. "We have the whole of Laurence's family here, her mother and her brothers and their wives. The place is filled to bursting."

"We must stay here," Elizabeth insisted. "We have nowhere else to go." She had to shout against his hammering.

"Oh well, you had better see Laurence. I dare say she will fix something up, though you can expect no British luxury."

She led me into an inner room. This room gave an impression of dark greyness. It was ill-lit by two small carbide flares on a long table where several children were doing their homework. There was a big double-bed in one corner. Elizabeth told me to put her rucksack on it. I did so, laying my little papier-mâché case from Strasbourg beside it, and my beret from Lyons. I was embarrassed. The room seemed at first sight to be full of women whose gaze was so uninquisitive that I found it hostile.

In such situations the only thing to do is to break the crowd into individuals. When I did this I found that there were only four women, one old and three young or youngish.

The old woman was perhaps more friendly than the others. She had an intelligent, deeply-wrinkled face, rather bronzed and with an aureole of steely hair.

"What a *queer* face," she said, staring at me through shell-rimmed glasses, with a round price-ticket sticking to one lens.

"He speaks perfect French," Elizabeth warned them quickly.

Too late. Laurence, the woman of the house, who sat by the fire weighing me up with scarcely concealed mistrust, had already demanded: "Who is this colourless young man (*ce jeune homme fade*)?"

"He is a British officer, a soldier escaped from Germany."

"It is for when, the Second Front?" one of them asked me.

"How should I know when those pigs of English will undertake it?" I answered, and drew an easy laugh.

Elizabeth began to talk to them about the Resistance. It was grim talk. The women listened and nodded. There were stories of betrayal, of torture, of burning farms, of the cruel Militia whose numbers in Annecy had recently been increased. Elizabeth called on Marie-Josèphe, the oldest of the three children, to fetch us some cider. Marie-Josèphe was a girl of sixteen, good-looking, wayward, sturdy. Her name was shortened to Mijo.

The cider had an exciting colour, greyish green. Elizabeth took the German water-bottle from the pocket of her *canadienne* and splashed an inch of marc into each glass before she filled it with cider. I was glad to drink. The others all refused with chilly smiles which said: "Let the English booze if they want to." The mixture was strong. I strove to be impersonal, to forget the hostile atmosphere.

I had managed to escape because French people had helped me. Not the least important part of their help had been the sympathy which they had poured out to me.

To forget these people who were not friendly, I looked around the room, letting their inanimate objects sink into my consciousness. In such peasant interiors you know the inhabitants by the worn, often astonishingly unfunctional, objects which surround them.

Laurence was cooking the usual potato soup on a small, box-shaped stove that stood out from the wall. The stove's primary function (which it performed inadequately) was evidently to heat the room, but there were two cooking spaces on the top. Beside it lay sabots and huge boots, with the farm-yard and country mud wet upon them. (The women, I noticed, all wore boots. So did the three children.)

There were two windows and a half-glazed door in one wall. The sash-bars that divided each window into four large panes of unequal size were crossed high up to give the effect of Christian crosses. I wondered if this were intentional, remembering that the mountain country outside was certain to be thickly studded with crosses.

While I thought of this I heard the two younger children repeating the catechism. They were learning slabs of it, parrot-fashion, as part of their home-work. One of the sisters-in-law was correcting the errors of the bigger, red-haired child, while the grandmother instructed the smallest girl. The woman crooned questions like: "What is death?" "What is the body?" "What is the spirit?" And the little girl brought out her automatic answers.

On the window-sills lay a litter of children's pencil-boxes, religious leaflets, books about the region, agricultural merchants' catalogues, and a too-pretty doll of the type that one used to see in thousands in the *grands magasins* of Paris at Christmas.

Three strings of tobacco-leaves hung drying from the ceiling of untreated white pine. The whole interior was new. The cement was still sweating on the walls and on the floors. It was very chilly in the room. I did not know which was the more chilled, my heart, or my body in its wet clothes.

I concentrated again on the furniture, glancing at an old sewing-machine, a chest-of-drawers, and a splendid, tall clock that stretched from floor to ceiling, widening reasonably gracefully from its small face down to a firm pedestal. It had a middle shaped like the waist of a guitar with an oval glass window in it. And through the navel of this distinguished clock you saw the pendulum slowly swinging.

"What's 'navel' in French?" I asked Elizabeth.

"Nombril."

"What's *nombril?*" asked the youngest child.

"It's a horrid word (*un mot très louche*)."

When the children had finished their home-work and their religious instruction, and not one moment before, the lot of us sat down to table. As is often the custom with country families in France, Clément, the *père de famille*, sat not at the end but in the middle of the table, with Laurence, his wife, on his right hand. Elizabeth, apparently the guest of honour, sat on Laurence's right, while I was tucked ignominiously away at

342

the end of the table, where I should not be able to interfere with the conversation. After being the centre of every table for such a long time, this was a healthy and probably much-needed pill. Furthermore, they had put me in among the ski-ing champions and their wives, and not among the children, with whom I should have felt at home, since children are without racial prejudices, at least up to the age of ten.

Elizabeth had already explained that Louis, the younger, and in a superficial way better-looking, of Laurence's two brothers, was the present ski-ing champion of France, while the other brother, Julien, was almost equally accomplished as a ski-er, although before the war he had worked in a factory in Paris. At any rate, both of them had super-healthy, pink-and-brown faces, steady, wrinkle-set eyes, and swinging, loose-limbed bodies.

They contrived to give to every gesture, even to rolling a cigarette or cutting the bread, that "I-don't-care-how-steep-it-is" look of your ski-ing champion. Naturally in their life at St. Gervais, a mountain resort much frequented by a certain type of Englishman, the Viallet family from which Laurence had sprung had learned that the English had clayey feet. And Clément remembered the Imperialists trembling on the mountains, or falling down and worshipping him because he was a master in the manly art of climbing. I cut *very* small ice.

In fact the only remarks that were addressed to me when the soup had been consumed were first the eternal one: "Are you British ever going to launch the second front—*ce débarquement problématique?*" and secondly, an expletive which they hurled at me and later explained: "Whisky shot!"

(The explanation was simple. There had been an English couple well known in one of their sporting hotels. This was a happy marriage, except in one small thing—the husband cared for drinking, the wife preferred that he remained without drink. So the husband had formed the habit in the course of each evening of leaving his wife, making some slight excuse such as fetching a handkerchief or making a telephone-call. On these occasions he always ran to the bar and shouted at the barman: "Whisky shot!" In the minds of those fine mountaineers the English were forever associated with that slightly unusual expression.)

Louis had married a local girl from St. Gervais. She was dark, good-looking, with a bronzed skin, and very much *enceinte.* Julien had married a Parisienne who had been in the

343

habit of going to St. Gervais for her holidays. She was thin, very tall, sharp and incisive. She had worked for the post office, and intended to do so again, in happier times. Both women were intelligent, and slightly antagonistic to me. The men were openly affectionate with their wives. Laurence often laid her head on Clément's shoulder. While I disliked them for their coolness towards myself (spoiled as I was, I was inclined to call it rudeness), I could not but admire their independent sturdiness and intelligence.

They had something in common with me and my people in that they were shy at first meetings, and they did not tell me anything of themselves until many days later, when they had begun to accept me.

Pepette had thrown into my parcel all sorts of luxuries to which these more Spartan people were unaccustomed—meats and fats and a bottle of Armagnac.

At Les Daines they ate simple, peasant fare. Plenty of soup and bread, and only occasionally meat. I was glad to face the prospect of living like that for a time, since life had been too fat for me at Pepette's.

Clément made one remark which amused me.

"Is he armed?" he asked Elizabeth, jerking his head at me. "No."

"That's bad. I'll lend him a gun."

Armed, armed, armed! What were these histrionics? Perhaps Clément thought he was armed with his little Swiss knife with a corkscrew on it which leaned now on the side of his plate to cut the food into neat segments or to make the sign of the Cross on the loaf. Perhaps he had a mother-of-pearl-handled opera-box revolver made in Belgium in 1870. Or a screw-gun strapped on to his muscular body and hidden by the overalls. Or perhaps there was an 88-mm. hidden in the loft. Was there a minefield sneaking out from the door there? And soon we might hear the roar of Whirlwind engines, warming up to take the tanks floating out through the ground mist to another dawn in the desert

I disliked Clément. There was something in him that fought against me. I did not see his worth for a certain hardness, a certain braggadocio that was in him. Yet, looking back now, I never remember meeting a finer or a braver man than Clément. Why did the war take men like Clément from the world, and leave normal men like me? Except that in his death he was nobler than a normal man could ever be. But that was later.

344

After dinner the ducks and hens were shut into a kind of work-room, full of joiners' and builders' tools, alongside the kitchen. The sheep and goats occupied the adjoining room, and all the human beings, including Elizabeth and myself, mounted in a stream to the dormitory on the first floor.

Before we went upstairs we trooped out into the dark yard where the men all pissed a few yards from the door, looking soulfully, as men often do on these occasions, at the wet heavens, while the women, bearing right a little for privacy or from prudery, must have done approximately the same thing.

The dormitory was not a large room. The window space was restricted to two small, newly-installed casements. There was a large double-bed for Clément and Laurence and a big wardrobe for the family's clothes. My own small metal bedstead and that of Elizabeth paralleled one wall. Two single beds (each, since our arrival, to be occupied by a young married couple) stuck out from another wall. A bed made by laying mattresses on the floor was occupied by two of the girls. The fine old walnut of a grandmother and the youngest child slept in the double bed below.

The two carbide lights could not be blown out without danger of explosion. They burned lower and lower until there was the tiniest flicker of blue flame on their nozzles. The window gradually steamed up, although it was cold in the room. My bed was pleasantly hard, and quite clean. I lay there in woollen vest and long pants, listening to the breathing and stirring darkness. When I thought of home and people who had cared for me, a lump and a loneliness formed inside me.

I could sleep no later than 7 a.m. In the early morning one is more susceptible to squalor than at other times. I noticed the great mud-encrusted boots and the grotesquely thick woollen socks lying in strange shapes on the floor by the connubial beds; the floor that was rough with mud and twigs and small, deeply brown, crushed cigarette ends. My own boots were so muddy and so grey that they looked like elephant's feet on the mantel-piece of a Southend boarding-house.

One of the children was awake. The nice, carroty-haired one. She was reading an adventure story, lying on her tummy.

"*Bonjour, ma petite,*" I whispered, thinking that here at least I might establish human relations.

"*Bonjour, Monsieur,*" she replied, with cold politeness, and pointedly returned to her book.

Elizabeth was sleeping deeply. She had told me that at Les

Daines she never considered getting up before eleven o'clock. I heard the grandmother downstairs beginning to break up sticks for the fire. I could stand my bed no longer. I climbed awkwardly into my damp trousers, which I had laid on top of the bed for warmth, and went downstairs.

The grandmother gave me an enamel basin. I filled it with icy mountain water at the spring outside and washed myself beneath a pear-tree that raised its knotted arms beside the rabbit-hutches. Twenty-three rabbits, most of them Belgian, munched stolidly as I washed and shaved, and each eyed me sideways with only one eye, as rabbits like to do. Also the ducks, which had come outside with me, pottered around me and even pecked and shovelled at my boots. The ducks looked happy and healthy, perhaps sinisterly so. I had never seen such a wet and muddy landscape.

Miserable landscape. Worse in the dirty daylight than the night before. The farm stood in the foot-hills of the Alps. But the Alps were hidden and all that was visible was a brownish-green, sloping basin. It was evidently sheep land, and fruit country in summer-time. The enclosures that existed were inadequately sheltered by wind breaks of stunted oak-trees and scrub, and about every tenth tree was a poplar. The poplars were weak and nipped by the sharp winds, but they stood up raggedly, far above the small oaks, and gave an unshaven look to the country. Here and there in the wilderness I saw a clump of sturdier trees, and there were other farms sheltered in these clumps.

Les Daines and the immediate precincts were wetter, it seemed, than any of the surrounding country, the reason being that three small, but very active, burns came down the hill-side, and flung themselves at the farm. There had evidently been partially successful attempts to lead all this water away. Deep new drains emerged from under the house and petered out farther down the hill-side.

The house itself reminded me instantly of the Stone Age dwelling shown in a bright blue children's history-book which I studied at the age of five in Cupar, Fife. It was a long building which staggered down the slope. It appeared to have been flung together by a mixed gang of amateur masons and giants. The masons built rubble walls, like farm walls in Yorkshire, and here and there the giants had stuck in enormous boulders. The jutting roof, of a heavy and ill-fitting type peculiar to that region, was in a bad state of repair, and through holes in the first-floor walls one could see a jumble of things which were kept in the loft—an old churn, a mildewed oilskin hanging from a hairy rope, a pile of worn-out motor-car tyres. In front of the house, in the yard, the fowls pecked around the remains of a Citroën car of first World War vintage which somebody had sawn in two, evidently with the idea, long since relinquished, of building a makeshift tractor. Beside the rusty chassis stood a home-made "horse" for sawing wood, and a hand-mill for grinding wheat into home-made flour, a devilish contraption for the person obliged to turn the handle.

As I stood there in the rain the two young men, loose and gracefully uncouth as ever, came out.

"Which one is it to be?" Louis shouted to Mijo, who was giving the rabbits their breakfast.

"Hélène. The one with the broken horn."

"Come, help us to kill Hélène. Then you'll be entitled to help us to eat her," he said to me.

She was a large ewe, with a black splash over the left eye.

They flung her, feet in the air, on the "horse". I held her back legs, thinking of Bernard Shaw, and how horrible ordinary humans really were. Is any meat-eater entitled to register horror at Nazi or other cruelties? I am a meat-eater, however, and I strove to harden my heart as Julien (who, like Tino, had been trained as a butcher) opened her jugular vein. I felt the life rush out of her with her blood.

I was so depressed that I considered the life fortunate to be able to leave such a place so quickly, so easily.

They collected all the thick blood in a basin (valuable stuff blood for making the *boudin,* a delicacy which they valued highly). I wondered if the life were in the basin with the blood, or if it had gone somewhere, or just ceased to exist.

We carried Hélène into the dining-room and the two young men sprang at her poor corpse with their sharp knives, skinning and peeling and tying some mysterious things carefully with string. Frenchmen are much more knife-conscious than Englishmen. By this time I had a razor-sharp knife myself (all part of my French personality), but alas, I did not know what to cut, so I awkwardly held Hélène's legs apart while they did the work.

"How fat, how beautifully fat she is!"

"Like a virgin ready for her lover."

"The kidneys look good."

"And the liver. It is good grazing here for sheep."

They told me that Hélène had died to celebrate the anniversary of Clément and Laurence.

"You have arrived at the right time, Georges. To-night there will be a feast with much meat."

That afternoon Elizabeth walked me into the dark village of Chaumont, topped by a sinister and mouldering ruin, to seek drink for the evening's festivities. Elizabeth could drink like a man, and she liked her dram. But although the *lambic* was functioning in the middle of the village, where the narrow street, overhung with heavy roofs, corkscrewed up the rocky hill, we could find no marc—or *la gnole,* as they called it—for sale. The *lambic* looked like two elderly traction-engines making love in clouds of steam and exhaling a queer, strangely heady, alcoholic smell. It was making marc from the skins of the wine grapes. At the top of the village in a café which was half baker's shop we managed to buy three bottles of *Roussette.* As we gloomily slithered down the muddy street past the red glow of the hissing *lambic* a peasant offered to sell us two bottles of *la gnole.*

He took us into his kitchen, where the brass shone brightly against the darkness. He and his wife fussed around us, giving us glasses filled with the warm new spirit and lumps of sugar to dip in it. From their talk they knew or guessed that we were "Resistance". They complained to us that there were too many *maquisards* quartered on the village, that they were always hungry, and that it was difficult to find them food.

We walked back again through the darkness. I felt no less a stranger to this place than on the previous evening. Approaching La Pepette's place I always had the impression that I was arriving at my home. Now I wanted to stay out in the rain. I felt that I was unwelcome.

Dinner passed with a lot of singing and serious drinking, for these were Savoyards. They sang less well than Italians, less sentimentally than the Austrians, but with the drink they acquitted themselves like well-mannered mountain people, and they had risen in my opinion when we went up to bed. The two girls lay on the floor, whispering and giggling together at the odd behaviour of the grown-ups.

Mijo, the oldest, had been in a convent in the mountains, but shortly before my arrival the Germans had taken over the place for use as a barracks. She was a well-educated sixteen-year-old, with more knowledge, more prejudices, more Shakespeare, and more sex than most British girls of her age.

Isabel and Michel, her younger sisters, were obliged to go to

348

the school at Chaumont, no matter what the weather. They got up at 7.30 and, after a bowl of warm milk and some bread, undertook the five-mile walk to their school. In water-tight aluminium containers they carried their midday meal, to be eaten in the class-room or in the street. They returned home in the darkness, about 6.30 in the evening, drank a little coffee or tea with slices of dry bread if they felt hungry, and settled down to their home-work. They slaved at this work, suffering, with awkward hands that did not love using pens and pencils, with tortured tongues that waved around under their noses, seeking to lick inspiration from the humid air. Much of their work was done from biased history-books. It was there, I perceived, that the anti-British feeling began, for every chapter seemed to end with the English being "chased out of France". These passages were often read aloud, in high mechanical childish voices, for my benefit.

On Thursdays they did not go to school. But it was a day devoted to religious work, and they were obliged to trail off, as early as on normal days, but to the priest's house. They worked all Saturday. Sunday was a rest day from school, but again they were obliged to make the long walk to the Mass in the morning, and Sunday afternoon was the only time they had for mending their own clothes (they were already, I noticed as an ex-prisoner, surprisingly handy with needle and thread) or for playing with their dolls.

Small wonder then that their faces were already as old in spirit as my own. They were over-worked. They seldom played and shouted like normal children. They were strangely young-old little girls, and strangely attractive with their tired poise. They only made a background to my life. Usually I can get near children, but they always stood me off. They had no time for me. There was too much to do.

On my third morning in that place I began to write short stories. Something forced me to write. Perhaps the urge was increased because at Pepette's I had been the handy-man around the place with plenty of work to do, whereas in this place all the men would have laughed at my efforts to cut wood or to dig in the garden. Again, here there were four women and little washing up or housework to be done. There was a super-abundancy of labour. I had to do something that sucked me away from their life, and I wanted to do something that they would not understand. At tea-time I awoke from my trance of work and looked at the short story which I had written. It was

349   M

a story called "Winter, 1940", about Paris at the opening of the war, a nasty, mean, twisted story written in vulgar, flashy English. It was hateful.

"Why the hell did I write that?" I asked Elizabeth.

"Were you not conscious of trying to write like that?"

"No, it just poured out."

"I wonder what it means. It's about an unfaithful woman. I think it's rather clever and quite horrible. It makes me sick."

"Me too."

"Why should you write that stuff? There must be something bitter in you, something wrong with you."

"No, nothing. Only . . ."

"Only what?"

"Only sometimes. . . . I wrote it automatically. It almost seems that somebody else wrote it."

"Quite mad," said Elizabeth kindly. "Now come and play some rummy with me, for I am bored to death, and to-morrow I leave for Paris and the north. Perhaps we shall never meet again. Clément has work to do in Paris. I am going to Vannes, in Brittany, on your wild-goose chase."

*   *   *   *   *

The chase she referred to had been started by a young Annecy *gendarme* who had approached me one day in La Pepette's bar.

"You Georges?" he had asked.

"That's me."

"If you ever want to leave France, go up to Vannes. My father is an officer in the *Gendarmerie* up there. He is in contact with England."

"How?"

"Speedboats of the Royal Navy come into the coastline around there, often several times a week. They take off evaders and other people. Just give this pass-word to my father. . . ."

*   *   *   *   *

"Then I am going to do some work near Paris," Elizabeth continued. "So to-morrow we had better say adieu."

"But how long have I got to stay in this place?"

"Just wait until Clément comes back. Wait patiently."

"I refuse to wait here, I would rather go into the Maquis, or make my own way south."

"You will do what you are told. Remember that you are a soldier, and obliged to obey orders."

The following morning we waded down the hill towards Frangy, five miles below, in the valley. The squelching fields were running with water. There were attractive twists in the ground though, where the vine-yards patterned the green slopes that swung so neatly together. I was aware that in better weather and with congenial company I could have liked the place. The big religious crosses pricking the outlines of the countryside seemed unpleasant and unhealthy. I even hated Elizabeth because she was leaving me alone in this streaming wilderness.

She would not let me descend out of the *bled* into Frangy; we stopped at the top of the final wooded decline, and I smoked a cigarette with her to conceal my exaggerated chagrin. It was my first cigarette in six weeks, and I loathed it. We transferred her rather vulgar brown-and-white rucksack from my shoulders to hers. Clément and Julien's tall wife came down the hill to join us.

Their ski-boots made sucking noises as they trod the wetness. They looked like two blue crows, for they both wore the heavy blue cloaks of the *chasseurs alpins.*

"Au revoir, Georges, soyez sage."

"Au revoir, Elizabeth, Clément."

I climbed gloomily up the hill, so tremendously discontented that I could revel in my discontent.

I was so conscious of being unwanted that I seriously considered running away from the farm. Then I thought of Xavier, and I knew that I could never do that. I stood pondering outside the front door of Les Daines. When I went in I saw that Laurence, sitting by the range stirring a pot of stew, was looking out at me from the shut-in privacy of her hard, half-noble, half-grasping face. Laurence might have modelled for a portrait of Joan of Arc. Her face was bare and thin and bony. None of the features was individually good, yet the effect was good. Yes, it was a face that carried more than its share of character and nobility.

She had been stout before the war, but now she was thinned down by hard rations and the drudgery of life. Her eyes had a film of ice over them when she looked at me. She thought I was ungodly, and a capitalist. I had never imagined that any intelligent person would take me for a capitalist.

I plunged into my bitter writing, and into the gloomy routine of winter life in the farm.

I continued to be the earliest riser, for the moment I awoke

in the dormitory I was anxious to leave its cold, damp fug behind me for the day. I washed at the spring a hundred yards
above the farm. Every second day I drew hot water from the
tap at one side of the kitchen range and shaved myself, not to
be British officerly, but because I wanted to be different from
the bouncing Julien and Louis, who did everything physical so
much better than I did, and who only shaved on Sunday
mornings.

When I had washed, the grandmother and perhaps one or two
of the younger women would be in the kitchen scratching the
sleep out of their eyes. Breakfast was a bowl of imitation coffee
with some milk and sugar. We ate this from a shelf. We cut
cubes of sour brown bread into the coffee, and we sucked it up
with great noise. I left the bread alone as much as possible; it
blew me up.

The inner room was aways cold. I had to wipe a film of
moisture off the surface of the table before I sat down to my
work with one of the children's pens and an exercise-book which
Elizabeth had given me. I wrote in minute characters to save
paper. At one o'clock the two young men would come in from
their work on the house or the steading. We ate quickly, un-
sociably. The men went out again when they had smoked. I
worked. The women sewed or mended. The darkness came
early. The children arrived home. The prospect of the dormitory loomed up as the home-work began and the potato soup
bubbled on the stove.

After a succession of such days a kind of numbness descended
upon me. And the people slightly changed their attitude towards
me. Laurence, for example, called me "Georges" instead of
"Monsieur l'Anglais", and I noticed that now she invariably
set me on her right hand at meals, and she saw that I got my
fair share from the vegetable- and meat-pots.

Julien and Louis, too, began to treat me less as some foreign
matter in the soup, and more like a man. I saw that there was
something strangely dramatic in the presence of this united
family, the Viallets, all hiding from the enemy, complete, so
far as lives went, down to the unborn child carried by the wife
of Louis.

Three weeks before my arrival at the farm they had been in
their own home, another but a much finer farm on the outskirts
of St. Gervais. Julien had not gone back to his job in Paris
after the fall of France. He refused to work for the Boches. He
had brought his wife to his mother's house. Louis, the ski-ing

champion, had done the same. The two men worked their mother's farm.

All summer and autumn they worked, laying in vast stores of vegetables and bottled fruits and wine and cider and *la gnole*. The women were busy bottling all the time. There were smoked hams too, hams with no fat on them done in the manner of Haute Savoie, and sausages and pickled pork and delicious *pâté de lapin*. There were apples in the loft and potatoes in the cellar. But all this food was not for them alone. The Viallet family organised the feeding of the Maquis that lived in chalets on the high mountain, and they gave largely from their own riches, the fruits of their own labour.

With the winter, and no more cultivating to be done, Julien and Louis began to work as woodcutters.

One fine morning a friend of Louis Viallet's, a man called Perry, arrived, and with him was a fine-looking blonde woman. They asked old Madame Viallet if Julien was at home. The mother would not answer because the blonde was a stranger. If it had been Perry alone she would have answered, for he had been a ski-ing *moniteur* like Louis, taking the classes of rich tourists who were clumsy at the game because they had not been born with skis on their feet. Perry was above suspicion. As she denied that her sons were at home, she saw with embarrassment that both of them were coming down the hill behind the farm.

Julien stopped up above to look at a pile of wood, freshly cut. Louis came on down. The blonde and Perry saw him and the woman made a signal to three men, who began to circle the orchard, closing in behind Louis.

Young, handsome, cocksure, Louis stood leaning easily on the fence at the end of the garden, near the summer-house. The blonde walked towards him, followed by an elderly man and Perry.

"Good morning," the blonde said to Louis. "You are Julien Viallet, are you not? I am anxious to get my husband into your Maquis."

"Maquis? I have no Maquis."

"Well, we can have a chat, can't we?"

"It is not for to-day, our chat," answered Louis, swinging off like a startled stag and flying down-hill.

"Shoot him. Kill him," cried the woman.

The elderly man fired twice, but Louis swerved as though he were on skis and went on downhill in a rush that nothing could check. Two other Germans in plain clothes fired at him. He was untouched.

But he was followed hot-foot by Perry, with whom he had grown up as a boy on the snow slopes near Chamonix, with whom he had paraded as a brother *moniteur* in front of the rich people from the lowland towns of France, Britain, America; against whom he had competed in less vital races. Perry followed desperately, and every now and then he paused to fire at his former class-mate. He knew that if Louis escaped it would mean his own life. After 200 yards he found that he was outpaced, but he still followed, leading five or six Germans in the hunt.

Louis came to a bridge, but something told him to avoid it, and he crossed lower down on two big pipes of the hydro-electric system. This saved his life. As he crawled across the pipe, a grenade thrown from above exploded on the bridge. He ran fleetly through fields and houses where men shouted at him: "Eh, Louis, where is the fire?" or: "Louis boy, there must be a girl waiting for you."

He circled and found the family again in the high woods. Even the grandmother Viallet had had the sense to escape. They had left the fruit and vegetables and meat, the furniture and the home where generations had built up stocks of comfort. But the whole family had escaped, even the unborn one.

*　　　*　　　*　　　*　　　*

On Tuesday, November 30th, Clément returned from Paris, or wherever he had been.

He waited until he had dined before saying to me calmly: "I don't know when you will go, Georges. You must have patience. I have just received this order concerning you." He produced a slip of paper on which was typed:

"Officers who escape are unimportant as compared with your normal work. It is understood that these officers feel that it is urgent that they should move on, but as far as you are concerned they are a secondary consideration. Pilots must be considered as more important, however."

Having read this I told him that I would like to take myself out of their hands and try to cross into Spain on my own initiative from the South of France.

"*Verboten*," was all he replied, looking across at me from the hill of his calm strength. I was glad that he was leaving the following day, and I told myself: "I shall wait one more week, then I'll go in the night and catch a train from Annecy to Perpignan."

I forced myself to write another story, and a damp kind of snow settled slowly upon the mud outside. That night Laurence said that she thought Clément had been a little hard with me. We began a long conversation. Laurence was supported by the remainder of the family.

They had heard that England was a rapacious and immoral country. America, according to them, was still worse. They had heard much of the dangers of "the great Trusts". It was odd, in that isolated farm, to hear them handling foreign names like Henry Ford, and General Motors, and I.C.I., and Lever Brothers, with French names like Renault, Schneider, and international names like Rothschild. They wanted France to return to an agrarian policy, with a build-up of the land and disintegration of the cities and factories. They despised the capitalist systems of England and America. They saw the weaknesses of those systems and disregarded the separate strengths and goodnesses of those countries. With much of what they said I agreed in principle.

These people did not follow Marshal Pétain or the Vichy Government. Laval was as repulsive a political figure to them as to me. They were essentially of the Resistance. But at the same time they pointed out to me that there was much that was good in the Pétain administration. It was an administration which (theoretically at any rate) despised money and upheld the Church and the home. It had done something to improve public health and education.

Julien asked me, for example: "When you were in Paris did you see any sex magazines on the bookstalls?"

"Now that you mention it, I don't think I did."

"You know the reason for that? Partly that the Boches have clamped down on the Jews, and partly the influence of the Pétain Government. There was much money in sex magazines, but they were immoral and they had a putrefying influence."

"But we don't have them in England. Or at any rate they are not obvious."

"No, because England still has remnants of public morality. But in America the sex magazine is as rife as in pre-war France."

"Rifer perhaps. But Hitler may also have cleaned up the sex magazines. Don't forget that Hitler built up German strength for aggression on the same cry as Pétain about the home and the family."

"The Boches are a law unto themselves. They are bullies."

"Yes, under Hitler. Were the French not bullies under Napoleon?"

"No."

"No?"

"Never. That was just British propaganda."

They pointed out the difference between the German youth movements and the *Compagnons de France* movement begun, apparently on the German model, by Marshal Pétain. The sight of boys in uniform is naturally sickening to a Britisher, and I had heartily disliked the *Compagnons*. They wore a blue uniform and berets with a badge showing a cockerel.

Clément wore this beret and this badge when he departed on his missions. I knew that he was a leader, a *chef*, of the *Compagnons*. Now they told me that he used the *Compagnons* as a cover for his dangerous work for the British and the Resistance, and that many of the *Compagnons* were doing the same thing. They extolled other merits of the organisation: it was rejuvenating French youth, it was training young men to work with their hands, it was hardening their bodies.

The young wife of Louis took up the case of Pétain's government. She told me that because she was expecting a baby she got help from the State in the shape of advice, special foods, money, and free space in a mothers' clinic when her time came.

I was pleased to attempt to colour their hard minds a shade, to change them if but slightly in their uncompromising attitude towards Britain and towards Russia. And pleased to listen to their arguments.

One Tuesday a code telegram arrived. Laurence became excited. She said that I might be leaving for the south the following day. Meanwhile I must go down with her at once to Frangy to act as interpreter. Five British airmen were due to arrive in a truck at the Hôtel Moderne.

We splashed down together through the mud. She told me that the airmen would spend that night in one room in the hotel. On the following morning we should set off in the truck for Perpignan. The petrol for the trip had been bought from the Gestapo at Perpignan at the extraordinary price of £4 a gallon.

It was already dark when we entered Frangy. The proprietress at the chilly Hôtel Moderne told us that the five *colis* (the French word for "parcel", which was the stock description for evaders who were being passed along an underground chain) had not arrived.

Laurence and I decided to eat there, in the bar. While we ate a small, bright-faced *gendarme* named Tournier came in with his buxom wife. He approached us at once and said to Laurence with a wave of his slender, hairy hand: "Who is this? Can I talk?"

"Go ahead," she said to my amazement. "This is a British officer, but where are the other five?"

"There has been trouble somewhere. There is a rumour that the Militia have heard that five 'parcels' are arriving at this hotel, and they think they are parcels of arms for the Resistance. At any rate, better clear out of here. Come along to the *Gendarmerie* with us. We have posted scouts on the outskirts of the village to stop the truck if it comes in."

The police station was long and imposing. Tournier and his wife had a fat child which howled the moment it saw me, although Laurence had asked me earlier to make a present to the father "for his son", and this led the good people to suppose that the child would naturally care for its benefactor.

To drown the child's indiscreet howls there were several bottles of particularly good *Roussette*. A tall, dark and handsome Frenchman, with a strangely wide face and liquid brown eyes, came in with his mother. These were Serge and Madame Avon. He was to leave with us for the south.

"Why are you going?" I asked him.

"To train either in Britain or America or North Africa to be a pilot."

"Do you want to be a pilot or do you want to kill Germans?"

To my delight he answered frankly:

"If I wanted to kill Germans I should stay here in the Maquis. I want to be a pilot, and, since the war has interrupted my studies, departure seems to be the only hope I have for a decent future."

Honesty is particularly refreshing in war-time, and on such topical subjects. Despite his pampered looks and the long side-whiskers that curled down from his luxuriant hair, I began to like Serge. His mother was a middle-aged widow with black hair and a fiery gaze. She told me that her husband had been a *cheminot,* and an engine-driver at that.

"He was a huge man, and a good Communist," she said. "I keep up his ideals now that he is dead." She brought this out with a sharp glance at Laurence, as much as to say: "*Your* politics stink."

The airmen did not arrive, and at 1 a.m. Laurence and 1 climbed up to the farm through a drenching downpour of rain.

Mijo, the oldest daughter, looked daggers at me the following morning. I wondered what possible reason she could have for this, and then realised with horror that she suspected that I was making love to her mother. I looked at her again and knew that I was not imagining things.

"What do you mean by keeping my mother out so late at night?" said her look. I wished I could reply equally well with my eyes in the trite sentiment: "It was not I, but duty, my dear, that kept your mother out so late." She had succeeded in making me feel thoroughly uncomfortable.

When Laurence said at midday that we must make another night expedition to Frangy I saw Mijo's face darken, and I attempted to withdraw, pleading that I felt tired, and that I had no dry clothes. It was snowing and half a gale was blowing across our hill face.

"Nonsense," said the unsuspecting Laurence. "We must have an interpreter. As for the clothes, I shall lend you some of Clément's."

I scarcely dared to face the wrath in Mijo's face that evening when I was called upon to parade in front of the family in mountain clothing, complete with ski-ing boots and blue *chasseur alpin* cape. Uncomfortably in these borrowed garments (for Clément was a smaller man) I faced the storm at Laurence's side. But I had not covered a third of the trudge to Frangy when I realised that I going to be very uncomfortable indeed. How Mijo would have gloated had she accompanied us! For the old ski-ing boots, hardened up to the consistency of steel in the leaking loft at Les Daines, were mangling my feet.

I had never been so thankful to sit down. I let myself gently into a chair in the Hôtel Moderne, took off the boots and examined them. The insides were splashed with my blood. Pieces of my feet, particularly around the heels, had literally been torn out. This worried me more than a little. I knew that I should have to depend on my feet to carry me across the mountains to Spain.

The airmen again failed to appear. It was two in the morning when I struggled, panting with pain, into the kitchen at Les Daines. I could hear angry words upstairs between Mijo and

Laurence, but I was beyond caring about such things. Of the few small feats of physical endurance in my life that five-mile walk had been the least spectacular and the most terrible. I tore off my bloodstained boots and bathed my feet for an hour and forty minutes in the icy water that ran in an improvised pipe from the spring above the farm to a basin in the kitchen.

Next day I could not walk, but sat working with my feet wrapped in handkerchiefs greasy with some form of unguent which the grandmother had given me. Mijo was sent off by her mother to confess to the *curé* her sins of jealousy. That night Laurence went down alone, and came back in time for dinner with the worst of news. The five pilots had fallen into an ambush. One had been killed by the Germans, shot dead on the spot, the guide and the others had escaped.

But although the evening had begun badly, it finished on a festive note. A friend brought in the local evening paper. He had tramped up from Frangy to show Julien and Louis a paragraph headed: "Terrorists Murder St. Gervais Ski Instructor." It was the vengeance on Perry of course. The paragraph simply stated that when Perry came out of a café in Mégève two men followed him with a Sten-gun and fired twenty-eight rounds into the small of his back.

This called for a celebration, and Laurence brought out the *bonbonne,* an enormous glass jar protected by wicker-work, filled with apple-jack. We drank Perry's health until two in the morning.

From then on telegrams from Perpignan began to arrive at the farm with alarming frequency—alarming at any rate from the security point of view, since the enemy obviously kept a watch on all postal traffic. I could see that Clément and Laurence were determined to get rid of me soon, and I could not help thinking that Mijo's misplaced jealousy might have something to do with it.

On December 7th Clément returned from the Midi and told me that arrangements were nearly complete for me to go down there whether the British pilots arrived or not. He and Laurence returned immediately to Annecy, whence they were leaving for Perpignan. I watched them pedal away down the Annecy road on a tandem bicycle belonging to Julien and his wife. They did not know I was watching them, for I was hidden in the vineyards overlooking the road. They looked a queer pair of saviours, struggling uphill on their tandem, with Clément in front and Laurence doing very little work behind. But I had

359

great confidence in them. Now in the intervals of working I had taken to roaming the countryside. I found that if I bound my feet up carefully I could walk, although several of the wounds inflicted by Clément's old ski-ing boots were slow in healing. I was afraid to lie up absolutely with the Pyrenees trip apparently so close.

Next day as I sat eating in the farm with only the grand-mother and my enemy Mijo as company, for the young men and their wives had gone to other relatives, there was a clatter of nailed boots on the stone floor of the kitchen, and Elizabeth swept in.

Her hair, her pink-and-white nose and her smart brown *tailleur* all dripped water, for it was raining heavily outside, and she had walked from Chaumont without a coat.

"Get your things," she barked at me. "You leave here at once."

"But Clément and Laurence expect to return from Perpignan in a day or two and then I was to go down there."

"You heard me, you are leaving. Pack your bag."

Mijo loaned me a thin white raincoat belonging to Clement. She would have loaned more than that to see the last of me, poor girl.

Elizabeth was in a highly nervous state. She had evidently had some close shave on her trip to the north. All she told me at first was that the escape route through Brittany was not work-ing for the moment. Then, as we splashed down the muddy road to Chaumont, she told me that her engagement had been broken, in fact her fiancé, a middle-aged Frenchman, was already married to "the other woman".

"Life is too hellish, George. I wish I were dead."

Mixed with my sympathy for this unhappy friend was some concern for myself. Elizabeth was in no safe frame of mind.

"Where are we going, and how?" I asked.

"To Pepette's. I told Xavier that you must be dying of cold, hunger and *cafard* up here, and that you had been here long enough. He said that you could move down to Pepette's again for the last few days."

Outside Chaumont she began to swear because she saw no car waiting for us. I hid in the lane while she went on into the village, and soon I saw a Peugeot rush down the hill in a cloud of spray from the wet roadway. It stopped about a quarter of a mile away from me, and I saw Elizabeth alight and give the "close on me" signal of the British Army, while two men got down from the front seat and pretended to tinker with the engine. They were Angelo and Edouard.

Pepette greeted me with tearful embraces. She told me that Ramon had left a week earlier for the Pyrenees. It had been decided that I must hide all the time in *la chambre bleue* so that my presence in the house could remain completely secret to outsiders. She had prepared a table for two up there and Elizabeth and I dined *à deux*. She was in a bad state of nerves.

I was disturbed to learn that on her last trip to the north Elizabeth had been accompanied by Tino. It seemed to me that Tino had looked at me in no friendly manner when I arrived, and his bearing when he brought us up our food and wine was much less pleasant than when we were sharing the work of the house in the old days. I noticed about him too, more than ever, the aura of death.

Elizabeth sniffed at my idea as "ghoulish nonsense". She thought that it was interesting to have a man of Tino's character as a bodyguard and confidant. I thought it dangerous and so did Pepette, who confided in me that Tino had brought a goldsmith from Annecy to the house. Unknown to Elizabeth, this man had valued her gold-fitted dressing-case. The estimated war-time price was one and a half million francs. Pepette feared that Tino had a fixation about the dressing-case and that he would stop at nothing to possess it. I was inclined to agree with her, but for that evening all that I did was to warn Elizabeth that he might be a dangerous companion, since a man of his *métier* might not stop short at blackmail. Elizabeth only smiled.

"If he tries that I shall kill him."

The following morning Elizabeth had an idea, which had come to her through the night, that the Gestapo were about to visit the house. Tino fanned the flames in her mind by coming back from Annecy with a story that the police there already knew that I was back with La Pepette. I took this calmly, for I believed that he would want to get rid of me, considering me to be a bad influence on Elizabeth from his point of view.

But she could not keep me there in the face of his story, which *might* after all be true. I said good-bye to Pepette and Bobby, and left on a bicycle accompanied by an unwilling Tino. We cycled to the bottom of the hill on which Chaumont stood. I left him there and watched him wobble away, leading my bicycle. I did not want him to know in which direction I intended to walk. The potato soup was just being poured out when I arrived at Les Daines.

Clément and Laurence returned from Perpignan, enthusiastic about the town, bringing delicacies from it such as noodles and *banyuls* and also good news for me. All was arranged at the Perpignan end, said Clément. Now it was only a matter of awaiting a signal which would come by telephone or telegram. Then I should leave Les Daines.

"You will leave from Annecy station with Serge, and Laurence will accompany you," he said, eyeing me very directly. I suspected that Mijo had passed on some of her unwarranted suspicions to her father. Fortunately, he was a strong enough character to refute them and to disregard them. The situation was awkward, nevertheless, and as the days passed with no message I began to fret.

On Monday, December 13, I went out with Laurence on a bartering expedition. I carried a rucksack filled with wool, and we exchanged this at different farms and villages against bottles of alcohol and large joints of pork. Wool was at a premium in the community, since it was unfindable in the shops and the only way to get fresh supplies was to buy it or grow it in the raw. The sheep-shearing in the farm was usually done in the dining-room, with the sheep slung upon a cradle by its middle, and gazing stupidly down on me while I wrote. When we returned to the farm that evening the kitchen was full of men.

They were trying a man for his life, but the accused was not there. Clément seemed to be judging the case. There were five other men in the room, all strangers to me. They were *maquisards,* and they demanded the life of a young man whom they charged with selling to the Militia arms parachuted for the Resistance. The evidence they produced was all of the so-and-so and such-and-such variety. My opinion was asked. I said that I found the case unconvincing.

And so did Clément. He closed the meeting, saying: "We cannot take French lives without definite proof of guilt. None of us has the right to shoot this man. It is true that by delaying I may be risking the lives of all my household, including Georges, who has been entrusted to me. But I still could not face the responsibility of taking a life that might be innocent."

His reasoning was unpopular with the other men. They had come to obtain a conviction and a death sentence. I saw that they were all armed. They had intended to kill the accused immediately. Clément called out the *bonbonne,* and while they drank the colourless alcohol and rolled themselves brown, untidy cigarettes, he told them gently that the young man might

362

be interrogated, but that anyone who laid hands on him would answer to a higher authority. Clément was a fine man, afraid of nothing, not even of public opinion. When I saw that he was just, even in the heat of the Resistance, even in the fear for his own home and children, I knew that he was a man of stature. It had made life seem very cheap to sit in the farm kitchen with six men and the women and children, and hear a life demanded while the soup hissed on the stove and the baby girl said her catechism. Then Clément had made things right again with his justice.

One of the men cocked his automatic before leaving and said: "You refuse to execute this traitor, but I warn you that if we meet him on the way down to Frangy I shall descend him myself." The others smiled approvingly, but Clément remained sitting like a rock at the table. He swallowed the marc that remained in his glass and never so much as glanced at them.

When they had gone he left with Mijo to see some cousins who lived twelve miles away. The following day the stout woman from the Chaumont Post Office came panting into the kitchen with a telegram which declared:

"Jules will arrive on Thursday."

Laurence became wildly excited, and I knew before she spoke that it was the signal for my departure.

"To-day is Tuesday," she said. "This means that you are expected in Perpignan on Thursday, so we must leave Annecy to-morrow night. We must go down to Frangy this evening to warn Serge, and to meet Clément and Mijo when they come off the bus."

My feet were still very sore, but I was excited this time, and nothing could have kept me at the farm. At Frangy we met the evening bus from Annecy on which Laurence expected to find Clément and Mijo. But they were not on it, so we went round to see the hospitable Tourniers at the *Gendarmerie*. As usual, Serge was there with his mother. They were eating sausage with a great deal of garlic in it and pickled cabbage. This dish inflamed our thirsts and everyone became sentimental about our impending departure. Madame Avon insisted, when we had finished Tournier's wine and drunk half his marc, that we go and attack the Armagnac in her little house.

Before we left, Tournier himself stood up on a chair and gave, in a voice that rocked the whole *Gendarmerie*, the toast: *"Nous n'avons qu'un chef, de Gaulle!"*

It was already 2 a.m. when Laurence and I began our long

walk home. There were two alternative routes. The normal one, by road and track, was slightly the longer but was easier walking. The other climbed straight out from the back of Frangy, and was mainly across fields and through vine-yards. Laurence wanted to take the first route, but, for some reason which I could not explain even to myself, I was determined that we should follow the other. I pointed out that although we had no torches, there was a fair moon, and in the end she gave me my way.

Something made me nervous on this walk. I kept imagining that I saw figures in the dark shadows of the pine-woods or along the ragged hedges. It was a bitterly cold night. This helped me to hurry along Laurence, who was normally a ruminative walker. I kept thinking to myself that Clément and Mijo might have arrived home. And if they had it would be suspicious to say the least of it for any husband to find his wife out with a foreigner at three in the morning in such a wild countryside. Furthermore, I told myself, Mijo would be certain to increase her father's nervousness under such circumstances. In the end, I voiced my fears. But the calm Laurence pooh-poohed them.

"If they had been coming they would have arrived on the bus," she said.

But I was right and she was wrong. For when we arrived at the farm we saw two shining new bicycles in front of the house. Clément and Mijo had evidently arrived by another route. There was something grotesque and frightening about those bicycles. For they were brand new, yet they had been flung down anyhow in the mud. And bicycles in France at that time were the most precious things on earth.

We tiptoed into the house. She asked me to wait in the kitchen while she mounted to the dormitory. I strained my ears to listen, feeling all kinds of a fool and cursing my bad luck. Soon I heard Mijo in tears and Laurence came downstairs.

"Go to bed normally," she said. "Clément must have gone mad. He and Mijo arrived only at one o'clock, and when they found that we were not here he left for Frangy on foot. How dared he! Does he think that he has to spy upon me?"

I wasted no time in getting to bed. Mijo lay motionless on the floor bed, beside her red-haired sister, but I could tell from her breathing that she was not asleep. She was lying raging at me.

Her misplaced jealousy might spell disaster for me. It occurred to me that I could not have felt more guilty, more worried about the situation had I really been guilty of committing adultery or something like it with Laurence. My situation was ludicrous, but it was also dangerous.

The trouble was that I was afraid of Clément. I admired him, and I remembered his justice towards the *maquisard* whom the others wanted to execute. But I knew also that he was a man of hot and sudden temper. He was a good deal my elder, but I was fairly certain that if it came to a fight he could tear me to pieces. And he was always armed.

We had evidently only missed meeting him in the windy darkness because I had insisted upon taking the rougher route. He had taken the other, considering that by doing so he would probably meet us.

That such a situation should arrive on the eve of my almost certain departure for Perpignan was more than maddening. Sleep was out of the question. I lay worrying and shifting in the darkness. But not for long.

Clément came up the staircase as solidly as my grandfather Morton striding around his house on a Sunday morning to wind up the tall clocks. I feigned sleep carefully as he entered the room. He passed my bed without faltering, sat down on the side of his own double bed and began to take off his boots.

"So you are back at last," he said quietly to Laurence.

"How dare you follow me about as though I were a criminal or a whore?" she demanded angrily.

"Shh," he soothed her. And they talked in whispers for a long time. I lay like some cringing slave waiting to be whipped or killed, listening to their whispering, realising that perhaps my life, certainly my immediate future depended upon its outcome.

"*Bonne nuit,*" I heard him whisper at last.

"*Bonne nuit.*"

I slept little and I had the feeling that their sleep was as troubled as mine. In the midst of my anxiety for myself, I was pained that it was my presence which had upset, if only temporarily, so fine and so remarkable a household.

The following morning, as I left the dormitory to wash, I noticed to my surprise that Laurence was alone in bed. I found Clément below, in the cold kitchen. He was cleaning and oiling his two pistols. He asked me to give him back the pistol which he had loaned to me on the night of my arrival. I did so without serious misgiving, for his face looked calm and set, although his voice showed the rough edge of strain.

Soon the grandmother had heated up coffee for us, and

Clément and I ate together in silence. While we ate storms of hysterics began in the dormitory above. It was Mijo. We heard Laurence remonstrating with her and then the sharp sound of a face being slapped. The hysterics changed into gales of weeping. Mijo was Clément's favourite child. This was more than he could stand. With a grim look at me, he left his breakfast and went upstairs. From then on, for an hour, I heard the constant murmur of voices from the dormitory, and occasionally the sobbing and wailing broke out.

I waited there in an agony to be away from Les Daines, and an agony of worry that Clément would postpone my departure because of this scene.

Madame Avon had asked Laurence and myself to lunch in her house before leaving for Annecy. After a time I could stand the uncertainty no longer. I went to the dormitory door and knocked. Clément opened.

"What do you want?"

"I thought I might go ahead, down to Frangy."

"Yes, go ahead. And tell Madame Avon that I shall be there too, for lunch. Hurry up and collect your things."

I went in and picked up my clothes from my bed, packing them into the little brown case from Strasbourg. I ignored Mijo, who lay stiffly stretched on her bed.

"Anything *else* you want?" asked Clément.

"Yes, I wondered if you would mind lending me the white raincoat. It might be much better for me to have a coat of some kind for the journey. I would send it back to you from Perpignan."

"Take it. I have two *coats*."

Was it my imagination, or had he unduly stressed the last word? I had expected him to add: "But only one . . ."

My agitation gave me wings. I covered the distance to Frangy in one hour.

Clément and Laurence were late for the meal. I could tell nothing by looking at them. Their faces were like lumps of granite. I noticed Madame Avon, who naturally knew nothing of the trouble between them (and me) looking from one face to the other and wondering.

It was a sad meal. Serge was worried at the prospect of leaving the good home he had enjoyed for twenty-three years. His mother was tearful at the thought of losing her only son. Clément, Laurence and I could do nothing to lighten their gloom.

The taxi which had been engaged to take us to Annecy failed

366

to arrive. Soon we had a telephone call to say that it had been requisitioned by the hospital to act as an ambulance. Clément telephoned to Annecy for another taxi. This was straining things too far. Now we had an hour to wait with nothing to do.

At first we sat all three in the big bar of the hotel. Clément ordered a *chopine* of white wine, and insisted that I should drink some of it, as though ostentatiously showing me that I was not regarded as an enemy.

Finally he seemed to make a decision.

"Come out with me for a moment, Georges," he said.

"Clément," said Laurence pleadingly.

"All right. You stay there. We won't be long."

He led me round to the back of the hotel. There was a big gravel court-yard with black wooden garages down one side and a bowling alley on the other. Beyond it were a few allotments, then the dark woods. It was a suitable place (I could not help feeling) for an execution. Clément walked up and down the bowling alley. He walked springily, but firmly in his ski-ing boots. I slid along beside him, noiseless in my rubber soles, taller than he, yet lighter.

"*Comme mari, je suis ni aveugle ni complaisant,*" he began. The words beat at my head and failed to register.

"I beg your pardon?"

"I repeat, as a husband I am neither blind nor complaisant."

"Why, I should never have thought that you were," I said weakly. He swept my weakness aside.

"I am sending Laurence with you to the south. It is a trip full of danger for her, and perhaps full of danger for me, for my household. There are five or six other women whom I could have sent with you. But none of them is of the calibre of my wife. I have two things to consider. The first is my duty. That impels me to look after you, so I am sending Laurence. The second is my marriage and my home. So I am sending Laurence to show that I trust her. I do not trust you. You are a foreigner and I do not know you. To Laurence I say: 'Go, because I believe in you.' But you I warn: 'The husband of Laurence is not blind. Be careful.' "

"Your confidence in Laurence is certainly not misplaced. As for me, I owe you so much. I should never dream . . ."

"My daugher Marie-Josèphe is a very intelligent and sensitive girl. . . ."

"Agreed, but I must insist that a great mistake has been made. Your daughter has exaggerated out of all bounds a situation

367

which was abnormal only in that I was obliged to accompany Laurence on walks through the night. I have never for one moment forgotten that she was your wife or treated her with anything but the respect . . ."

"Let us admit it frankly, Georges," he interrupted a shade more bitterly. "The English are supposed to be tongue-tied, but you can certainly juggle about with words and sentiments when you begin to talk. I am a simpler man than you. I am more direct. Am I more honest? That question I will leave for you to answer in your secret soul. And I hope that the answer is: 'No.'

"My daughter thinks that you are trying to take her mother away from me. I believe that there at any rate she exaggerates. There was nearly a terrible scene at the farm this morning. Marie-Josèphe had written a letter, telling you what she thought of your conduct in my house. She showed me this letter, it is in my pocket now. But I refuse to show it to you, because I still regard you as my guest, and I consider that some of the terms she has used are too strong."

"But does Laurence not deny all this?"

"She does."

"And do our joint denials mean nothing to you? Do you accept the opinions of your daughter, opinions which there is no reasonable evidence to substantiate, against the denials of your wife?"

"On the contrary. I accept your joint denials. But I hope that you are sorry for what you have done, for wittingly or unwittingly you have done a terrible thing. You have been the cause of doubt in a household where, before your advent, no doubt existed."

"I am sorry, if you put it like that."

"There is the taxi at last."

"At last."

Laurence looked at me searchingly as she came out of the hotel. Serge sat beside the driver. Clément put me in the middle of the back seat, between himself and Laurence. It was odd to pass Pepette's. There was nobody about outside "*Ma Baraque*", and Angelo's garage opposite seemed to be shut.

We ate dinner in a small restaurant under the arches in one of the back streets of Annecy. It was near the offices of the *Compagnons de France* and it was filled with young *Compagnons*. They made a great fuss of Clément and Laurence. They called him *Chef*.

A tall, thin railway policeman who had stayed at Les Daines ate with us. He was Laurence's cousin. She had dressed up for the journey now, changing her personality with her identity-card, for she travelled with a false name and address. She wore a beaver coat and a large black hat. Beneath the coat she wore a white blouse with a cameo brooch at the throat and a black skirt. Her mouth was reddened for the first time since I had met her.

When we arrived at the station our friend the policeman went on ahead.

"There is a German control," he told us. "I shall take you two young men in by the back way."

He led us round the back of the station, through the railwaymen's quarters and on to the end of a long platform. We strolled down this, past the German soldiers who were examining the papers of all who entered.

Clément was standing outside a third-class compartment.

"You will find Laurence in there," he said. "Serge, you will sit opposite her, and Georges will sit beside her. In the event of danger, Georges, you must pretend to make love to her. That always disarms suspicion. Well, I suppose that is about all. Good-bye and good luck. I mean that."

"Good-bye, Clément." We gripped each other's hands. His powerful face with its broad brow was calmer now. I could say nothing more to him in front of Serge and the policeman, but I tried to put into my hand-clasp and my expression the admiration and the gratitude that I felt for him.

That was the last I saw of him, standing there, stocky and square in his long blue army cape, a big beret tilted on his fine head. There was a quiet man, a strong man, a jealous man and a generous one. And above all a *man*.

I leaned out of the window until he was only a deep blue blur in the station's splash of light.

CHAPTER XXII

I

WHEN Germans came round the train looking into the carriages Laurence caught me in her arms.

"Act like a lover," she said. "And for goodness' sake look as though you like it."

369

"So embarrassing in front of all these people."

The carriage was filled with Serge, three most respectable-looking women, and a youth-movement lad with a cropped skull and a dagger hanging from his belt.

"And besides, I feel that Clément is looking over our shoulders. What a ghastly mistake has been made, thanks to your daughter."

"Oh, don't worry about that. If Clément had been a more petty man it might have mattered. Even so, I was extremely frightened, because he has a very jealous nature. Up to now such a question has never arisen. I have never looked at another man. Clément is strong and admirable. At one time this morning I feared that he would not let us go. But I quickly realised that I was mistaken. He regarded it as his duty to pass you on your way, and even if what Mijo believed, poor dear, had been true and proven, Clément would have sent you to Perpignan just the same. Only after the war he would have searched you out and killed you. He is a headstrong man."

The Germans passed our carriage with rude guffaws. It was only a snap control, examining identity-papers here and there down the train. We travelled all night and arrived at Narbonne too late to catch our connection for Perpignan.

We had been warned that Narbonne junction was a dangerous place, and that the short railway journey from there to Perpignan would be the most dangerous that I had hitherto undertaken. But the station was crowded to overflowing. That was a good sign. There were a lot of German soldiers about, and a good many men who looked as though they might be Gestapo. The waiting-rooms would be too dangerous. Laurence led us to the station buffet, a large, dingy, classical room with a double order of doric pilasters and much graining in the paintwork.

"You will be in Britain for Christmas," Laurence told us.

"Oh, no, we won't; we shall have to wait three weeks in Perpignan," I said.

"I assure you that you will do nothing of the kind. Perpignan is extremely dangerous, and the organisation will see to it that you pass on immediately. Let's see, we arrive there this evening. You will leave either to-morrow or the next day, or perhaps even to-night."

"What organisation?"

"That I cannot tell you. Except that the man who is running your part of it is the *Chef* of the *Compagnons de France* at Perpignan."

370

"Another *Compagnon.*"

"Yes. His name is Pierre Cartelet, and he is a professor. He, Clement, and Xavier are the three finest men I have met."

How pleasant it was to be in the Midi again with its brightness, its dust, and its sparkling, chattering, singing people. It was plain that the black market flourished here even more than in the north. Everywhere along the station platform were crates and boxes holding pigeons, rabbits, fowls, and young porkers. Everybody who travelled seemed to carry some kind of container which emitted rustlings or animal noises or from which urine silently oozed.

When the train for Perpignan came in we saw that it had probably been as well that we had missed our proper connection. There were two German controls waiting to board this one, one lot in *Wehrmacht* uniforms, the others in plain clothes; but the train was long, and it was fairly evident that they would not be able to carry out more than a cursory check.

When everybody had squeezed and cursed and shouted and laughed himself or herself on to the train, it was in fact so crowded that the Germans were unable to pass down the corridors or to enter the compartments. So we arrived in Perpignan, hot but unquestioned.

Laurence led us on foot to a small hotel in a back street, the Hôtel du Centre. A large dark woman with a Spanish accent checked us in. There was a double room for Serge and myself. The *Chef* (Cartelet, of whom Laurence had spoken to us in the waiting-room) was away for the night, so Laurence could sleep in his room. We were obliged to register in the names given on our false identity-cards, and when we went to bed at night we must leave the cards with the night porter. This arrangement was against my principles. Supposing the Gestapo raided the place, I should not be able to destroy my card and protect the Mayor of Tiercelet. But there was nothing to be done about it. Anyway, Laurence said it was only for two nights at the maximum.

A young dark man, Estève, was there to meet us. He was Cartelet's assistant at the *Compagnons de France* (and in the work which lay behind that harmless façade). I liked Estève from the first handshake; he was quiet, self-possessed with the cold self-possession of a matador, and self-effacing (a rare quality in a Frenchman from the Midi). He took us out to lunch. We walked across the centre of the town.

And I fell in love with Perpignan. Perhaps a little because

371

it was the final gateway to my hopes, my freedom and my wife. But also because the winter sky was always blue while I was there. And because the river was clean and brisk and brought right through the centre of the town a whiff of the snow-covered mountains, so easily visible to the south. The only unpleasant thing about the place was the number of German troops, well-disciplined ones and well-dressed ones at that, to be seen everywhere. And the militians, who had chalked their sinister sign on all the pavements and many of the buildings.

We never saw a German in Valencia, though. It was to this small, narrow restaurant in a place that was half-ground floor, half-cellar, that Estève led us. The walls were grey and discoloured. The tables were marble-topped, and no cloths were supplied.

But we ate blue trout, followed by a huge Spanish omelette, then salad, then pastries, then bottled peaches. There was good *grenache* for an *apéritif* and excellent red wine in strangely-shaped, pointed carafes. The bill came to 1,300 francs, and Laurence paid up handsomely. She appeared to feel the influence of the south and the sun. She was a different Laurence from the tight-lipped woman whom I had watched bartering with the peasants near Frangy.

That evening she met somebody, she would not tell us who, and she was able to guarantee that we would leave Perpignan within two days.

When she had finished her work we drank *banyuls* in the Palmarium, the extraordinary glasshouse built over the river which is the central café of Perpignan. Compared to the north, the drink was plentiful and potent. The Germans were thoroughly enjoying it. The Palmarium was packed with them. But there was no drunkenness. They were too well-disciplined for that. And probably the rocky-looking Gestapo men, whom Estève carefully pointed out to us, had a lot to do with the discipline. The Gestapo men sat in pairs and often played chess or draughts to pass the time.

Estève told us several horror stories about the place. The German prison at Perpignan, the Citadelle, was always full. The German Governor was reported to be drunk every morning by eleven o'clock. But before that hour he dispensed ruthless "justice", sending off his daily quota to the Citadelle. The beautiful town was held under a reign of terror.

Laurence left the following evening for home, laden with Christmas presents for the children. These mostly took the form of religious books, pictures of saints, and small models of the Nativity. Serge and I accompanied her to the station, and we said good-bye in the draughty booking-hall. Clément might have been relieved had he seen the lack of emotion in our farewell. Yet I was desperately sorry to see her go. Eager as I had been to leave Les Daines, the people there had made an impression upon me far deeper than my liking for them. They were spiritually clean and admirable people. I felt chilled, lonely and sad when I saw her heavy fur coat pass through the iron gates which led to the trains. She did not look back.

Serge and I drowned our sorrows in another gargantuan meal at Valencia. I paid for this. Elizabeth had given me another 5,000 francs, and I felt that I had more than enough money to see us through.

Everybody told us that the trip across the Pyrenees was liable to be unpleasant, and advised us to eat all we could and to "drink as much good wine as possible".

(The French and Spanish, in fact all Latins, have an idea that wine is a wonderful tonic and stimulant. I think that wine is a wonderful thing, wonderful in itself and raising food to æsthetic heights to which it could never attain unaided. But I can still only believe that if one seeks the height of physical strength the body is better without wine, unless some harmless form of tonic is required to tone and soothe the nerves.)

At this, and subsequent meals at Valencia, Serge and I drank a litre each of the red wine of the country, thirteen degrees in alcoholic strength.

I found to my embarrassment that Laurence, who had been paid by Xavier so much a day to keep me, had provided no rations for my journey across the mountains, although it apparently had been stipulated that we must each carry rations for three days. But fortunately Madame Avon had given Serge enough for the two of us. In his small suitcase he had a loaf of the hard dry bread that France sent to prisoners in Germany, two cakes of sweet brown honey-bread, a big slab of ham, sausages, cold lamb, butter, jam, and cheese. We decided that if we bought some bread before starting we should have supplies for four days' walking.

On Sunday, December 19th, Pierre Cartelet came to see us in our hotel bedroom. He was not a Southerner, he came from somewhere on France's north-east frontier. Like his assistant, Estève, he was smallish, dark, and quiet. He had an intelligent face with an extremely mobile mouth, and long unruly hair that tumbled over his collar and over his brow—the sort of hair that one might expect to see on the King's Parade at Cambridge. Cartelet was peculiarly unattached to appearances. He wore old clothes, and wore them anyhow. He did not bother if there was egg all over his lapels and if both shoe-laces were undone.

I had the feeling that he had taken a dislike to us. But later I thought that this impression was only given because he was nervous.

He showed me on a large-scale map of the town a street corner with a public lavatory. He would be there to meet us at eight o'clock the following evening. He would lead us to a party which would leave for Spain directly, and on foot.

"You will be well advised to sleep all to-morrow," he said. "There is snow on the mountains, and the rivers are very swollen. Many *colis* have been lost through exhaustion and exposure recently. You will have one Spanish guide. He has a good reputation, and you must all obey him to the smallest detail. You, Millar, must act as interpreter and chief of the party. The remainder will probably be Americans, and they rarely speak French.

"I regret that the method of crossing the *zone interdite*, the forbidden zone, by car, has had to be abandoned. It was too costly, and now the roads have been made impassable by German road blocks. The forbidden zone begins at the Tech river, about half-way from here to the frontier. No ordinary civilians may circulate there, and you will be fired upon instantly if seen by the Germans. The plan is to cross all the country between here and the foot-hills of the Pyrenees in the dark to-morrow night. Until to-morrow then.

"Oh, and by the way," he ended in more personal tones, "I am informed that you eat at Valencia. Be very careful of the young woman who lives in this hotel and who often eats there. She is a *femme légère,* and she is doubtful. Don't speak to her."

At eight o'clock, as directed, we were sitting in the dark on a wooden bench outside the public lavatory. Cartelet came riding up on a bicycle and introduced us to a man with a strong Spanish accent (no novelty this, for since the influx of Spaniards following the Civil War in Spain the population of Perpignan was fifty per cent Spanish) and led us around a corner.

A body of men were drawn up in this dark lane. They stood in file, paired off as though for a girls' school "crocodile". They all appeared to be identically dressed—a small beret, a long blue overcoat, a brown-paper parcel in one hand.

When I got in among them and looked at their fresh faces, I whispered: "American or British?"

"American," came back in a storm of whispers which ended with a kind of croak, "Belgian".

Cartelet left us, and the guide with the Spanish accent asked me to tell the others that they must split up into pairs, each pair just keeping the pair ahead in view. In that manner we would walk clear of Perpignan, where we would meet our guide for the big journey. The first guide, a kind of mud-pilot, remained on his bicycle—obviously so that he could drop us in the event cf trouble—and shepherded the long-strung line through back streets until we were well into flat open country.

At the corner of a big ploughed field I was introduced to the man who was to lead us into Spain. He was a willowy, bronzed creature with a thin line of moustache on his upper lip. His large eyes stuck out prominently from his thin face. There were hollows in the backs of his hands where the skin sagged between the bones.

He directed us to take off our boots and wear *espadrilles*. (Enough of these rope-soled canvas shoes for all of us had been brought by the Americans from Paris.) I kept on my Harrods' half-boots, for their rubber soles made no noise, and from experience I knew that *espadrilles,* probably the most comfortable shoes on earth, could play hell with your feet on a long walk.

The Americans numbered five. They were boisterously hearty, and I saw that they had no conception of the ordeal that lay ahead of us, always a bad frame of mind for a start. The five of them, and the old Belgian who was with them, had travelled down from Paris in that day's train. They had arrived in Perpignan only an hour before I met them.

I was dressed less warmly than they in their thick overcoats. I had been obliged to leave the white raincoat with Estève, to be returned to Clément on his next visit to Perpignan. So I wore the grey suit from Hayange, across the German frontier, the blue checked shirt from Harrods' in London, the blue tie given me by Philomène's son at Villerupt, the beret given me by the old man in the slum outside Lyons, and the R.A.F. blue pullover which I had found when scrabbling with Wally Binns in the German litter pile at Gavi prison camp. I had two pairs of English socks on my feet, and a third pair in my pocket. As you may imagine, all these garments were dear to me, and had a certain character and meaning for me that no clothes have had before or since.

375

Less dear to me, but never more necessary, were a set of heavy Red Cross underwear, with the big woollen pants which the Americans describe so colourfully as "long Johns", and a lighter set of English underwear which I wore inside the wool. I would have given a lot for some gloves and some kind of overcoat.

I carried the small rucksack belonging to Serge. This held part of our store of food and two wine bottles from Valencia. One bottle held wine, the other water. Serge had made his suitcase into a pack by fixing two leather straps on it. He was the best-dressed of the party, since he had a fine store of thick clothes and a black leather *canadienne* with a fur collar, a handsome, weather-tight garment which had belonged to his engine-driving father.

The guide whispered last-minute injunctions in halting French.

"Complete silence . . . never smoke unless I tell you yes . . . follow in single file . . . walk springily on the balls of the feet . . . avoid rattling stones or cracking branches . . . lie down if I do . . . run if I do . . . don't separate if we meet a German patrol . . . just run after me into the darkness . . . if the Germans shoot and wound one the others must not stop, run on . . . there is much walking to-night. . . ."

"How much?"

"Forty-five kilometres (28 miles) and six rivers to cross."

My companions did not appear to be a whit abashed by this, except for Serge, who had some conception of what walking meant. After the first few hundred yards I knew that this party could never cover before daybreak the distance the guide had mentioned.

The going was appalling. There had been heavy rain. We were crossing a flat plain covered mostly with vineyards, and the rain had laid a deep paste of mud over everything. In this heavy going I soon heard bellows-to-mend behind me (I followed immediately behind the guide so that I could quickly interpret his orders) and I knew that the guide, Serge and myself were the only fit men there.

Our guide padded rhythmically in front of me with short, springy strides, each footprint falling dead ahead of the last. He was a practical figure. He carried a biblical-looking stave with which he tapped the ground ahead in dark or difficult places. He wore a small rucksack in the centre of his back, a haversack slung on one side of his body, and a coat and a strange-looking raincoat of oiled silk rolled up together and slung round one shoulder in the manner that a French *poilu* carried his blanket. Opposite the haversack hung a large Spanish drinking-skin from which the drinker can shoot a jet of wine into his mouth without touching the neck with his lips. Rolled up on the top of his head was a thick blue Balaclava helmet.

He kept up a fast pace for one hour exactly, then halted in the shelter of some pine-trees, sat down, and told me that we might smoke.

A small and evil-smelling figure came clumping up to me, and sagged down half on me. His body felt like a sack of offal. I asked him in English why he had not changed into *espadrilles*.

"If you want to kill me, tell me to try to walk in *espadrilles*," he replied in French.

I examined him carefully in the half-light. He was a wizened, elderly man with a long grey stubble on his chin. In his youth he had been fat and powerful, for he still carried a barrel and a broad squat frame, and when he walked he rolled like a sea-faring man. His breadth was enhanced by the fact that he wore two suits and over them a very thick, very long, black leather coat. He had already broken out into a profuse sweat, and as he sat beside me I smelled distinctly the smell that I had known on the battle-fields of Rethel, the Marne and the desert, and recently on Tino—he smelled of death.

I told myself angrily that I was being over-imaginative, but my heart sank when he got sufficient breath to cough and to talk.

"A poor old man like me cannot continue at this mad pace. I am nearly sixty and I am ill. I have rendered great service to the British. It is your responsibility now, young man. Tell the guide to go slower."

While he spoke he frequently broke into the most appalling fits of coughing, the noise of which soon angered the guide. It was a racking cough which seemed to tear his insides out, and with it there came to me on his breath the unmistakable smell of strong alcohol. I explained his difficulties to Pedro, the guide.

"Why do they send such an old hulk on a hard trip like this?" he answered bitterly. "At present this is child's play. We must go fast here or we shall never reach the frontier. Up there on the hills the snow is deep."

He took a good look at the Belgian and told him to follow immediately behind him and to make every effort to keep up. As he spoke he sniffed.

"I do not like the smell of this man," he whispered to me.

377

"I think he is an alcoholic. Mark my words, it would be better if he turned now."

Meanwhile the Americans were giving some trouble. They appeared to be city dwellers, and they were making far too much noise. They were all airmen, and had little notion of moving quietly across country at night. However, they were fairly amenable when I asked them to be quiet and to be careful how they lit their cigarettes. They carried large stocks of red wine, which they passed with loud insistence down the line. I could see that disaster loomed ahead, and I would have given the world to be making the trip with my brothers or with six little riflemen.

It grew darker as we moved on. The guide maintained his swift pace. I have good night vision, but I could see nothing. The guide knew the route yard by yard and inch by inch. It was a complicated route, for he often left the small tracks to cut across a field or a vineyard where the stubbly vines reached out sharp claws to tear at our legs. He never faltered. Occasionally he stopped for a moment or two, dropping on one knee to silhouette anything that might lie ahead, and to listen. We passed through showers of heavy rain.

About eleven o'clock we came to a fair-sized stream. The guide stopped to roll his trousers above the knee.

"This one is nothing," he said, and waded in. We splashed through after him. I was wet to well over the knees and the Belgian fell into a hole and wet himself to his navel. We sat for a few minutes on the other side, wringing out our trousers and passing the red wine.

"The Tech will be very high," said the guide. "I doubt if we shall get across it. I've never seen this river as high as to-night. If we hurry we shall be at the Tech soon after midnight."

He told the Belgian sharply to stop coughing so loudly, and that he must walk faster from then on.

"I am finished," replied the old man in a whining voice. "You are responsible for me. You cannot leave me here."

The guide muttered something under his breath, and we resumed walking. Shortly afterwards the night cleared beautifully, and ahead of us, a long way ahead, we saw the snowy, magnificent ridges of the Pyrenees.

The Belgian began to hang back and to stagger obviously as he walked. He was apt to burst into talk or fits of coughing which resounded dangerously in the frosty night air.

Passing a farm-house, at a point where the guide had

378

demanded absolute silence, the cough suddenly burst out and two or three dogs began to bark. The guide broke into a swift trot, and, afraid of losing him, I passed the Belgian and followed on his heels. He covered perhaps half a mile, trotting, and then squatted down beside the track in some low currant-bushes. We had to wait twenty minutes before the Belgian arrived.

"I am finished," he exclaimed, flopping down amongst us.

"There is a village only two kilometres from here," said the guide, leaning over him persuasively. "I shall take you there and leave you in a cottage where you can sleep and eat. Thence you will be able to make your way back to Perpignan. You must rest and get well before you make this crossing. You speak French, you can easily fend for yourself."

"What would I do in Perpignan?" the old man replied angrily. "I was sent direct from Paris. I know nobody in Perpignan and have no means of getting help there. I should be obliged to return to Paris. It is my life that you ask of me." He burst into tears.

"It is perhaps all of our lives if you go on," said Pedro, with a deep sigh. "This expedition is ill-fated. You will ruin all of us."

"The guide is right," I told the Belgian. "If you do not turn now you will die in the mountains. Look, I can give you some money; then you can stay in Perpignan until you are stronger. The guide will give you an address perhaps."

But he would not listen.

"I shall cross the Pyrenees to Spain," he said. "Even if you have to carry me."

We went on, but with frequent halts to allow the Belgian to catch up. He and two of the Americans were complaining now of sore feet. The pace became so slow that I could not keep warm. I pulled the beret down over the tops of my ears and kept my hands in my pockets. Partly from my Army training and partly to pass the time I tried to memorise our route as we went along. But it was too complicated and the guide's manœuvres were too minute. I knew from the stars that we were always heading south-east, and from observation that we were keeping in the open country between two roads which must have made a kind of wish-bone on the map.

It was nearly two o'clock when Pedro led us through a thick screen of rushes, as tall as a row of small trees, and down a slope to the banks of a river which was broader than the Thames at

Kingston. It was a turbulent stream with a racing current. In parts it was shoal, but there were strips that looked dangerously smooth and deep. The far bank was lined with dark woods. The moon shone with gloomy blues and greys on the racing water.

When the Belgian saw this he moaned piteously.

"You cannot ask me to cross that."

"Choose then. Stay on this bank if you like," Pedro replied roughly, taking off his trousers. He told us to strip everything off below the waist and tie the garments round our necks.

"Keep your boots on, though, for the bottom has stones that would cut your feet. Everyone must hold hands to form a chain. We should have a rope. But if you hold hands properly we may manage. Whatever happens maintain your grip so that if one gets swept off his feet he need not be lost.

"We shall only get this old man across if you two get on either side of him," he said to Serge and me. "You follow me, and the Americans can go behind."

We edged out into the stream with the guide in front tapping and sounding with his long stick. The water was inconceivably cold. It came straight from the snow and ice of the mountains. Its touch burned my legs at first and soon numbed them. A strong wind bored in gusts down the river and clawed at the clothing tied clumsily round our necks. What a wonderful target we would have made for any German on the far bank! The current was swift, and it was most difficult to walk and to stand up when the water came above our knees. After a few minutes of this, the Belgian moaned continuously and frequently lost his footing. Serge and I were obliged to catch him below the armpits and hold him up.

The river at this part had two deepish channels with a wide hump of shoal in the middle. The first channel wet us to our hips, but we negotiated it successfully and staggered in our ungainly line across the shoal to the channel on the far side. This was only some thirty feet wide, but when we were in the water as far as our navels the guide poked with his stick and found that the depth was increasing. He therefore turned with the line struggling after him, and moved up-stream to try again.

We had been in the water twenty minutes and all feeling had left the lower half of my body and my wet hands when Pedro, endeavouring again to find a crossing, ventured a little too far, lost his footing and vanished in the dark water with a scream. Serge let go of him and was himself torn from the Belgian.

Fortunately the American behind me hung on, stoutly anchored by the chain of men behind, and the Belgian and I swung round with the current in a slow, agonising arc. I just managed to hold on to the old man and to keep my feet on the river-bottom. And by good luck an eddy swept Serge and Pedro round to us, so that we were able to pull them out of deep water.

"Only one thing to do," Pedro chattered, the water running over his cadaverous cheeks from the soaking blue Balaclava. "Go back."

Accordingly we began the bitter shuffle back to the northern bank. Half-way across the Belgian collapsed utterly. Serge rallied himself from his immersion like a man, and he and I carried the old sack of flesh and bones across, his legs dangling loosely in the water.

It was only when we left the water on the sandy bank among the clumps of rushes that we realised how desperately cold we were. Fortunately everyone but myself carried a bottle of spirits. Serge and I shared his bottle of marc. This alcohol must have kept us alive.

Although more lightly clad than the others, I was now better off than most, for the clothes around my neck were still dry. The Belgian's huge leather coat had been lost, swept from his neck by the river, and one of the Americans had lost his trousers in the same manner. When we had dried and dressed ourselves as best we could, Pedro led us into the thickest bank of rushes. He chose a diagonal path through them, and in the middle he beat them down to form a circular resting-place about eight feet in diameter. There we sat down, huddled together for warmth, and partially sheltered from the wind by the swaying rushes.

The Belgian seemed to be dying. He lay on his back with froth bubbling from his lips and occasionally he burst into a chattering form of hysteria. The only way to make him stop this was to slap him hard on both cheeks. The Americans were good to him, covering him with coats which they could ill spare. I noticed that the Belgian was not quite so helpless as we at first supposed, for every time that anybody produced a small bottle of alcohol he would begin to shout: "Give, give. Poor old man."

Pedro was one of the coldest, and when we had been there an hour he attempted to make a fire from the damp rushes. Serge and I went outside the rushes to gauge the effect of this and saw to our horror that it was most spectacular, lighting up the rushes for thirty yards on either side, and sending a glow into the sky.

We ran back in and made him extinguish it. Shortly afterwards we heard footsteps passing along the river-bank. Pedro crawled across our circle to put his hand over the Belgian's mouth.

"German patrol," he whispered, when the noise had ceased. "We shall only sleep a little if we drink," he continued. "Produce all the wine. I shall get more to-morrow."

We drank all the wine that remained. Then Pedro brought out a litre of spirits.

"Not more than one mouthful each of this," he counselled. It was "36", the immensely potent alcohol which is used for making some liqueurs and which is fairly popular as a stimulant in those parts.

I was far too cold to sleep, but all the others did. While they slept I "marked time" in the centre of our clearing, straining my eyes into the waving rushes, and listening for the returning clump of German boots. At dawn Serge awoke and gave me for breakfast a slab of wet bread and a cube of fatty ham. It promised to be a fine day. The sun was rising powerfully, but too slowly for us.

Pedro slipped out of the rushes about eight to reconnoitre. He came back, considerably perturbed, to tell us that a patrol *had* passed during the night. He had examined their tracks and those of "a dog with great feet". He decided that we must wait all day where we were and attempt to cross the river again at last light that evening. This time we would have a rope, and one of us would swim the river and attach the rope to a tree on the far bank.

"This I do not like," he continued. "For to obtain a rope I must go to one of the farms near here. And the peasants in this area are not to be trusted."

At all our halts he had taken great pains to see that we left nothing lying on the ground, not even the butt of a cigarette.

"I do not like the peasants to know that we have passed. And I think it dangerous to wait in this place. You must follow me."

He led us up-stream for about a mile. The Belgian walked with the greatest difficulty. He said that his leg muscles had "frozen", and indeed he made a creaking noise as he walked. The strange smell which he emitted was stronger than ever, and none of us could bear to remain for one second to leeward of him.

We followed a rough path with the river on our left screened by rushes. In gaps in the line of rushes on our right we caught glimpses of vineyards and small farms. We stopped in the centre of a big clump of rushes and all of us took off our damp clothing, hanging it up to dry in sunshine that was already a little warming.

Serge and I ate some more ham and bread. Then we lay down to sleep. We were soon awakened by shouts and the noise of scythes or sickles. The peasants were cutting the rushes, and they were working on the far side of the very clump in which we lay. Pedro began to sniff about like a good gun-dog, and soon he crept away, leaving us there. It was obvious that we would be obliged to move. We dressed ourselves and had everything ready when Pedro returned.

"Follow me."

We ran after him up the river-bank. In some places there was no undergrowth between us and the river, and we were exposed to the view of anybody on the opposite bank. I was running about the middle of our line when I saw a German sentry on the far bank.

He was walking up-stream, in the same direction as us and a little ahead of us, by good luck. He wore a long greatcoat and the muzzle of his slung rifle tapped against his big helmet. The others were too engrossed with their running to notice my gestures, and Pedro was far ahead. I did not reach him until the whole party was once more screened from the river by a line of rushes.

Pedro was greatly upset when I told him about the German. He led us into a scrubby, low wood, near the river-bank. We crawled in for some fifty yards. Then he began to stamp out a circle in the prickly bushes about the same size as the circle in the rushes where we had passed the night. It was considerably less comfortable. The bushes grew upon mud which soon became soggy beneath us.

"You will have to remain here for the rest of the day," said Pedro. "I must leave you and post myself farther up-stream. If the Germans have seen us they will probably send a patrol down from the bridge which is three kilometres up-stream from this point. If they do that I shall come back and lead you away. Tell the others that they may smoke, using the utmost caution. I shall return about five o'clock and we shall attempt to cross the river then."

When he was leaving he paused and added: "I have never lost a man on this trip yet. But I would give anything to lose this Belgian, for with him we shall never cross the mountains."

Serge and I were not quite comfortable at Pedro's departure, especially after his last remark, but he had left more than half of his possessions in our care, including his big yellow waterproof, his long stick, and the rucksack which held his food.

It was damnably cold. We huddled together. Serge and I made a good lunch off bread, sausage, and cheese. I tried to make the others eat too, but they were all more interested in smoking and having nips at the different bottles which they had been given in Paris. The long wait gave us an opportunity to talk to the Americans.

All of them had been shot down in Flying Fortresses operating over the north of France. Two of them were officers. One of the officers had German parents, and Serge and I in our conversation always called him Fritz, while his brother-officer we called Clark Gable for some reason, maybe the combination of his size, his ears and his metallic voice. Another was born of Polish parents, on the Canadian frontier. Him we called the Trapper. He was a good type, considerably older than the others, with a charmingly twisted face. Then the one who wore no trousers (since the Tech) we called the Chauve Souris. He was a decent fellow, and you really scarcely noticed that he wore no trousers—his "long Johns" were so thickly encrusted with caked mud. Last of the Americans was Charlie.

Charlie was the youngest, and at that time I disliked him, but only because he complained more than the others. In a few days I understood their difficulties.

These were the difficulties. All of them were, you might say, green and new from their own country. They had not been flying long over Europe when they were shot down. They had not had time and opportunities to form any coherent impression of Britain. Their talk about that island was limited to sketches of bleak airfields and things they called Piccadilly Commandos, and of course criticism of everything in war-time Britain that was different from its counterpart in their country. Their impressions of France were still less coherent. All of them had been saved by individual French patriots, farmers, shop-keepers, business men. These Frenchmen had passed them from house to house, and all of them had been hidden in Paris, awaiting the convoy to the south. Two of them had spent nearly six months in Paris bedrooms. There was nothing for them to do in Paris but lie in bed.

So all of them were soft and unhealthy and carried too much

384

fat. All of them were feeling liverish too, and they were dazed by being out-of-doors and so suddenly flung into stern physical endeavour.

At first I was put out by their habit of open complaint against discomfort. Then I realised that this was a mannerism. In Britain a boy and a man are expected to suffer discomfort—it may be a blister, it may be a tooth-ache—in silence.

This was a national habit which I had never remarked. But walking with the Americans I remembered how as children we would have died rather than admit, still less complain, that we were tired or footsore when we were climbing the Cairngorms with our mother, or rowing a dinghy on the Clyde. I had been used in the Army to working with men who would drop from fatigue before they would admit to being tired.

Now that we had time to size each other up I got plenty of amusement out of them. They contrived to laugh at the dampness and misery of our situation. Even young Charlie, who never ceased to moan about the state of his feet and his doubts about his own ability to cross the mountains, had a volatile sense of humour. Charlie was more adaptable than the others. He was the only one who had learned a few words of French.

As 5 p.m. approached we packed our things, and began thinking of the cold grey water that we must cross, and the snow mountains beyond it. We were all chilled to the bone. The cold day darkened to a colder evening with a stiff north wind. The Belgian began to smell more thickly than ever, but he was cheerful. I failed to understand this until Charlie gave me a nudge and pointed to the old man, who had left the zareba, ostensibly to have a piss. He was standing behind a bush and was taking a long swig at a large black bottle which he replaced in his bosom with a guilty look around him to see that he was unobserved. When he came back he announced that his legs felt better.

Five o'clock, and no Pedro. The Americans became a shade worried, and insisted that the God-damned Spanish so-and-so had left us in the lurch. Just before darkness we heard people moving about in the vicinity, and we all lay down maintaining silence. Eventually they moved away, and we never knew whether they were Germans or peasants. There was nothing for it but to spend the night in that horrible place. We settled ourselves in a line, wedged tightly together for warmth. Since I had no coat, and knew that I should not sleep, I chose the end of the line.

Most of that night I stamped up and down, swinging my arms, or "ran on the spot" to keep my circulation going. Meantime I made up my mind what to do the following day.

It seemed fairly certain that Pedro had either left us deliberately or that some accident had befallen him. Before he went away he had shown me an automatic, and told me that he had once been a prisoner of the Germans and that he had escaped from the Citadelle. "They will never take Pedro again," he said. If he had been picked up by a German patrol our situation was clearly dangerous. The Germans might search the neighbourhood the following day. I could see no prospect in our attempting to cross the river, the forbidden zone and the Pyrenees on our own, without a guide. Had I been with a stronger party, or alone with Serge, I should have tried it. But I knew from all that we had heard in Perpignan that the ground between us and the frontier was most difficult in itself and also closely guarded. Furthermore, our food was running extremely low, and all of us were in a semi-exhausted state from exposure. Early in the previous evening we had finished the last of our water.

The one thing to do was to return to Perpignan. But how were we to return? And what could we do there with five Americans who spoke no French?

First, we must go in the darkness. That would mean waiting until the following night. And the only way to get there would be to walk north-east until we found a house. Then I would send Serge in to ask if there was a track or path leading towards Perpignan. If we could get into the town in darkness but before the eleven o'clock curfew, Serge and I could see Cartelet at the Hotel and ask for his help. I would hide the Americans for the night in some wood just outside Perpignan. Then at 5 a.m. when the curfew lifted I would go out to them again and take them to a hiding-place designated by Cartelet. If we could find neither Cartelet nor Estève I thought that we might go to the Valencia Restaurant since I had spent a great deal of money there. The future was not rosy.

Two hours before dawn it began to rain heavily, and it rained throughout the day. When the others awoke I made them eat a large breakfast of sodden bread sandwiches. All of them complained of thirst. I warned them that we were certainly in grave danger from German search-parties, and that nobody must speak above a whisper. I then laid my plan before the assembly. It was accepted by all but two of the Americans, but I knew that it would eventually be accepted by everybody, since it was the only possible course of action.

Fritz and Gable felt it their duty to say that they were going on alone and nothing would stop them. It was no use telling them that nothing, not even murder, was going to stop me from crossing those mountains, but that this time we must cut our losses. I moved out to reconnoitre the river-bank. We had to get water for drinking.

When I had crawled cautiously to the top of the bank and slowly parted the leaves, I at once saw two German posts on the far bank. The posts were well enough camouflaged with turf sods and earth. They were built up out of the bank, and each was manned by two men with a machine-gun. One was directly opposite me, and I slid back into cover when I saw that a German was sweeping our bank with a pair of gleaming binoculars.

Fritz and the Trapper cut a very long stick from a tree near our hiding-place. The three of us crawled to the river, but downstream from the German posts. Then, while I watched the Germans, the two of them tied wine bottles to the end of the stick and submerged them in the muddy stream. We made several such trips during the day and I "disinfected" the greenish water with a little of the "36" alcohol from the guide's bottle. The taste of this mixture was loathsome, and remained with us all for days. Charlie said it tasted of frog's piss.

The Belgian, who had a sense of humour as macabre as his person, suggested that after the war we might form the committee of a spa to sell Tech water. He insisted that we should only have to bury some German babies in the shingle of the upper reaches to give our water a flavour and aroma which would sell it with the finest beverages in Europe.

We had to wait until 6.20 p.m., when I judged it dark enough for us to leave. We travelled in single file, with me leading, until we found the path by which we had reached the Tech with Pedro. After following this for a short distance, I saw a farmhouse, and halted the party, well concealed, and at a discreet distance, while Serge went boldly in.

My heart lifted to see him go. He had been admirable all through this difficult trip. I was proud to have him as a companion, and comforted that I had him to help me through whatever lay ahead. He returned with good news. The family in the farm had taken him for a young communist, freshly escaped from Spain. We could follow the lane which passed the farm as far as the first village, La Tour, and thence there was a small secondary road to Perpignan which was seldom patrolled by the Germans.

Accordingly I split the party into groups of two and three. Serge and I took the lead in case there was any talking to be done. We also collected all available water-bottles, since everybody still had a raging thirst. I promised to fill them at the first fountain.

The lane was about two feet deep in mud. Serge and I pushed ahead, but at short intervals we were obliged to wait for the others to catch up with us. The Belgian was in the second group. And already he had begun to moan.

In the outskirts of the village of La Tour, Serge and I turned up a lane to fill the bottles. While we were thus engaged the others walked on past us. At a road junction in the village there was a group of youths standing just as, in a British village, you might see a small crowd in front of a public-house. I feared that the others might have taken the wrong fork, so I told Serge to ask the strangers if our friends had passed. They did not reply at first and appeared to be both surly and suspicious.

Then one of them came forward and said: "Yes, they took the right fork. The road to the left is blocked by several Fritz posts," he added meaningly, with a glance at our mud-stained clothing. We moved on smartly, but apparently we had lost more time at the fountain than we thought. We met a single man, walking in the opposite direction, and Serge asked him: "Have you seen six comrades of ours farther up the road?"

"Yes," answered the man. "I just passed them." The accent was heavy, and peering closely at him we saw that he was a German soldier. When we were round the bend from him we ran until we found the Americans and the Belgian, stumbling along in an untidy group. I separated them into couples again, and we moved off.

From the kilometre-stones we saw that there were twelve miles to cover to the centre of Perpignan, and we had slightly less than three hours to do it in. Alone of course Serge and I could have done this easily. But the others had to keep up. I therefore explained the situation to the Belgian. He was rebellious and refused to be left.

"And I refuse to endanger the whole party for you," I told him flatly. "If you cannot keep up you must just drop behind. You risk nothing. You are an old man, you have money, and you speak French."

He suddenly gave in, and lay down at the side of the road, gently weeping.

"I see that none of you want me. I am only a nuisance. When I was young I was a better man than any of you. Well, I will meet you to-morrow morning at 11.30 in the café opposite the station in Perpignan."

We all shook hands with him and wished him luck. I told him that if we found a good hiding-place for the Americans I would leave a man beside the road to stop him while he was walking into Perpignan. He was already asleep, lying snoring on the damp grass.

Now we pushed on up the road at a great pace, but the kilometre posts still seemed to come towards us with agonising slowness. My rubber-soled half-boots were in such a dreadful state after their immersions that I had put on *espadrilles* before leaving the Tech. My feet soon began to go sore on the hard roads. The old wounds made by Clément's ski-ing boots were reopened. Otherwise I felt no fatigue, and was only obsessed with the idea of getting to Perpignan before the curfew.

The Americans did their best, but we continually had to slow down or wait for them. Charlie refused to go any farther at ten o'clock. After several exhortations he agreed to "kill himself to get there".

At eleven, curfew hour, we were still four kilometres from Perpignan. I dared not remain on the road any longer, for I had been told that every night after curfew patrols came out from the large garrison in the town. So I led the party up a bank and into a muddy vineyard which was at least hidden from the road. They all lay down and sank into an exhausted sleep. I walked restlessly up and down beside them in the mud, for I was uneasy and obsessed with my responsibility for the American lives.

I was now ruefully aware that I had been over-optimistic in hoping to hide the American party under cover near Perpignan. There were only two patches of cover between Perpignan and the Tech. One patch was on the first river and the second was on the banks of the Tech itself. I decided therefore that the only thing to do was to walk the Americans into Perpignan at 5 a.m. After all, we should then have several hours of darkness in which to dispose of them. It was a terrible risk. But it would clearly be fatal to leave them in the open country. When I wakened them I told them of the plan.

They were very nervous at the idea of entering the town,

but more so at the idea of stopping where they were without us.

By the light of Serge's petrol-lighter we scraped the mud from our clothes with knives and wiped our faces and hands with damp handkerchiefs. I made Serge lend a pair of trousers from his suitcase to the poor Chauve Souris, who had been bravely walking all night in his "long Johns".

Split up into pairs, we walked quickly into the town. Most fortunately we were no sooner on the outskirts than I recognised a beautiful church which I had visited with Laurence. I knew the route from there across the complicated old town to the Hôtel du Centre. It was easy to hide with the Americans in the lane beside the hotel. Serge went in to find Cartelet.

It was 5.45 a.m. and Pierre Cartelet, a man who had reason to fear alarms in the night, was sound asleep when Serge banged upon his door. But he reacted straight away, brave soul.

"Take them into some café until 8.15," he said. The offices of the *Compagnons de France* open up then. You must make your way to these offices singly and at intervals. Do you know how to find the offices?"

"Yes, Monsieur Cartelet. Madame Laurence showed them to us."

"Right. Good luck! I'm going back to bed."

We took them to a small café between the hotel and the headquarters of the *Compagnons*. It was a working-class café used by the drivers and conductors of the buses and by passengers too, for the terminus was close at hand. This was fair camouflage for us and even for our muddy clothes. We might pass for peasants who had just come in to sell black market goods, and who were now waiting for a bus going back into the country.

Serge and I bundled them on to the *banquettes* and ordered round after round of coffee. It was remarkably wonderful to drink hot liquid. When we tired of coffee we drank cognac.

One by one we went into the lavatory to shave and scrub the worst of the dirt off our faces, clothes and boots. The *Compagnons'* offices were in an otherwise empty building in a wide street. They were between the main Post Office and the German Headquarters. And immediately behind them was the big *Gendarmerie*.

Serge drew a plan of the ground between the café and the offices, and I explained the route to the Americans. I went ahead to prepare the way. One of the Americans kept me in sight. There was only a young secretary in the office. He wore a blue ski-ing suit with the cockerel badge on it, and he was most suspicious.

"I have no instructions, I have no instructions," he kept repeating.

However, while I hesitated there, Cartelet himself, hatless and untidy as usual, came bounding up the wide stairs. He showed me into a long dirty room. It was evidently a kind of board-room where they held occasional meetings. There were two portraits of Marshal Pétain and a photograph of Cartelet himself, in uniform, receiving a flag at the hands of the Supreme Chief of the organisation. There were three large windows. The room was furnished with a long deal table, four benches, a desk and an upright piano. There was a little iron stove, but the pipe of this had broken away from the wall.

One by one the Americans arrived and finally Serge.

Cartelet carried in the electric heater from his office next door. We were greatly taken by the calm way in which he received us. He knew, of course, that he was running a fearful risk in thus sheltering us. We might even have been followed to his offices.

He took us down to derelict store-rooms on the floor below. There we found Army blankets and several old mattresses, enough to make a big communal bed in our room above. Cartelet and Estève went out to search for food. They dared not buy too much, for that would have aroused suspicion.

They brought us long loaves of bread and tins of sardines and the French Army bully beef, usually called *singe*. These provisions vanished instantly, for all of us were ravenous. A woman who taught English in a local school came in with more food. She was leaving that day to go on holiday, and she brought us what remained in her larder—a sack of potatoes, a tin of haricot beans, some dripping and a big tin of butter which had been melted down so that it would keep.

The Trapper put the reflector of the bowl-shaped electric heater horizontal instead of its normal vertical, and began to bake potatoes in it.

All of us peeled off our outer clothes and our boots. The door was locked from the inside. We agreed with Cartelet and Estève only to open it on the V knock—ta-ta-ta-TUM.

We lay down in a row, and I fell instantly asleep, sleeping with the fevered relaxation of exhaustion. So ended our first attempt to cross into Spain.

Only one thing disturbed my sleep. Thoughts about the old Belgian. When I had told Cartelet that I had a rendezvous with him in the café outside the station he replied at once: "Quite out of the question. It might be a trap. There are so many people hunting us. I beg of you not to go."

So I had gone to bed. After all, the old man had enough money to return to his friends in Paris. And, anyway, it would have meant certain death for him to cross the Pyrenees.

But he still disturbed my sleep.

Had he not implied that Paris probably meant death for him too? He knew that it was a hundred to one against his ever crossing the mountains. Yet he had wanted to go on.

The head of the organisation of *passeurs* called on me that evening. I was taken alone into Pierre Cartelet's office to meet him. He was a tall Spaniard, astonishingly handsome in a dashing brown *canadienne*. His pseudonym was Louis. He spoke perfect French in slow, balanced syllables.

"I cannot imagine what has happened to Pedro, your guide. He was one of the best men in our organisation. He once was a doctor with a large practice in a Spanish town. Now, since I have engaged to pass you across the frontier, pass you I will."

(I knew that he had been handsomely paid for each one of us.)

"You may have to wait for some days, however," he continued. "You see, the *passeurs* are temperamental gentlemen. They earn good money for their dangerous work. What do they do? They pass one party from Spain, and they arrive in a French town, say this town. So they celebrate here. They taste all the delights. Their money is finished. So they take another party back into Spain, and they do exactly the same thing that end. For us, who have to run the thing with such material, life is a bedlam. We never know when or where a *passeur* is to be available.

"If possible I should like to send you across on Christmas Eve. On that night every German between here and Spain should be soundly drunk. In the meantime, I beg of you all to remain here as calmly as possible. I shall try to find houses to hide you in, but it is really most difficult, since this is the holiday season."

We had to arrange blankets and cardboard over all the windows so that not a chink of light showed outside when we turned on the lights. We stopped the endless baking of potatoes in the heater, stood it on the table, and trained it on our communal bed. Then we all went to sleep again. For the moment none of us could get enough sleep or enough warmth into our chilled bones.

The next day passed in the big room, not badly for me because Cartelet had some good books, but interminably for the Americans, none of whom could read French. They passed their time with discussions about the rates of pay in their armed services, the merits of different allied aircraft, different automobiles, and different women.

Cartelet moved us the following day. He had been warned that a government commission might arrive to inspect the building with a view to removing the *Compagnons* and installing another organisation there. Louis had found a house which could take three of the Americans; Serge and myself moved to our old hotel; and Estève and the young secretary were each to look after an American.

It was fine to be at large again in Perpignan, and Serge and I celebrated with a slap-up dinner at Valencia, followed by drinks in the Palmarium. The following day was Christmas, and I remembered sadly how Laurence had promised that we should eat our Christmas dinners in London. However, we certainly had a very much better meal than anything war-time London could offer. Valencia provided hors d'œuvre, trout, turkey, tournedos, salad, Gorgonzola (bought from Italian soldiers) and peach jam.

As we finished our meal, a flashily pretty woman sat down at our table and ordered everything that she saw on our bill, which lay in front of her. She looked at us both keenly and attempted to draw us into conversation with some of the usual openings, asking the time, and so on. Her presence there worried us both. She was the *femme légère* against whom Cartelet had warned us. She lived in the hotel and her bill was paid by a rich business man. Other lovers visited her, but not too often. Why should she interest herself in us? Serge, with all the ardour of race plus side-whiskers, suggested that her interest might be purely physical, that it was difficult elsewhere in all Perpignan to find so personable a pair of young men. There he was certainly wrong. Perpignan is a centre of Rugby football. And its interesting streets were filled with male gorillas of all shapes and sizes, everything calculated to attract a woman such as our fair table companion. Christmas afternoon we spent at a cinema, where I saw for the second time a film about the Spanish Legion, "La Bandera".

A phrase in it had remained in my memory, since I had seen it five or six years previously in London. The *légionnaire* is with his native sweetheart, the girl in the brothel. He is about to make love to her. And he says gently to her: *"Tu ne sais pas attendre. . . ."* I was glad to see the film again, and the phrase again made a great impression on me. The rest of the film was only a background for it.

On the morning of Monday, December 27th, Pierre Cartelet told us that we should leave that night. High time, so far as I was concerned, for I was beginning to fear that I might run out of money. Serge had very little, and I could not bear to see him paying for things. He would need his money when he arrived on the other side. I had been rich when we first arrived in Perpignan, but I had been spending more than £6 a day there, and now only a few thousand francs remained in my note-case.

We provisioned ourselves this time at Valencia. Immediately before our rendezvous we ate a large meal there, and the proprietor made for us three days' rations in the shape of vast sandwiches containing steak, fried eggs and endives. In a black market baker's we had bought several stodgy and nutritious cakes. With two bottles of wine and two of water we thought that our supplies would be adequate.

Cartelet himself led us to the rendezvous. It was in a bosky lane on the outskirts of Perpignan. There we met a young and handsome Frenchman who told me that he was an officer in the Mercantile Marine. He was to accompany us to Spain.

When I saw our two guides my heart fell. I had expected something like Pedro, but this time the head guide looked more like a French stockbroker. He was a powerfully built man with a squashed face, tightly cut civilian clothes, and a light overcoat. His assistant was a weedy youth of seventeen. Neither of them appeared to carry provisions. This aroused my fullest suspicions.

"You do not intend to eat on the way?" I asked the guide.

"Oh," he replied airily, "as for us, we shall be at the Spanish frontier to-night, and to-morrow we shall be back in our own homes on this side."

"But Louis has given me to understand that you will lead us to a farm well inside Spain and that you will take a message from there to Barcelona, a message asking the British Consulate to send cars for us."

"Ah, how nice, what a beautiful plan, for *you.*"

"That is the arrangement. Your organisation has been well paid. Louis will be angry if the arrangement is not adhered to."

"But my dear Englishman, you certainly all have Spanish money?"

"What for?"

"Why, to take the train from Figueras to Barcelona. When you stand on the frontier Figueras shines out like an illuminated round jewel below. I shall point it out to you. You will descend to it, take the train, and, *presto*—you are in Barcelona."

"You know well that you speak nonsense. Figueras is closely surveyed by the Spanish police and German agents. None of us speak Spanish. How are we to take tickets? And beside all this," I added, lowering my voice, "there are three Frenchmen with us. For us Anglo-Saxons, being caught at Figueras would mean only an unpleasant term of imprisonment in Spain. For the Frenchmen it might mean death, for they have no powerful government to protect them, and they might easily be handed back to the German guards on the frontier."

Our conversation had not been overheard by the Frenchmen. I was afraid that if they heard they would refuse to go, and I was anxious to depart, thinking, perhaps foolishly, that once under way the guide would fulfil his mission. One of the Spaniards who had guided other members of the party to the rendezvous was still there. I spoke to him and he indignantly told the surly guide that he must deliver us safely to the Spanish farm and then see that the message went to Barcelona.

"But these are strange guides who are not equipped and who have not even food for the trip," I protested.

"Do not fuss," said the guide. "I shall take you by an extra fast and extra simple route. As for food, my companion and I each have a packet of sandwiches, and if we need more we shall get it in the houses of friendly peasants along our path."

"I do not like it."

"Now, now, Englishman. Cheer up! You will find that I know my business." He now called the remainder of the party around him and addressed them in his comical Catalan-French.

"We go into grave danger. But we are all men, yes? Our danger lies in the dogs that the Boches use on this frontier. If a dog runs at you fling up your left arm, so, protecting your throat, for he will always spring at the throat. When you feel his teeth close on your arm, but not before, stretch your right hand under his belly and tear off his balls, *thus* . . ."

The Americans, excited by his vivid gestures, were clamouring for a translation. When they had it they began to practise in a fantastic shadow mime.

"Hah," exclaimed the guide. "I perceive that we shall get along. These men have marrow in their bones."

I was beginning to have serious doubts of his sanity. I warned him gravely that several of us, especially Charlie, had tender feet, and that it might be advisable to set a steady pace.

"Coward's talk that," he replied angrily. "To reach the frontier at all we must travel like the lightning that strikes once and is never again seen in the same place. Lightning, the soul of the storm. . . ."

With this he set off through the suburbs. We made a great noise, for all my companions wore heavy boots this time. They were determined not to repeat the agony of the *espadrilles*.

If this guide could do little else, he could at least walk. He was one of the fastest walkers that I have ever seen. He progressed like a gigolo, his heels almost brushing the ground throughout the forward swing and his insteps brushing each other as his feet passed. He had a fluid stride.

This night, by the mercy of Heaven, the sky was clear, and I was able to check our direction as we advanced swiftly in a long-drawn line from which came cries of pain. The ground had dried after several days without rain, and there was a hard, slightly slippery crust on it. Protests that gradually rose to howls came from the Americans behind me, and especially from Charlie, who finally ran forward, caught the guide by one arm, and dragged him to a bank.

"What is this?" demanded the guide.

"They say that they cannot continue at such a pace."

"Then tell them they must turn back."

"They ask if they may smoke."

"No, no, no. No smoking."

Soon he was away again, and going as fast as ever. After a time I saw from the stars that he was turning more and more to the east, while I knew from our first trip with Pedro and from maps which I had studied in Perpignan in the interim, that we should follow roughly a south-easterly course. By this time the guide had lost all paths and was simply crossing vine-yards and climbing and descending banks. The pace was murderous.

I became certain that the man was lost when I saw that we were going almost due north. I stopped the party and asked:

"Why are we walking north?"

"How do you make that out?" he asked, with a laugh.

"Because there is the North Star," I said, pointing. To my amazement, no storm of corroboration came from my companions. I could understand that the Americans, pilots and gunners, might not know the stars. But what about the handsome Frenchman? He had said that he had his second mate's ticket in the French Merchant Marine. Had everybody gone mad? Or was it more sinister than that?

The guide laughed immediately.

"You are a know-all, my friend. You think you know everything, even the way. I tell you that must be the South Star. We are now heading towards Spain, and everyone knows that Perpignan is north of Spain.

"Listen," he continued, with a dramatic gesture. "You can hear the sea—the Mediterranean, in case you don't know—on our *left*."

It was true that we could hear the sea, and much too loudly, I thought (for we had been told in Perpignan that it was dangerous to venture too near the coast because of the German coastal defences and mine-fields). Whether the noise came from the left or from the right was impossible for any of us to tell by listening. But I, knowing that we were facing north, knew that it must come from the right.

The guide now became truculent.

"Who is leading this party?" he asked. "You must give me the total responsibility and your total trust. Then you will arrive in Spain. Let me *be*. Do not *bother* me."

When we had walked a little longer, still due north, we struck a wide road with tramway-lines running along one side of it. This could only be the road running north-east from Perpignan to the coast, and we must be well to the north of our starting-point, and farther from Spain than two hours earlier.

Even the guide could be in no two minds about this. He threw both hands over his face and tears oozed through his writhing fingers with the broken words:

"*Merde*. I am completely lost."

This caused an upheaval among the Frenchmen, who up to then had thought that the guide must be right. The second guide came up to tell squashed-face that there was a sign-post 100 yards down the road. After carefully examining this, the guide led us at a tremendous pace along a secondary road to Perpignan.

At 11.30, three hours after our departure, we arrived back at our starting-point. And our circular race had already exhausted three of the Americans, while it had unfuriated everybody, including the guide himself.

The guide now led our long file straight down the main road from Perpignan to the frontier. I stood this for some five minutes and then all my principles got control of me. I had not gone through all this trouble with Wally and alone in order to be caught stupidly on a main highway because it was too uncomfortable to walk across country.

Once more I stopped the guide.

"Is there no danger from patrols on this road?"

"Yes, patrols of the *Feldgendarmerie*. The trouble with those *salauds* is that they come silently on bicycles without lights. Like that they are upon you before you know it."

"Then what in the name of God are we doing upon this road?"

"Listen carefully to me," he said. "The route that I know is down the railway as far as the River Tech. But since the last time I went that way the railway has been closed. The Boches have put posts on it and it is lousy with guards."

"So now you do not know the way?"

"No. That is, I don't know it as far as the Tech. Once over the Tech I know the *zone interdite* like my wife's face, for that is my own country."

"Well, the first thing to do is to get off this road."

"Yes," he agreed, and we took to the fields.

He led on rather doubtfully for a bit.

"Am I going too far to the east?" he asked.

"Yes."

"*Nom de Dieu!*" he cried, beating his head. "I must have some devil in my head to-night which makes me want to roam in circles. Listen, Englishman. Walk immediately behind me, and every time I lead off too much to the east you will warn me."

"All right."

We walked on disconsolately, crossing terrible country. With Pedro every inch of our way had been selected for us and it had still been hard going. Now, although the ground was drier, the going was ten times worse. We had to fight our way through dense vine-yards and muddy swamps.

It was 3 a.m. when we reached the north bank of the first stream. I knew that the cover at that point was all that existed before the Tech, and it seemed unlikely that we could reach the larger river before dawn. Our only hope therefore would be to hide where we were until the following night. An extremely unattractive proposition. It was the coldest night that we had yet struck. Although I had "borrowed" Pedro's strange raincoat made of felt-lined oiled silk, the wind whistled through it to my kidneys.

The guide chose this moment to tell the Frenchmen that he himself was a wanted man in Spain, and that it would be "criminal folly" for him to venture his person on Spanish soil. He would lead us to the frontier, and once there he intended to leave us to our own devices. Serge and the so-called sailor said that if that was the way things were to be they refused to go on.

I told him that if the Frenchmen, quite properly, refused to go on, he must still lead the five Americans and myself.

"Oh, no," he replied. "I either take everybody, or I take nobody."

A fearful, whispered, three-sided argument ensued in the bitter darkness, with continual alarms, for we were all highly strung and imagined that every rustle was a footstep and that every shadow was a German.

At one point the Frenchmen agreed to come on with us and to risk themselves in Spain. The guide then told them how dangerous that would be, and they changed their minds. I could not blame them much, and I was beginning bitterly to see that we.had no chance of reaching the frontier with this charlatan, and indeed that he was determined to ditch us.

"What are your plans?" I asked him.

"My young friend and I will now walk to the nearest station, when we will catch the milk-train to our homes. To-morrow, after some rest and food, we shall together return to Perpignan, where I shall give a full explanation to the Chief of the Organisation of my conduct and yours."

"Your conduct will cost you your life, and I am tempted to kill you now and throw you in the river," I told him. "Louis will certainly exterminate you when he hears of this. At any rate, you surely cannot desert us like this. You must lead us back to shelter in Perpignan."

"I am lost. You know the stars. You can lead them back much better than I could."

"But you do not understand. We have five Americans here who speak no French. How are we to hide them?"

"That is your affair," he replied with a yawn. "Now I long for some hot soup and then my bed."

We shouted threats after him as he led the young lad away towards the sea. Then, marching on Cassiopeia, I led the hobbling, cursing party back across the vine-yards.

The young Frenchman from the Merchant Navy proved to be most helpful in rallying our party and in finding dry routes across some of the more swampy fields. Serge, who had been so energetic and full of spirit right through the first trip, was now discouraged, and would do nothing except moan at the organisation which had promised to get him to Spain and landed him with a guide who did not know the way.

Charlie's feet were in a terrible state, and he whimpered with every step.

At 5.30 a.m. the Americans stopped and sent forward a deputation to say that they were certain that we had passed Perpignan, for they imagined that they had seen its lights on their right some half-hour previously. I replied haughtily that this was quite impossible, and that I had great experience in marching on the stars—experience gained in the Libyan Desert (this was an exaggeration). They continued, protestingly, to follow, and some twenty minutes later we struck the outskirts of the suburbs of Perpignan.

All the way back I had been wondering what to do with the Americans. I was unwilling to saddle Cartelet with them again. It seemed to be asking too much of fate.

My doubts seemed to be providentially resolved for me by the young sailor, who said that he had been staying in an hotel near the place where we had met at the start of this maddening night. This hotel, he assured me, worked with the organisation, and would take all the Americans.

The hotel was shut when we arrived there, although it was already after six and beginning to get faintly light. We waited there for an hour, with the Frenchman occasionally ringing the bell, and doubts growing in my mind.

It kept worrying me that this sailor, and an officer at that, did not know the stars. Then he had seemed quite eager to return to Perpignan. And why was he so eager to have the Americans? Was it all patriotism? And why was he so insistent on wanting to know where else we thought of hiding them? And where Serge and myself were going to stay? I decided that if he were false he would almost certainly say that his hotel would not take them in, for then he might hope to find out more about the other people who helped us.

Eventually the *patron* stuck his head out of a first-floor

400

window, and there was some parley. The sailor came back to me.

"He says he will take me, but no strangers. I am sorry. Is there anything I can do to help?"

"Nothing at all, thank you. See you this evening, I expect. Good-bye."

"Au revoir then." He strolled off doubtfully towards his hotel. I hurriedly wakened Serge and the Americans. They had fallen asleep sitting on benches.

"We have to go back to the same place," I hissed at them. "And we have to hurry. It's already daylight. Serge. You must lead them to the café where we went last time. Give them coffee and get them cleaned up. I'll go and see Cartelet in the hotel."

With a good deal of effort I got the lot of them shambling off in the right direction. Near the hotel I saw to my horror that the sailor had added himself to the tail of our group. Serge was useless. A prey to his depression, he moped along like a lump of frozen suet.

When I had seen them all, including the sailor, enter the café, I went to the Hôtel du Centre, and climbed to Room 6. Cartelet came sleepily to the door when I had knocked several times.

"'My God, Georges, I have been having nightmares about you all."

All in a rush the funny side of the affair took possession of me, and I could scarcely outline the story to him for laughter.

"Do exactly as you did last time," he said. "It's a risk we must take."

When I got back to the café I found that we were one American short. Who was it? The Trapper. He had sore feet and must have lost us in the town through lagging behind. I was furious with Serge. This was disaster of the highest magnitude. Apart from the Trapper's personal worth, if they caught him they might torture him and he knew two addresses, one of which we were all going to immediately.

Poor little Charlie, completely worn out, slept with his dirty head flopped anyhow on the marble table-top. I gave him a sharp kick on the shin to wake him up. He was too conspicuous like that. They were drinking coffee laced plentifully from a bottle of cognac which the charming young French sailor carried.

I took Serge into the lavatory.

"Pull yourself together. Have you mentioned to this sailor the words 'Cartelet' or *'Compagnons'?"*

"Don't think so."

"On no account mention them. I don't trust him. At any rate, we don't know him, and we owe it to Cartelet and Estève to take every precaution."

"Oh, all right, but he seems a good sort. And he has given us an address to go to. A family address."

"You have not mentioned the Hôtel du Centre to him?"

"No."

I firmly said good-bye to the sailor. He left, apparently for his hotel, and I watched Serge and the Americans leave individually for the *Compagnons'* offices. I waited to see that there was no sign of the sailor following us, then I went up there myself.

Five minutes after my arrival the clever Trapper walked in. He had lost us in the darkness, so he had walked the town until he recognised the Post Office building, and from there he had found the *Compagnons'* place.

It was not easy to settle down again in the big room that still smelled of baking potatoes. By this time all the Americans were thoroughly bloody-minded, and worse than any of them was my friend Serge.

I tried to draw him into picturesque conversations about the bravery of his mother, the delights of his native department, the extravagant charms of so-and-so's mistress. But his lethargy persisted. He told me that he intended to leave Perpignan for his home at Frangy.

"Only to spend a few days. Then I shall come back with gloves and a scarf for you, and lots of food for the trip, and money and bread coupons and clean linen."

"All those things are unimportant. Can't you see how trivial they are? The first thing is to escape."

But, alas! I could not change him, although I badly wanted to. The prospect of Perpignan without him was terrible. I liked him. I associated the place with him. I could not think of escape without him. I did not like to think of the Americans' company without the pepper, salt and mustard of Serge's gallicisms.

Things were clinched, however, that evening, when Louis arrived, immaculate as ever, with polished apologies for all that had happened.

"That guide will pay for last night with his life," he assured us. "I had found it impossible to get any of my regular guides to take you. This man had been trying for some time to work for me. I only took him when he had given me an absolute assurance that he would pass you safely to Barcelona.

"Now I ask you to wait a further six days. Then I shall have the finest guide in the south of France or the north of Spain. He is the man with whom I always pass myself, and I am a hunted man in both countries."

He gave Serge permission to leave instantly on the evening train to the north. Serge promised to return in five days. At my suggestion a code telegram was arranged in case we should need him sooner.

Louis then told me that the body of Pedro had been found in the River Tech.

"He was apparently drowned, but we suspect foul play. He was wearing his trousers, and if he had been attempting to find a crossing his legs would probably have been naked.

"Another thing. I have agents in every hamlet between here and the frontier. I must tell you that you were all more than fortunate to arrive back in Perpignan the first time. You remember you spoke to some youths in a village called la Tour?"

"Yes, we asked if our companions had taken the Perpignan road."

"Three minutes later a German patrol arrived at that road junction. Their arrival coincided with that of a German soldier from whom you had also demanded directions. The officer in charge of the patrol asked this soldier his opinion of your band. 'Just a few more Spaniards trying to get work in Perpignan,' said the soldier. 'Not worth following them then,' the officer decided."

Louis hoped to be able to find us accommodation in private houses. He and Cartelet were both extremely nervous when I told them about the sailor who did not know the stars. Louis knew nothing of him except that he had been "sent down from Paris and paid for".

Cartelet and Estève did their best to cheer us. They brought us a lot of bread and *singe* and a big *bonbonne* of red wine. At the New Year the bakers of Perpignan exert themselves to make bread flavoured with caraway seed. This tasted good with the wine, which we mulled gently. The Americans were unused to strong wine. Young Charlie crawled over to a corner and was violently sick on the floor. Cartelet and Estève, coming in shortly after this with more provisions, were too polite to notice

403

anything. That night three Americans were taken away by one of Louis's helpers to stay in a private house.

Next day they sent me to the home of a physical culture expert who taught rhythmics and gymnastics in Perpignan. He and his wife were a charming young couple. I never knew their name. The flat was sunny and pleasant too. There were many novels, and the walls were hung with pictures of the body beautiful and photographs of the wife in bathing-costumes and the husband executing spectacular ski-ing turns.

I slept in a comfortable room with a wood fire. But in the night there were shots and screams. They told me not to worry, and pointed out that the Gestapo headquarters were in the big villa next door.

It was a florid, expensive villa with sweeping front steps and a carriage-way in which two black front-wheel-drive Citroëns usually stood. Most of the Gestapo men looked fat and comfortable. They seemed to like wearing tweed coats and grey flannel trousers, like middle-class Englishmen at the week-ends. Their chief, or the man who was pointed out to me as the chief, was in the late twenties or early thirties. His face was thin, his eyes slanting, his forehead high. His head was quite bald and sunburned. The Gestapo in Perpignan had the reputation of being particularly active and cruel at their vicious work.

On Sunday, January 2, Cartelet arrived at the flat for dinner and told me that I was to leave with the Americans the following night.

"Have you sent a telegram to Serge?" I asked at once.

"Absolutely out of the question. Far too dangerous. He must try again another time."

"Then I refuse to go."

"Just wait till I explain. To-day there has been a major disaster. We are all expecting every minute to be arrested. I don't know whether it was your sailor friend who found us out or not, but he has been sniffing around the *Compagnons'* offices.

"The Gestapo have been hunting Louis's organisation for months. This morning they raided four houses belonging to him, including the house where he was living himself, although by great good luck he was out when they called. They caught nobody, but they have collected a great mass of papers, a lot of money, 200 gallons of petrol, and two lorries. Now do you see that it would be madness to send telegrams? You will be lucky if you get out of Perpignan. If you do you should cross the mountains all right. Your guide this time has been crossing them as a smuggler for the last twenty-six years."

"What about Louis?"

"Going about Perpignan heavily disguised. He's in process of winding up his affairs and will probably move to another town not far from here. He has been decent in taking so much trouble to get you across."

"Well, third time lucky."

3

Eight o'clock the following night found us once more at the corner of the ploughed field outside Perpignan where we had met Pedro.

The guide this time was a small, wizened man with a very high voice that had a hollow, conch-like tone. He spoke only the Catalan tongue, with a sprinkling of French, but thanks to my sketchy knowledge of Italian I clearly understood him. There was another man with him, a tall husky fellow who smelled strongly of wine. This man carried an enormous rucksack which clinked when he covered rough ground, and which probably contained contraband in the shape of bottles of alcohol or perfume.

Our little guide gave no melodramatic instructions with regard to dogs. He only asked me to advise the Americans to relax as much as possible while they walked and to forget that they were covering the ground, because from then until dawn they would be walking all the time.

"How can we forget?—ask him that," said Charlie.

"Think of God, or a woman," replied the old man.

"Ask him how we cross the river Tech."

"We will cross nearer the sea than you did on your attempt with the ill-fated Pedro, and you will see that it is not difficult. Only I shall demand absolute silence, especially on the far bank, which is apt to be closely guarded."

He set off, padding smoothly in *espadrilles* down paths which we had followed with Pedro. If anything, this man was more cautious than Pedro, and we reached the first river in good time without causing a dog to bark. The Americans were thoroughly broken in by this time, and they were walking well, although I knew that their feet must hurt. Mine did.

The guide took off his shoes at the river, and waded it barefoot. I was glad, because I had earlier decided to do that in order to preserve my boots and make the walking more comfortable between streams. Also the level of this stream was much lower than it had been with Pedro.

He would not let us sit down for more than two or three minutes at a time.

"When you rest too much your legs get stiff. Just sit long enough to relax all the muscles. Then walk on. That is the way."

He himself seemed to flow across the ground with tiny, smooth steps. Like Pedro, he carried a long stick. He said that he was fifty-five, but the assistant whispered: "The old one is vain, very vain, and likes to think that he is still young. He is sixty-five."

This time we reached the north bank of the Tech before midnight. The river looked wider and shallower at this point. The guide asked us to follow him at thirty-yard intervals in case the enemy saw us and began shooting. The water was terribly cold and the stones cut our feet. I counted 290 steps on the way across.

We sat down in dense undergrowth on the south bank and were drying ourselves and putting on trousers and boots and socks when a terrible shouting broke out. After a moment we realised what had happened. The old man had crossed first and had arrived further down-stream. His assistant had followed him and all of us had followed the assistant. Now the old man (who had demanded absolute silence) could not find us, and was screaming insults at the assistant, who answered in kind.

When we linked up with him ten minutes later three of the Americans had got lost. There was more shouting until they arrived.

We walked on into the forbidden zone. We had not gone far when the old guide stopped so suddenly that we all cannoned into him. Three figures were crossing a field towards us. In a flurry the guide turned, barged his way through the Americans, and dashed back along the path we had been following. We all followed him in a mad rush for some 300 yards, when he cut off to the left down another track. He made a big circle, and soon we were on our original path.

By this time the Pyrenees were coming closer. But the closeness was deceptive. To get to the mountains it was necessary for us to act as counters in some diabolical game of "Snakes and Ladders". The rungs in our ladder were rivers which had to be waded or roads which had to be stalked and then crawled across. The guide was most careful with the roads. At one of them he turned to me and whispered: "I once lost a bottle of Napoleon brandy here. A German bicycle patrol came round that corner just as I was crossing. I ran so fast that I left the bottle behind."

"Was it real Napoleon brandy?"

"Of course not. It never is. But it was marked clearly on the bottle, and it would have fetched a Napoleon price in Spain. I won it at bowls: the bottle I mean. The brandy I had put in from something a little newer and more shapely in the way of bottles."

We began climbing when we came to the olive-groves. It was hard work on the terraced ground. Then we left the olives and climbed up woodland paths. At one of our short halts I took off Pedro's oiled silk coat, which I had carried in a roll over one shoulder. I took it off to make a seat on the damp ground. And when we went on I forgot it. That forgetfulness might have cost me my life.

At 5 a.m. we cleared the woods, and the bare mountains were above us. The guide told us to sleep in some bushes while he and his assistant went to a cottage farther up the hill. We had been walking for nine hours. All of us went to sleep among the sparse bushes and were awakened by strange noises like the barking of a small lap-dog. They were made by the guide.

"More climbing now," he said. "Fill your water-bottles passing the cottage. I apologise for leaving you outside. But there are often German patrols here. If they found us they would take us for visiting shepherds. If they found you they would kill everybody, burn the cottage, rape my friend's wife, and eat his sheep."

At the back door of the cottage a thin woman wearing a jacket of sheepskin and trousers of some soft leather filled our bottles with earthy-tasting water. Then we went on climbing up a narrow path over and through big rocks. Often tough thorn-bushes closed behind the man in front, lashing those who followed with tearing branches. It was bitterly cold, although we could see a strong-looking sun beginning to rise over the sea horizon. We were tired, but would have liked to go on climbing to keep warm. At eight o'clock, however, the guide said that it was getting dangerously light.

He shepherded us into the thorn-scrub below the mountain path.

"You will enjoy several hours of sunshine here to-day," he said. "Tell your friends that if they get a good sleep and eat solidly in the evening, they should be in Spain to-morrow morning. Warn them not to drink too much water, because that is bad for crossing the mountains, and this crossing is never easy in winter. My friend and I are going back to sleep the day away in the cottage below. Au revoir, and don't move about. That big house down there is the headquarters of the German frontier guards. They occasionally send patrols over the hills during the daytime, and some of them have dogs."

I faithfully transmitted his instructions to the Americans. They had borne up bravely all through the night. Now they seemed to have an enormous thirst. Before the end of the morning all our water had been drunk. I attributed their thirst to their unfit condition. The one we had called Clark Gable looked quite ill. He lay near me, heavily asleep, his face a greenish-grey against his mossy pillow.

The air at that height was cold and crisp, even when the sun was on our hill-face. A heavy coastal battery of German guns had firing practice during the afternoon. The shells fell a long way out to sea. The guns themselves were sited nearly a mile inland.

From our high resting-place we could see all our little milestones of the past three weeks stretched out below us in a huge relief map. We could see Perpignan, the first river, the Tech, and the subsequent rivers. There were the two roads making a wish-bone forking towards us from Perpignan. And down below us, where the hills ran into the sea, lay Port Vendres, such a dramatic little port in the Spanish Civil War. Pale wisps of wood smoke rose from its distant chimneys against the pale winter blue of the Mediterranean.

Although I could not sleep, I ate all that I carried and lay as relaxed as possible on the slope. At the beginning of this attempt I had not had enough money to buy provisions. I had left Perpignan with two tins of French Army meat, two small loaves and one of the cakes that Serge and I had bought for the second attempt. The Americans wondered to see me finish my provisions, but I told them that it was better to have a full stomach before we set off on the worst part of the journey than to save up for a meal when we were across.

Within myself I felt an immense exultation, for I was convinced that in twenty-four hours I should be safe from the Germans.

The guides arrived promptly at five, but we had to wait until six before the old man considered it dark enough for us to begin climbing. The early going was good on a bare, rocky path.

We stopped at a spring to fill all our water-bottles. While we were there, three of the Americans got down on their knees and lapped at the water like dogs. When he saw this the guide stood on a rock above them and jabbered at them in his high voice.

"Bad, bad, bad. Water is bad on the hills. Much better drink wine." He offered his wine-skin, but nobody felt like drinking wine.

The guide now wore a kind of fluffy woollen helmet, which covered all but his sharp nose and his restless eyes. He led us up small paths made perhaps by goats, perhaps by men. Sometimes he left the paths to slither across steep hill-faces. He explained that he did this to avoid German posts which were often placed on the high ground.

A bitter north wind cut into our backs. I deeply regretted the loss of Pedro's coat, for even with the climbing I could not keep warm.

"This wind is the *tramontane*," said the guide. "It will get much worse and it will bring snow."

"To-night?"

"When else?"

We had been walking and climbing for two hours and a half when we stopped to rest in a small dark pine-wood. All of the Americans were extremely tired and were feeling their feet.

"Of what do they speak?" asked the guide.

"They speak of the possibilities of victory next year," I lied.

"I know that they are talking about their tired limbs. That is because they have drunk too much water. Tell them they drink no more water. Let them ask for wine. Eh, *amigo*, pass your skin."

His companion passed the wine with some grumbling, and this time we all drank, including the guide himself.

"Tell your comrades to have courage, for with courage man conquers all," he continued with a chuckle. "Tell them I lost my brother here one year ago."

My translation of his morbid injunction was met by hollow groans from the Americans, for their extreme fatigue could not yet prevent them from laughing at everything, including themselves.

After this rest we slithered down a hill so steep that it just

409

failed to be a precipice. At the bottom was a raging torrent which had to be crossed by leaping from boulder to boulder. Two of the Americans, the Chauve Souris and Gable, fell heavily but followed on. The Chauve Souris had been lagging for some time.

We had not, it appeared, traversed the main block of the mountains, and we turned west, paralleling what the guide said was the last ridge before the Spanish frontier. This paralleling was the most arduous work of all, for there were continual high ridges running across our path so that we were like some infinitely small animals climbing in and out of the squares of a giant honeycomb. Now too, we were walking in snow, although it was not deep enough to present much of a handicap.

I explained to the Americans that we were working along the high ridge on our left, keeping well below the summit because there were German frontier posts and patrols there, and that the guide would turn up it at a place where he knew it would be safe to cross. But an exhausted man finds it difficult to reason and easy to complain. Our line grew more and more strung out. The guide frequently had to halt to allow the Chauve Souris, Charlie and Gable to catch up. I would have liked to push on much faster, for it was the cold, not fatigue, that worried me. My back was freezing in the *tramontane*.

Charlie told me at one point that he had seen cows and I thought he must be going mad.

"Can't you tell a cow from a goat?"

But a little later I saw them myself, a large half-wild herd of small cows. And I suddenly remembered Laurence talking with Alpine scorn of the Pyrenees as *"Montagnes des vaches"*.

The blizzard became so bad and so heavy with wet snow that the guide led us into a small cave in the hill-side. Here there was just room for all of us to rest, squeezed together and dripping water from our soaking clothes. The others smoked. Some shepherd had left a crude oil-lamp there. The guide lit it and I was able to look at my companions.

My heart would have bled for them had I been less intent on surmounting this final obstacle. Except for Fritz, who seemed to thrive on the work, they were plainly in the last stages of exhaustion.

Gable, the biggest and toughest-looking of us all, told me that he could not go much farther.

"Why not?"

"My legs are passing out on me."

The Chauve Souris and Charlie seemed to be equally miserable. The Trapper was little better, although he complained less since he came from tougher, less citified stock.

They begged me to ask the guide if we could either stop there for the night or if he could take us by a quick, direct route to the frontier.

"If we wait here we shall die from the cold," he answered. "I must take you by the proper route. Tell them it is only one hour from here to the frontier if this blizzard dies down, as I think it will very soon."

The going was more difficult when we started out again, and the Americans, excepting Fritz, were slower than ever. At one short halt, when the guide left us for a moment to look at the crest of the ridge, Gable lay down on a patch of snow and shouted: "I can't go on, I can't go on."

Fritz and I went back to him.

"My legs have given out," he said. "Ask the old man if he can give us five minutes' rest."

"Certainly not," said the guide indignantly. "Tell him to be a man."

He now noticed that some of them were stuffing lumps of snow into their mouths. For although it was deathly cold and eerie and wet on the mountain-top, we were parched with thirst. "If you drink like that you will die," shrieked the guide.

So we moved on slowly to what he said was the last slope. It was very steep, and the snow was deeper and softer. The four weak Americans were all in grave difficulties. Fritz and I had to divide all that they carried between us. They struggled bravely at the slope. But there were times when they all lay down in the bitter cold, and we despaired of ever getting them over.

The guide and his assistant did nothing to help. They only got angry, screaming at us and jabbering in fast, incomprehensible Catalan. I have never given so many encouraging discourses in such a short time. They sounded false to me, up there in the whistling wind, and they had little effect on Gable who, poor soul, was now almost unconscious with pain from his powerful legs. The others somehow, little by little, managed to drag themselves up. The Trapper and Charlie hung together and kept going inch by inch with a rest every few yards. The Chauve Souris, brave spirit, negotiated the whole slope on hands and knees. This left the two of us to deal with Gable.

At first he lay on the snow saying: "I can't, I tell you."

Fritz gave him a "You're doing fine, boy," piece of nonsense.

He responded by walking with our help for twenty yards, then he sank down again. While he lay there Fritz talked to him and the Chauve Souris passed us, crawling. I was reminded of the hare and the tortoise and burst out laughing. The old guide chose this moment to come back and scream that this was the most dangerous part of the whole trip.

"Kick him into activity. Does he want to kill us all?"

"Ask him to let me rest here for a half-hour, just a half-hour," moaned Gable, his voice trailing away slowly into a sleepy drawl.

"Rest?" yelled the guide (I had not dared to translate the "half-hour" request). "Rest, I'll give him rest, the pig."

He danced down the slope and slapped Gable sharply several times on the face. This roused the poor man, and, supported by Fritz and me, he did another fifty yards.

Then he collapsed finally. Fritz and I tried everything we could think of, praise, vilification, encouragement, massage, wine from the Spaniard's skin, alcohol from Fritz's little bottle. The big man would not move. Tears oozed from his eyes.

"Leave me here to die, you fellows. I can't go on."

The Chauve Souris passed us again, going bravely on hands and knees. I pointed him out to Gable.

The only comment this drew was: "Just give me a half-hour and I think I'll be O.K."

Charlie and the Trapper were nearly over the ridge. The guide and his assistant were ahead of them. The Chauve Souris was nearing the top.

Fritz and I managed to raise big Gable. He sagged. We each got a shoulder under him, twining his heavy thick arms like dead pythons round our straining necks. We gathered ourselves together and managed to stagger up to the top and over the ridge. He kept saying maddening things like: "Let me be, fellows. Just let me rest."

The summit of the ridge was narrow and smooth; below it lay a few yards of scrub, then stunted pine-trees. The three of us fell in a heap. I lay there with the blood pounding in my ears.

When I picked myself up Gable again was asking for "a half-hour's rest."

Fritz and I worked on him. We ran the full gamut of first-aid, we talked to him lovingly, angrily. Nothing happened. The other three lay around us in the scrub, offering advice. The two Spaniards stood sourly under a tree, watching us. Occasionally the guide hurled piping invective at us. At last he came over to look at the prostrate giant.

"The Spanish frontier is thirty minutes' easy walking from here," he said. "We go down to the burn below us, over it, up on the other side, and then across that plateau. At the far edge of the plateau is the frontier, and you can see the lights of the Spanish town of Figueras from there."

"Why don't you leave me then?" said Gable. "I'll make it when my legs get some strength back in them."

"We won't leave you. You must come with us now. It's too cold to lie here."

"I'll cover myself with leaves. See," he began to scrabble leaves over his legs. "After an hour or two I'll go on down to Spain. Now I got to get some rest. . . ."

"Enough of this foolery," screamed the guide. "I have been taking men across all this winter and I never saw such women. This is the worst part. Sooner or later Germans will pass here. Are you all going to throw your chance away for one weakling?"

He suddenly darted on Gable.

"I will *make* you go on," he shouted. Before we could stop him he seized two handfuls of Gable's black hair and began to bash his big head against a tree-trunk. Gable only moaned gently.

"I don't care what you do to me. I can't go on."

When I had translated the guide's remarks about German patrols to him he only replied: "What do I care about Germans? My legs hurt so badly. Please go on without me. I'll be O.K. I see the way. You none of you'll make it if you take me along. It's the only hope, to leave me. When I've rested I'll go on down into Spain . . ."

After all the ground that had been covered I could practically see the Spanish frontier. After the help of Wally Binns, the French prisoners, the Strasbourg café plotters, Ramon and Alban, Greta, Scherb, Dolores, Pascal, La Pepette, Xavier, Elizabeth, Clément, Laurence, Serge, Estève, Cartelet—after all that, I was stuck here, almost within jumping distance of the frontier. Stuck, stuck, stuck! Because one American had been too lazy to do three deep knee bends each day that he was hidden up in Paris. Was my duty to this man, or to all that lay behind me and all that lay ahead?

I could not decide. I asked Fritz.

"I reckon we should leave him as he asks. He may make it in the morning. If we stop here it may mean all of us get lost."

I asked the Trapper, Charlie, and the Chauve Souris. They were all of the same opinion as Fritz. By this time the guide, who did not understand what this talk was about, was screaming: "To perdition with you all, you bunch of women! I am going on. I will not throw myself away for you. . . ."

We covered Gable's body with leaves and left him what food and wine remained. We showed him the road to the frontier again.

The others moved off. He had relaxed, and looked much better now that he knew he was to be allowed to rest. When I was hurrying after the others, I bumped into a man in the darkness.

"Who is it?"

"It's me," said the Chauve Souris. "Listen, lieutenant. I was in the same house with him for six months in Paris. I'm going to stay with him. Furthermore, my legs are just about all in too, and I would be a drag on the rest of the party. I could never make the frontier to-night. We'll go on down together in the daylight. See you in Spain. . . ."

"Keep each other awake," I told him. "It's too cold, dangerously cold, to go to sleep. If you go to sleep you may never wake. Drink all the wine and eat the food. Rub each other's legs and get on down as soon as you feel you can move. I'm glad you're staying with him. It's a good thing to do. A decent thing. . . ." But already we had separated in the wood, and I was running down towards the burn, after the others.

The Trapper and Charlie were both in a bad way, and the effort of carrying Gable had taken a lot out of Fritz and me. We worked our way slowly up the wooded slope beyond the burn. There seemed to be a numbness in my legs. The guide was nervous and ill at ease. He repeatedly hissed at us to be silent or to hurry.

At last we came out on the plateau. It looked unnatural, like the face of the moon. The bitter wind swept across it, bludgeoning us forward, stabbing us forward. The guide nudged me and pointed to a kind of hillock at the far edge of the plateau.

"Keep that on your left hand," he said. "It marks the Spanish frontier. But you must make them run across here. We are in full view. It's not far. Look. Only 300 metres."

He and the other Spaniard began to run away in front of us. "Run," I shouted. "That's the frontier. Run. Run."

The Trapper and Fritz ran on. Charlie was too tired. He stumbled after them. A wild exaltation gripped me, filled me, maddened me.

"Just 300 yards now, Charlie boy," I shouted at him. "Run with me."

"I can't."

"Run. Run. Run."

I took him by the hand and pulled him as you might an unwilling child. The pair of us broke into a shambling trot. I pulled and the wind pushed. Charlie responded nobly. Our speed increased. We crossed the plateau; and suddenly we were running away with ourselves as we dropped over the edge of the plateau—into Spain.

CHAPTER XXIII

I

BUT were we in Spain?

It was true that far below us, beyond the slope of the hills, stretched a great plain with splashes of light on it from towns and villages, startling splashes to eyes accustomed to war-time darkness. Louis had warned me, however, that we could not be certain that we were in Spain until we had actually descended to the plain itself. He had also hinted that the Spanish frontier guards might hand over to the Germans anybody whom they captured actually on the frontier.

When we stopped at a spring to fill our water-bottles I realised for the first time that I had seriously twisted my left knee, possibly when we had fallen with Gable. It was difficult to stand up again.

The spring was high up in the hills. I had doubts about my ability to walk far.

"How far to the farm?" I asked.

"A good fifteen kilometres (nine miles)," replied the guide.

"Is it certain that we are in Spain?"

"Certain. This is your first trip. I have been crossing these mountains for twenty-six years. But we must walk on, and fast, because here in Spain I am in more danger than in France. And you are all in danger too, at any rate in danger of going to Miranda jail and having your heads shaved and catching a dose of the pox."

"I'd a hell of a lot rather catch that than keep on walking," said Charlie when I had translated. But they did keep on, he and the Trapper, although their feet were raw and they were nearly dropping. Crossing the frontier seemed to have given them a second wind, whereas for me there was emptiness and pain. True, every fifty yards I told myself that I was FREE, but my whole body seemed to be sagging, and the pain in my knee made me gasp for rest. After a time the guide noticed how lame I was, and he bound the knee up tightly with a crêpe bandage.

Descending the hills on a good, wide, stony track the *tramontane* came whistling down into our backs again, cutting into my kidneys. Despite the labour of walking, I was desperately cold and shivery. I imagined that I was sickening for some illness. Through the short temper and unreasonableness of fatigue we became very angry with the guide and his companion.

At one point, just before leaving the hills for the plain, the two of them dumped us in a small wood and went off "To see if there were any of the *Guardia Civil* in the neighbourhood". They came back when we had shivered for a miserable hour, and we were positive that although they said that they had found no sign of the *Guardia Civil* they had certainly found some good fellowship and much liquor, for of the latter they both smelled strongly.

The provident Spaniards had refuelled their large wine-skins, and the farther we progressed the better-tempered they became. They were generous with their skins and I drank freely of the wine, which had a tart, resinous tang that murdered thirst.

When we were on the plain the little man drove straight on for a time and then turned east towards the sea. Usually we were on tracks or small roads, but he avoided villages, and there were more icy streams to ford. The walk seemed endless.

It was 5 a.m. when we arrived in a large village and the Spaniards pushed us into an old cow-shed.

"Wait here, please," the guide said. "There is a sale of wine in this village and I can assure you that it is a village famous for its wine."

"But you cannot ask us to wait here. The floor is one metre deep in dung."

"Dung does not bite. And we go to buy wine not only for ourselves but also for you."

"Let us accompany you."

"My friend, you would have me hanged. But listen. Here I will meet my son, who will take the message to have you met by your friends from the British Consulate in Barcelona."

To pass the two hours that we waited in the dung we ate a tin of sardines which Charlie carried in his pocket, and the remnants of the bread the three of them had brought from Perpignan. The Americans were all three in good spirits, though we speculated grimly on the fate of Gable and the Chauve Souris, still up there in the cold wind.

Our Spaniards arrived, singing, and arm in arm. The guide began by hanging a large, full wine-skin around my neck.

"This is my son," he said, presenting a dark young man in white shoes. "He has been in touch with your people and to-night you will meet at ten o'clock a representative of the British Consulate. He has also arranged for you to have a splendid dinner to-day. Now we will continue our promenade, but ask your friends to be quiet, for there is much police vigilance about here."

We walked south-east for another two hours, and day was breaking when the guide stopped in a lane, pointed to a thicket of bushes and young trees on the left and said: "You will be very comfortable in there."

"For how long?"

"Only a short while. Do not fret now."

Obediently we climbed through a fence and disposed ourselves about the thicket. The three Americans lay down to sleep. But my leg hurt me too much and the cold had bitten too deeply into the small of my back. I stamped to and fro in the thicket, working myself into a really bad temper. The guide's companion had remained in the lane, as though he were keeping guard on us. My movements evidently worried him.

"For the love of God, keep still," he hissed into the bushes.

"I refuse to keep still. I am too cold. How long are we to remain here?"

"All day."

"All day! I refuse to remain here all day. Are we not going to a farm-house?"

"Yes, to-night. What is the matter?"

"I am freezing, and I think I am sick. If we must remain here I will light a fire."

The Spaniard stood up and peered in at me. Finally he shrugged his shoulders.

"It is your own suggestion, so why not? And I will gladly help you," he said.

Fritz and I built shelter walls by hammering in long uprights and weaving brushwood, while the other three gathered wood. In this way we soon had a small enclosure, well sheltered from the piercing wind, and with an enormous fire in the middle.

I lay beside the fire and let the blessed heat soak into my back and my knee. All that remained in the way of food was French tinned meat, *singe*. We divided this into four portions, toasted it on long sticks, and ate it without bread. Then, having banked our fire, all four of us went to sleep. That was a life-saving fire.

Soon after 4 p.m. I awoke. The others were sitting up, complaining of hunger. My leg was very stiff. Otherwise I was stronger. We recalled the guide's promise to give us a fine meal that day. We laughed at his promise.

But at 4.30 he arrived with two more wine-skins and a large basket which he handed to us, saying: "We bought these few things for you on the black market."

The things were fried sausages, the English type of sausage, bananas, tangerines, and long loaves of white bread. We toasted the sausages until they were burning hot and tasted faintly of wood smoke, and I do not think that I have ever eaten a more delicious meal by way of contrast to what had gone before. He also produced for the Americans long black cigarettes.

At 6 p.m. the guide led us out of the thicket and headed southwest, tearing across fields and on the beaten tracks around vineyards with his now familiar dancing quick little steps, and heading for the silver line of a big river in the distance.

"How far are we going?" I asked.

"We shall be there in four hours at this pace."

Four hours! All of us had thought that we were going perhaps one mile, perhaps two.

"Ask him if there are many rivers to cross," said Charlie, for that was now our chief dread.

"Only two, but they are big ones."

The four hours slowly passed and we stopped in a hollow beside another stream, but this time we were not going to wade it. The guide's companion was going to his home by another route. Before he left he embraced us warmly, insisted that we finish all the wine that remained in his skin, and then embraced us once again.

A few miles farther on, the guide tapped with a long stick on a farm-house window. A light went on inside and then vanished. He tiptoed round to the front of the house, motioning to us that we must follow at his heels. When he had waited there for a few minutes to make sure that we were unobserved, he led us quickly through the front yard into a byre where there were two cows and a bull, through the byre to a stable occupied by a pony, a mule and a draught horse, through the stable to a cellar filled with wine-casks and demijohns, and thence up a spiralling stone staircase to a long living-room where several people were gathered around an open fireplace.

A thin, nondescript Spaniard came forward, said in French that he was from the British Consulate in Barcelona, and asked us to fill in our particulars, rank, regiment, etcetera, on a paper he carried.

The Catalan women took charge of us. They gave us warm water to wash with and cooked us a copious meal on the open fire.

The firelight sparkled in a decanter of red wine, a decanter with a narrow glass jet sticking out of its normal neck.

"All black market—a fine place this," the Spaniard from Barcelona remarked to me.

"Fine, fine," agreed our old guide testily. "But not so fine as my home, Englishman. Only I am outlawed. Here I am twelve kilometres from my home, and not allowed by the government to sleep with my own buxom wife—I am an old man, but I believe in young wives, none of your scraggy old hens for me."

"Where are you going now, then?" For he had eaten a little, had drunk considerably, and was now dressing for the road.

"Where am I going? Why, home, of course. Nobody can prevent me from climbing in at my own bedroom window. And to-morrow I cross the mountains again. Au revoir."

"An astonishing man," I said to the Spaniard from Barcelona.

"There are many astonishing men in Spain, but not many like him."

"He was divinely made," said one of the women. "He forgets that he is old, so he is as young as his grandsons."

They led us off to sleep in the hay. One of the sons forked down a lot of it; they spread blankets over this when we had flattened it out to make a big bed. All four of us lay down together; they put more blankets on top of us and more hay on top of that.

419

"You will sleep more comfortably to-morrow night if all goes well," the Spaniard told us. "Try to sleep most of to-morrow. I shall return in the evening and we shall journey on together. We have to be very careful. I should warn you that the Spanish Police are more clever than the Germans."

We slept until midday, when one of the squarely-built farm women brought us a splendid golden-brown stew with mutton, beans, garlic, onion, and pimento in it. There were beakers of a strange pinkish wine, strong and sweet.

Our new guide returned at five o'clock. He led us into the country for a few miles and then made us crouch beside him in a wood not far from what appeared to be a mixture between a level-crossing and a station. Perhaps in England it would have been called a "halt".

"That town is Figueras," he said, pointing to a glow of lights in the distance. "We are not going to board the train there. But if the police search the train and arrest you, then you must say that you boarded it at Figueras and your tickets, which I now give to you, will bear out that statement. Is that understood?"

He waited while I translated.

"Next thing. We must not be seen by anybody outside the train while we board it at this station. We shall therefore leave this hiding-place just before the train arrives. It will slow down well before the station and we shall jump in while it is moving. You will follow me into a long carriage like a Pullman car. You will separate, and will sit singly in opposite corners of the carriage. You will speak to nobody. I shall leave you in that carriage and sit in the carriage nearer the engine. The trip will take about two hours. When it is time to alight I will walk back through the carriage. I will say nothing, I will not even look at you, but you must all individually get up and follow me. Is that understood?

"Now listen carefully. We must not be seen alighting from this train. You will follow me out on to the rear platform of the carriage. The last of you will shut the door behind him, and we shall all jump off while the train is moving. Be careful how you do this. We will drop off the right side of the train. Let your right foot gently down until it touches the ground, then run. We have no time for accidents. Is that understood?

"We will then find ourselves in a town. You will follow me at one-hundred-metre intervals, but staggered. That is to say that the man who follows me will be on the opposite pavement, and so on. When we pass the main hospital of the town we shall find a car waiting for us, a large black car. The car will allow us to pass, then will follow us to a piece of waste ground, where we shall all jump in. Is that clearly understood?"

"Oh boy," said Charlie, when I had translated the last bit. "Does that car sound good!"

Although his plans had sounded a little fantastic to tired men, everything went exactly as he had predicted—until the bit about the car.

We passed the main hospital, we turned up a side street, we arrived at the piece of waste ground. But not a car was to be seen. Our guide was so angry that he could scarcely speak intelligible French.

"There has been some accident. Wait here while I telephone for instructions. Remain standing against that wall, motionless and in absolute silence."

It was so cold out there in the moonlight that it was impossible to remain motionless without demanding frost-bite. He had placed us against the wall because the moon was casting dark shadows. We stood there doing the cabman's exercise, and stamping our feet on the iron-hard ground.

Our position was made the more uncomfortable by contrast in that there was a large block of wide-windowed flats at the edge of our waste ground. Through the plate-glass windows we could see men and women sitting around, talking or reading or sewing or warming their buttocks by the dancing flames of large wood fires.

The guide's bad temper had not abated with his telephone conversation. All he would say was: "That creature has trains on the brain."

At length he calmed down sufficiently to tell me that our plans had been changed; we now had to jump a freight train.

"This is no easy matter. How many of you have jumped freight trains before? Have *you?*"

"No," I said.

"No," said Fritz.

"No," said Charlie.

"Yup," said the Trapper.

"Ah, one at least. That one must mount last of all. You, Englishman, since you have a bad leg, will mount first. Now follow me."

He led us to the dark shade of a shelter in a cluster of miserable allotments. We were a few hundred yards outside a large marshalling yard and our shelter was fifty yards from the line. This guide was certainly an expert on trains. We waited for over an hour, and whenever a train pulled out of the marshalling yard he would peer at it in the moonlight.

"Confound it, not that one," he exclaimed. "These Spanish railways are really damnable. Always late, never on time, I earnestly assure you."

At last he shouted: "This is ours. Follow me closely."

He darted down to the railway, scaled the fence, and soon we were running with him alongside the train, which was picking up speed. I was carrying Charlie's parcel, and my first jump for the little iron ladder at the back of a truck failed because the weight of the parcel swung me round. At the second attempt all went well. The others followed me. The guide hung on to the ladder for a minute.

"Count the stations," he shrieked at us above the roar of the train. "Just before the *sixth* station, jump off. I shall remain on the truck behind this one." He vanished, climbing over the buffers.

Those Spanish freight trucks had tiny brake cabins stuck at the back, the roof of the cabin being raised some three feet above the roof of the truck. There was just room for the four of us to stand upright beside the heavy iron brake-wheel. Any movement was out of the question. The top of the truck, stretching in front of us, was covered with a five-inch layer of gleaming white frost. There were no windows on the cab. As we stood squeezed there, like tinned asparagus in a refrigerator, little icicles formed on our hair and our eyelashes. The language in our cabin was terrible. When the train stopped at small stations, railwaymen would walk or run past us tapping at the wheels, unhooking a wagon behind, or shouting at somebody in the distance.

We saw the guide leap from the train like an elongated monkey, and scuttle off the track. We all did our best to emulate him, and followed him along a path that circled the sixth station and then rejoined the railway.

"We have a walk of three hours in front of us, going fast," the guide told us. "Most of it will be easy walking along the railway line."

By this time my leg appeared to have got accustomed to walking, but otherwise I knew that I had a chill and no amount of fast walking could warm me.

We arrived in the early hours of the morning at a handsome

farm-house with shuttered windows and beautiful wrought-iron-work on balconies and gates. The guide found a key in the garden and opened the door of a garage containing, of all things, an Austin 7. From there he led us through a hall which held a lot of shining old furniture and a suit of armour, and then into a large kitchen.

A middle-aged couple came out in woolly dressing-gowns to meet us. They lit a huge fire of brushwood and gave us coffee and white, home-baked bread with a lot of butter. The wife was pleased with me because she was French and I spoke her language.

"You have the red lights of fever in your cheeks and you must go to bed," she told me. She explained to the Americans in English with a powerful French accent: "The Englishman must have the single bed to-night because he is sick. You three will have to sleep in the double bed, but it is a very beeg one."

On the upstairs landing there was a portrait of General de Gaulle with the British, American and French flags hanging above it. The bedroom was airy. French windows opened to a balcony with a view of moonlit hills and vineyards. There were linen sheets on my bed and coloured blankets edged with silk.

The following morning they gave me some kind of draught, but nothing to eat. I slept most of the day, half-conscious only that my American friends were being spirited away from me.

I was alone when I awoke at three o'clock and Madame gave me a treble brandy with warm milk.

"You will be well enough to eat dinner," Madame said. "Many of our young men arrive in your state. Sometimes we get the doctor and he says that it is a physical state, but I do not agree. He says it is a plain chill caught in the mountains and exaggerated by physical exhaustion. That is why it always passes quickly, he says, when the sick man has time to rest and sleep in a good bed.

"But I look at the young men who arrive like that, and I believe that the thing he calls a chill is a symptom of mental strain, nothing physical. It is because the young man has been wanting so much to cross the mountains, and for so long. He crosses them and something that was taut inside him suddenly sags. The doctor says it is a chill. But doctors are still groping in the dark. Now you are all right. I will bandage your bad leg (the doctor must see it in Barcelona), then you will put on your new clothes which you see laid out there, and you will come down and eat a solid meal with us. Just me and my son. My husband has gone to Barcelona with your friends. We like eating, my son and I.''

While I memorised a plan of the route from Barcelona station to the British Consulate, Madame made a few quick alterations in my clothes. They were new clothes, Spanish ones, so that I should not arouse suspicions on the way to Barcelona. Then we ate.

We ate first a risotto with mussels and oysters. Then for the three of us she brought in a platter with twelve large steaks upon it. Each of us ate four steaks, underdone, rubbed with garlic and pepper and salt, and cooked in butter. Then we had salad with dressing made from olive-oil grown and pressed on the farm itself. I was surprised to find that I still wanted to sleep.

It was a small village station, and the passengers waiting on the unsheltered platform when I arrived early next morning were going to Barcelona for the day's work. It was still dark. Now I was respectably dressed (according to the standards prevailing locally) and they had given me a second-class ticket, since those were the least crowded carriages on that train.

The only thing that worried Madame about my appearance was my long, straw-coloured hair, which stuck out in a kind of ruff over the back of my collar. I had not been able to have it cut properly since *le cocu* had taken me to the barber's shop near the cathedral in Strasbourg, three months earlier. It had been cut once at Les Daines by the tall railway policeman who had helped us to leave Annecy station. He had been a barber in civil life, and he claimed a barber's altitude record, for he had cut the hair of *maquisards* high up on Mont Blanc. But he had asked me: "I suppose you want *la coupe anglaise?*" And when I replied in the affirmative he shaped the hair around my ears but left the back uncut.

Long before my train arrived in Barcelona my carriage was filled with suburbanites. Once again I was obliged to feign sleep in order to avoid being drawn into conversation.

I hurried through the station, well-lit and imposing, and crossed the town by memory from the plan Madame had made me memorise at the farm. They had told me that I should have no help on this walk unless I lost my way, but that I should be watched. And half-way to the Consulate I saw our train-jumping expert on the other side of the street. He stopped to light a cigarette, and cast one glint from his black eyes at me.

I found the Consulate without difficulty and, as instructed, walked quickly past the Spanish policemen who sat in the hall and up the staircase. At the top there was a man behind a desk, and rows of well-dressed townspeople waiting to make inquiries or to see people.

I gave my name to the man behind the desk.

"Just step along to that door marked 'Waiting-room', Mr. Millar."

A young Englishwoman came into the waiting-room to find me.

"You are George Millar. We have been waiting for you for a long time."

I was almost home.

2

What did it mean to be free?

I was driven around in big cars with chauffeurs and escorting Spaniards who smiled at me. I was given dinner by a tall, hospitable Englishman who was kind to me, I think, because of my regiment. It should have interested me to eat off English china and to sit in a well-studied English room (although it was in Barcelona), and to talk to an Englishman who was carefully dressed, and whose shoes were as polished underneath the insteps as they were on top. I went to see a doctor. I was taken to have my hair cut, I was photographed, I lived in a quick, efficient whirl of administration. And it was difficult to know whether to be happy or sad.

We, my three American friends and I, were quartered in a comfortable family house. It was a house with more amenities than any in which I had stayed on my journey from Munich. There were bathrooms and family dinner-parties and a gramophone with records of "Il Trovatore" and the "Clock" and "Pastoral" symphonies. Surely all that ought to have meant something to me. At least I should have gone out and bought, in honour of my late cell-mates at Gavi and Padula, three dozen tins of condensed milk.

Up to our crossing of the frontier I had been the most positive member of our inter-allied party. Now the roles were reversed. Now Fritz and Charlie and the Trapper were happy already in the happiness that was to come. They knew what they wanted to do, and I was a ghost trailing after them, sucked after them in their slip-stream. Perhaps I had influenza.

"Was there a *war* here lately?" asked Charlie.

We were motoring from Barcelona to Madrid, and the car had stopped above a ruined village to let us eat. The railway passed close to the road. Near the place where we sat eating our ham sandwiches and oranges the railway had crossed a ravine on a feathery viaduct.

The viaduct had been blown up at our side where the supports began to lengthen out of the slope. It was being mended. The work was being done by two men in wide-brimmed hats. They had a mule to help them, and two deep baskets which fitted into panniers on the mule's back. The two men with the mule collected stones from a place back down the road where another man was breaking stones with slow thuds of a hammer. Then they walked up to the gap and tumbled the contents of their baskets over the edge.

Every few days they must have varied their work by going down below to arrange the stones they had dropped from above. The pile of stones below already reached one-third of the height to the level of the railway.

The two men had evidently been doing this work for a long, long time. Their movements were as simply correct, as effort-saving, as those of the mule. They wore thin, short trousers, which showed a length of brown-black shank on each leg. Their feet were long and bare with upturned toes and flat, wide, light-coloured soles, and from our distance they looked beautiful and comfortable, the bare feet.

"How long have they been working there?"

"Maybe one year, maybe two," said the Spaniard who was with us.

"Don't they *want* to get this country straight after their war?" asked Fritz.

"After a war it is difficult to work, and often it is difficult to want anything at all."

4

In Madrid I was having a hot bath when they told me that Joan, whom I had known with her husband in peace-time, wanted to see me. When I was not being bustled round efficiently to get papers and railway tickets, I went out with her to dinner, and to places where we drank champagne before eating and ate sucking pig.

I think I should rather have gone to the Prado, but it was easier to play the conventional role of the escaped prisoner who wants the delights of the flesh. I knew that I did not want such delights, but that I wanted quickly to be home. I bought a great many pairs of silk stockings for Anne, and a cheap suitcase to carry them in. For I had learned some things from my civilised friends in Madrid. One was that women in London would do almost anything at that time for silk stockings.

They told us in Madrid that Gable and the Chauve Souris had managed to cross the frontier. Now they were interned, with shaven heads, in the Miranda prison.

We stayed, after all, only a very short time in Madrid. Then we took the train for Gibraltar, sitting up all night in cold first-class carriages. I had an overcoat now, and money, and a welcome wherever I went. I was no longer frightened of the immediate menace of the present. I was sheltered and protected and free. All those dreams in prison had been realised. Wally was not with me, but for me they had been realised.

What more could a man want?

But of course realisation is much less satisfying than the dream or the desire from which it springs. I was thankful that for me there was something behind the realisation, that I had not just escaped to escape. There was Anne.

5

The gateway to Gibraltar was a gateway to memories which had become neglected in the need for action. In the gateway stood a British military policeman, and there were many other battle-dresses and uniforms, even kilts, moving behind him to carry me back to the earlier days of the war.

My reaction was a sharp revulsion from such things. When I had been thoroughly examined by an Army doctor (an apologetic doctor who said: "I'm so sorry, but it is surprising how many of you people arrive with all sorts of diseases on you") I went to the transit camp where I was to stay.

Mine was a bare bedroom with windows overlooking the unnatural town's main street. There were three beds covered with grey Army blankets. I chose the bed farthest from the windows, and lay down, although it was only eleven o'clock in the morning. I lay there for a bit in the room's twilight—the shutters were closed—listening to the noises of the street outside and trying to pacify my mind into some sort of numbness. After a time I could hold myself on the bed no longer. I went to a window and parted the shutters a little so that I could see into the street.

There were all manner of British people below me, hurrying and dallying, men in business suits, men in uniform, women in naval uniform. An Army lieutenant passed on a motor-cycle, wearing a silly-looking crash-helmet. (New regulations since I had ridden a motor-cycle in the Army.) An 8-cwt. truck, like the one Mike had in his Company Headquarters before we left England, scurried down the crowded street and I recognised the note of its klaxon.

Instead of going down to lunch in the hotel reserved for British officers, I lay on my bed. I was afraid of the crowds in the dining-room.

That afternoon I met two fellow-prisoners from Gavi, "Stump" Gibbon, a tall, drawling tank officer, and Dan Riddiford, a conservative New Zealander. They had done remarkable things since the night of September 18th, when they and all the occupants of their truck had escaped from the train taking us to Germany. Stump and Dan had collected a party of stray British troops in the north of Italy, and had led them down through Jugoslavia. In both of them I detected a little of my own shyness at being back in a British world. I was glad to meet them because in their company I did not mind going to meals, and I was hungry.

There was something odd about me in Gibraltar. I had three manifestations of this oddness.

The first manifestation was Pearson.

Pearson was a man who had worked with me in the middle thirties. Like myself he was a newspaper reporter who had been at sea. There the resemblance ended. When I arrived in Gibraltar I certainly had not thought of Pearson for years.

Then, walking down the street one day, I said: "Just one moment, Dan. There is a man over there whom I must speak to." As I approached this man his features changed.

"Can Pearson really have altered as much as all that?" I asked myself. It was not Pearson. In fact, this man was nothing like Pearson; he was not stout, he had no moustache. I had committed myself by my advance. I had been so certain.

"I am sorry," I said to the stranger. "I mistook you for somebody else."

The following day, however, I met Pearson. He was in khaki

uniform. The moustache was the same, the portliness. We had little to say to each other. We had a drink.

The second manifestation was Alan Moorehead.

I had nothing to do on my second afternoon in Gibraltar, so I walked up to the Rock Hotel and asked at the desk for Alan.

"But were you expecting Mr. Moorehead? We have no notice that he is arriving, and he has not stayed here for a very long time."

Yes, I had expected to find him there. But why? Alan had been no particular friend of mine, although I had known him fairly well and had liked him. Shut up in prison since January, 1942, I did not even know that he was still alive. I thought of him as the Alan I had known in 1939.

The following afternoon I met another newspaper man down in the town.

"Yesterday I had a feeling that Alan Moorehead was here," I said to this man.

"He *is* here. He arrived unexpectedly last night in the nose of a Fortress with Alex Clifford of the *Mail*. They are staying at the Rock."

Alan was in battle-dress on a deck-chair. It was warm on the terrace of the strangely empty hotel. He and Clifford were surprised that I was "well-informed" about the war. Alan told me that Anne had looked well the last time he had seen her in London. I learned that he had written several books. We had nothing very much to talk about because so much had happened since we last met. We had lunch together at a table looking out over the docks to the sea.

The third manifestation was my elder brother.

I had not seen him for nearly five years, since our work in peace-time had taken us to different countries. I had had no idea of what he was doing until I met "Stump" and Dan, who told me that they had met him in Italy.

On the evening after my meeting with Alan I went into the Bristol Bar.

"Good Heavens," I said to somebody. "Excuse me, there is my brother, but what on earth is he doing in naval uniform?"

But when I approached the man in naval uniform he bore no resemblance to my brother. I saw that he even had black hair and dark eyes.

Next evening, though, at the same time, and on the identical bar stool, I found my brother. He was a major in the Army.

We had no time to talk and a great deal to talk about. He had a through passage by air to England, whereas I had to wait for a fresh aircraft to leave Gibraltar. He left quickly, taking with him a short letter from me to Anne (and, I was told later, the impression that I had become more serious and contemplative).

"Whom am I going to see next?" I asked the man who had worked for the British Broadcasting Corporation before working for the British Government.

"If only to-morrow afternoon you could imagine that you were about to see God," he replied.

But the next day I was busy preparing unregretfully to leave Gibraltar. I bought a white kit-bag at the officers' shop and filled it with lemons, bananas, Tio Pepe sherry and elastic, all things that they told me were wanted in London.

I had no time for further manifestations.

6

When I am going somewhere in an aircraft I am seldom conscious of any feeling of nervousness. On the other hand, when I am returning I often remember that both the aircraft and myself are heavier than air.

It seemed to me on this journey that it would be silly if, after all the chance and luck of my journey from Munich, this particular Sunderland flying-boat should, for any reason, lose its speed and with it the lift that kept us travelling above the sea. It would have seemed a queer twist of fate that all those people in Germany and France and Spain should have put themselves out to help me get free, and that I should perish on the final easy bus-ride.

But would it have been so silly? Are not those strange tweaks of fate the things that make life more than bearable? As for the people who had helped me, although I had tried to make their help a personal thing, to appropriate it to myself, had they not in fact helped me because they wanted to do something? because they hated the Germans?—because they thought that they had been too nice with the Germans and now must even the balance by being nice with the British?—because they obeyed the instinct to help the weakling who gets the worst of a fight?—or just because they had nothing to do and wanted to do something? And if you regarded those people as having any personal stake in me, then it was perfectly proper under

430

the rules of life that their stake should be in danger right up to the very last yard of my journey.

"It can't happen to me."

What a comforting phrase that is for the inexperienced.

I looked around the swaying, slightly vibrating cabin of the old flying-boat. It was uncomfortable, since this aircraft had been intended to carry material, not men. My companions were two brigadiers, both elderly, a Royal Air Force flight-sergeant, and some kind of nurse who had a Scots accent and wore a grey uniform with a lieutenant's badges of rank on the shoulders. It was much less liable to happen to them than to me.

Nothing happened.

"There is something so *satisfactory* in returning to Britain," one brigadier remarked to the other.

I looked over their broad shoulders at the grim anchorage and grimmer buildings of Pembroke Dock.

I was not at all sure that I wanted to go ashore.

"After you," I said to the nurse.

"Please go ahead, I have so many bits and pieces."

"No, after you."

CHAPTER XXIV

THE exiled Millar, day-dreaming in the prison camps of Italy and Tripolitania, had frequently pictured his home-coming.

With the successful escape from the train near Munich and the prolongation of that escape to freedom, his day-dreaming had ceased. The present had taken the place of the future.

But the grimness of the Royal Air Force mess at Pembroke Dock, the waitresses in their organised clothes, the bacon and sausages turned out by machines, the tea from a great urn with a brass tap, the greyness, the solidity, the artificiality of England, brought back his dreams. They came in a shuddering, shivering rush, unwillingly, like preparatory schoolboys running across a wet stone floor to brave the discomfort of the cold tub on a December morning.

There were two stock day-dreams. There were others, of course, since he had read enormously in prison, and many of the situations encountered in books and plays he had adapted to his own situation. He was a situation-lover.

But the two stock dreams had so persisted that to him they amounted to reality.

In the first dream he arrived on a sunny morning at that platform in Victoria Station where all the boat-trains used to arrive. (Note that it was Victoria Station, the least unpleasant and the most agreeably and conveniently situated of all the London stations.)

He leaned from the window but he could not see her. He collected his belongings and left the compartment, sometimes alone, and sometimes with a former cell-mate.

Anne stood at the end of the platform, peering at the crowds in that peculiarly expressive, myopic way, the body slightly tensed forward, the eyes a little screwed up. (She would not want to wear her glasses when she knew that he was going to see her there for the first time in three years.) Sometimes he was glad to present a prison companion or two to her. Sometimes they were alone, an island in the crowd.

They kissed each other two or three times. They bundled his things and her poodle into a taxi. (There were plenty of taxis, because of course he dreamed of the last London that he had known, the London of 1940, when the streets were filled with taxis and shops still contained some reasonably-priced articles made by craftsmen.)

What a very clean taxi! It smelled of polish and seasoned wood like the interior of his grandmother's old car.

The sun flashed into the dark blue interior, picking out the bright daffodils and the dog, such a white, freshly-bathed dog, with a hint of gold in the shadows of his whiteness.

They arrived at her flat looking out over the Thames. There were odd pieces of furniture which he recognised from their former life together. They had a meal alone, sitting on a balcony in the sun looking out over the dancing Thames. On the far south bank the industrial buildings and the Chinatown of slum dwellings behind them were obscured in haze.

Later they would agree to go somewhere quieter than the flat above the Thames. You could be quiet in London if you did not answer the telephone. But only to a degree. Later, they would go to the south of Ireland or the north-west of Scotland, where there was deep quiet and where, although you did not have to think of such things, you were not living on the top of drains and telephone-wires and electric light cables. To say nothing of all the old skeletons and people going home after work on underground railways.

In the second dream he arrived unexpectedly and he had to ask the porter how to find her flat. He rang an unknown door·

bell, waited, rang again. Then he heard her hesitating, slightly heavy step within. She opened the door, her eyes puckered with their effort to see who stood there on the dark landing. He saw her silhouetted against the sunshine of the windows, with a rim of gold showing round the small hairs on the outline of her head. He stood there waiting—and then anything might happen, depending upon his mood while he dreamed.

He built and rebuilt upon the situations according to his moods. Sometimes he began at the end and worked back.

When he was exercising around the paddock at Padula or up and down the stone ramp at Gavi he found it easy to pass the time with one or other of the day-dreams. Remark that in these dreams Anne was an idealised version of the most beautiful Annes he had known, a mixture of all the Annes; the gentle one with whom he had eloped in 1935; the wild one on the boat in the Mediterranean in June, 1939; the smooth, sad one in Paris just before the Germans broke through the crust of France; the efficient, motherly one at Aberdeen in 1941.

Remark too that in his imaginary scenes all did not always run smoothly between them. For what could be duller? He was quick and apt to imagine many different types of horror, many fantastic situations, many wordy battles. But right (himself) always triumphed as though his dreams had been Victorian novels. Right, in the torrid dialogues, always produced the sharpest, hottest thrusts.

In France it had occasionally been suggested to him that his wife might now love somebody else. The suggestion had usually been made in the light, practical manner in which French people reason such things out, and he had accepted it laughingly, although fully realising its reasonableness.

They told him that no woman was likely to remain physically faithful for three years; particularly a young woman obliged to live through the strained artificialities of war conditions in London. He had agreed, as any sensible person would, with all that they said. One night in summer, 1943, when he was drinking his glass of sour red wine before the prison dinner, he made up his mind that he would condone any physical infidelities. But while he took out this mental insurance policy he never really considered that it was necessary, for he believed strongly and proudly that their love and affection had been well-founded, had been basic, had been passionate, had been clean, and that it was everlasting.

Another thing. The returning husband was always looking

433

his best in the day-dreams. Bronzed and bleached by summer suns, he was thinner than he had been when she had last seen him. His face was older, less babyish. She, who knew it so well, would surely (he hoped) be able to detect in it the signs of suffering and the development of character in the contemplative self-discipline of prison.

Then his clothes might vary in the dream between uniform and civilian clothes. But they inevitably carried an aura of tattered and picturesque charm.

Now reality.

He arrived at Waterloo Station at midnight, and nobody knew that he was arriving except the authorities of a London transit camp where he was obliged to spend the night.

There were no taxis. There was nobody to meet him.

He was obliged to carry his luggage to a bus. The conductor at first refused to take him because of his suitcase and his kit-bag. This was in keeping with the British Customs. They had made him pay heavily for every dutiable thing which he had bought for Anne. He crossed the greater part of London in the bus, and then had to walk a mile to the transit camp. The commandant welcomed him (with astonishing friendliness as compared to the Customs and immigration authorities) and offered him a meal and drinks. He refused the offers and climbed to his bedroom, an old-fashioned, polished-mahogany hotel room with a private bathroom.

Shut securely away in his bedroom, with only the night noises of London to remind him that he had at last reached the end of his long journey, he looked at himself in the mirror.

And the day-dreams fell to pieces, finally shattered.

Everything about him was wrong.

There was no doubt about it, he looked terrible. No shadow of doubt.

Really everything was wrong. His hair had been cut so that it stuck out in pathetic blond tails all round the head. It was short in the wrong places and long where it should have been short. His face could never have been described as "bronzed" and still less as "interesting". No woman in her senses could detect in those round, rosy cheeks, those clear, baby-blue eyes, the faintest hint of hidden suffering, the remotest sign of fasting or self-discipline.

Alas, the only mark that he carried from his escape was a pronounced limp, and the rest of him looked so healthy that the limp appeared to be a piece of theatrical clap-trap. He had actually (oh, horror!) turned the rich food of Dolores, Pepette, and the Restaurant Valencia into firm, bouncing flesh.

Then his clothes! Those Spanish shoes, twisted round as though pointing at each other in sympathy or scorn. Those baggy grey trousers, so wide, and made apparently of a species of sack-cloth. The coat which was much too wide and which was made of checked tweed. If only he had been able to keep his escaping clothes. They at least were old and famously worn, they were friends, they would have supported him in his doubts.

He got into a hot bath, scrubbed himself from head to foot, washed his hair, shaved, dried himself and looked in the mirror again. Terrible!

No wife could love such a husband. He went to bed but could not sleep. He lay thinking that some time during the next twenty-four hours he would probably meet Anne. He was extremely thankful that, as a returned prisoner of war, he was obliged to go through certain formalities and interviews before seeing any relatives or friends. At the same time he wanted desperately to see her of course.

But as he thought it out in bed such a meeting appeared to be stacked with all manner of terrible difficulties—difficulties which had been ignored or smoothed over in his dreaming.

What happened when lovers separated? The separation was pain and then, later, it was a numbness, since all pain in the end burned out either itself or the sufferer. When the pain was ended the waiting period began. During the waiting period each party built up a dream, idealised the other party.

Millar was aware that while he had been in prison he had ceased to love the real Anne. He had set another Anne in her place.

He had set a photograph of the real Anne beside the bed, and another photograph of her on the top of his cupboard. He often looked at her picture, he was pleased when his friends admired it, furious when the Italians made disgusting, slobbering noises as they walked past it. He was proud that she wrote to him more than other wives wrote to their prisoner husbands. His love had increased in prison.

Had it increased healthily? He now asked himself this question: Was he still in love with the real Anne? And the answer was: "I do not know, for I do not know the real Anne. I have obscured her with an ideal, an imaginary woman, who is cleverer, deeper, more charming, more beautiful than the woman whom I shall soon meet again. . . ."

And of course Anne herself was facing the same problem. But did she realise it? he wondered.

To soothe his inferiority complex he got out of bed and examined the things that he had bought for her in Spain and in Gibraltar. There was something reassuringly physical about silk stockings.

At the end of the next morning's interviews with Intelligence Officers he realised that he would be free after 5 p.m. By telephoning old friends who were amazed to hear his voice, he obtained the address and telephone number of her new flat. (He had been cut off for so long from all news from England that he had not known where she lived.)

The telephone-booth was in an old box-room. It was necessary to put twopence in the slot each time he tried her number. When he held the telephone to his face a faint odour of disinfectant came to him. Each time that he dialled her number there was no reply. He rang it six times during the break in his interrogation from midday to 2 p.m.

"Why is she not there?" he wondered. "She must have known two days ago" (from the message carried by his brother) "that I would be home any day. Ah, but she will be working, she must be at the factory."

He did not know the name or the address of the factory where she worked.

His interviews were exhausting. The rooms were stuffy and the interrogators puffed at pipes. His head was bursting. When he glanced in the mirror he was infuriated to see that he looked grotesquely healthy, grotesquely unlike the way he felt.

At 4 p.m. one interviewing officer finished with him.

"May I telephone my wife?" he asked the fresh interviewer.

"Certainly; you have been patient with us."

They smoked away at their pipes, and he wondered if they realised how important this telephone-call was to him; probably they did. The receiver was lifted at the other end.

"Hullo!" It was her voice.

"Hullo! I've arrived."

"Oh! Yes, I knew that you were on your way. I expected you all yesterday. I was beginning to be afraid that you had had an accident. Are you all right?"

"Very much so."

"Where are you?"

"I can't tell you where. How are you?"

"I'm all right, I suppose. It's a bit of a strain all this."

"I know it."

"Yes, you must be tired out, poor thing."

"A little tired."

"When shall I see you?"

"In about an hour." He wanted to say that he had presents for her, but he wanted also to hold them against the awkward moment of meeting.

"In about an hour," she echoed.

Her voice had sounded cold, almost stunned. But then her voice had always been strangled by the telephone.

Until then he had been able to provide clear answers for the Intelligence Officers. But after the telephone conversation all that was finished. They persevered for a little, trying to prod him gently back to common sense. At last the senior major said: "I think we had better resume this discussion to-morrow. You are evidently a little tired. Most understandable. Good luck."

His things were packed and ready in the bedroom. He found a taxi without difficulty. He was surprised at his inability to look at the London streets which he had not seen for so long. Going through the park he forced himself to notice obvious things like guns and barrage-balloons and Americans.

When he looked down he was surprised to see that his hands were trembling. He was filled with an almost unbearable exaltation and at the same time with an almost unbearable nervousness. He felt as though he were a piano in the middle of an immense silence. Every note of the piano was struck at the same time and the noise went on; it felt as though it would go on for ever in that vacuum of silence.

His face, unnaturally elongated and a little dirty, stared back at him from the small vertical mirror between the windows of the taxi. He would have changed it willingly for any face in the world. Ramon's thin, dark one would have suited him nicely. What an entrance he would have been able to make with Ramon's face! Through Ramon's gash of a mouth he would have rolled out smooth, slightly aloof, sentences and sentiments.

For he had seen that at first he must be aloof with her. There was no possibility of allowing himself to be anything but aloof.

"You are absurd. You are middle-class. You have inhibitions. You are a ridiculous introvert," he told himself. "Remember that evening at the Gare de l'Est, when you went down

437

to look at some of the French troops returning on their first leave from the front? You stood in the shadows, away from the blue light that fell upon a long strip of platform. You were curious, you did not quite know why, to see how such men would greet their wives. Most of them were disappointingly matter-of-fact about things. One solid, squashy kiss on the mouth, perhaps a smack on the woman's behind, and off they walked with the crowd, chattering at each other, perhaps already quarrelling about ancient histories of letters or parcels or tobacco. But those young ones! You had really felt like a Peeping Tom when you saw them, and when you went on watching, to see the outcome. The man was leaning out of the window as the train came in. He was very young, but broad and powerful. Everything about him was wide, his head, his hands, his nostrils. He collected his woman before the train stopped. She seemed to fly at his mouth as though it were a magnet. She was small, and he caught her by the waist, dragging her up to the window. When the train stopped there were shouts of anger from inside the compartment. Unwillingly, he stood aside to let his companions get out. He did not mind or did not hear their crude jokes about his female companion, jokes which told you that the woman was his wife. When you left the platform they were still there. He was sitting on a porter's barrow. His wife was on his knee and their lips were again locked together. All the way back to the Palais Royal, slipping the car through the narrow back streets you had thought about that pair. What a *natural* way to come back to one's wife, and what a strange way to come back! After all, it was bestial. They had not exchanged six words. What were they going to talk about at breakfast the following morning? The power and potency of their kiss would surely strain the after-relationship. Ugh! What insensitive people!''

Yes, aloofness was the only thing. After all, the young soldier at the Gare de l'Est had only been separated from his wife for a matter of months. But he, Millar, was returning as a stranger. He and his wife must give each other time to fall in love all over again.

Only there were handicaps to falling in love. Surely it would be easier to fall in love with a complete stranger than with somebody you had once loved and later idealised?

The taxi smelled musty; and although the street in which they stopped was a most respectable one in decent Kensington, it seemed to him that it smelled infernally of cats. If only it had

438

been a known vehicle, going to a known house. He had never lived in or contemplated living in such a street.

He squeezed in at the street entrance, awkwardly carrying the now dirty white kit-bag and the cheap suitcase, one lock of which was already broken. He tried the bell of the ground-floor flat first, and there was no reply. He mounted the stairs in a swirl of excitement, and at once he knew that he stood outside the right door. He recognised his wife's perfume, the smell of her home, the aroma which had once encased him. But now it was *her* home.

He rang and she opened.

And everything was so ordinary and normal. It was not difficult any more. Like all dreaded scenes, difficulties faded away in the execution. He had not heard her step as he had dreamed, for it had been muffled by carpets. He was too shy to look hard at her. He left his luggage outside the door and took her in his arms in the hall.

He felt nothing, absolutely nothing. He was astonished at himself. No tenderness, no rush of love? No, only a blankness. Her body felt thinner, harder than he remembered it.

She was evidently manœuvring in the same, dazed way; memory against reality.

"You are so big, bigger than I remember you," she said.

He felt divorced from the large warm room that she led him into. He recognised the furniture, of course, and there were far too many pictures of him about the place. A book of Toulouse-Lautrec's strange, twisted drawings lay open on a big chair beside the fire. Was that how she had passed the time, awaiting his arrival? Or had the book been left there for effect?

Occasionally he looked at her, wondering: "Is that my wife?"

To conceal his embarrassment, he produced the things from the kit-bag and the suitcase. Stockings, sherry, lemons, bananas, olive-oil were scattered about the place.

He sat in a chair, trying to relax, fighting an inclination to walk about the room, to kick the dog that looked so mistrustfully at him. He saw objectively that both he and Anne were sick. Sick with inward tension that tautens and twists.

Apart from being objective, apart from being with somebody who was at the same time his wife and a stranger, he noticed that she was very cold, that she was almost wary with him. That she never touched him. He wanted to touch her. Not for the physical contact. He needed her sympathy and kindness, and he knew that she was kind.

439

"After all," he repeated to himself. "When two people love each other for five years they form something which is almost stronger than love. The deep feeling that comes from doing the same things together and liking the same things, from suffering and worrying and playing together. Can one not recover this *basic* sentiment immediately, even if one must wait for the other kind of life?"

They got along quite nicely together. Another woman came in and said that he looked like his pictures. Then she went away. They drank some of the Tio Pepe he had brought from Gibraltar. There was only one small scene.

"What do you intend to do now?" she asked.

"Ask for two months' leave."

"Yes, but after the leave?"

"I am still in the Army of course. But . . ."

"But what?"

"I want to go back into France, to fight with the Resistance there. But I won't do it if you . . ."

She let out a long sigh and lit a cigarette before she spoke to him. He noticed that the war had changed little things and habits about her. She smoked more. She smoked in a different way, more quickly, as though she needed something from the cigarette.

"There you go again, always the little Boy Scout," she said in a tired voice. "You are hopeless, really hopeless."

"I'm sorry. It was just an idea I got, on my way here from Germany."

"It's not much fun for the wife, you know. She stays at home and has to work, and is lonely . . ."

"I know. Don't let's talk about it now. I'm tired."

Yes, he was tired. And his mind was searching for loopholes. It kept trying to slip off, to slip back to France.

There was something irresistible in the idea of going back into France, to try to work like Xavier. And to repay some of the people who had helped him. There was a matter-of-factness about the war in Britain which did not please him, although there was an intensity of effort in Britain which was clearly lacking in France. There was something which drew him to the muddle of the war in France, something which repelled him in the machine-like precision of the war in Britain. In France everybody claimed that they were fighting against the Boches, and not so many of them were doing anything about it. In Britain most people were mobilised to fight against the Germans, but only the minority were doing anything important about it. Even the people in uniform often gave the minimum of effort. It was the same thing really as in France. The heroes that the British press yelled so much about were an infinitesimal minority if you put them beside all the soldiers and sailors and airmen who clung greedily to comfortable jobs at home, or even abroad.

Then he had told Xavier and Dolores and Pepette; Ramon and Tino and Clément and Laurence that he was going back to France.

Where were all those people as Millar sat in his wife's chair?

Wally Binns was continuing his language studies in Switzerland. He had been recaptured by the Germans but had escaped from Strasbourg jail, leaving a note which said: "I do not care for the accommodation here, I think I can do better elsewhere."

Robert Cahin, the well-to-do grain merchant from Metz, was still helping people to make escape plans in Stalag VIIA at Moosburg.

In the Munich goods yard his friends were still operating. They had packed many more evaders into goods trucks bound for Strasbourg, and two of them at least were British, Buck Palm and George Sukas. Buck had returned to England some weeks before Millar.

Eugène and his wife had been denounced for helping Millar by the café plotter, the artist Dédé, and were both in a German concentration camp.

Greta survived in the Hermanngoeringstrasse, and worked in Hayange.

Ramon Delgado languished in the Spanish prison of Miranda, and was soon to see his beloved North Africa again.

Alban was engrossed in several intelligent combines in the Dordogne.

Scherb and her family awaited the Allies in Paris, listening four times daily to the news broadcasts from London, and now fairly confident that the Gestapo had not traced Millar to their Passy flat.

In Lyons a handsome French naval officer was paying court to Dolores, who was on the point of asking Henri to go back to his wife. Barbarossa rarely called now at the bistro, and the maid who resembled a field of waving corn had left under a cloud. Pascal still carried his razor-sharp blade quietly about the streets.

La Pepette had been obliged to leave "Ma Baraque" and to

take to the Maquis, where she employed her culinary genius beneath the leaves and the stars.

Tino, the gold-topped bottles of Elizabeth just slipping through his fingers, was about to be killed in an underworld fight in Lyons. His wife, Joséphine, again worked for him in a brothel.

Elizabeth was in danger of her life, and was soon to be imprisoned in the terrible jail at Fresnes.

Clément and Laurence were in the Citadelle in Perpignan. Soon after Millar had crossed the mountains the Gestapo had caught them in that beautiful town while they were shepherding British airmen. Now Clément was under torture, and Laurence, half-demented, was forced to witness his stubborn agonies. Stubborn because he took all "blame" from his wife's shoulders. Soon they would tire of torturing him, and would kill him, sending his wife off to Ravensbrück concentration camp, to the undeserved prospect of a filthy death.

Serge was crossing the Pyrenees, and was to become an air cadet in California.

Pierre Cartelet, the untidy young professor, was still going about his dangerous business in Perpignan, but he was probably already being tracked by the Gestapo, and he was destined to be killed by them in Toulouse twenty-four hours before that town was liberated by the Americans.

Xavier was carrying on.

An air-raid on London began while he sat there. It was the last big raid carried out by ordinary German bombers. There was a tremendous noise which he could not recognise.

"I never heard that before," he said. He was glad of the air-raid. It seemed to make things easier between them.

"It's the rockets they shoot up now," she explained. "All sorts of wire and metal fragments come crashing down. It's dangerous if you are out in the street."

She asked if he would mind eating dinner in a near-by restaurant. He agreed to do that; and he thought that she did not want to be alone with him.

It was one of those "continental" restaurants that are so popular with sections of the London populace. The food was bad, but that did not matter. She bent her head down in the old, exciting way to peer at the contents of her plate.

He made great efforts to talk smoothly, to reassure her, to let her see that he was nervous and only wanted to rest. His talking soothed him, lulled him like self-hypnosis. He began to forget his fear of her, he even tried to explain it to her and to laugh at it with her.

Sometimes the building shook with the bombs, but neither of them paid any attention. She had always been brave and he was too deeply engrossed in other things. Indeed, nobody seemed to pay attention to the bombs. The place was full, and there were people waiting, drinking synthetic vermouth.

Then everything crashed in on him.

He was attempting to explain to her something of what he had felt in prison, and then on the previous night, and lastly, when he had sat drinking Tio Pepe in her big room.

"The only thing that would end everything," he said to her, "would be if you had fallen in love with somebody else . . ."

"Perhaps I have."

She had answered in a hard, pondering voice. He looked into her face. He felt like an oyster, torn from its shell and wobbling ludicrously there in front of the table. He began then to wish that he had not come home.

THE END

443